Exploring the Great Lakes States through Literature

Exploring the United States through Literature Series

Kathy Howard Latrobe, Series Editor

Exploring the Northeast States through Literature
Edited by P. Diane Frey

Exploring the Southeast States through Literature
Edited by Linda Veltze

Exploring the Great Lakes States through Literature
Edited by Kathy Howard Latrobe

Exploring the Plains States through Literature
Edited by Carolyn S. Brodie

Exploring the Southwest States through Literature
Edited by Pat Tipton Sharp

Exploring the Mountain States through Literature
Edited by Sharyl Smith

Exploring the Pacific States through Literature
Edited by Carol A. Doll

Exploring the Great Lakes States through Literature

Edited by Kathy Howard Latrobe

State Editors
LaVonne Hayes Sanborn, Illinois
Barry Lessow, Indiana
Gail Beaver, Michigan
Mary Alice Anderson and Elsie Husom, Minnesota
Carolyn S. Brodie, Ohio
Jane Roeber, Wisconsin

Exploring the United States through Literature Series
Kathy Howard Latrobe, Series Editor

Oryx Press
1994

The rare Arabian Oryx is believed to have inspired the myth of the unicorn. This desert antelope became virtually extinct in the early 1960s. At that time several groups of international conservationists arranged to have 9 animals sent to the Phoenix Zoo to be the nucleus of a captive breeding herd. Today the Oryx population is over 800 and nearly 400 have been returned to reserves in the Middle East.

Copyright © 1994 by The Oryx Press
4041 North Central at Indian School Road
Phoenix, Arizona 85012-3397

Published simultaneously in Canada

All rights reserved
No part of this publication may be reproduced or transmitted in any form or by any means, electronic or mechanical, including photocopying, recording, or by any information storage and retrieval system, without permission in writing from The Oryx Press.

Library of Congress Cataloging-in-Publication Data

Exploring the Great Lakes states through literature / edited by Kathy
  Howard Latrobe.
  p. cm.—(Exploring the United States through literature
series)
  Includes bibliographical references and index.
  ISBN 0-89774-731-3
  1. Lake States—Juvenile literature—Bibliography. I. Latrobe,
Kathy Howard. II. Series.
Z1251.G8E97 1993
[F551]   93-2486
016.977—dc20   CIP

Contents

Series Statement vii

Preface ix

Contributors xiii

Illinois 1
  by LaVonne Hayes Sanborn

Indiana 18
  by Barry Lessow

Michigan 33
  by Gail Beaver

Minnesota 48
  by Mary Alice Anderson and Elsie Husom

Ohio 75
  by Carolyn S. Brodie

Wisconsin 94
  by Jane Roeber

Directory of Publishers and Vendors 115

Author Index 125

Title Index 131

Subject Index 141

Series Statement

The *Exploring the United States through Literature Series* comprises seven annotated regional resource guides to selected print and nonprint materials for grades K-8. Each regional bibliography is divided into state sections identifying materials that relate to the history, culture, geography, resources, industries, literature and lore, and famous figures of the states in the region. The seven volumes cover the following regions and states:

- *Exploring the Northeast States through Literature:* Connecticut, Delaware, District of Columbia, Maine, Maryland, Massachusetts, New Hampshire, New Jersey, New York, Pennsylvania, Rhode Island, Vermont
- *Exploring the Southeast States through Literature:* Alabama, Arkansas, Florida, Georgia, Kentucky, Louisiana, Mississippi, North Carolina, South Carolina, Tennessee, Virginia, West Virginia
- *Exploring the Great Lakes States through Literature:* Illinois, Indiana, Michigan, Minnesota, Ohio, Wisconsin
- *Exploring the Plains States through Literature:* Iowa, Kansas, Missouri, Nebraska, North Dakota, South Dakota
- *Exploring the Southwest States through Literature:* Arizona, Oklahoma, New Mexico, Texas
- *Exploring the Mountain States through Literature:* Colorado, Idaho, Montana, Nevada, Utah, Wyoming
- *Exploring the Pacific States through Literature:* Alaska, California, Hawaii, Oregon, Washington

The materials included in these resource guides were selected because they can be used by teachers and librarians to enrich young people's understanding of the histories and contemporary cultures of the 50 states, and because they are suitable for use with young people from any of the regional or ethnic groups of the contemporary United States. Each annotation includes a brief description of the particular work, a comment on its usefulness or appropriateness, and at least one learning activity compatible with the identified interest level of the resource.

Purpose

The *Exploring the United States through Literature Series* offers teachers, school library media specialists, and public librarians valuable assistance in resource selection and user guidance. The suggested activities demonstrate each title's potential for involving young people in creative thinking and problem-solving and for inspiring teachers and librarians to invent other imaginative uses for the title. The series can also be used effectively by school library media specialists and teachers as they work together to develop curricular units and plan learning experiences on the geographic regions of the United States or on specific states. Reading, language arts, and social studies teachers will find the series particularly useful.

The series addresses needs created by the following recent and important educational trends:

1. The whole language approach to learning, especially the integration of literature, the arts, and social studies curricula
2. Rapidly changing social environments that demand flexible curricula and multiple learning resources
3. Multicultural education with an emphasis on multicultural diversity and a recognition of the importance of leading young people to accept and appreciate diversity
4. The position of the Curriculum Task Force of the National Commission on Social Studies (NCSS) that the social studies curriculum should include both breadth and depth

The NCSS emphasizes the discovery approach to learning and maintains that young people should develop an overview as well as immerse themselves in the details of history and social studies.

Scope

Each regional editor coordinated the contributions of state editors who brought to the series a familiarity with and understanding of the notable and special features of their states and regions. The state editors used their own judgment in selecting materials that could most effectively assist young people in learning and understanding the many dimensions of each state. The editors' goal was not to include a predetermined number of entries, but rather to select pertinent items of merit. Because there are similarities across the regions, a few titles appear in more than one state bibliography. These duplicate entries serve to reinforce students' experiences with the region or to take the title in a new direction with a different activity.

Each state editor valued diversity—in subject matter, in time period, and in media. The editors sought to capture the past and present of each state by including not only books, but also such items as periodicals, computer programs, sound recordings, and videocassettes. A major goal of the series is to bring alive to young people each state's sights, sounds, tastes, music, stories and legends, natural environment, and people.

Activities

The state editors, who are all professionally involved either directly or indirectly with the education of young people, have devised learning activities that can appropriately extend the work being described. Denoted by a diamond (♦) in each entry, the activities are designed to enhance young people's understanding of each state and to encourage further exploration of the topic at hand. The activities relate the work to young people themselves, to specific geographic areas, to associated disciplines and subjects, or to broader concepts within social studies.

Sources of Materials

Because of the diversity and regional or state focus of materials, no single jobber can deliver all the included items upon request. Therefore, a "Directory of Publishers and Vendors," including specialized sources for state and regional materials, has been included in each volume. The agencies and departments of state and local governments, state and local historical societies, and other state and local organizations are also excellent sources of informational materials.

Organization

Each volume is organized first by the states within the region (arranged alphabetically). Each state section is then subdivided into Nonfiction (by Dewey Classification), Biography (collective biography, then individual biography, alphabetically by subject), Fiction (alphabetically by author), Periodicals, and Professional Materials (by Dewey Classification). Reference works listed in the Nonfiction section are identified immediately following the Dewey number.

In general, each bibliographic entry identifies Dewey Classification number, author, title, publisher or producer, ISBN or ISSN, date of publication or release, number of pages, black-and-white or color illustrations, cost of nonprint materials, any special purchasing information, and running time and format specifications for nonprint items. Each entry also includes an interest level designation and relevant subject headings.

Three indexes provide access by author, title, and subject. The state-by-state division allows teachers and librarians to access materials by state, and the Subject Index provides access to materials appropriate to more than one state and to topics with regional significance. Subject headings are based upon *Sears List of Subject Headings*.

The Dewey Decimal Classification numbers, while appropriate for each volume's organization, are not offered as recommendations for cataloging/classification purposes. Many items are open to classification in more than one area.

—Kathy Howard Latrobe
Series Editor

Preface

Illinois

The 95 literature selections about Illinois focus on notable individuals, the exploration and settlement of the state, and the contrast between rural and metropolitan lifestyles. The "Land of Lincoln" is well represented by a significant body of literature about Abraham Lincoln. Numerous well-known inventors, political leaders, authors, poets, and scientists are also presented in both individual and collective biographies. Many titles address the significant contributions made by African Americans such as Jean Baptiste Point du Sable, the first settler of Chicago.

Books for young readers about the exploration and settlement of Illinois include both famous individuals and significant events. Many of these works describe the explorations of Louis Joliet, Sieur de La Salle, and George Rogers Clark. Other titles describe such events as the Chicago Fire, the Black Hawk War, and the Haymarket Riot, or economic developments such as the development of the railroad industry.

Also prevalent in the literature about Illinois is the contrast between rural and metropolitan lifestyles. Because half of the state's population lives in or near Chicago, many books address that city. Fewer titles represent the rural culture, but the important role of agriculture is emphasized by the inclusion of titles about the dairy and corn industries.

Although there are many excellent information books about Illinois, there are fewer works of fiction, and many of those items do not offer information about the state or its people. Except for picture books, works of fiction are included only if they significantly illuminate Illinois history or geography.

Indiana

A variety of excellent resources, both print and nonprint, acquaint young people with this diverse midwestern state. The history of Indiana and the state's significance during the pioneer era provide the subject for numerous items. Many of the 86 entries present the roles in Indiana history of Native Americans, particularly the Miami. Others focus on the Hoosier State's natural resources (including limestone and coal), geography (from tornado alley to the Indiana Dunes), culture, and famous citizens. Resource materials address Indiana's modern role as a center of transportation, manufacturing, mining, farming, and amateur and professional sports. This section also includes materials about unique Hoosier phenomena such as the Indianapolis 500 Race and the nineteenth-century utopian community of New Harmony.

Michigan

The focus of most of the 89 Michigan selections is on the Great Lakes, reflecting Michigan's unique geographic position and the influence of the Lakes on all aspects of Michigan life. The name "Michigan" is generally translated from the Ottawa as "great water." The boundaries of the two peninsulas that make up the state extend into parts of Lakes Superior, Michigan, Huron, and Erie. Furthermore, the geologic forces that forged the Great Lakes also gave Michigan thousands of inland lakes and connecting rivers that provide access to both peninsulas.

Consequently, the French and the Indian legends, explorers' journals, and the settlers' diaries reflect the all-important presence of the great waters. These stories of heroic acts, lost ships and shipwrecks, great storms, and harrowing canoe journeys have been retold to inform and delight young readers.

Well represented in the bibliography is the early history of Michigan as well as the hallmarks of Michigan's last century, including the rise and decline of the automobile industry, an increasing social consciousness, and the development of tourism as the state's second largest industry. The selected biographies, histories, and travel films also provide excellent information for young people. However, there are few suitable titles about unionism and union leaders, inner-city unrest, and Michigan's most recent ethnic and cultural groups.

This section includes films and books featuring Great Lakes ecological and environmental information. Although not all of the materials were developed specifically for young people, they are excellent, easily accessible resources. The stewardship of these great water resources will inevitably be a part of Michigan's social and political future.

Minnesota

Minnesota is more than the "Land of 10,000 Lakes." It is a land of diversity, as reflected in its literature.

Even though the 11,000 plus lakes have been Minnesota's "claim to fame," the Northwoods, the Bluff Country, the Plains, and the Iron Range also serve as popular settings for much of the writing. Weather plays an important role in the settings of fiction and nonfiction works. The cold, snowy winters and warm summers create many opportunities for enjoying outdoor activities and portraying Minnesota's natural beauty through photography and the written word; yet, the seasons also bring blizzards and drought that evoke survival accounts.

Minnesota's earliest known culture was Native American. In the 1800s, major immigration brought a European influence. During the twentieth century, particularly the latter half, many Hispanic, African-American, and Pacific-Asian peoples made Minnesota their home. Minnesota is now culturally diverse, especially in the metropolitan areas; however, there are still many communities throughout Minnesota that typify the predominant European influence. Multicultural resources are therefore important because they provide some young people with their primary exposure to other cultural and ethnic groups in the state.

The editors' evaluation of resources about Minnesota revealed a wealth of information in many formats, especially for the upper elementary and middle school audience. However, more resources address historical topics than contemporary life, and more resources cover longer established cultural and ethnic groups than more recent ones, such as the Hmong and Vietnamese peoples. Overall, 161 materials selected provide many possibilities for creativity and for meeting diverse learning needs.

Ohio

The 120 literature selections for Ohio reflect a strong sense of history, and the prestigious contributions of individuals dominate the numerous quality materials related to the state. Because Ohio was the home for eight United States presidents, there is a substantial biography selection. The history of flight from early beginnings to astronauts has important connections to the state, including the Wright brothers, John Glenn, and Neil Armstrong. Legendary characters Annie Oakley, Mike Fink, and Johnny Appleseed are also linked to the state. Literary figures of the state have included Harriet Beecher Stowe and Paul Laurence Dunbar, and the state has been the home for Newbery authors Virginia Hamilton and Cynthia Rylant.

A wealth of historical nonfiction exists, especially for upper grades. Excellent nature and wildlife resources that reflect the beauty of the state are available in different formats. There are Native American information materials, including biographies. Useful reference materials are available, and especially valuable are recently published almanacs.

The fiction selections include picture books and chapter books that feature both contemporary and historical settings. There are few collective resources of Ohio folklore and legends, other than recently published ghost stories.

Wisconsin

Although Wisconsin's Northwoods traditions and agricultural heritage are portrayed in some depth in this selective compilation, the state's urban milieus are less well represented. Historical fiction is more plentiful than contemporary fiction, conveying a unique sense of place. Similarly, nonfiction about the past is more abundant than works about the present. There are gaps in coverage of the many ethnic groups who are part of the state's past and present. The availability—or absence—of authentic, accurate, and appealing materials inevitably influenced the content of the section.

With the above caveats in mind, readers will find here a collection of 126 resources that speaks with Wisconsin's voice. It speaks, for example, of people such as John Muir and Gaylord Nelson, Belle Case LaFollette and Golda Meir, and Georgia O'Keeffe and Frank Lloyd Wright. It tells of farm year cycles, describes state Capitol architecture, and identifies place name origins. It introduces such creative works as the novels of Anne Pellowski and the videos of Jocelyn Riley. With these resources and many more, it says, "Welcome to Wisconsin!"

The Wisconsin editor gratefully acknowledges the insights of Ginny Moore Kruse, director, Cooperative Children's Book Center, University of Wisconsin-Madison, and Evelyn Weible, library media specialist, Northside Elementary School, Middleton, Wisconsin. The strengths of this section are rooted in their willingness to share their knowledge of books and children. Ginny Moore Kruse provided invaluable and generous assistance by making available the draft of *On Wisconsin* (described in Wisconsin's professional materials section).

Contributors

Series and Regional Editor

Kathy Howard Latrobe is an associate professor at the University of Oklahoma School of Library and Information Studies where she teaches children's and young adult library media services. She is coauthor of three books on reader's theater for young people, including *Social Studies Readers Theatre for Young Adults: Scripts and Script Development* (Libraries Unlimited, 1991). She is coeditor of *Public Relations for School Library Media Centers* (Libraries Unlimited, 1990) and *Multicultural Aspects of Library Media Programs* (Libraries Unlimited, 1992).

State Editors

Mary Alice Anderson is a media specialist at Winona Middle School, Winona, Minnesota. She is a member of the Library Science and Services Consulting Committee, World Book Publishing; author of the technology column for *Book Report;* and contributor to other professional publications. She frequently works with the Minnesota Department of Education on technology projects and often speaks at media/technology conferences.

Gail Beaver is a school library media specialist at Huron High School in Ann Arbor, Michigan and an adjunct lecturer in the School of Information and Library Science at the University of Michigan. She serves on the advisory board of *Biography Today,* a periodical providing contemporary biographies for young readers, published by Omnigraphics, Inc. Her teaching, performing, and research interests include folk literature and the art of storytelling.

Carolyn S. Brodie is an assistant professor in the School of Library and Information Science, Kent State University, Ohio. She regularly offers the graduate credit workshop "Ohio Children's Literature." She is coauthor of *Many Faces, Many Voices: Multicultural Literary Experiences for Youth* (Highsmith Press, 1992), a book based on the Virginia Hamilton Conference held each spring at Kent State University. She edited *Exploring the Plains States through Literature* and contributed the Arkansas section to *Exploring the Southeast States through Literature*, both published by Oryx Press.

Elsie Husom is director of media technology for the public schools in Brainerd, Minnesota. She has written a number of journal articles; has spoken on a variety of topics at state, national, and international conferences; and has piloted innovative educational projects on the local and state levels.

Barry Lessow is an assistant professor of Education at Indiana University, Bloomington, Indiana. With a focus on elementary social studies methods, he has received university awards for outstanding teaching. He is a member of the National Council for the Social Studies Committee on Science and Society.

Jane Roeber is coordinator of youth services at the Wisconsin Division for Library Services, Department of Public Instruction (DPI), Madison, Wisconsin. In addition to editing annual Summer Library Program manuals (Wisconsin DPI, 1989-1993), she has written the *Wisconsin Public Library Trustee Handbook* (Wisconsin DPI, 1989; revised 1991) and coauthored *American Indian Resource Manual for Public Libraries* (Wisconsin DPI, 1992). She is currently a member of the Discover Wisconsin Writers Week Committee of the Wisconsin Library Association.

LaVonne Hayes Sanborn is an assistant professor of children's literature at Western Illinois University. She is coauthor of *Using Children's Books in Reading/Language Arts Programs* (Neal-Schuman Publishers, Inc., 1992).

Illinois

by LaVonne Hayes Sanborn

Nonfiction

331.88
McKissack, Patricia and McKissack, Frederic. *A Long Hard Journey: The Story of the Pullman Porter.* Walker (0-8027-6884-9), 1989. 144p. B/W photos. (Interest level: 5-8).

Twenty years after George Pullman debuted his first sleeping car with a run between Bloomington, Indiana, and Chicago, he established a special community for 12,000 white employees in southern Chicago. Thousands of African-American porters who served on the Pullman sleepers, the railroad car designed by George Pullman, struggled for fair treatment and formed the first African-American-controlled union. Numerous photos and a well-written text make this work an excellent research resource for transportation, labor, and early civil rights activity.
♦ Students can list working conditions (hours, pay, tasks) as presented in this text, and then invite a railroad, bus, or airline employee to discuss current conditions for comparison.
1. Porters—History 2. Pullman Company—History 3. Railroads—History 4. Labor unions—History.

385
Flatley, Dennis R. *The Railroads: Opening the West.* Watts (0-531-10682-9), 1989. (A First Book). 64p. B/W and Color illus. (Interest level: 5-8).

In this outline of railroad development from 1800 to 1865, one chapter explains the rapid development of the Illinois railroads which affected the growth of Chicago. A federal land grant to the Illinois Central Railroad made available two and a half million acres of land along proposed routes. This attractive, informative book is useful for research or browsing.
♦ Students may develop a visual railroad museum by duplicating illustrations from this book and other resources and replicating models. They may especially want to include the Pullman sleeper, which was developed in Illinois.
1. Railroads—History 2. West (U.S.)—History.

398.2
Kellogg, Steven. *Johnny Appleseed.* Morrow (0-688-06418-3), 1988. Unpaginated. Color illus. (Interest level: K-4).

John Chapman (Johnny Appleseed) traveled from Pennsylvania through Ohio, Indiana, and Illinois, clearing the land and planting apple orchards for future pioneers. Through entertaining illustrations and text, Kellogg shares biographical facts and many tall tales that developed around this historical figure.
♦ Students may celebrate Chapman's contribution by eating Golden Delicious and Jonathan apples, which are this state's leading varieties. They may read more about Chapman and locate these two types of apples on the "Apple Varieties" chart in Charles Micucci's *The Life and Times of the Apple* (Orchard, 1992). They may continue the celebration by reading Reeve Lindbergh's beautifully illustrated poem *Johnny Appleseed* (*see* Ohio—Fiction).
1. Appleseed, Johnny, 1774-1845 2. Apple.

574.5
Stone, Lynn M. *Prairies.* Rourke (0-86592-446-5), 1989. 47p. Color photos. (Interest level: 3-6).

Introduced with Louis Joliet's reaction to the prairie of northern Illinois in 1673 ("the most beautiful one can imagine"), the book explains that "prairie" is the French word for "meadow." This useful text then addresses three types of grasslands, the importance of fire in forming and maintaining prairie, and various plants and animals. Concluding the work are a helpful glossary, student activities, a listing of prairie sites and conservation organizations, and a brief index.
♦ Because tall-grass prairie in Illinois primarily exists in tiny relict patches, students may be able to visit railroad right-of-ways, which this book explains are the best places to locate tall grasses. If students do

not have access to prairie in their state or locality, they may wish to debate why it is important to protect it.
1. Prairie ecology 2. Ecology.

581.5
Lerner, Carol. *Seasons of the Tallgrass Prairie*. Morrow (0-688-22245-5), 1980 (out of print). 48p. B/W illus. (Interest level: 4-6).

This poetic presentation of the prairie across four seasons, enhanced with realistic drawings of more than 50 plants and grasses, explains how more than 200 individual plants are able to grow together in a square yard of earth. This is an excellent book to read aloud for a science, ecology, or Westward movement study.
♦ Students may take turns being Professor Prairie, who answers student-generated questions about grasses and plants.
1. Prairie plants 2. Ecology 3. Fire ecology.

599
Wild Mammals of Illinois. (Multimedia kit). Illinois Department of Conservation, 1991. (12-minute video, 4-minute cassette of Illinois Mammal Sounds, 22" x 17" poster, trivia and bingo games, teacher's guide). Free to Illinois public and private schools. A limited number are available to other educational institutions for a $30 donation. (Interest level: K-8).

The introductory video presents eight of Illinois' 64 known wild mammals: white-tailed deer (the state animal), coyote, beaver, raccoon, opossum, badger fox squirrel, and the bobcat (which is on the state's threatened list). This video has child appeal because the narrator wears animal costumes and performs camera tricks, and its educational value is ensured by the well-written script and excellent camera footage.
♦ Students may use numerous resources to identify as many of the remaining 56 Illinois mammals as possible. They may also plan and produce a video similar to *Wild Mammals of Illinois* for another state.
1. Mammals—Illinois 2. Illinois—Description.

599.74
Arnosky, Jim. *Raccoons and Ripe Corn*. Lothrop, Lee & Shepard (0-688-05456-0), 1987. Unpaginated. Color illus. (Interest level: K-2).

Striking illustrations and minimal text show a mother raccoon and her almost-grown kits sneaking into a cornfield in autumn for an all-night feast. Because both corn and raccoons are so prevalent in Illinois, this is an appropriate information book to share with young children.
♦ Students may listen to additional Arnosky titles, such as *Come Out Muskrats* (Lothrop, 1989) and *Deer at the Brook* (Lothrop, 1986). These same mammals can be seen in the excellent video titled *Wild Mammals of Illinois* (*see* preceding entry).
1. Raccoon 2. Corn 3. Autumn.

630
Bial, Raymond. *County Fair*. Houghton Mifflin (0-395-57644-X), 1992. 39p. Color photos. (Interest level: 3-7).

The Champaign County, Illinois, fair is the focus of this photo essay by an Illinois author and photographer. After a brief introduction explaining the origin of the word "fair" (from the Latin word "feria," meaning "holiday"), the book is divided into four distinctive parts: "The Livestock Barns," "The Exhibit Hall," "The Grandstand," and "The Midway." Each aspect is briefly presented through striking photos and informative text.
♦ To learn more about state and local fairs, rural students may invite representatives from the local 4-H, Future Farmers of America, or nearest county fair association to share their insights. Other students may write to state fair associations or interview adults who have participated in state and local fairs.
1. Fairs 2. Agriculture—Exhibitions.

630
Demuth, Patricia. *Joel: Growing Up a Farm Man*. Photos by Jack Demuth. Putnam (0-396-07997-0), 1982. 144p. B/W photos. (Interest level: 3-6).

This photo essay introduces farm family life in northwest Illinois (near Scales Mound) and portrays the incredible amount of work involved. Thirteen-year-old Joel, youngest of six children, plants and harvests field crops and assumes complete responsibility for the care of the pigs. More than 100 photos and lively text make this an inviting book.
♦ Students may compare their personal lists of chores with Joel's list. Rural students can compare Joel's farm with their own. Just for fun, they may share the author's picture book entitled *The Ornery Morning* (Dutton, 1991), in which the farm animals refuse to do any work but change their minds when the farmer refuses to feed them.
1. Farmers 2. Farm life—Illinois 3. Agriculture—Middle West.

631.3
Bushey, Jerry. *Farming the Land: Modern Farmers and Their Machines*. Carolrhoda (0-87614-314-1), 1987. 39p. Color photos. (Interest level: 3-6).

Large photos and minimal text blend well to introduce the many pieces of farm equipment needed to plant, maintain, and harvest farm crops such as corn, wheat, soybeans, and hay. Included are several photos of machinery by John Deere, a company that is home-based in Moline, Illinois. A glossary adds to the book's usefulness.
♦ Students may examine a crop map, which can be found in most general Illinois resources, to determine where corn, wheat, and soybeans are grown in the state. Students may also make a list of known

farm machinery brands other than John Deere and research the location of their home-bases.

1. Agriculture 2. Agricultural machinery 3. Farmers.

633.1
Bial, Raymond. *Corn Belt Harvest*. Houghton Mifflin (0-395-56234-1), 1991. 48p. Color photos. (Interest level: 4-8).

This Illinois author and photographer has created a brief photo essay about the Corn Belt. Emphasizing the needed equipment, sharp, clear photos show the step-by-step process of planting, growing, and harvesting. Of special interest are all the photos of the Ivesdale, Illinois, grain elevator. Although this book will encourage browsing for all ages, the well-written text is most appropriate for upper elementary and older students.
♦ Starting with the uses for corn listed in this text, students may develop competitive teams charged with finding as many uses for corn as possible.

1. Corn 2. Agriculture 3. Agricultural machinery.

637
McFarland, Cynthia. *Cows in the Parlor: A Visit to a Dairy Farm*. Atheneum (0-689-31584-8), 1990. Unpaginated. Color photos. (Interest level: K-3).

Although the photos in this book were not necessarily taken in Illinois, they represent well the daily routine at dairy farms in the northern part of the state. Photos of farm machinery, milking equipment, and a calf add to this book's appeal. The simple illustrated text is an appropriate introduction to modern dairy farm life.
♦ Students may be introduced to the many different types of maps that explain information about a state. Students can use an encyclopedia or general state book to search for the dairy farm symbol on a "farm and mineral product" map of Illinois or of their state or region.

1. Dairying 2. Agriculture 3. Agricultural machinery.

690
Balterman, Lee. *Girders and Cranes: A Skyscraper Is Built*. Whitman (0-8075-2923-0), 1991. Unpaginated. Color photos. (Interest level: 3-6).

Fifty photos detail the three and a half years it took to build one of Chicago's tallest buildings. In this step-by-step explanation, there is emphasis on the equipment used and the many people needed as well as safety precautions followed. A world record for concrete pumping was set when construction reached the roof. Concrete was pumped 67 stories from the ground through a pipeline. The color photos and minimal text will be appreciated by browsers, but this book is also useful for research because special construction vocabulary is defined.
♦ Students may increase this book's research usefulness by creating an index for it. Or they may consult other skyscraper construction books, such as Vicki Cobb's pop-up book, *Skyscraper Going Up!* (Crowell, 1987), to discover what a "topping out" ceremony is.

1. Skyscrapers—Design and construction 2. Building.

780
Terkel, Studs. *Giants of Jazz*. Rev. by Milly Hawk Daniel. Harper (0-690-00998-4), 1957, 1975. 210p. B/W photos. (Interest level: 6-8).

The history of American jazz is outlined through the lives of 13 individuals, including four who spent extended time in Illinois: Joe Oliver, who came to Chicago from New Orleans in 1918; his friend, Louis Armstrong, who joined him in 1922; Bix Beiderbecke, who attended Lake Forest Academy and went into the Loop to hear numerous bands; and Benny Goodman, who had his first clarinet lesson at Jane Addams' Hull House when he was 10 years old. The interrelated lives of many of these famous musicians adds to the appeal of the work.
♦ Public, school, or individual music libraries may have some of the jazz albums listed in this book's discography. Students may listen and reflect on the special importance of Chicago, as well as New Orleans and New York, to the development of jazz.

1. Jazz music 2. Jazz musicians—Biography.

784.4
Goodman, Ailene S. *Abe Lincoln in Song and Story*. (Audiocassette). Eliza Records (0-9620704-0-8), 1988. (Includes guide). $11.88. (Interest level: 4).

These 11 lively tunes, well performed by a company of six singers and four instrumentalists, include songs sung by Lincoln's mother (e.g., "Buckeye Jim"), those liked by Lincoln (e.g., "Hoosen Johnny"), and representatives from the years Lincoln lived in Illinois (e.g., "Goober Peas"). Brief narration gives a clear historical perspective for each song, as does the 11-page guide.
♦ Children will enjoy listening to and singing these lively songs. Older students may locate the many illustrated folk songs available in libraries and investigate the historical perspective of each. Of special interest may be Robert Quackenbush's *There'll Be a Hot Time in the Old Town Tonight: The Great Chicago Fire of 1871* (*see* following entry).

1. Lincoln, Abraham, 1809-1865 2. Songs, American.

784.4
Quackenbush, Robert. *There'll Be a Hot Time in the Old Town Tonight: The Great Chicago Fire of 1871*. Harper (0-397-32267-4), 1974, 1988. Unpaginated. Color illus. (Interest level: K-8).

Great disasters are often commemorated in ballads, and the Chicago fire has been a familiar subject throughout the years. To the traditional ballad Quackenbush adds lively verses, the musical score, brightly colored illustrations inspired from authentic period prints and photographs, and useful information about fire survival.

♦ After students have been introduced to the background details, they may sing the ballads to another class and share the history of the fire.
1. Chicago (Ill.)—Fire, 1871 2. Folk songs 3. Fires—Chicago (Ill.).

796.357
Fertig, Dennis. *Take Me Out to the Ball Game*. Photos by William Franklin McMahon. Whitman (0-8075-7735-9), 1987. Unpaginated. B/W photos. (Interest level: K-2).

This photo essay introduces Ryan, who attends his first major league baseball game at Chicago's Wrigley Field when the Chicago Cubs play the Atlanta Braves. His adventure includes riding on a train, purchasing a scorecard, obtaining an autograph from Bobby Dernier, and trying to catch a foul ball.
♦ Because professional sports teams are very important to tourism, students may discuss teams and players. If students have visited Wrigley Field or other baseball fields, they may compare personal experiences to Ryan's.
1. Baseball—Chicago (Ill.) 2. Chicago Cubs (Baseball team).

811
Brooks, Gwendolyn. *Bronzeville Boys and Girls*. Illus. by Ronni Solbert. Harper (0-06-020651-9), 1956, 1967. 40p. B/W illus. (Interest level: 2-5).

This African American, who is the Poet Laureate of Illinois, presents a collection of 36 poems, each one titled with a child's name. For example, Eppie yearns for something of her very own, and Lyle envies a tree because it has not had to move seven times as he has. Although these poems are Chicago-based, they reflect the experiences of children anywhere, at any time.
♦ After students have heard several of these poems, they may write poems about themselves or friends, expressing their dreams or disappointments. Students may search through anthologies to locate other poems that have a child's name as the title.
1. African Americans—Poetry 2. Poetry, American.

811
Siebert, Diane. *Heartland*. Illus. by Wendell Minor. Crowell (0-690-04732-0), 1989. Unpaginated. Color illus. (Interest level: 3-8).

This tribute to the characteristics of the Midwest includes farmland and animals, small towns and large cities, and nature's contributions (seasonal changes) and challenges (drought and tornadoes). Beautifully written and illustrated, the poetic text begs to be shared orally. Teachers and librarians may wish to stress Wendell Minor's association with Illinois because he states, "The pictures I've painted try to capture what I remember as the good life: the farming community in my hometown, Aurora."

♦ The teacher may play instrumental listening music as background when reading this book aloud to young people and plan a special poetry-reading event featuring many young people reading poems about Illinois and the region.
1. Middle West—Poetry 2. Poetry, American.

909
Rahn, Joan Elma. *Animals that Changed History*. Atheneum (0-689-31137-0), 1986. 114p. B/W illus. (Interest level: 6-8).

This book explains that rats, horses, and beavers have played important roles in world and United States history. Although horses were important to the development of the prairie states, the chapter about beavers has special significance to Illinois because of its details about the Mississippi River exploration by Jolliet, Marquette, and LaSalle.
♦ After the teacher or librarian reads aloud excerpts about beaver and horse history, students may wish to debate which animal was most important. They can also compare the current uses and importance of these two animals.
1. Animals and civilization 2. Horses 3. Rats as carriers of disease 4. Beavers.

910
Haskins, Jim. *Against All Opposition: Black Explorers in America*. Walker (0-8027-8138-1), 1992. 86p. B/W photos and illus. (Interest level: 5-8).

One chapter in this work is devoted to Jean Baptiste Point du Sable, usually regarded as the founder of Chicago. After leaving Haiti as a young man, du Sable lived in New Orleans and British-controlled St. Louis. In 1774, du Sable and his family traveled north and built a trading post at Eschikagou.
♦ Using other resources about Chicago's history, young people may investigate further how John Kinzie was erroneously credited with Chicago's settlement for many years. They may read other chapters in the book to determine how the empathy between Native Americans and African Americans helped in the exploration of America.
1. Explorers 2. African Americans—Biography 3. America—Exploration.

917.73
Davis, James E. and **Hawke, Sharryl Davis**. *Chicago*. Raintree (0-8172-3025-4), 1990. (World Cities). 64p. B/W and Color photos. (Interest level: 3-6).

This overview of Illinois' largest city includes its history, an examination of the suburbs as well as the metropolis, a discussion of the city's culture, and a projection of its future. Numerous photographs and lively text make this book appealing.
♦ After reading about Chicago's future plans, students may invite their local mayor or city manager to discuss current concerns and future plans of their

own community, which could be compared to those of Chicago.
1. Chicago (Ill.).

917.73
Davis, Lauren. *Kidding Around Chicago: A Young Person's Guide to the City.* Illus. by Sally Blackmore. John Muir (0-945465-70-X), 1990. 63p. Color illus. (Interest level: 3-5).

Historical, geographical, and cultural information is provided about Chicago and its suburbs. Street maps are included for some regions: Lake Michigan, downtown Chicago, and the Loop. Other special features include a monthly calendar of special events and addresses for the most popular sites. This sightseeing tour has definite child appeal.
♦ Students may browse the many possibilities available for sightseeing before they determine their 10 favorite historical or geographical locations.
1. Chicago (Ill.)—Description—Guides.

917.73
Stewart, Gail. *Chicago.* Rourke (0-86592-538-0), 1989. (Great Cities of the USA). 47p. B/W and Color photos. (Interest level: 5-8).

After a brief history of Chicago, three sections of the city are described: Downtown (e.g., the Loop and the John Hancock Building), North Side (e.g., the Carl Sandburg Village and the Cabrini-Green housing project), and the South Side (e.g., Chinatown and the Irish and Polish neighborhood of Bridgeport). Numerous photos make Chicago come alive.
♦ Chicago is a city of world statistics, including the tallest building, largest lighted fountain, and busiest airport. Students may consult numerous Chicago resources to compile a comprehensive list to be put into a "Chicago Book of Records."
1. Chicago (Ill.)—Description.

973.5
Hargrove, Jim. *The Story of the Black Hawk War.* Illus. by Ralph Canaday. Childrens Press (0-516-04696-9), 1986. (Cornerstones of Freedom). 31p. B/W illus. (Interest level: 3-5).

In 1832 the last great Indian uprising east of the Mississippi River was led by the Sauk Indian chief, Black Hawk, who struggled to prevent settlers from pushing his people out of Illinois. Using numerous quotes from the writings of Black Hawk, the complicated story of his defeat is successfully retold from his perspective for young readers.
♦ The Black Hawk War is frequently referred to as the saddest event in Illinois history. Students may determine reasons for this statement.
1. Black Hawk War, 1832 2. Black Hawk, Sauk chief, 1767-1838 3. Sauk Indians.

973.6
McGovern, Ann. *If You Grew Up with Abraham Lincoln.* Illus. by Brinton Turkle. Scholastic (0-590-42230-8), 1966. 79p. Green/White illus. (Interest level: 1-5).

The author notes, "In this book I want to give you an idea of what it was like to grow up with Lincoln and to live in the same places that he lived." In a question/answer format she includes high-child-appeal topics, such as occupations, illnesses, homes, and entertainment.
♦ This book concludes with "some important changes that happened during Lincoln's lifetime." Focusing on one of the topics presented, students may interview a parent or other adult to determine what changes that person has experienced during his or her lifetime. They may add illustrations to enhance their written report of the interview.
1. Lincoln, Abraham, 1809-1865 2. Illinois—History 3. Presidents—United States.

977
Aylesworth, Thomas G. and **Aylesworth, Virginia L.** *Western Great Lakes: Illinois, Iowa, Minnesota, Wisconsin.* Chelsea (0-7910-1046-5), 1987, 1992. 64p. Color photos and maps. (Interest level: 3-6).

The separate treatment of Illinois is divided into four sections ("The Land," "The History," "The People," and "Of Special Interest"). This well-illustrated book includes a map highlighting the largest cities as well as photographs of the state bird, flower, flag, and capital.
♦ "The People" section of this book gives the hometown for several well-known politicians, reformers, writers, and entertainers. Using this resource and others to determine additional names, students may create Illinois maps highlighting names and hometowns of famous people.
1. Illinois 2. Iowa 3. Minnesota 4. Wisconsin.

977
Great Lakes Region. (Sound filmstrip). Eye Gate/Nystrom, 1987. 3 color filmstrips, 3 cassettes. (15 min. for each filmstrip). $128 for the series. (Interest level: 4-6).

Illinois is among the five Great Lakes states examined according with respect to people and resources, geography and climate, and cities. Chicago, Rockford, Peoria, Springfield, and East St. Louis receive coverage. A well-written script and clear, relevant photographs communicate the state's and region's economic activities, including transportation, steel, corn, hogs, dairy farms, beef cattle, soybeans, and farm machinery production.
♦ Students may wish to prepare transparency maps to identify regions within Illinois that are known for specific economic activities.
1. Great Lakes region 2. Geography 3. Middle West—Description.

977

History of the Great Lakes States. (Sound filmstrip). National Geographic Society, 1990. (Part I of three filmstrips in the series History of the United States). Color, (18 min.). $97 for Part I. (Interest level: 5-8).

These 56 frames present a brief overview of the history of the five states surrounding the Great Lakes from the time of the mound builders through the 1980s. Of special significance to the study of Illinois are Marquette and Jolliet, Black Hawk, John Deere, Abraham Lincoln, and the cities of Galena and Chicago. Excellent photographs and a well-written script make this a worthwhile historical overview.

♦ This filmstrip is a good introduction to the history of this region. As students listen, they may choose one person or event for further research. Then, as the filmstrip is repeated, individual students may orally contribute new facts to the filmstrip's brief overview.

1. Great Lakes region 2. Great Lakes region—History.

977

McCall, Edith. *Biography of a River: The Living Mississippi.* Walker (0-8027-6914-4), 1990. 162p. B/W photos and illus. (Interest level: 6-8).

Thirteen chapters give a comprehensive history of this mighty river, which is the western boundary of Illinois. The work addresses early explorations of the area and the settlements established. Of current interest is the vast investment of work and money to make the Upper Mississippi as navigable as the Lower Mississippi. The author's writing style more than compensates for the lack of quality in some photograph reproductions. A 10-page glossary and extensive index increase the work's usefulness.

♦ The preface includes a five-page "The River Speaks" section in which the river is personified. Students may model this writing technique by choosing another river and describing where it begins, what sites are along its banks, and where it ends.

1. Mississippi River—History.

977

The Mississippi. (Sound filmstrip). National Geographic Society, 1985. (The Water's Edge: Life Along the Great Rivers Series). Color, (17 min. for each filmstrip). $97 for the series. (Interest level: 5-8).

Beautiful photographs plus an interesting script make this a well-produced visual description of the land along the Mississippi River, the history of river transportation, areas of interest, and river control projects. A map enables students to understand how the Mississippi forms the boundaries for 10 states, including the western border of Illinois. Of special interest is a sunset scene from Cairo, Illinois, where the Ohio River flows into the Mississippi.

♦ Working in groups, young people can research the various geographic regions of the United States, identifying the sets of rivers that serve as state boundaries. They may also explore the importance of those rivers for transportation, irrigation, recreation, and hydroelectric power.

1. Mississippi River.

977

Stein, R. Conrad. *The Story of Marquette and Jolliet.* Illus. by Richard Wahl. Childrens Press (0-516-04630-6), 1981. (Cornerstones of Freedom Series). 31p. B/W illus. (Interest level: 3-6).

This description of the 2,500-mile expedition to find the Mississippi River and claim new lands for France presents Louis Jolliet, the first New World explorer to be born in America (near Quebec). This work includes references to Quincy, Chicago, the Illinois River, and the Illinois Indians. It is especially useful for comparison of what landmarks were called in the 1600s and what they are called today.

♦ On his way back to Montreal, Jolliet shot the Lachine Rapids (St. Lawrence River) and lost his strongbox containing expedition maps and notes. Using the text and maps from this book, young people may replicate the contents of his strongbox and celebrate its discovery.

1. Mississippi River—Exploring expeditions 2. Jolliet, Louis, 1645-1700 3. Marquette, Jacques, 1637-1675 4. Explorers.

977.3

Aylesworth, Thomas and **Aylesworth, Virginia.** *Chicago.* Rosen (0-8239-1209-4), 1990. 64p. Color photos. (Interest level: 4-6).

Following a brief introduction and a long chapter about the city's history, famous or influential Chicago-born writers, musicians, comedians, and entertainers are noted. The "On the Tour Bus" section emphasizes museums, parks, buildings, and churches. Several double-page and numerous full-page photographs make this book pleasurable for browsing. A time line and a comprehensive index add to the book's usefulness for research.

♦ Students may discuss the Chicago-born people they recognize and use other resources to enlarge the list. Shel Silverstein will be known by many young people, and they may wish to share his humorous verse and song lyrics.

1. Chicago (Ill.).

977.3

Carpenter, Allan. *Illinois.* Rev. ed. Childrens Press (0-516-04113-4), 1979. (New Enchantment of America). 96p. Color illus. (Interest level: 4-8).

This comprehensive coverage of Illinois includes chapters about its history, natural resources, famous people, historic and recreation sites, and cities. The "Handy Reference Section" includes instant facts, a historical timetable, a list of important people, a list of governors, and an index. Although some basic infor-

mation like population. and the current governor will be out-of-date, the historical information is still very useful. The numerous illustrations also make this a pleasurable book for browsing.
♦ Using the historical timetable or general book information, students may illustrate and label one historical event to add to a collage titled "It Happened in Illinois."
1. Illinois.

977.3
Fradin, Dennis B. *Illinois*. Childrens Press (0-516-03813-3), 1991. 64p. Color photos. (Interest level: 2-5).

Useful for browsing and research, this work addresses topography, history, industries, historic sites, and famous Illinoisans. A "Did You Know?" section contains interesting facts about softball, the original Ferris wheel, and Miss America winners. Especially useful are the photographs in the "Illinois Information" section, a time line of historical events, and a full-page map of major cities and rivers. A glossary and index are included.
♦ Because the historic site chapter is arranged according to northern, central, and southern divisions, students may plot a bus trip to their favorite section, determining mileage, expenses, and time involved.
1. Illinois.

977.3
A Guide to Free and Inexpensive Materials on Illinois History. Illinois State Historical Society and Illinois State Historic Preservation Agency, 1990. 13p. (Interest level: 3+).

This booklet lists materials about Illinois available from various governmental agencies. Of special interest are "My State Reader" (a set of six pamphlets suitable for students in second and third grades) and "Stories from Illinois History" (a set of six pamphlets for students in grades four through six).
♦ Young people may write for free materials and contribute them to a vertical file in the school library media center.
1. Illinois—History—Sources.

977.3
Historical and Cultural Agencies and Museums in Illinois. Congress of Illinois Historical Societies and Museums, annual. Free. (Interest level: 5+).

This directory is a guide to Illinois' cultural heritage presented in museums, historic sites, and nature/science centers. Its arrangement is alphabetical by town, but there is also a helpful county index. Each entry contains an address, dates and times open, and a contact person.

♦ Young people may create individual maps of Illinois or an Illinois county, featuring sites for (1) museums, (2) science centers, and (3) historical places.
1. Illinois—Description—Guidebooks 2. Museums—Illinois 3. Historic sites—Illinois.

977.3
Misselhorn, Roscoe. *Illinois Sketches*. Edited by Elaine Stratton. Swiss Village Book Store (0-9615744-0-2), 1985. 160p. B/W illus. (Interest level: 5-8).

Seventy-six pencil sketches, each accompanied by a one-page description, help portray Illinois history and culture. Sites commemorated include the George Rogers Clark statue, three former capitol buildings and the current one in Springfield, the Ulysses Grant home in Galena, important bridges and forts, architectural designs by Frank Lloyd Wright and Buckmaster Fuller, and the eight-sided schoolhouse in Randolph County. The realistic art and brief highlights of important events and people encourage browsing.
♦ Students may locate each of these sites on an Illinois map. The state may be divided into sections so that groups of students can plan a sightseeing trip (mileage, overnight stops, food and lodging expenses) to last a designated length of time. This book contains an invitation to submit further information about any site for consideration in a second edition.
1. Illinois 2. Historic sites—Illinois.

977.3
Pfeiffer, Christine. *Chicago*. Dillon (0-87518-385-9), 1988. (Downtown America). 60p. Color photos. (Interest level: 3-7).

This work provides a detailed explanation of the city's ethnic diversity; a listing of festivals and parades; an overview of its schools, churches, homes, and historic areas; a description of cultural opportunities (zoos, museums, sports, theaters); and a listing of places to visit (with complete addresses and phone numbers). Numerous photos, lively text, and several special lists make this a very useful book.
♦ Students may wish to use this book to determine and justify places they would like to visit in Chicago. They may also wish to compare the cultural opportunities in Chicago with those in other major American cities.
1. Chicago (Ill.).

977.3
Simon, Charnan. *The Story of the Haymarket Riot*. Childrens Press (0-516-04740-X), 1988. (Cornerstones of Freedom). 31p. B/W and Color photos and illus. (Interest level: 3-6).

Rapid industrial growth in American cities produced unrest, leading to the formation of unions to fight for improved working conditions. In Chicago on May 4, 1886, as police arrived to break up a peaceful labor rally, a bomb exploded, setting off a riot when police opened fire on the crowd. This short overview of a very

complicated incident will provide background information for researchers.
♦ Students may consult other Illinois history resources about this riot to acquire further facts and then debate if the eight men accused should have been held responsible when the bomb thrower could not be determined.
1. Haymarket Square Riot, Chicago, (Ill.), 1886 2. Labor disputes 3. Riots—Chicago (Ill.).

977.3
Stanek, Muriel. *We Came from Vietnam*. Photos by William Franklin McMahon. Whitman (0-8075-8699-4), 1985. 46p. B/W photos. (Interest level: 3-6).

This photo essay introduces the Nguyen family, who are Vietnamese refugees attempting to adjust to Chicago life. Shared is information about Vietnam, how they became boat people, and their adjustments to Chicago's weather, a new language, and different schools and food. Also discussed are strong family ties and respect for elderly people. Numerous photos and meaningful text make this an excellent introduction to the Vietnamese culture.
♦ Students may compare this true story with Eve Bunting's fictional account *How Many Days to America?* (Clarion, 1988) in which well-conceived illustrations help tell the story of Caribbean refugees who also came to the United States as boat people. Students may list similarities between the two cultural experiences.
1. Vietnamese Americans 2. United States—Immigration and emigration.

977.3
Stein, R. Conrad. *Illinois*. Childrens Press (0-516-00459-X), 1987. (America the Beautiful State Book). 144p. B/W and Color photos and illus. (Interest level: 4-8).

Ten chapters describe Illinois history, geography, government, economy, culture, and important people. Twenty-four pages of "Facts at a Glance" summarize the highlights of the earlier 10 chapters. Nine different maps present information about major highways, population density, counties, rivers, and resources. Numerous illustrations, a well-written text, and a good index make this a very useful resource, especially for Illinois history.
♦ Illinois history includes several serious conflicts involving labor, race, and war protest. Students may be challenged to locate the highlights of the riots in this text and then create a timetable of "Moments of Conflict."
1. Illinois 2. Illinois—History.

977.3
Stein, R. Conrad. *The Story of the Chicago Fire*. Illus. by Richard Wahl. Childrens Press (0-516-04633-0), 1982. 31p. B/W illus. (Interest level: 2-5).

This brief overview of the nation's deadliest fire includes its causes, physical and economic toll, and information about the rebuilding. The large print and many sketches make this book especially useful for younger students. All students will benefit from the many eyewitness quotes that are included.
♦ Teachers and librarians may introduce students to information about National Fire Prevention Week, which is celebrated on the anniversary of the Chicago Fire. Students may add to the three causes listed in this book by doing further research to determine the many speculated causes of the fire.
1. Chicago (Ill.)—Fire, 1871 2. Fires—Chicago (Ill.).

977.3
Thompson, Kathleen. *Illinois*. Raintree (0-86514-452-4), 1988. (Portrait of America). 48p. B/W and Color photos. (Interest level: 2-5).

This work provides a broad historical overview of Illinois, emphasizing individuals, both well-known (e.g., Abraham Lincoln) and lesser-known (e.g., Jesse White, who established a successful tumbling team in a Chicago housing project). Although the text is fragmented, the numerous photos and emphasis on people make the book useful for curriculum-related activities.
♦ Students will be interested when they read that Illinois is the number one state in candy manufacturing. They may report to the class when they see an Illinois address on a candy wrapper and add the brand to a developing list. Their first item can be Wrigley's gum.
1. Illinois.

977.3
Warburton, Lois. *The Chicago Fire*. Illus. by Maurie Manning and others. Lucent (1-56006-002-6), 1989. 64p. B/W photos and illus. (Interest level: 5-8).

Following a detailed account of the 24 hours during which the fire destroyed much of Chicago and killed more than 300 people is a brief explanation of how such a fire would be handled today. Of special interest are the numerous drawings that depict Chicago, the insert boxes that explain technical concepts, and eyewitness anecdotes.
♦ This book's preface states that disasters have always aroused human curiosity. Students may investigate other international, state, and local disasters (e.g., earthquakes, floods, volcanic eruptions) through interviews and research. Of special interest may be other fires that are listed on page 9 of the book.
1. Chicago (Ill.)—Fire, 1871 2. Fires—Chicago (Ill.)

Biography

920
Aaseng, Nathan. *The Problem Solvers: People Who Turned Problems into Products*. Lerner (0-8225-0675-0), 1989. 80p. B/W photos. (Interest level: 5-8).

Among the nine people included in this work is Illinois' John Deere, who "visited a sawmill in 1837 and noticed a broken circular saw made of steel." Using that piece of steel and designing a better shape, he invented a plow for Illinois soil.

♦ Many other Illinois people have solved problems as Deere did, and students may investigate other resources to discover who they were. They may create a student-produced book of "Illinois Problem Solvers." Students may also think about products that they could invent to solve current problems in the home or school.

1. Business people—Biography 2. Problem solving.

920
Aaseng, Nathan. *The Unsung Heroes: Unheralded People Who Invented Famous Products.* Lerner (0-8225-0676-9), 1989. 80p. B/W photos. (Interest level: 4-7).

Among the featured unsung hereoes are Mac and Richard McDonald, who owned a popular eatery and sold a franchise that enabled Ray Kroc to open the first McDonald's in suburban Chicago in 1955. This work also includes unsung heroes associated with Coca-Cola, General Motors, Hoover (vacuum cleaners), Bingo, Superman, and Hummel (figurines). Brief highlights and photos make this enjoyable reading.

♦ If a McDonald's restaurant is nearby, students may invite the manager to explain quality control and franchise details.

1. Business people—Biography.

920
Collins, David R. and **Witter, Evelyn.** *Notable Illinois Women.* Illus. by Michael J. Payne and David R. Collins. Quest (0-940286-52-1), 1982. 152p. B/W illus. (Interest level: 4-8).

These six- to nine-page sketches of 12 women who made a contribution to society's welfare include Jane Addams, Mary Ann Bickerdyke, Marguerite Brooks, Lorraine Hansberry, Mahalia Jackson, Mother Jones, Harriet Monroe, Archange Ouilmette, Bertha Palmer, Lucy Perkins, Myrtle Walgreen, and Frances Willard. Bibliographies follow each presentation. In addition, there are thumbnail sketches of 28 other women. This collection provides useful read-aloud or research material.

♦ Using the 28 additional names listed, plus any others discovered through library research, young people may brainstorm and justify who should be in *More Notable Illinois Women* (an imaginary second volume).

1. Illinois—Biography 2. Women—Biography.

920
Haber, Louis. *Black Pioneers of Science and Invention.* Harcourt (0-15-208565-3), 1970. 181p. B/W illus. (Interest level: 6-8).

Of the 14 scientists described, Illinois can claim at least three: Lloyd Hall, a pioneering food chemist; Daniel Williams, who attended medical school in Chicago and later taught there; and Percy Julian, a chemist who worked for Chicago's Glidden Company before opening his own lab. These factual overviews emphasize schools attended, company affiliations, societal memberships, and prejudices encountered.

♦ At the time of publication, both Lloyd Hall and Percy Julian were still alive. Students may consult other resources to determine their death dates and additional contributions that could be inserted into the book for future researchers.

1. Scientists—Biography 2. Inventors—Biography 3. African Americans—Biography.

920
Jacobs, William Jay. *Great Lives: Human Rights.* Scribner (0-684-19036-2), 1990. 278p. B/W photos. (Interest level: 4-8).

Among the brief biographical sketches of Americans who fought for human rights are three individuals associated with Illinois: Jane Addams, who founded Hull House in Chicago; William Jennings Bryan, who awakened the nation's sympathy for the poor and farmers during his three unsuccessful presidential candidacies; and Clarence Darrow, renowned defense lawyer who championed the rights of organized labor and criminals. These sketches provide useful and enjoyable reading.

♦ Students may choose one of these three individuals and create a collage of his or her life, emphasizing whom they helped and why.

1. Reformers—Biography 2. Human rights.

920
Katz, William Loren. *Black People Who Made the Old West.* Crowell (0-690-01253-5), 1977. 181p. B/W photos. (Interest level: 6-8).

Of the 35 African Americans briefly described in this text, two have special significance to Illinois: Jean Baptiste Pointe du Sable, the first settler of Chicago, and John Jones, who ran a prosperous tailoring business in the nineteenth century and fought for equal rights by assisting underground railroaders, delivering speeches against slavery, and working for the repeal of an Illinois law that forbade blacks to enter the state. This book contains information not easily found in other sources for young people.

♦ Because information was not as readily recorded in the past as it is now, the amount and degree of detail of the experiences of earlier Illinois settlers vary. Students may consult numerous Illinois history books to discover the conflicts in information about du Sable.

1. African Americans—Biography 2. Frontier and pioneer life—West (U.S.) 3. West (U.S.)—Biography.

920
Lomask, Milton. *Great Lives: Exploration.* Scribner (0-684-18511-3), 1988. 258p. B/W photos (Interest level: 4-8).

Among the 25 world explorers presented in brief, biographical sketches is La Salle, the French explorer who led the expedition that traced the Mississippi River to its mouth, founding several Illinois forts in the process. Included is a reproduction of a George Catlin painting depicting the expedition's departure from Canada. Because of its brevity and readability, this overview will be helpful for research.
♦ Students may reproduce a map of the Great Lakes area and the Mississippi River so that La Salle's various journeys can be visually traced and displayed.
1. Explorers—Biography.

920
Lomask, Milton. *Great Lives: Invention and Technology.* Scribner (0-684-19106-7), 1991. 262p. B/W photos. (Interest level: 4-8).

The lives of 27 world inventors are briefly sketched. Although several of them attended college in Illinois, two especially are claimed by the state as "native sons." Enrico Fermi helped build the world's first atomic reactor at the University of Chicago. Element number 100 was named fermium in his honor. Cyrus McCormick invented a successful wheat reaper and built a factory in Chicago. Because these sketches cover the highlights and are so readable, they will be of much use to researchers.
♦ The teacher or media specialist may invite an attorney to explain the patent process. If the community includes someone who is attempting to improve a product or invent something new, he or she may be asked to discuss with the group the problems encountered.
1. Inventors—Biography 2. Inventions.

920
Peavy, Linda and **Smith, Ursula.** *Dreams into Deeds: Nine Women Who Dared.* Scribner (0-684-18484-2), 1985. 148p. B/W photos. (Interest level: 5-8).

Of the nine National Women's Hall of Famers briefly described, three have significance to Illinois: Jane Addams, who established Chicago's Hull House; Alice Hamilton, who assisted at Hull House and fought for safer working conditions in factories; and Mother Jones, who was a labor activist. Each chapter presents a well-written overview of their dreams and achievements, as well as two photos.
♦ Because this book's emphasis is on childhood dreams that were achieved, students may create a collage of personal dreams they want to achieve in the future.
1. Women—United States—Biography.

920
Shiels, Barbara. *Winners: Women and the Nobel Prize.* Dillon (0-87518-293-3), 1985. 254p. B/W photos. (Interest level: 6-8).

The 21 women who were Nobel Prize recipients between 1903 and 1983 are listed in this book. Among them is Jane Addams, who established a settlement house in Chicago. She is one of 11 recipients who receive brief sketches in Appendix A. This book's main emphasis is on eight females, one of whom is Maria Geoppert Mayer, the 1963 Physics Prize winner. She was born in Germany and worked at the University of Chicago's Institute for Nuclear Studies for many years. At the University of Chicago she became "the first physicist to be able to explain clearly how the particles in an atom's nucleus are arranged." This book presents very readable material about twentieth-century heroines.
♦ Because this book only lists female Nobel Prize winners to 1983, young people may research to determine if additional females have won since then and if they have a tie to Illinois.
1. Nobel prizes 2. Women—Biography.

92 Addams, Jane
Kent, Deborah. *Jane Addams and Hull House.* Childrens Press (0-516-04852-X), 1992. (Cornerstones of Freedom). 32p. B/W and Color photos. (Interest level: 3-5).

This overview of Addams' life begins and ends in Cedarville, Illinois, where she was born in 1860 and buried in 1935. Narrative and numerous quotes tell of her popular settlement house in the industrial slums of Chicago and her unpopular crusade for world peace. This biography is useful for both research and read-aloud purposes.
♦ Many of the people who became involved in Hull House work went on to become well known. Students may list the many people mentioned in this text and determine their main contributions to society.
1. Addams, Jane, 1860-1935 2. Social workers 3. Hull House (Chicago, Ill.)—History 4. Reformers.

92 Addams, Jane
Mitchard, Jacquelyn. *Jane Addams: Pioneer in Social Reform and Activist for World Peace.* Gareth Stevens (0-8368-0144-X), 1991. (People Who Have Helped the World). 68p. B/W and Color photos and illus. (Interest level: 5-8).

Particularly emphasized in this account of Jane Addams' life is her establishment, with Ellen Gates Starr, of Hull House in a poverty-stricken immigrant Chicago neighborhood. Through the years, they and many other volunteers provided whatever support they could through funds raised at educational and cultural events.
♦ The index of Mitchard's work identifies the names of many influential and famous people (e.g., John Dewey, Booker T. Washington, James Garfield, and Abraham Lincoln). Young people may choose one

of these individuals and determine his or her relationship to Jane Addams.
1. Addams, Jane, 1860-1935 2. Reformers 3. Social workers 4. Hull House (Chicago, Ill.)—History.

92 Black Hawk, Sauk Chief
Oppenheim, Joanne. *Black Hawk, Frontier Warrior.* Illus. by Hal Frenck. Troll (0-89375-157-X), 1979. Unpaginated. Brown/White illus. (Interest level: 3-5).

Having proven his abilities as a hunter and warrior, 15-year-old Black Hawk was awarded feathers and paint. After his father's death, he led his people as they defended their Illinois land against white settlers. Students will find the full-page map of Illinois useful as they read this simple biography.
♦ Students may consult state and Native American resources to determine whether surrounding states had chiefs who became as famous as Black Hawk. Did they defend their land with the same vigor? They may create a gallery of famous Native Americans from the Great Lakes area.
1. Black Hawk, Sauk chief, 1767-1838 2. Sauk Indians.

92 Clark, George Rogers
DeLeeuw, Adele. *George Rogers Clark, Frontier Fighter.* Illus. by Russ Hoover. Chelsea (0-7910-1456-8), 1967, 1992. (A Discovery Book). 80p. Color illus. (Interest level: 3-5).

This biography covers Clark's life from age 12 to his death. At age 24, he was a major in Kentucky's new militia. Clark's relevance to the history of Illinois is that he successfully captured, without any bloodshed, the British-controlled forts at Kaskaskia and Cahokia, bringing Illinois country under control of the United States. Although the book has a simple vocabulary and sentence structure, the text is fast-moving.
♦ Because Clark's military endeavors were helpful to several states, announcement of his death in each state would have had a different interpretation. Students may write such an announcement for a local newspaper emphasizing his accomplishments relevant to the appropriate state.
1. Clark, George Rogers 2. United States—History—Revolution, 1775-1783 3. Illinois—History.

92 Deere, John
Collins, David R. *Pioneer Plowmaker: A Story about John Deere.* Carolrhoda (0-87614-424-5), 1990. 64p. B/W illus. (Interest level: 4-6).

Although this biography by a Moline, Illinois, author lacks integrated detail, it presents many aspects of John Deere's life. Born in Vermont, he traveled to Grand Detour, Illinois, at age 32. There he built the first steel plow, and eventually his work involved into a large, many-faceted business in Moline.
♦ Young people may interview a farmer or agricultural representative to determine the cost of owning and operating specific farm equipment today.
1. Deere, John 2. Inventors 3. Agricultural machinery.

92 Disney, Walt
Selden, Bernice. *The Story of Walt Disney, Maker of Magical Worlds.* Dell (0-440-40240-9), 1989. 90p. B/W photos. (Interest level: 3-5).

This biography covers the life of one of Illinois' famous native sons, highlighting his struggles (coping with an abusive father and poverty) and achievements (in film, television, and amusement parks). Eight pages of photographs accompany the readable text.
♦ Young people may celebrate Disney's popularity by bringing their memorabilia (clothes, stuffed animals, books, records, etc.) for display.
1. Disney, Walt, 1901-1966 2. Motion pictures—Biography 3. Animation (Cinematography).

92 Dunham, Katherine
Haskins, James. *Katherine Dunham.* Coward (0-698-20549-9), 1982. 158p. B/W photos. (Interest level: 6-8).

Born in Glen Ellyn, this African-American dancer, choreographer, and anthropologist returned to Illinois at the end of her world-renowned career to establish the Performing Arts Training Center in East St. Louis. Also located in this area is the Katherine Dunham Museum.
♦ Dunham's life included much travel because of her dancing and research. Using a world map, students may locate these travel sites, which will include many European nations, Japan, and numerous islands (Martinique, Haiti, Jamaica). Additional information about Dunham can be found in Haskins' *Black Dance in America: A History through Its People* (Harper, 1990).
1. Dunham, Katherine 2. Dancers 3. Choreographers 4. African Americans—Biography 5. Women—Biography.

92 Grant, Ulysses
Kent, Zachary. *Ulysses S. Grant, Eighteenth President of the United States.* Childrens Press (0-516-01364-5), 1989. (Encyclopedia of Presidents). 100p. B/W photos and illus. (Interest level: 4-8).

Eight chapters outline this Civil War general's life. His problems with alcohol and maintaining employment are described, as well as his heroic return to Galena, Illinois, where residents presented him with a large home which is now open for public viewing. A detailed index and numerous illustrations make this a useful research tool.
♦ The nine-page chronology of American history lists numerous world events that occurred during Grant's life (1822-1885). Students may choose one of the listed events, research details, and write a story

about the event for a special newspaper titled *The Life and Times of Grant*.
1. Grant, Ulysses S., 1822-1885 2. Presidents—United States.

92 La Salle, René-Robert Cavelier, Sieur de
Nolan, Jeannette Covert. *La Salle and the Grand Enterprise*. Grey Castle Press (1-55905-087-X), 1991. 173p. B/W illus. (Interest level: 5-8).

This large-print reproduction of a 1951 Simon and Schuster book focuses on the adult life of the explorer who became famous for proving that the Mississippi River flowed into the Gulf of Mexico. La Salle's greatest strength was his respect for Native Americans, which led him to learn many of their languages and assisted him in achieving his goals. The large print compensates for the sophisticated language and few illustrations, making the book useful for an in-depth look at early Illinois history.
♦ Accused by his friends of being too trusting of people, La Salle often included undesirable men among his collegues during his explorations. Students may brainstorm about how La Salle could have improved his judgment when selecting traveling companions.
1. La Salle, René-Robert Cavelier, Sieur de, 1643-1687 2. Explorers 3. Large-print books.

92 Lincoln, Abraham
Abraham Lincoln. (Videocassette). Atlas Video, 1990. VHS, 1/2", Color, (35 min.). $19.95. (Interest level: 5-8).

Period photographs, paintings, political cartoons, and live shots of historical sites in New Salem and Springfield tell the story of Lincoln's life from birth to death. This realistic presentation covers the many facets of his personality, family life, and significant events. Of special interest is the coverage of restored New Salem Village, Lincoln's home in Springfield, and the Old Capitol. Excellent music and a good script make this a worthwhile investment.
♦ This video serves as a vicarious field trip to New Salem Village and Springfield because young people may preview footage from all of the restored sites.
1. Lincoln, Abraham, 1809-1865 2. Presidents—United States.

92 Lincoln, Abraham
Abraham Lincoln. (Sound filmstrip). Spoken Arts, 1982. Color, (12 min.) Includes teacher's guide. $39.95. (Interest level: 1-4).

This filmstrip duplicates, word for word, Ingri and Edgar Parin D'Aulaire's Caldecott-winning book of the same title (Doubleday, 1939) in presenting biographical facts covering Abraham Lincoln's birth to the end of the Civil War. In presenting Lincoln's most positive experiences and personality traits, this work also emphasizes the lifestyle of the time. A well-done narration and good sound track make this an excellent production.
♦ The teacher's guide contains both discussion questions and instructional suggestions. One suggestion is for students to create a diary for a fictional person living during Lincoln's time, based on the many facts about lifestyle given in the text.
1. Lincoln, Abraham, 1809-1865 2. Presidents—United States.

92 Lincoln, Abraham
Adler, David A. *A Picture Book of Abraham Lincoln*. Illus. by John and Alexandra Wallner. Holiday (0-440-84746-X), 1989. Unpaginated. Color illus. (Interest level: K-3).

The highlights of Lincoln's life from birth to death are presented. This straightforward telling is greatly enhanced with many double-paged spreads.
♦ After young people enjoy this book's illustrations, they will profit from seeing photos and prints from Russell Freedman's *Lincoln: A Photobiography* (see following entry).
1. Lincoln, Abraham, 1809-1865 2. Presidents—United States.

92 Lincoln, Abraham
Freedman, Russell. *Lincoln: A Photobiography*. Clarion (0-89919-380-3), 1987. 150p. B/W photos. (Interest level: 5-8).

This Newbery Award winner covers Lincoln's childhood and early law and political career as well as his presidency during the Civil War. Appendices include a sampling of his most notable quotes, a listing of historic sites, and other works about Lincoln. Numerous photos and prints plus a well-written text make this book a totally enjoyable reading/research experience.
♦ Young people may view the excellent video *A Visit with Russell Freedman* (Houghton Mifflin Author Videotape Series, 1990, 18 min.) in which he describes his visit to Springfield and his research for this book. *Lincoln: A Photobiography*, a 65-minute videocassette (B/W, VHS, 1/2"), is available from American School Publishers (1989).
1. Lincoln, Abraham, 1809-1865 2. Presidents—United States.

92 Lincoln, Abraham
Greene, Carol. *Abraham Lincoln, President of a Divided Country*. Childrens Press (0-516-04206-8), 1989. (Rookie Biography Series). 48p. B/W and Color photos and illus. (Interest level: 1-3).

This volume covers Lincoln's life from age seven to his death. Large print, numerous color and black-and-white sketches, and historic and current photographs of restored sites make this appealing to browsers and useful as a first informational book for younger students.
♦ This text contains a photo of a toy wagon that Lincoln made for his son, Tad. Students may create

92 Lincoln, Abraham
Gross, Ruth Belov. *True Stories about Abraham Lincoln*. Illus. by Jill Kastner. Lothrop, Lee & Shepard (0-688-08798-1), 1973, 1990. 46p. Color illus. (Interest level: 2-5).

Twenty-two one-page segments outline Lincoln's life from birth to death. Each vignette is accompanied by a full-page informative illustration, making this book a useful visual representation of Lincoln's life.
♦ Using this same one-page-with-an-illustration format, young people may want to research and create more vignettes about Lincoln, another famous person, or themselves.
1. Lincoln, Abraham, 1809-1865   2. Presidents—United States.

92 Lincoln, Abraham
Hargrove, Jim. *Abraham Lincoln, Sixteenth President of the United States*. Childrens Press (0-516-01359-9), 1988. (Encyclopedia of Presidents). 100p. B/W photos and illus. (Interest level: 4-8).

Two of the work's six chapters detail Lincoln's move to Illinois at the age of 21, his years in New Salem, and his career as a lawyer and politician in Springfield. Many photos and authentic quotes bring this history to life.
♦ The seven Lincoln/Douglas debates conducted throughout Illinois in 1858 brought national attention to Lincoln. Using this source and others, students may collect quotes from those debates to use in a debate reenactment.
1. Lincoln, Abraham, 1809-1865   2. Presidents—United States.

92 Lincoln, Abraham
Jacobs, William Jay. *Lincoln*. Scribner (0-684-19274-8), 1991. 42p. B/W photos. (Interest level: 3-6).

Although this biography spans Lincoln's entire life, there is a large focus on the years he spent in New Salem and Springfield. Despite a somewhat glorified presentation of Lincoln, the brief text and appropriate photographs have child appeal.
♦ Students may select and read one of the many biographies about Lincoln. As the teacher or librarian reads the Jacobs biography aloud, pausing to encourage participation, the young people may orally share additional details they found in the biography they read.
1. Lincoln, Abraham, 1809-1865   2. Presidents—United States.

92 Lincoln, Abraham
Ostendorf, Lloyd. *Abraham Lincoln: The Boy, The Man*. Lamplight Publications (No ISBN), 1962, 1988. 157p. B/W photos and illus. (Interest level: 4-8).

One hundred and fifty one-page episodes are accompanied by original drawings by the author or by historical prints. The back cover contains a three-state map in which all significant sites concerning Lincoln are numbered with a guide included as the last page of text. Although the map is isolated from the text and the lack of an index deters researchers, browsers will enjoy the brief stories and 225 illustrations.
♦ After students have studied the "Lincoln Heritage Trail" map on the back cover, they may make one that represents their own life or someone else's (birthplace, homes, schools, workplaces).
1. Lincoln, Abraham, 1809-1865   2. Presidents—United States.

92 Lincoln, Abraham
Weinberg, Larry. *The Story of Abraham Lincoln, President for the People*. Illus. by Tom LaPadula. Dell (0-440-40411-8), 1991. 102p. B/W illus. (Interest level: 3-5).

Lively text and several full-page sketches enhance this biography of Abe Lincoln that begins with his grandfather selling his Virginia farm to move to Kentucky. It concludes with the full text of the Gettysburg Address and an extensive timetable of highlights of Lincoln's life.
♦ Students may make a likeness of Lincoln's head, using a tin can (10-16 oz size) which can easily be covered with construction or contact paper. Using the book's cover illustration as a model, facial features and a hat may be designed from miscellaneous materials and added to the covered can.
1. Lincoln, Abraham, 1809-1865   2. Presidents—United States.

92 Pinkerton, Allan
Wormser, Richard. *Pinkerton: America's First Private Eye*. Walker (0-8027-6964-0), 1990. 119p. B/W photos and illus. (Interest level: 4-8).

Before opening his own detective agency in Chicago, this immigrant from Scotland was a barrel maker, ran a stop on the underground railroad, and served as a lawman. Of much interest is how he discovered a plot to kill Lincoln as the president made his way to Washington. Numerous illustrations, well-written text, and many references to Pinkerton's case notes make this a biography with much reader appeal.
♦ Wormser claims that Pinkerton's greatest contribution to law enforcement was that he made police detection a science. Students may invite a local police officer to explain which of Pinkerton's innovations are still used and how they have been improved.
1. Pinkerton, Allan, 1819-1884   2. Detectives.

(continued on facing page)

a museum of homemade toys or replicate the making of a wooden wagon like Lincoln's.
1. Lincoln, Abraham, 1809-1865   2. Presidents—United States.

92 Reagan, Ronald
Devaney, John. *Ronald Reagan, President.* Walker (0-8027-6932-4), 1990. 137p. B/W photos. (Interest level: 5-8).

Illinois was the birthplace and home of Ronald Reagan for his first 21 years. Seven of the 16 chapters outline his Illinois years as he attended grade school, high school, and Eureka College. These chapters emphasize his roles as lifeguard, football player, and actor. Despite the matter-of-fact text, the many photos help maintain interest.
♦ Because Reagan's father was an alcoholic and had employment problems, the family frequently moved. After reading the first seven chapters of this biography, students may list the many times Reagan moved around Illinois and discuss the feelings they would associate with these experiences.

1. Reagan, Ronald, 1911- 2. Presidents—United States.

92 Reagan, Ronald
Kent, Zachary. *Ronald Reagan, Fortieth President of the United States.* Childrens Press (0-516-01373-4), 1989. (Encyclopedia of Presidents). 100p. B/W photos and illus. (Interest level: 4-8).

One of the book's eight chapters details Reagan's birth in Tampico, Illinois, and his many moves within the state before settling in Dixon, where his childhood home is now open to the public. Numerous photographs complement this account of Reagan's life.
♦ Students may design a postcard for young Reagan and write to a make-believe friend explaining why the family has made one of their many moves, where the new home is, and how he feels about his new home.

1. Reagan, Ronald, 1911- 2. Presidents—United States.

92 Reagan, Ronald
Sullivan, George. *Ronald Reagan.* Messner (0-671-60168-7), 1985. 126p. B/W photos. (Interest level: 6-8).

This comprehensive biography depicts Reagan's life from birth until the beginning of his second presidential term, addressing his childhood, college years in Illinois, his experiences in film, and his political career. The strength of this biography is the realistic presentation of what his critics had to say and speculation as to what history will say about his presidency. Many photos and a very readable text add to this book's appeal.
♦ Because this book reveals that Reagan was the oldest president, students may investigate the ages of the other presidents to determine such interesting statistics as who was the youngest president and what is the average age of a president

1. Reagan, Ronald, 1911- 2. Presidents—United States.

92 Sandburg, Carl
Mitchell, Barbara. *"Good Morning, Mr. President": A Story about Carl Sandburg.* Illus. by Dane Collins. Carolrhoda (0-87614-329-X), 1988. 56p. B/W illus. (Interest level: 3-6).

Sandburg's fascination with Lincoln, which eventually won him a Pulitzer Prize, began with the stories he heard about the Lincoln/Douglas debate held over 30 years earlier in his hometown of Galesburg. At 18 Sandburg left home to travel the country as a hobo, collecting stories and songs that later appeared in his poems and books. Mitchell's appealing coverage makes this work useful for budding authors who need role models and motivation.
♦ Students may investigate current poetry anthologies for young people to determine which Sandburg poems are most often included. These may be illustrated for a student-produced book titled *Long Live Sandburg!*

1. Sandburg, Carl, 1878-1967 2. Poets, American 3. Authors—United States—Biography.

92 Sandburg, Carl
Sandburg, Carl. *Prairie-Town Boy.* Illus. by Joe Krush. Harcourt (0-15-263332-4), 1955, 1990. 208p. B/W illus. (Interest level: 6-8).

Excerpted from his book titled *Always the Young Strangers*, this autobiography covers Sandburg's first 20 years. Described in memorable ways are everyday life and notable events, such as Robert Lincoln's speech at Knox College's anniversary celebration of the Lincoln-Douglas debates.
♦ During his first 20 years, Sandburg had many different jobs. Young people may recall the diversity and especially his "first secret ambition"—to be a professional baseball player. They may then poll available adults about their childhood ambitions to determine whether any of those desires were fulfilled.

1. Sandburg, Carl, 1878–1967 2. Poets, American 3. Authors—United States—Biography.

92 Washington, Harold
Roberts, Naurice. *Harold Washington, Mayor with a Vision.* Childrens Press (0-516-03657-3), 1988. 32p. B/W photos. (Interest level: 2-4).

This very brief overview of Chicago's first African-American mayor includes information about his early years and family, his college and army years, his five terms in the Illinois House of Representatives, and his two terms as U.S. congressman. The many photographs will capture the attention of browsers and researchers who are interested in famous African Americans or politicians.
♦ Since Harold Washington was Chicago's first African-American mayor, students may investigate other African Americans who were "first" in a certain occupation or field. Noted African Americans

are featured in most almanacs and encyclopedias for easy reference so a gallery could be featured.
1. Washington, Harold, 1922-1987 2. Mayors 3. African Americans—Biography.

92 Wells-Barnett, Ida B.
Van Steenwyk, Elizabeth. *Ida B. Wells-Barnett, Woman of Courage.* Watts (0-531-13014-2), 1992. (An Impact Biography). 128p. B/W photos. (Interest level: 7-8).

This founder of the National Association for the Advancement of Colored People (NAACP) spent her adult life in Chicago, and in 1950 she was named one of the city's most outstanding women. A complete index and glossary add to the research value of this comprehensive biography.
♦ Ida Wells-Barnett's contribution to society has been honored in numerous ways: Chicago named a housing project for her, her home has been designated as a National Historic Landmark, and a 1990 postage stamp was issued. Students may inquire about street and building names in their own community to determine whom they honor.
1. Wells-Barnett, Ida B., 1862-1931 2. Civil rights 3. African Americans—Biography.

Fiction

Anderson, Joan. *Joshua's Westward Journal.* Illus. by George Ancona. Morrow (0-688-06681-X), 1987. Unpaginated. B/W photos. (Interest level: 3-8).

After Samuel Carpenter read that the prairie was paradise, he packed up his Pennsylvania family and belongings to travel to his uncle's home in Illinois. The diary entries, dated from July to September 1836, and the many photos make this living-history presentation so realistic that young readers may suffer along with Joshua and Becky when their mother dies and is buried along the trail.
♦ This book provides an excellent opportunity for adults to introduce young people to photo essays. Young people may wish to develop a photo essay of their own.
1. Frontier and pioneer life—Illinois—Fiction 2. Illinois—Fiction.

Bauer, Marion Dane. *On My Honor.* Houghton Mifflin (0-899-19439-7), 1986. 90p. (Interest level: 5-7).

Twelve-year-old Joel has promised never to go near the dangerous Vermillion River. But his friend Tony convinces him to stop for a swim when they are biking to Starved Rock State Park. Confronting Tony's death and explaining the details to his family provide an intense emotional experience for Joel and for young people.
♦ Because this Newbery Honor novel mentions that the Vermillion flows into the Illinois and then into the Mississippi, students may trace this progression on a map. Other geographical extension ideas about the Oglesby, Illinois, region can be found in Joanne Kelly's *On Location: Settings from Famous Children's Books—#1* (Teacher Ideas Press, 1992).
1. Promises—Fiction 2. Obedience—Fiction 3. Accidents—Fiction.

Diller, Harriett. *Grandaddy's Highway.* Illus. by Henri Sorensen. Caroline House/Boyds Mills (1-878093-63-0), 1993. Unpaginated. Watercolor illus. (Interest level: K-3).

When Maggie and her grandfather hear just the right truck, they fantasize about boarding it to head as far west as they can go on Highway 30 West. Part of their imaginary trip takes them by Lake Michigan, through Chicago, and then across the Mississippi River.
♦ Highway 30 West crosses all of upper Illinois so students may use a highway map to identify the many towns Maggie and her grandfather would have passed. Students may also list the special sightseeing possibilities along the route, such as President Reagan's boyhood home.
1. Fantasy 2. Trucks—Fiction.

Fiday, Beverly and **Fiday, David.** *Time to Go.* Illus. by Thomas B. Allen. Harcourt (0-15-200608-7), 1990. Unpaginated. Color illus. (Interest level: K-3).

This picture book by an Illinois author begins: "The acres of my family's farm stretch endlessly before me. We've been here for as far back as anyone can remember. But today all that will change. Today we are leaving." Before the young narrator leaves, he takes one last look at and reminisces about several sites, including the cornfield, henhouse, barn, windmill, and his tree house. Although young children can appreciate the pencil drawings and identify with the well-portrayed sadness associated with leaving a favorite home, older children who have studied the details about the declining number of farms will benefit as well.
♦ Students can vicariously experience another family farm loss in a second picture book with more text, Jan Andrews' *The Auction* (Macmillan, 1991), in which a grandfather and grandson do the same type of reminiscing the evening before the farm is to be auctioned. Students can speculate on the future of the young boy portrayed in each of the two books.
1. Farm life—Fiction 2. Moving, Household—Fiction.

Herman, Charlotte. *Millie Cooper, 3B.* Illus. by Helen Cogancherry. Puffin (0-14-032072-5), 1986. 73p. B/W illus. (Interest level: 3-5).

Third grader Millie Cooper dreams of owning the latest invention, an ink pen called Reynolds Rocket which costs $3.98. While Millie struggles to determine her best qualities so she can write a school assignment about them, the reader learns of her life in Chicago in 1946: radio shows, breakfast cereals, candies, comic books, favorite places like the Brookfield Zoo, and

special activities like sledding. This lighthearted presentation will encourage young people to consider societal changes over the years.
♦ Has life changed much for a third grader? Young people may reflect on everything they learn about Millie and then determine what has changed (comics cost more than 10 cents now) and what has remained the same (Lifesavers candies are still popular). Students or teacher may bake and share favorite carrot cake.
1. Individuality—Fiction 2. School stories.

Herman, Charlotte. *A Summer on Thirteenth Street.* Dutton (0-525-44642-7), 1991. 181p. (Interest level: 5-7).
Eleven-year-old Shirley Cohen is experiencing the frustrations of coming of age in a Chicago neighborhood where the lifestyle is changing because of World War II. Her life centers around her good friend Morton, her secret love for teenager Manny, and her pregnant cat, Stinky. Period detail and strong characterization are this novel's strengths.
♦ Students may wish to replicate Shirley's neighborhood through a drawing or model as she mentions the many streets and businesses. Students may also list the period detail as it relates to radio shows, music, movies, and the cost of items.
1. Chicago (Ill.)—Fiction 2. World War II, 1939-1945—United States—Fiction.

Howard, Ellen. *The Chickenhouse House.* Illus. by Nancy Oleksa. Atheneum (0-689-31695-X), 1991. 52p. B/W illus. (Interest level: 3-5).
This story, inspired by the memory book of the author's great aunt, tells of Alena's dismay when she discovers that her first winter home on the prairie is the chickenhouse from which the family will move when their new house is completed. In the spring, family and neighbors come to help frame, roof, and side the new house and, once again, Alena has to adjust. Large print and full-page illustrations make this story appealing to newly independent readers.
♦ Students may be introduced to the concept that fiction often contains much fact. They can list or illustrate the mentioned prairie plants, animals, weather, and activities in Hancock County, Illinois, in the late 1800s. Alena's younger sister, Faith, is featured in *The Cellar* (Atheneum, 1992) which affords the same readability. Junior high girls can read about Alena's maturation and marriage in *Sister* (Atheneum, 1990) and *Edith Herself* (Atheneum, 1987).
1. Frontier and pioneer life—Fiction 2. Houses—Fiction.

Hunt, Irene. *Across Five Aprils.* Follett (0-695-80100-7), 1964 (out of print). 223p. (Interest level: 5-8).
A farm in southern Illinois is the home for nine-year-old Jethro, who is left with tremendous responsibilities as each older brother leaves to fight in the Civil War. Conflict also comes when brother Bill decides to fight for the South. This Newbery Honor novel's strength is its strong characterization. The book is also available as a sound recording cassette ($14) from American School Publishers (1973).
♦ Students may determine the date when a glacier left "a line that separated the rich black loam culture of northern Illinois from the poor hard-packed clay culture to the south" (p. 22). Geography extension ideas about this book's setting—Jasper County, Illinois—can be found in Joanne Kelly's *On Location: Settings from Famous Children's Books—#1* (Teacher Ideas Press, 1992).
1. Illinois—Fiction 2. United States—History—Civil War, 1861-1865—Fiction.

Locker, Thomas. *Family Farm.* Dial (0-8037-0489-5), 1988. Unpaginated. Color illus. (Interest level: K-4).
Because a family farm is experiencing financial problems due to low corn and milk prices, each member of the family must make sacrifices. When Sarah and Mom successfully sell their flowers and pumpkins, the whole family considers diversifying their farm produce for the next growing season. Locker's distinctive oil paintings were inspired by the farm in the Galena area where he lived in the early 1970s.
♦ Young people may replicate Sarah and her mother's farm stand in their classroom. They may brainstorm what products would be available from an Illinois farm and check the local grocery for prices. Locker's art is also worthy of an in-depth study.
1. Farm life—Fiction.

Naylor, Phyllis. *One of the Third-Grade Thonkers.* Illus. by Walter Gaffney-Kessell. Atheneum (0-689-31424-8), 1988. 136p. B/W illus. (Interest level: 3-6).
The title of this novel relates to a club formed by Jimmy Novak and his third-grade friends. Jimmy lives in Joliet, where his father is first mate on a towboat that pushes barges down the shipping canal from Chicago to New Orleans, using the Des Plaines, Illinois, and Mississippi rivers. The characterization will captivate young readers.
♦ This book contains many interesting facts about Mr. Novak's job as first mate and about the dangers of a river. Students may search for and list these factual details and discuss why authors of fiction need to do research. Students may also write a front-page newspaper article about the towboat's accident or clip articles about river accidents.
1. Courage—Fiction 2. Cousins—Fiction 3. Clubs—Fiction.

Pevsner, Stella. *Keep Stompin' Till the Music Stops.* Seabury (0-395-28875-4), 1977. 136p. (Interest level: 6-8).

Twelve-year-old Richard, who has learning disabilities, is sympathetic to his great-grandfather's predicament as the grandchildren meet to discuss moving him from Galena, Illinois, to a retirement home in Florida. This well-paced story with just the right touch of suspense emphasizes the warm relationship between Richard and his great-grandfather. It also contains references to Galena's past—Sac Indians, Chief Black Hawk, Ulysses S. Grant's home, and the Galena River, which carried ore from lead mines to Chicago.

♦ This book says Galena was bigger than Chicago at one time. Students may compare the populations of these two communities over time. Other resources can be consulted to determine the historical significance of lead mining, Chief Black Hawk, and U.S. Grant.

1. Learning disabilities—Fiction 2. Family life—Fiction 3. Grandfathers—Fiction.

Sandin, Joan. *The Long Way Westward.* Harper (0-06-025206-5), 1989. (I Can Read Book). 63p. Color illus. (Interest level: 2-4).

In this high-interest, low-vocabulary historical fiction book, three non-English-speaking, emigrant brothers from Sweden are among those hoping to make a new home in Minnesota. When they leave the New York boat dock, they travel inexpensively in a crowded, dark, and cold "emigrant train car." While changing trains in Chicago, they are aided by a member of the Svea Society, who helps them find the right train and avoid those who would cheat them out of their money.

♦ Students may pretend to be one of the brothers and write a letter to someone back home in Sweden, explaining how a fellow Swede in Chicago assisted them. Teachers may introduce Sandin's earlier book about their boat trip from Sweden, *The Long Way to a New Land* (Harper, 1981).

1. Immigration and emigration—Fiction 2. Swedish Americans—Fiction.

Periodicals

977.3

Illinois History, A Magazine for Young People. Illinois Historical Society, quarterly (October through May). Available from the Subscription Clerk, Illinois Historical Society. $8/year. (Interest level: 5-12).

Each thematic issue contains 10 essays written by Illinois students. One copy is sent free upon request to all Illinois teachers using it in their classroom.

♦ Illinois students may wish to submit an essay for publication. Using the format of *Illinois History*, young people in other states may work in groups to develop a similar issue for their own state.

1. Illinois—History.

Indiana

by Barry Lessow

Nonfiction

069
Kriplen, Nancy. *Keep an Eye on that Mummy.* The Children's Museum of Indianapolis (0-9608982-0-4), 1982. 217p. B/W photos. (Interest level: 5-8).

This lively description of the founding of the Indianapolis Children's Museum focuses on the history and construction of the museum, but also offers glimpses of the museum's many exciting collections and exhibits.
♦ If possible, young people may take a field trip to a children's museum and witness firsthand what the museum has to offer. As a group, students might also design a floor plan or single exhibit for their own children's museum.
1. Children—Museums 2. Museums—Indiana.

289.7
Faber, Doris. *The Amish.* Doubleday (0-385-26130-6), 1991. 45p. Color illus. (Interest level: 3-8).

The largest Amish communities in the United States are located in Pennsylvania, Ohio, and Indiana. Large, full-color illustrations enhance the discussion of the history, culture, daily lifestyle, and future of the Amish people.
♦ Because quilting by Amish women is a practical activity as well as a social and artistic outlet, young people may create their own quilt block design on paper bookmarks, prepare a group fabric quilt, or make an edible quilt using colored icing on graham crackers.
1. Amish.

394.2
Anderson, Joan. *Christmas on the Prairie.* Illus. by George Ancona. Clarion (0-89919-307-2), 1985. Unpaginated. B/W photos. (Interest level: 2-6).

This photo essay presents the re-creation of Christmas Eve and Christmas morning of 1836 at the living history museum at the Conner Prairie Pioneer Settlement near Noblesville, Indiana. The lively text and outstanding photographs authentically relate nineteenth-century life, including children's boisterous departure from a one-room school, cookie making, and a meal shared by candlelight.
♦ Young people may bake cookies, using cookie cutter shapes like those pictured in the book, or they may make simple ornaments, using materials that would have been available in 1836.
1. Christmas—Indiana.

394.2
Anderson, Joan. *The Glorious Fourth at Prairietown.* Illus by George Ancona. Morrow (0-688-06246-6), 1986. Unpaginated. B/W photos. (Interest level: 2-6).

This photo essay re-creates the Fourth of July in 1836 in the fictional village of Prairietown, Indiana, to show how the holiday was celebrated in a typical frontier community. Capturing the spirit of what was then the nation's only holiday, the work is accurate in every detail, including descriptions of rock candy on a string, a roasted pig, and a game of hoops.
♦ As a group, young people may collect or illustrate items that symbolize the Fourth of July today and create a collage to display on a bulletin board.
1. Fourth of July.

398.21
Jagendorf, M. A. *Sand in the Bag and Other Folk Stories of Ohio, Indiana, and Illinois.* Vanguard Press (No ISBN), 1952. 192p. (Interest level: 5+).

This older collection of folk stories includes diverse stories from Indiana. These brief stories on topics such as the Underground Railroad and ghosts are appropriate for storytelling.
♦ Students may collect local stories or select them from this book and tell the stories to others. Page 4 in the September/October 1988 issue of *Library Talk* features Ruth Gilbert's article "Teaching Children to

be Storytellers," which provides concise hints and tips for beginners.
1. Folklore—Old Northwest.

549
Secrets of Limestone Groundwater. (Videocassette). Indiana University Audio Visual Center, 1980. VHS 1/2", Color, (14 min.). Available from Indiana University Media and Teaching Resources. $15, rental. (Interest level: 4-8+).

Much of Indiana exhibits karst topography (i.e., regions shaped by limestone formations, including caves and sinkholes). A substantial amount of groundwater flows through this vast connected network of springs, wells, and underground rivers. This video uses animation and live-action scenes to illustrate how the water supply is threatened by bacteria and waste chemicals from polluted rainwater runoff. The need for control of the pollution coming from septic systems, sanitary landfills, barnyard wastes, and garbage dumped in sinkholes is stressed.

♦ The class may examine a geological map of their region to locate areas with caves, sinkholes, and other karst features and trace the potential flow and impact of pollutants dumped in a particular area. Class speakers might include spelunkers or environmental scientists who can share firsthand accounts of experiences with polluted groundwater.

1. Geology 2. Water pollution 3. Water supply.

551.483
Simons, Richard. *The Rivers of Indiana*. Indiana University Press (0-253-17476-7), 1985. 224p. B/W and Color photos. (Interest level: 6-8).

Colorful photographs and informative text explain how the rivers of Indiana have played a major role in the history of the state. The different contemporary uses, names, and geologic origins of each river are presented. An Indiana map, prior to each section, helps the reader locate each of the 30 rivers.

♦ The class may investigate a nearby river, examining its role in their state's history and future. Students may include a study of environmental concerns that affect the river.

1. Rivers—Indiana 2. Indiana—Description 3. Indiana—History.

551.55
Chasing the Tornado. (Videocassette). Coronet, 1987. (Knowzone). VHS 1/2", Color, (30 min.). $250. (Interest level: 4-8).

Part of a series hosted by David Morse, this film focuses on the scientists who track and study these violent windstorms. Tornadoes are a major destructive force in Indiana and other regions of the Midwest, causing serious loss of lives and property.

♦ Students may investigate what is required to pursue a career as a tornado scientist or other meteorological professional. A local television or radio station may be able to provide a meteorologist as a class speaker; the class could also visit a local studio where the weather is broadcast or an airport where forecasts are determined and distributed.

1. Tornadoes 2. Storms 3. Weather.

551.55
Violent Storms. (Videocassette). Coronet, 1986. (Atmospheric Science Series). VHS 1/2", Color, (14 min.). $250. (Interest level: 5-8).

Indiana and much of the Midwest experience frequent sightings and significant damage to towns and farms from tornadoes and violent windstorms. Dramatic cinematography and time-lapse photography show how thunderstorms, tornadoes, and hurricanes develop. Also presented are the efforts of atmospheric scientists to strengthen the power of satellites and radar to spot developing tornadoes and provide early warnings.

♦ Students may research the history of tornadoes and violent windstorms in their area for the past 10 years. Discussions might include a comparison of the frequency of tornadoes in a given month, the type of destruction, and tornado safety procedures to be used at home and at school.

1. Storms 2. Weather 3. Tornadoes.

574.5
May, Julian. *Moving Hills of Sand*. Illus. by John Hawkinson. Hawthorn (No ISBN), 1969. Unpaginated. B/W and Color illus. (Interest level: 3-6).

This beautifully illustrated portrait explains the ecological history and formation of Indiana's dunes, or "moving hills of sand," located on the northern shore of the state. The recognition of the unique plants and wildlife in this habitat led to the creation of the Indiana Dunes National Lakeshore State Park.

♦ Students in Indiana may locate state parks on a map of Indiana and take a class field trip to one closest to them. Literature obtained from the state Department of Natural Resources would allow them to identify the features, wildlife, and history for each park. They may also examine the process required to designate an area as an official Indiana state park. Students in other states could build a diorama of the sand dunes.

1. Sand dunes—Indiana 2. Indiana Dunes State Park (Ind.).

598.2
Brock, Kenneth J. *Birds of the Indiana Dunes*. Photos by Peter B. Grube. Indiana University Press (0-253-31201-9), 1986. 178p. B/W illus. (Interest level: 8+).

Focusing on birding sites, this comprehensive resource provides insights into the geology of the northern Indiana dunes and background on 50 families of birds. For each bird, an occurrence histogram is given along with additional facts about the species. A bibliography and index are also provided.

♦ If possible, students may visit a local bird habitat. After conducting library research about local birds, students might also use a field guide to go bird watching on the school grounds or in a nearby park.
1. Birds—Indiana Dunes State Park (Ind.) 2. Bird watching—Indiana Dunes State Park (Ind.)

622
Limestone. (Videocassette). Indiana University Audio Visual Center, 1978. VHS 1/2", Color, (13 min.). Available from Indiana University Media and Teaching Resources. $120. (Interest level: 4-8).

The quarrying of limestone is a major industry in Indiana. This film depicts the formation of limestone and explores its importance as a natural resource. Major quarries are indicated on a map. The entire quarrying process is explained, including the use of limestone by-products in soapmaking, in the preparation of medicines, and in the manufacture of cement, paint, paper, and steel.
♦ Students may make a sequence chart of the steps involved in locating and quarrying limestone. They can locate a quarry on a map and trace the route blocks of limestone would have taken to such destinations as Washington, DC, and New York City for use in famous buildings. They can also determine why limestone is a popular building surface.
1. Lime 2. Natural resources.

662.6
The Role of Coal. (Videocassette). Indiana University Audio Visual Center, 1979. VHS 1/2", Color, (17 min.). Available from Indiana University Media and Teaching Resources. $240. (Interest level: 7-8+).

Coal has been an important natural resource in southern Indiana, supporting steel manufacturing in northern Indiana. This film explores the characteristics of coal as a natural resource and its use for generating electrical power and making steel. The economics, production, and distribution of coal are compared with other sources of energy.
♦ Students may trace the history of current efforts to "scrub" or remove the high amounts of sulphur impurities from Indiana coal so that it may be burned without contributing to the acid rain problem. The class may also explore the implications of higher energy prices resulting from this type of technology, including the search for alternative fuel sources.
1. Coal 2. Energy resources.

728
Be a Building Watcher on the Street Where You Live. (Pamphlet). Historic Landmarks Foundation of Indiana, 1986. 7p. $.65 for out-of-state orders; free in Indiana. (Interest level: 4-8).

Young people can learn to become "building watchers" by reading this introductory publication. Explanations of architectural styles and terms, elements to look for in buildings, and pictorial descriptions of Indiana buildings—with architectural styles dating from the early 1800s to the mid-1900s—are included.
♦ Students may identify architectural elements in the buildings in their community.
1. Architecture—Indiana 2. Historic buildings.

741.5
Hubbard, Kin. *The Best of Kin Hubbard: Abe Martin's Sayings and Wisecracks.* Edited by David S. Hawes. Illus. by Frank McKinney. Indiana University Press Media and Teaching Resources (0-253-10611-7), 1984. 144p. B/W caricatures. (Interest level: 4-8).

This highly entertaining book is dedicated to the work of American humorist Frank McKinney Hubbard, the creator of the comic cartoon character Abe Martin. The caricatures and examples, many set in Indiana, illustrate Hubbard's philosophical humor.
♦ The class can compare the humor of Kin Hubbard to that of contemporary comic writers, looking for similarities and differences in style, subject matter, and tone.
1. Hubbard, Kin 2. Cartoons and caricatures.

789.5
On the Downbeat—A Jazz Heritage. (Videocassette). Indiana University Audio Visual Center, 1982. VHS 1/2", Color, (29 min.). Available from Indiana University. $150. (Interest level: 7-8+).

Indiana University Professor David Baker narrates parts of this lively review of the history of jazz in Indiana. Beginning with its roots in ragtime at the turn of the century, the saga of jazz continues with the big-band era of the 1930s, bebop after World War II, and on to more recent forms. Artists highlighted include Jesse Crump, Russel Smith, Julia Niebergall, Freddy Hubbard, Virgil Jones, and Wes Montgomery.
♦ Students may listen to additional works by these and other jazz musicians. They can compare the music in each major decade with modern jazz, rock, and pop, discussing the way in which events and culture of the time are reflected in music.
1. Jazz music 2. Musicians, American.

796.323
Batson, Larry. *An Interview with Bobby Knight.* Creative Education (0-87191-574-X), 1977. 31p. Color photos. (Interest level: 3-6).

This early interview with Bobby Knight presents a candid and interesting profile of the well-known coach of the Indiana University basketball team. Knight's belief in concentration and hard work to achieve leadership and a person's full potential is revealed through quotes and personal anecdotes. The lessons he tries to teach his players are the same ones he learned as an athlete and then as a coach.
♦ Students may nominate a favorite personal hero for an award, describing the characteristics and actions that they admire and reasons for their choice.
1. Knight, Bobby 2. Basketball—Biography.

796.323
Hoose, Phillip M. *Hoosiers: The Fabulous Basketball Life of Indiana.* Vintage (0-394-74778-X), 1986. 292p. B/W photos. (Interest level: 6-8).

This overview of Indiana's most popular sport presents great basketball players, coaches, and Indiana rivalries. Historic moments include African-American players fighting for the chance to play in the state tournament. Ample black-and-white photos show some of the best players and memorable events in Indiana basketball.
♦ Students may choose a favorite basketball star or team and do further research. Many may wish to research how the game of basketball began.
1. Basketball—Indiana—History.

796.323
McKee, Carl R. *Indiana University: Basketball Trivia.* Quinlan Press (1-55770-027-3), 1987. 184p. B/W photos. (Interest level: 5+).

A question-and-answer format introduces basketball fans to such details as statistics, records, coaches, tournaments, Big Ten teams, and players. Indiana University is described as a major force in college basketball, winning 16 Big Ten championships and five NCAA titles from 1901 to 1987. A section of 42 photographs accompanies the text.
♦ Students may study the impact of basketball in their own state, looking at attendance figures for both high school and college games, the coverage of games by the media, and the amount of revenue generated by ticket and souvenir sales. They could also prepare a biography of their favorite player.
1. Indiana University 2. Basketball.

796.323
Rosenthal, Bert. *Sports Stars: Larry Bird, Cool Man on the Court.* Childrens Press (0-516-04312-9), 1981. 45p. B/W photos. (Interest level: 3-6).

Although Larry Bird became a professional basketball player for the Boston Celtics, he spent his high school and college years playing in Indiana. This entertaining biography features quotes from the player and his coaches and photographs from many of Bird's games, including those at Indiana State University in Terre Haute.
♦ Larry Bird spends considerable time and resources for charitable events and causes in his home state. Students may identify and examine the role of other professional players who have had a positive impact in their home communities. They can determine what they would do as a public official to recognize these contributions.
1. Bird, Larry 2. Basketball—Biography—United States.

796.323
Schwomeyer, Herb. *Hoosier Hersteria (A History of Indiana High School Girls Basketball).* Mitchell-Fleming Printing (No ISBN), 1985. 451p. B/W photos. (Interest level: 6-8).

Basketball has played an important role in the sports history of the Hoosier state. This companion volume to *Hoosier Hysteria* provides a perspective that covers Indiana High School Girls' Basketball from 1893 to the 1985 season.
♦ Students may study the history of girls' basketball in their community high schools. Using the pictures, information, and statistics provided in the book as a guide, students can trace the history of girls' high school basketball in the nation as a whole.
1. High School Basketball (Girls)—Indiana 2. Basketball.

796.332
Roberts, Rich. *Sports Stars: Eric Dickerson, Record-Breaking Rusher.* Regensteiner (0-516-04349-9), 1985. 44p. (Interest level: 3-4).

This readable account of the life and professional football career of Eric Dickerson includes a chronology of his involvement with sports, beginning in high school. Photographs and quotes add personal interest. Dickerson recounts growing up with his great-aunt and credits her with his development of good sportsmanship.
♦ Students may develop a chronology of the professional career of another well-known sports figure, either past or present. Biographies, current events, or interviews may be used to look at factors that influenced the person's choice of sports as a career. They may also wish to examine the issue of the responsibility of famous sports figures to provide positive role models.
1. Dickerson, Eric 2. Football players—Biography 3. African American athletes.

796.332
Rothaus, James R. *The Indianapolis Colts.* Creative Education (0-88682-025-1), 1986. 47p. B/W photos. (Interest level: 4-8).

It is unusual to move an entire NFL football team to a new state. This chronological story of the Colts traces the team's controversial and historic move from Baltimore to the Indianapolis Hoosier Dome in 1984, with quotes from key players and highlights of important games.
♦ Once students determine the major factors affecting the Colts' decision to move, they may portray in a skit the mayor, team owner, coach, players, fans, business owners, and residents of a hypothetical city whose football team wishes to leave.
1. Indianapolis Colts 2. Football.

796.72
Dolan, Edward R. and Lyttle, Richard B. *Janet Guthrie: First Woman Driver at Indianapolis.* Doubleday (0-385-12526-7), 1978. 79p. B/W photos. (Interest level: 5-8).

Interesting dialogue and photographs enhance this account of the first woman race car driver to compete in the prestigious Indianapolis Motor Speedway Race. In this portrait of personal courage and perseverance, Dolan credits Janet Guthrie's determination, intelligence, skill, and patience for her success in proving that female drivers could compete in championship events.
♦ Students may write an account of another individual who triumphed over a major personal challenge. This could be someone who founded an organization, faced a disability or catastrophe, or created equal opportunities for others. Students should identify characteristics that helped that person overcome difficulties and succeed.

1. Guthrie, Janet 2. Automobile racing drivers—United States 3. Indianapolis Motor Speedway Race.

796.72
Murphy, Jim. *The Indy 500*. Ticknor & Fields (0-89919-151-7), 1983. 96p. B/W photos. (Interest level: 5-8).

This behind-the-scenes look at the challenging Indianapolis Motor Speedway Race explains the design and testing of race cars as well as the roles of the mechanics, pit crews, sponsors, and drivers. A chronological history of the "Indy 500" is provided, including the stories of individual races and drivers, successes, failures, and the efforts to make race car driving a safer sport.
♦ Students may examine the history of automobile design and manufacture, including the continuing introduction of regulations to make passenger and racing cars safer. Students may investigate the economic and publicity roles of a driver's sponsor and then design and videotape their own promotion and advertising campaigns.

1. Indianapolis Motor Speedway Race 2. Automobile racing.

796.72
Olney, Ross R. *Janet Guthrie: First Woman at Indy*. Harvey House (0-8178-5882-2), 1978. 54p. B/W photos. (Interest level: 4-8).

Through a personalized account of the life of Janet Guthrie, the reader discovers the challenges, disappointments, and successes she faced in the male-dominated world of professional race car driving. A graduate physicist, commercial pilot, and adventurer, she eventually triumphed in 1978, finishing in the top 10 as the first woman to compete in the Indianapolis Motor Speedway Race.
♦ Students may investigate the lives of other women who have created new opportunities and served as role models. They may also identify the challenges faced by each of these women in their chosen cause or career. Students may create designs for commemorative stamps, coins, or posters.

1. Guthrie, Janet 2. Automobile racing drivers—United States 3. Indianapolis Motor Speedway Race.

811
Lindbergh, Reeve. *The Legend of Johnny Appleseed*. Illus. by Kathy Jakobsen. Little, Brown (0-316-52618-5), 1990. 32p. Color Illus. (Interest level: 1-3).

A rhymed text and colorful folk art paintings relate the life of John Chapman. The detailed illustrations convey the daily activities of pioneers and the nature of their homes and farms. The work's value for young people is further extended with a closing biographical summary and end papers depicting a map of the states he visited, including Indiana, where he died at Fort Wayne in 1845.
♦ The book's end note explains that he established nurseries across the Midwest to raise and care for apple trees. Young people may take a field trip to a tree nursery in their area, or perhaps a tree nursery manager could visit the group, explaining how trees are nurtured today.

1. Appleseed, Johnny, 1774-1845 2. Apple.

811
Riley, James Whitcomb. *The Gobble-Uns'll Git You Ef You Don't Watch Out!*. Illus. by Joel Schick. HarperCollins (0-397-31621-6), 1975. 32p. Color illus. (Interest level: 2-5).

Among the narrative poetry of Indiana poet James Whitcomb Riley (1849-1916) is "Little Orphant Annie," the basis of this picture book. Originally published in 1890 in *Rhymes of Childhood*, this cautionary poem is about a servant girl who tells about "gobble-uns" that steal misbehaving children.
♦ Young people may compare the illustrations in this book with those by Diane Stanley in *Little Orphant Annie* (Putnam, 1983, out of print). They may also create another rhymed cautionary tale like those that Annie tells, sharing theirs aloud with the well-known refrain.

1. Poetry, American.

912
Indiana Puzzle. (Map puzzle). Indiana Department of Natural Resources, n.d. Color. $9.95. (Interest level: 3-6).

This 20" x 30" puzzle indicates the outline and county seat of each county in Indiana and presents some historical facts about the state. The cardboard pieces are sturdy, and, when assembled, rest on a thick cardboard base.
♦ Young people may work individually or in small groups to solve the puzzle. They may explore the geography of Indiana in more detail with the following maps also available from the Indiana Department of Natural Resources: *Indiana Map* (A color map showing cities, waterways, highways, counties,

and contour lines. $4.00); *Explorers' Routes Map* (A United States map with routes of explorers from 1501 to 1844 traced in color. $2.50); *Indiana Historic Indian Map* (A map of the state of Indiana with line drawings indicating Native American villages, treaty lines, and other important features. $2.00); and *Hoosier Historic Map* (A full-color map of Indiana with important events and places in history identified. $2.50).
1. Maps 2. Indiana—Maps.

913.7
Marston, Elsa. *Mysteries in American Archeology.* Walker (0-8027-6627-7), 1986. 115p. B/W photos. (Interest level: 5-8).

This valuable work presents archeological sites across the United States. Two Indiana sites that are highlighted are Angel Mounds near Evansville and Mounds State Park in Anderson. The index, site listings, glossary, and maps make this book an indispensable resource for archeology buffs or those interested in Native American cultures.
♦ If possible, students may plan to visit an archeological site. They may research famous archaeologists, especially those from Indiana. Class presentations could include maps of excavation sites and reports of major findings.
1. United States—Antiquities 2. Indians of North America 3. Archeology—United States 4. Excavations (Archeology)—United States.

917.72
Aylesworth, Thomas G. and **Aylesworth, Virginia L.** *Indiana.* Photos by John R. Savage. Bison (0-86124-240-8), 1985. 96p. Color photos. (Interest level: 4-8).

In this oversized book an accessible text accompanies the color photos of different attractions in Indiana. The book is divided into eight sections: beauty, history, homes, architecture, commerce, education, recreation, and people.
♦ Young people may use this book as a resource when studying the history of Indiana or any of the different aspects of Indiana that are covered. The photos will support the book's use by a wide range of readers. The class may make a photo book with text of their city.
1. Indiana—Pictorial works.

917.72
Thompson, Kathleen. *Indiana.* Raintree (0-86514-430-3), 1986. (Portrait of America Series). 47p. Color photos. (Interest level: 4-6).

A wealth of historical photographs extends the textual portrayal of the history, diversity, and national contributions of the Hoosier state. Highlights include a lengthy interview with a farmer who shares his life story, quotes from people involved in major events, sections on the architecture of Columbus, and projections of the future of Indiana.

♦ Students may interview an Indiana native and write an oral history. Students can relate their histories to major events in the state by using the book's extensive reference section. As an alternative activity if no one from Indiana is accessible, young people may wish to develop a profile of their community, also using quotes from family, friends, and neighbors.
1. Indiana.

917.7252
Berry, S. L. *Indianapolis.* Dillon (0-87518-426-X), 1990. (A Downtown America Book). 58p. Color photos. (Interest level: 3-5).

This portrait of the thirteenth largest city in the United States chronicles the recent development of Indianapolis from an isolated farming community to a national metropolis. People and events that have shaped the cultural diversity of "The Circle City" and contributed to its status as a national crossroads and amateur sports capital are emphasized.
♦ Students may research and create a time line of important people, events, and resources that shaped the development of Indianapolis. This framework may be compared to the growth of other metropolitan areas in the country. An appendix provides addresses for useful historical resources and organizations.
1. Indianapolis (Ind.).

970
Jacobson, Daniel. *The North Central States.* Watts (0-531-04731-8), 1984. (A First Book). 90p. B/W photos. (Interest level: 4-8).

The geography and economic history of 12 "heartland" states (Ohio, Indiana, Michigan, Illinois, Wisconsin, Minnesota, Iowa, Missouri, Kansas, Nebraska, North Dakota, and South Dakota) are summarized. Because information about Indiana is integrated with that of other states in the readable text, the concepts of a region and interrelationships of states can be understood.
♦ The final chapter looks to the future. Students may read the business news in a local or national publication to see whether they can find evidence of job growth and new businesses in these states.
1. Middle West.

970.004
Myths and Moundbuilders. (Videocassette). PBS Video, 1981. (Odyssey). VHS 1/2", Color, (58 min.). $68.45 with shipping. (Interest level: 8+).

Angel Mounds, located in southwestern Indiana, is just one of many such sites created by early Native Americans. This documentary presents the work of Cyrus Thomas, whose research and discoveries (circa 1897) furthered understanding of the Midwest Mound Builders and explored their relationship to their Native American descendants. The film presents evidence to support Thomas' theory that more than one tribe built mounds.

♦ Students may research to compare the mound sites in Indiana with those in other states (e.g., Oklahoma's Spiro Mounds). Possible topics for exploration are the cultures that built them, their discovery, and their preservation.

1. Archaeology—United States 2. Indians of North America 3. Mounds and Mound Builders.

970.1
Baxter, Nancy Niblack. *The Miamis!* Illus. by Richard Day. Guild Press of Indiana (0-9617367-3-9), 1987. (Hoosier Heritage Series). 108p. B/W photos and illus. (Interest level: 4-8).

Told in first person by a Miami girl and boy, this book gives the reader an exciting and factual look at the Miamis' woodland survival skills, folktales, and customs. A glossary of Miami words is particularly helpful.

♦ Students may further investigate the skills and culture of the Miami and their significant role in the history of the Midwest. Using the book and other resources, students may locate where the Miami once lived.

1. Miami Indians.

970.1
Lamb, E. Wendell and **Schultz, Lawrence W.** *Indian Lore.* Light and Life Press (0-8395-3358-6), 1959 (out of print). 192p. B/W photos, maps, and illus. (Interest level: 4-8).

This resource book on Native Americans includes charts, maps, pictures, pictographs, sign language, stories, and lists of names and their meanings. It is an invaluable resource for investigations of Native Americans, particularly the Miami and Potowatomi of Indiana.

♦ Students may study the sign language vocabulary of a Native American group and create the signs for their own stories. Students can also use maps to locate Native Americans that lived nearest their hometown.

1. Indians of North America.

976.9
Cavan, Seamus. *Daniel Boone and the Opening of the Ohio Country.* Chelsea (0-7910-1309-X), 1991. (World Explorers Series). 112p. B/W and Color illus and photos. (Interest level: 6-9).

This account of the life and times of Daniel Boone reveals the important role he played in the exploration of the Ohio River territory, which was divided into the states of Ohio, Indiana, and Illinois between 1803 and 1818. Numerous illustrations and maps add to the textual information.

♦ Students may wish to research the staples of a pioneer's diet during the mid-1700s or explore what life may have been like for Boone and his party traveling in a Conestoga wagon through the Cumberland Gap in 1769. Following the events in the book, students may chronologically chart Boone's travels.

1. Boone, Daniel, 1734-1820 2. Old Northwest—History 3. Ohio River Valley—History 4. Frontier and pioneer life—Old Northwest.

977
Aylesworth, Thomas G. and **Aylesworth, Virginia.** *Eastern Great Lakes: Ohio, Indiana, Michigan.* Chelsea (0-7910-1045-7); (0-7910-0534-8 pbk), 1991. (State Reports Series). 64p. B/W and Color illus. (Interest level: 3-6).

This brief work introduces geographical, historical, and cultural aspects of Ohio, Indiana, and Michigan. The biographical sketches of prominent state residents and the quick reference tabular format for facts are very useful.

♦ Beginning with the information and illustrations provided in this book, students may look for similarities and differences among these three states. They may focus on the influence of the Great Lakes and other geographical features that have affected population growth.

1. Great Lakes region 2. Michigan 3. Indiana 4. Ohio.

977
Children of the Wagon Train. (Videocassette). Centron Corporation, CRM/McGraw-Hill Films, 1960. (Children of American History). VHS 1/2", Color, (19 min.). Available from CRM Films. $99. (Interest level: 5-8).

This grim and realistic film follows a wagon train on part of a 2,000 mile trip to Oregon. The story is told from the perspective of a 14-year-old boy, Jim, who along with other children works on daily chores such as gathering wood and water and drying buffalo chips for the fire. During the trip the settlers experience rain, cold, heat, dust, sickness, and the death of Jim's younger sister.

♦ Young people may trace the Oregon Trail on a map of the United States, identifying major geographic obstacles in Indiana, such as rivers and mountains, that the settlers had to overcome. Students would also benefit from working with the computer software program "Oregon Trail" (MECC, 1985), which allows students to choose provisions and strategies for accomplishing the journey.

1. Frontier and pioneer life 2. United States—Territorial expansion.

977
Experiencing Indiana. (Audiocassette). Experience America, 1991. (30 min.). $9.95 per tape, plus $2 for shipping and handling. (Interest level: 4-8).

This informative presentation provides an auditory tour of the Hoosier state, focusing on its history, geography, and scenic regions. For each town, city, or recreational site that is depicted, interesting highlights

and major features are explained through anecdotes and local trivia.
♦ After listening to the tape, students may design their own tour of any region of the state, complete with a brochure and trip itinerary.
1. Indiana.

977
Great Lakes Region. (Sound filmstrip). Eye Gate/Nystrom, 1987. 3 color filmstrips, 3 sound cassettes, Color, (15 min. each). $44 each, $128 for series. (Interest level: 4-6).

Organized by geography/climate, people/resources, and cities/states, this set of filmstrips presents an overview of Illinois, Indiana, Michigan, Ohio, and Wisconsin. Although the set includes a supplementary set of follow-up activities and discussion questions, it will be most valuable when used as background material for specific areas of study.
♦ Indiana is often referred to as the "Crossroads of America." Young people may use a map of Indiana to trace the number of major highways intersecting in the middle of the state. They may also draw three circles around Indianapolis with radii of 100, 200, and 300 miles, and locate major cities, waterways, and other resources within proximity.
1. Geography 2. Middle West—Description 3. Great Lakes region.

977
The Great Lakes Region: The Heartland. (Sound filmstrip). National Geographic Society, 1979. (Geography of the United States Series). Color, (12 min.). Available from National Geographic Educational Services. $68, with shipping. (Interest level: 4-6).

This filmstrip presents the region's major cities, industries, crops, and natural resources. The filmstrip successfully uses representative photographs to demonstrate the relationship between the region's geography and its people and industries.
♦ As students watch this filmstrip, they may keep a list of all the products for which the Midwest is known. Later they may compile their individual lists into a single list and discuss the various ways the products are interrelated.
1. Geography—Middle West 2. Agriculture—Middle West 3. Great Lakes region.

977
Life in a Midwestern Small Town in the 1910s. (Videocassette). AIMS Instructional Media Services, 1976. (Had You Lived Then). VHS 1/2", Color, (17 min.). $49.95. (Interest level: 4+).

This excellent portrayal of the life of a family in a typical small midwestern town at the beginning of the century is told through the eyes of a woman recalling her childhood. The film emphasizes daily life, including cooking, school, and work. Changes emerge in the form of automobiles, packaged goods, manufactured clothes, electrical appliances, and other modern conveniences.
♦ After viewing the film, students may assume the role of reporters announcing a new product or convenience that was introduced around 1910.
1. United States—History, 1865-1918 2. Middle West—Social life and customs.

977
Pioneer Living: Education and Recreation. (Videocassette). Coronet, 1970. (Pioneer Living). VHS 1/2", Color, (11 min.). $195. (Interest level: 3-6).

Part of an excellent series on the lives of early pioneers, this video presents the educational and recreational facilities of the 1800s. The viewer is taken to a one-room school, quilting bee, box social, and hayride.
♦ Students may compare the events in the film to other accounts of pioneer life in Indiana, exploring why schooling and social activities centered around planting and harvesting time for these agricultural communities.
1. Frontier and pioneer life.

977
Pioneer Living: Home Crafts. (Videocassette). Coronet, 1970. (Pioneer Living). VHS 1/2", Color, (10 min.). $185. (Interest level: 3-6).

Performing certain crafts and skills was a necessary part of daily life in the 1800s. Some of the pioneer activities that are depicted and explained in this video are sheep shearing; the washing, carding, spinning, and weaving of wool; rug braiding; furniture building; candle dipping; and quill pen and ink making.
♦ Students may make quill pens and berry ink or weave paper strips into a simple mat. Local weavers may be available to visit the classroom, demonstrating the preparation and spinning of wool. These activities should build an appreciation of the amount of time it took to perform even simple tasks.
1. Frontier and pioneer life 2. Handicraft.

977
Pioneer Living: Preparing Foods. (Videocassette). Coronet, 1970. (Pioneer Living). VHS 1/2", Color, (10 min.). $185. (Interest level: 3-6).

Pioneers of the 1800s needed to preserve foods from the summer growing season to last through the long winter. This informative video illustrates how pioneers prepared the farm harvest and gathered other foods in order to survive the winter. Activities presented include maple sugaring, preserving apples, smoking meat, churning butter, and baking bread.
♦ Students may determine what types and quantities of staple foods their families would need to survive the winter if they could not shop during the entire winter season. Students may discuss the hunting of

game for extra meat. They may also churn butter or bake bread.

1. Frontier and pioneer life 2. Food.

977

Pioneer Living: The Farm. (Videocassette). Coronet, 1970. (Pioneer Living). VHS 1/2", Color, (10 min.). $185. (Interest level: 3-6).

The livelihood of most pioneers of the early 1800s was based on farming. This video shows the various processes involved in raising crops, including clearing land, plowing fields, planting, and harvesting. Viewers will have an opportunity to consider the amount of time and hard work that was done by hand, without the benefits of later machinery such as tractors.

♦ Students may determine the steps necessary to plant and grow a vegetable garden, estimating the amount of time to do everything by hand. Using the average number of daylight hours during the spring or summer for their region, students may calculate the number of vegetables they could plant entirely by hand in one day. Discussions may focus on the necessity of cooperation for pioneers to produce enough food to feed their families and to trade for other supplies.

1. Frontier and pioneer life 2. Farms—History.

977

Pioneer Living: The Home. (Videocassette). Coronet, 1970. (Pioneer Living). VHS 1/2", Color, (11 min.). $195. (Interest level: 3-6).

As pioneers expanded into new territories in the 1800s, they staked out and claimed new homesteads. This video portrays how families selected a new site and built the log cabin. Common household chores such as cooking over open fireplaces and making soap and candles are shown.

♦ Students may discuss why pioneers traveling across the country to a new home were usually able to bring only a few necessities and treasured possessions from their former home. Students may brainstorm what they would bring on a move to a new home across the country if they could only have one suitcase.

1. Frontier and pioneer life.

977

Pioneer Living: The Village. (Videocassette). Coronet, 1970. (Pioneer Living). VHS 1/2", Color, (11 min.). $195. (Interest level: 3-6).

This video depicts the type of activities that were common in a typical pioneer village of the 1800s. Some of the crafts, trades, and services shown include a cobbler making shoes, a broom-maker tying brooms, a blacksmith shoeing a horse, and residents bartering at the general store.

♦ Students may be able to visit a living history site or museum in their state that features displays of pioneer life and activities. Students may also compare their clothing to the types of clothing children wore as depicted in books, photographs, and catalogs of the time.

1. Frontier and pioneer life.

977

Pioneer Mill. (Videocassette). Indiana University Audio Visual Center, 1972. (Pioneer Life). VHS 1/2", Color, (12 min.). Available from Indiana University Media and Teaching Resources. $161. (Interest level: 1-4).

Corn was a major crop even in Indiana's pioneer days. This video shows how the tedious nature of grinding corn at home spurred the creation of large water-powered mills. Farmers brought corn by horseback to be milled in exchange for a portion of the product. The entire process of grinding the corn to flour is explained as the miller does each step.

♦ While farmers were waiting, they often caught up on the latest news. Students may discuss places that they go to talk and "catch up on news" with their friends.

1. Frontier and pioneer life 2. Mills and millwork.

977

Settling the Old Northwest. (Videocassette). Encyclopedia Britannica Educational Corporation, 1990. (Settlement of the U.S. Series). VHS 1/2", Color, (18 min.). $99. (Interest level: 6-8).

This historical portrayal of the development of the Northwest Territory focuses on such issues as the growth of government, educational systems, transportation systems, and land ownership resulting from the Northwest Ordinance of 1787. The contributions and cooperative spirit of pioneers is illustrated through the living conditions and problems they faced in settling and developing the area into a major farming region.

♦ Students may research the Northwest Ordinance, including the history and major figures behind its creation. They may locate the Northwest Territory on an historical map and discuss how the history of the country might have been different without the Ordinance.

1. Frontier and pioneer life—Old Northwest 2. United States—History—1783-1865.

977

United States Regions: The Midwest. (Videocassette). Encyclopedia Britannica, 1989. VHS 1/2", Color, (20 min.). $103, with shipping. (Interest level: 4-6).

Using live footage, graphics, and paintings, this videotape emphasizes the Midwest's central location, productive farmlands, and abundant resources. Contemporary in its perspective, the video portrays a multicultural population coping with changes—e.g., the loss of the family farm, migration from cities, and the rise of service industries.

♦ Students may compare photographs in older works from the 1970s and earlier with the present-day

industrial plants portrayed in the video. Points to discuss could include the types of technological advances that are evident, such as the use of robots to spot weld automobile chassis and the advantages and disadvantages of each advance from the perspective of the company, the worker, and the consumer.
1. Agriculture—Middle West 2. Industrialization 3. Middle West—Indiana.

977.2
Baker, Ronald L. and **Carmony, Marvin**. *Indiana Place Names*. Indiana University Press (0-253-14167-2), 1975. 196p. (Interest level: 4-8).

This collection of 2,271 place names of the counties, cities, towns, villages, and some lakes and streams in Indiana includes pronunciations as well as historical, linguistic, geographic, and folkloric data for each place name given. A map of Indiana is provided in the appendix.
♦ Students may use this guide as a resource for further information about the places they are studying, including specific Indiana cities.
1. Geographic names—Indiana 2. Indiana—History, Local.

977.2
Burke, Carol and **Light, Martin**. *Back in Those Days: Reminiscences and Stories of Indiana*. Photos by Jackie Ullman. Indiana Writes (No ISBN), 1978 (out of print). 112p. B/W photos. (Interest level: 4-8).

One hundred and thirty people from west-central Indiana share their reminiscences of the past through well-told stories. This remarkable resource covers topics ranging from one-room schoolhouses to descriptions of courtships and early parties. The Indiana Arts Commission, the Department of English at Purdue University, and the magazine *Indiana Writes* served as sponsoring agents for this oral history project.
♦ Students may create a class reminiscences book. The students may record stories, jokes, and past remembrances that will give the future reader a sense of the class as a whole and the era in which the class book was written.
1. Indiana—History 2. Oral history—Indiana.

977.2
Carpenter, Allan. *Indiana*. Childrens Press (0-516-04114-2), 1979. (New Enchantment of America). 96p. Color photos and illus. (Interest level: 4-7).

Anecdotes, legends, stories, and quotes add personal interest to this account of Indiana's past and present. This is a comprehensive source of information on Indiana's history and notable figures, as well as its present-day cultures, education, geography, natural resources, and manufacturing.
♦ Students may investigate one of the many Indiana events or discoveries that had a national impact. Robert Owen's New Harmony utopia may provide ideas for the creation of a utopion community. Students could also trace the use of Bedford limestone to the Empire State Building in New York City and many famous buildings in Washington, DC.
1. Indiana.

977.2
Cavinder, Fred D. *The Indiana Book of Records, Firsts, and Fascinating Facts*. Indiana University Press (0-253-14001-3), 1985. 358p. B/W photos. (Interest level: 4-8).

This comprehensive book documents famous firsts, records, and fascinating facts associated with Indiana. Topics range from disasters to sporting and stunt records.
♦ Young people may select a city in Indiana and locate the records, firsts, or fascinating facts about it.
1. Indiana.

977.2
Fradin, Dennis B. *Indiana: In Words and Pictures*. Illus. by Richard Wahl. Maps by Len W. Meents. Childrens Press (0-516-03912-1), 1980. 48p. Color photos and illus. (Interest level: 2-3).

This profile of Indiana highlights periods and events of interest to younger children, including pioneer life, early school days, and the Indianapolis 500 race. State trivia and "firsts" as well as major cultural attractions, industries, crops, and wildlife are presented through the use of lively text and colorful photographs.
♦ Students may use the index and appendices to devise a state trivia game. They might also wish to create a state map indicating major crops and products, wildlife areas, or cultural attractions.
1. Indiana.

977.2
Hanfield, F. Gerald. *History on Tape: A Guide for Oral History in Indiana*. Indiana Historical Bureau (No ISBN), 1979. 18p. (Interest level: 3-8).

Oral histories of everyday people discussing important events of their lives capture the "slice of life" not often included in school textbooks. This "how-to" resource, created for the Oral History Project by the Indiana State Library, provides practical advice and insights for those wishing to use oral histories in their classrooms. Although information on available technology may be dated, lists for planning and conducting the interview are helpful. Sample historical events in Indiana and the United States are included as possible topics for oral history discussions.
♦ Students may interview an older relative or community member to collect an oral history. They might also begin to collect their own oral histories on tape for future generations. Comparisons between the two histories could lead to a class discussion concerning change and progress.
1. Oral history—Handbooks, manuals, etc.

977.2
Henry, Joanne Landers. *Log Cabin in the Woods: A True Story about a Pioneer Boy.* Illus. by Joyce Audy Zarins. Four Winds (0-02-743670-5), 1988. 60p. B/W illus. (Interest level: 4-7).

This delightful tale of childhood in early Indiana creates an authentic and memorable picture of the life of the first settlers. The story begins in 1832 and follows Oliver Johnson, age 11, through routine daily life as well as blizzards, log rollings, cabin raisings, a Fourth of July trip, and the fall preparations for winter. A period map and accurate historical references are provided.
♦ Students may participate in making candles, soap, or corncakes and practice other pioneer activities described in the book.
1. Johnson, Oliver, 1821-1907 2. Frontier and pioneer life—Indiana 3. Indiana—History.

977.2
Hoosier Landmarks: Indiana Properties Listed in the National Register of Historical Places. Historic Landmarks Foundation of Indiana (No ISBN), 1985. B/W photos and architectural drawings. 17p. (Interest level: 3-8).

This account of churches, cemeteries, schools, theaters, and homes designated as historic sites in Indiana is in an accessible format. Included with the properties are an address and the date of its declaration as a site to be preserved. Beautiful photographs and intricate architectural drawings enhance readers' understanding of the famous structures.
♦ Students may locate a specific historic site on an Indiana map and write to the Indiana Historic Landmark Foundation for information. They may also examine the process by which a site becomes an historic landmark or interview members of their own community who have encouraged the preservation of such landmarks.
1. Historic sites—Indiana 2. Indiana—History.

977.2
New Harmony: An Example and a Beacon. (Videocassette). Indiana University Audio Visual Center, 1971. VHS 1/2", Color, (29 min.). Available from Indiana University Media and Teaching. $15.90 (16mm film, for rent), $360 (16mm film, for purchase); $150 (videocassette, for purchase). from Indiana University Audio Visual Center. (Interest level: 8+).

Within this comprehensive portrayal of the utopian community founded by Robert Owen in New Harmony, Indiana, is the history and evolution of the commune from its origins to its status as an historic landmark. A major focus is the effort of Owen to gather thinkers who could conceptualize a new social order based on intellectual freedom.
♦ Students may read more about New Harmony as well as similar efforts to establish utopian communities. They can compare the goals, methods, outcomes, and achievements of each of these social experiments.
1. Collective settlements—Indiana 2. New Harmony (Ind.) 3. Indiana—Religion.

977.2
Ogden, R. Dale. *Indiana.* Childrens Press (0-516-00460-3), 1990. (America the Beautiful Series). 144p. B/W and Color photos and illus. (Interest level: 4-8).

This informative book presents the geography, history, government, economy, industry, culture, historic sites, and famous people of the Hoosier state. Photographs of architecture, people, paintings, and sculpture provide high visual interest and an interdisciplinary approach.
♦ Students may use the resource sections and maps in the book to plan an itinerary for either a cultural or historic tour of Indiana. They might also write a biography or prepare a mock interview for one of the 68 famous Hoosiers profiled. Many of these people, such as Dan Quayle, Jane Pauley, Larry Bird, and Michael Jackson, are visible, contemporary public figures.
1. Indiana.

977.2
The State House: 1888 to Present. (Pamphlet). Indiana Department of Commerce, 1987. Color photos. 11p. Free. (Interest level: 5-8).

This full-color document traces the history of Indiana State Houses from the first one in Vincennes to the current State House. Photographs of marble hallways and stained glass atriums provide a glimpse of the building, and anecdotes and charts of the state government organization inform readers about what happens behind those closed doors.
♦ Students may use a current daily newspaper to identify an important issue or bill facing their state legislature. They may then trace the bill's progress from the realization of the need for such a law, through the outcome of the votes in the legislature, to the governor's decision to sign or veto the measure.
1. Indiana State Capitol (Indianapolis, Ind.) 2. Indiana—Politics and government.

977.2
Swain, Gwenyth. *Indiana.* Lerner (0-8225-2721-9), 1992. (Hello U.S.A. Series). 72p. Color photos. (Interest level: 2-5).

Filled with both obscure and well-known facts, this resource takes readers on a trip detailing modern life in the Hoosier state. Special attention is devoted to environmental issues: how the Till Plain region was formed by glaciers and what steps must be taken today to preserve resources such as the Indiana Dunes State Park. Color photos, maps, graphs, and an index of famous Hoosiers increase the usefulness of this work.

♦ Students may research glacial history to identify how glaciers changed land formations and what contributions these flowing ice masses made to the soil. They may discuss the economic effects of those glacial changes. They may also prepare relief maps or three-dimensional cross-cuts of the land.
1. Indiana 2. Conservation of natural resources—Indiana.

977.2
Thompson, Charles N. *Sons of the Wilderness: John and William Conner.* Conner Prairie Press (0-9617-3676-3), 1937, 1988. 283p. B/W photos and illus. (Interest level: 7-8).

Set in Indiana, this work of historical fiction depicts the lives of William and John Conner, beginning in 1750 with the Conner family's dealings with the Delaware Indians and Moravian missionaries. It chronicles John and William's eventual work as trade, business, and government leaders in the state of Indiana. Helpful resources include a 1935 map of Indianapolis, notes, a bibliography, index, and illustrations and photos of the Conners.
♦ Some Indiana students may be able to visit Conner Prairie (about six miles northeast of Indianapolis), the restored living history museum that features the Conners' actual home and a working pioneer village. Students unable to visit Conner Prairie may compare this work with other writers' accounts of early Indiana.
1. Conner, John 2. Conner, William 3. Indiana.

977.2
Wilson, George R. *Early Indiana Trails and Surveys.* Indiana Historical Society (0-87195-005-7), 1919, 1986. 114p. B/W illus. (Interest level: 6-8).

A former county surveyor in Indiana, Wilson traces early lines of travel through the state in the 1800s, providing anecdotes and legends concerning travelers. The account of General William Henry Harrison is of particular interest.
♦ Students may choose one of the trails documented in the book and brainstorm possible challenges early settlers would have faced making the journey. Students could also make the connection to the present day by discussing what transportation challenges the United States and its neighbors are addressing now.
1. Roads 2. Indiana—Transportation—History 3. Travelers.

977.2
Wilson, William E. *Indiana: A History.* Indiana University Press (0-7837-3731-9), 1966, 1977. 243p. B/W photos and illus. (Interest level: 4-8).

This visual portrait covers many facets of the development of Indiana from the early exploration of the land to the transition from an agricultural to an industrial state. Ample black-and-white illustrations and photos add an extra dimension to the history of Indiana.

♦ This book may be used as a primary source for Indiana history. Students may use the photos to generate ideas for other topics of study.
1. Indiana—History.

Biography

920
Peat, Wilbur D. *Pioneer Painters of Indiana.* Art Association of Indianapolis, (0-317-29200-5) 1954. 254p. B/W reproductions. (Interest level: 6-8).

Some of the active painters in Indiana from 1800-1885 are highlighted. The book is arranged by regions, chronologically presenting facts about each painter's life and an assessment of his or her style and skills. Many black-and-white photos of the works by these Indiana painters are included as well as an index, a roster of the artists and a short biographical sketch for each.
♦ Using this book as a resource, students may compare the styles of several Indiana painters. They may also determine how this book's information about the painters and their paintings reflects the history and the culture of the 1800s.
1. Painters, American—1800-1899—Biography 2. Painters—1800-1899—Indiana.

92 Appleseed, Johnny
Brandenberg, Aliki. *The Story of Johnny Appleseed.* Simon and Schuster (0-671-66298-8), 1963. 32p. B/W and Color illus. (Interest level: K-2).

The brief text emphasizes the personal qualities of Johnny Appleseed—his love for nature, children, peace, and apples. Bold, childlike illustrations further reinforce these characteristics of this legendary pioneer who lived and worked in Indiana and surrounding states during the early 1800s.
♦ Young people may have a tasting party, sampling slices of several different varieties of apples and learning their names.
1. Appleseed, Johnny, 1774-1845 2. Apple.

92 Grissom, Virgil I.
Chappell, Carl L. *Virgil I. Grissom: Boy Astronaut.* Illus. by Robert Doremus. Bobbs-Merrill (No ISBN), 1971. 200p. Color illus. (Interest level: 3-5).

This biography recounts the life of Virgil Grissom (a pioneer of space exploration) from his birth in Mitchell, Indiana, to his death at Cape Kennedy, Florida, in 1967 aboard the Apollo spaceship. A glossary, additional recommended reading, and a time line of the life of this pioneer of space exploration are included.
♦ Students may research other American astronauts. They may also investigate the current qualifications for becoming an astronaut.
1. American astronauts 2. Grissom, Virgil I. 3. Outer Space—Exploration.

92 Harrison, Benjamin

Clinton, Susan. *Benjamin Harrison*. Easton Press (0-516-01370-X), 1989. (Reilly and Lee President Series). 100p. B/W illus. (Interest level: 5-6).

This detailed biography of the twenty-third president of the United States begins with his military successes during the Civil War and includes his service as a senator and president and his defeat for a second presidential term. The author successfully integrates the power and influences of various political forces on Harrison's career.

♦ Using Christine Fitz-Gerald's biography *William Henry Harrison* (*see* following entry), young people may compare and contrast the lives of Benjamin Harrison and his grandfather, William Henry Harrison.

1. Harrison, Benjamin, 1833-1901 2. Presidents—United States.

92 Harrison, William Henry

Fitz-Gerald, Christine Maloney. *William Henry Harrison*. Childrens Press (0-516-01392-0), 1987. (Encyclopedia of Presidents Series). 100p. B/W illus. (Interest level: 5-6).

This thorough biography addresses Harrison's army service in the Northwest Territory, role in the War of 1812, encounters with Tecumseh, and his election to the United States Congress and the presidency. Ample illustrations, a chronology of events, and a detailed index increase the book's usefulness for research.

♦ Young people may play the role of Harrison's campaign publicist during his election for the presidency in 1840 and, drawing from the candidate's past achievements, create a campaign poster.

1. Harrison, William Henry, 1773-1841 2. Presidents—United States.

92 Lincoln, Abraham

Boyhood of Abraham Lincoln. (Videocassette). Coronet, 1987. (The Boyhood Series). VHS 1/2", Color, (11 min.). $195. (Interest level: 2-6).

Set in an authentically reconstructed village and home in Rockport, Indiana, this personal portrait of Abraham Lincoln focuses on his boyhood of near poverty and his long hours of hard work. The production makes a point of showing how he developed qualities of honesty, responsibility, and humor—qualities that contributed to his becoming a great president.

♦ Groups of students may each select and read a different biography of Abraham Lincoln (*see* the "Illinois" section). They may then compare which major events each biographer stressed and which were omitted or downplayed, discussing what type of image each portrayal provided.

1. Lincoln, Abraham, 1809-1865 2. Presidents—United States.

92 Teale, Edwin Way

Teale, Edwin Way. *Dune Boy: The Early Years of a Naturalist*. Illus. by Edward Shenton. Indiana University Press (0-253-11860-3), 1966, 1987. 275p. B/W photos and illus. (Interest level: 6-8).

This autobiographical account of Teale's childhood explores his years on the Indiana Dune farm owned by his grandparents. Photographs of Teale's grandparents lend historical significance.

♦ Students may write their own autobiography, including how their lives have been influenced by their grandparents, other relatives, or special adult friends. The book may include pictures, remembrances, or other memorabilia pertaining to the person selected.

1. Teale, Edwin Way 2. Naturalists—Indiana.

Fiction

Chambers, Catherine E. *Indiana Days: Life in a Frontier Town*. Illus. by John Lawn. Troll (0-8167-0056-7), 1984. 32p. B/W illus. (Interest level: 2-4).

This readable story portrays travel by train in the mid-1800s. Twelve-year-old Kristi journeys from the Iowa prairie to an Indiana town to live with relatives and get her education.

♦ The class can compare life on an Iowa prairie to life in Indiana in the mid-1800s, including going to school.

1. Frontier and pioneer life—Indiana—Fiction 2. Indiana—History—Fiction.

Clifford, Eth. *Help! I'm a Prisoner in the Library*. Illus. by George Hughes. Houghton Mifflin (0-395-28478-3), 1979. 105p. B/W illus. (Interest level: 4-6).

In this Young Hoosier Book Award winner, two young sisters are accidentally locked in a library. After a night of unexplained sounds and happenings, the girls are finally rescued and reunited with their father. The story takes place in Indianapolis, and the author uses actual happenings of the time to make this tale believable.

♦ Students can brainstorm and write about how they could have fun and keep busy if they were locked in a library overnight. They may also research and map the history of major blizzards or other storms in their state, using newspapers and other sources.

1. Libraries—Fiction 2. Blizzards—Fiction.

Friermood, Elisabeth Hamilton. *The Wild Donahues*. Doubleday (No ISBN), 1963 (out of print). 208p. (Interest level: 5-8).

Using articles from Indiana newspapers given to her by friends, Friermood has devised an exciting historical melodrama. The story centers around colorful characters in the house in which Friermood's father had lived. References to the Underground Railroad are an important and useful component of this work.

♦ Students may study the history of slavery and the origins of the Underground Railroad. They might also wish to read and share such stories about the Underground Railroad as Virginia Hamilton's *The House of Dies Drear* (Macmillan, 1968) and its sequel, *The Mystery of Drear House* (see Ohio—Fiction, Hamilton).
1. Underground Railroad—Fiction 2. Slavery—United States—Fiction 3. Indiana—Fiction.

Hale, Janet. *The Conners of Conner Prairie.* Illus. by Richard Day. Guild Press of Indiana and Conner Prairie Press (0-9617367-5-5), 1989. 127p. B/W illus. (Interest level: 4-8).

This historical story of the Conner brothers relates the daily activities and events of early pioneer life on the frontier. The boys grew up among the Delaware Indians in Ohio but set out for the Indiana Territory in 1800. The role of each brother in the developing state is vividly described: They became senators, traders, guides, and interpreters; fought in the War of 1812; and established a milling business.
♦ The Conner homestead, located about six miles northeast of Indianapolis, has been preserved as an operating living history museum. Indiana students may visit the 1823 William Conner home and experience pioneer life in the 1836 village as interpreters role play in period costume. Young people in other states may create a diorama of one of the Conners' daily activities illustrated in the work.
1. Conner, William 2. Conner, John 3. Frontier and pioneer life—Indiana 4. Indiana—History.

Henry, Joanne Landers. *A Clearing in the Forest: A Story about a Real Settler Boy.* Illus. by Charles Robinson. Four Winds (0-02-743671-3), 1992. 64p. B/W illus. (Interest level: 3-5).

Based on an unpublished manuscript by Elijah Fletcher and on his father's diaries, this biographical novel is about a settler boy, Elijah, growing up in Indianapolis in the 1830s. The strengths of this brief novel are its lively characters and authentic detail.
♦ Young people may wish to locate on maps the various geographical sites mentioned in the novel, including Indianapolis and its streets (Delaware Street, Washington Street, the Circle, and Ohio Street) as well as Fort Wayne and Cincinnati. From the work's pencil illustrations, young people may also make a list of the items that are not commonly seen today (e.g., steamboats, covered bridges, and washstands).
1. Fletcher, Elijah 2. Indianapolis (Ind.)—History—Fiction.

Long, Eleanor Rice. *Wilderness to Washington: An 1811 Journey by Horseback.* Reflections Press (0-89917-324-1), 1981. 167p. B/W maps. (Interest level: 5-8).

This work of historical fiction is based on the true story of Jonathan and Ann Jennings and their trip on horseback to Washington, DC, where Jennings was to serve in the Congress of 1811. As the lives and romance of Jonathan and Ann unfold, the reader gains an understanding of the times.
♦ The class may trace the trail Jonathan and Ann traveled on the way to Washington and discuss the obstacles the Jennings could have encountered while traveling in the wilderness on horseback. The maps in the book could be used for this activity.
1. Jennings, Jonathan 2. Jennings, Ann 3. Voyages and travels.

Major, Charles. *The Bears of Blue River.* Illus. by A. B. Frost and others. Indiana University Press (0-253-10590-0), 1984. 277p. B/W illus. (Interest level: 4-8).

Balsa, a young pioneer boy in Indiana during the early nineteenth-century, has many adventures while exploring the woods with his brother. At one exciting point, they find themselves face-to-face with a notorious one-eared bear. The illustrations add to the drama of this tale.
♦ As a prewriting exercise, students may brainstorm possible adventures and dangers pioneer children might have encountered on a journey through the woods. After reading the book, they may write how they would feel if they were in the same situation as Balsa and his brother. What would they have done differently?
1. Indiana—History—Fiction 2. Frontier and pioneer life—Indiana—Fiction 3. Bears—Fiction.

Nicholson, Meredith. *The House of a Thousand Candles.* Illus. by Howard Chandler Christy. Indiana University Press (0-253-32852-7), 1905, 1986. 382p. (Interest level: 8+).

This thriller, set in fictitious Wabana County in rural Indiana, centers around John Glenarm, heir to his grandfather's mansion. In order for John to inherit the supposedly haunted mansion, he must reside in it for one year. John encounters strange noises, ghosts, and a burglar attack, but in the end he survives and receives his inheritance.
♦ The class can discuss attitudes, dress, language, values, and romances of the characters in the book, comparing them with contemporary ways.
1. Mystery and detective stories 2. Ghosts—Fiction 3. Indiana—Fiction.

Tarkington, Booth. *Penrod.* Illus. by Gordon Grant. Indiana University Press, (0-253-34311-9), 1914, 1985. 306p. B/W illus. (Interest level: 6-8).

This entertaining tale presents the exploits of Penrod, a 12-year-old boy growing up in the early 1900s. A sense of the social attitudes of the time are evident in Tarkington's subtle references to prevailing prejudices.

- Students may select an activity, event, or attitude presented in the novel and compare it with a contemporary counterpart.

1. Indiana—Fiction.

Professional Materials

977.2
Madison, James H. *The Indiana Way.* Indiana University Press (0-253-32999-X), 1986. 361p. B/W photos, maps, and figures. (Interest level: Teacher resource).

Ideal for use as a teacher resource, this volume gives a solid insight into the history of Indiana. The book is divided into four parts: Before There Was a State, Pioneer Indiana (1816-1850), Indiana in Transition (1850-1920), and Continuity and Change Since 1920. This book is well written, carefully organized, highly accurate, and interesting.
- The teacher may use this book for background information or as a supplement to any history lesson on Indiana.

1. Indiana—History.

977.2
Sayers, Evelyn M. *Handbook on Indiana History.* Indiana Department of Education (No ISBN), 1987. 224p. (Interest level: Teacher resource).

Organized chronologically, this resource presents the changes in Indiana landscape, culture, and inhabitants from Paleo-Indian culture (12,000-14,000 years ago) to the present day. Brief summaries appear on the right-hand side of every page to allow skimming and browsing of the text. Each chapter is divided into two distinct parts: general comments and points to emphasize. The Indiana Department of Education sponsored the compilation; therefore, special attention is paid to government in the Hoosier state.
- The governing body for Indianapolis and Marion County is called Uni-Gov, a mechanism that combines city and county systems and funds. Students could research that landmark form of government (it was the first of its kind in the country) to discern the motivating factors responsible for the change. They may discuss advantages and disadvantages of the program.

1. Indiana—History—Resource guide.

Michigan

by Gail Beaver

Nonfiction

363.1
Stonehouse, Frederick. *The Wreck of the Edmund Fitzgerald*. Avery Color Studios (0-932212-05-0 pbk), 1977, 1982. 208p. (Interest level: 5-8).
  This is a detailed and fascinating retelling of a twentieth-century disaster, the wreck of the *Edmund Fitzgerald* in Lake Superior. The author successfully weaves the story with known facts and speculation.
♦ After reading the account, students may re-create news broadcasts for the day of the event, beginning with weather reports for the Great Lakes region and incorporating other events of the time.
1. Edmund Fitzgerald (Ship) 2. Shipwrecks—Superior, Lake 3. Great Lakes—History.

387.1
Hyde, Charles K. *The Northern Lights: Lighthouses of the Upper Great Lakes*. Photos by Ann and John Mahan. Two Peninsula Press (0-9419-1209-4), 1986, 1990. 208p. Color photos. (Interest level: 5-8).
  Illustrated with photographs that highlight the differences in design of various lighthouses, this collection of stories emphasizes the value of lighthouses and the roles of those who operate them. One such story tells of a young girl, Emily Ward, who was marooned on Bois Blanc Island in Lake Huron during a storm in 1838. She saved all of the equipment from the lighthouse tower, then watched the tower fall.
♦ Students may write a newspaper account or prepare a broadcast script about Emily Ward's experiences.
1. Lighthouses 2. Great Lakes region.

391
Hartman, Sheryl. *Indian Clothing of the Great Lakes: 1740-1840*. Eagle's View (0-943604-16-8 pbk), 1991. 132p. B/W illus. (Interest level: 1-8).
  This collection of full-page black-and-white drawings of Great Lakes Indian clothing and paraphernalia presents identifications of the various items by their English and Indian names. Clear instructions for their construction and explanations of their history and significance are included.
♦ Young people can use this resource in a study of Indian culture at any level. They may draw and color the items described, construct models, or make costumes. They may wish to expand the collection with drawings of clothing worn by Native Americans in other regions.
1. Indians of North America—Great Lakes region—Costume and adornment.

398.2
Gage, Cully. *The Northwoods Reader*. Avery Color Studios (0-932212-11-5), 1977, 1992. (Interest level: 5-8).
  Michigan's north woods at the turn of the twentieth century is the setting for this collection of short stories. With the ease of a seasoned storyteller, Gage provides a unique sense of the region and its appeal in the portrayal of the people and events.
♦ After reading the stories, young people may make a list of the new understandings they have gained about the era and region. Using *The Northwoods Reader*, they may also wish to adapt some of the tales and stage their own version of "Prairie Home Companion" (Garrison Keillor's radio program). They can model their storytelling after Keillor's easy storytelling style.
1. Michigan—Social life and customs 2. Short stories.

398.2
Gringhuis, Dirk. *Lore of the Great Turtle: Indian Legends of Mackinac Retold*. Illus. by author. Mackinac Island State Park Commission (0-911872-11-6), 1970, 1984. 89p. (Interest level: 3-5).
  The setting for this collection of 19 illustrated stories is early Mackinac Island. The title story features the Indian legend that describes the island as a great turtle lying between Lake Huron and Lake Michigan, a place sacred to the Ojibway Indians. Varied in content and

authentic in detail, this collection should appeal to young people.
♦ Young people may find other Indian names and legends based on the animal-like shape of an island, mountain, or lake. They may wish to create a visual image of the formation by using an appropriate artistic medium (e.g., charcoal, watercolor, clay, or computer graphics).
1. Ojibway Indians—Legends 2. Legends—Mackinac Island (Mich.).

398.2
Land of the Sky Blue Waters. (Audiocassette). Performed by Sheila Dailey. Rumpelstiltskin Productions. Available from Hillsdale. 1 cassette, (80 min.). $19.95. Includes booklet. (Interest level: 3-8).

This well-respected Michigan storyteller presents the best-known legends of the Great Lakes. Included are the legends of Sleeping Bear Dunes and the ship, the *Griffon*. This excellent production is accompanied by a spiral-bound collection of illustrative background materials and activity suggestions.
♦ After young people hear the legend about LaSalle's ship ("The Legend of the Griffon"), they may brainstorm the possible fate of the lost ship and of those who were waiting for its return. They may wish to write a short story based on their speculations.
1. Great Lakes region—Legends 2. Folklore—Great Lakes region.

398.2
Newton, Stanley D. *Paul Bunyan of the Great Lakes*. Avery Color Studios (0-932212-42-5), 1946, 1991. 188p. (Interest level: 1-3).

This collection presents the best-known and most traditional versions of the Paul Bunyan tales, introducing favorite characters like Sourdough Sam and including such accounts as drinking the Blue Lake dry and installing the Northern Lights. Well-written and authentic to their Michigan origins, these tales are valuable for any tall tale unit, and young people will enjoy hearing and reading them.
♦ After discussing the varied aspects of Michigan's topography and climate, young people may write a new Paul Bunyan tall tale about a feature not addressed in this collection.
1. Bunyan, Paul (Legendary character) 2. Folklore—Great Lakes region.

398.2
Otto, Simon. *Walk in Peace: Legends and Stories of the Michigan Indians*. Illus. by Kayle Crampton. Michigan Indian Press (0-9617707-5-9), 1990. 50p. B/W illus. (Interest level: 3+).

The author, son of a Michigan Ojibway father and Ottawa mother, has recorded his memories of stories told by elders, medicine men and women, friends, and his parents as they gathered to share their tribal culture. The simple but appealing presentation makes these tales excellent tools for imparting Native American culture.
♦ Each student may retell one of the two-page stories in a storytelling session.
1. Indians of North America—Legends 2. Indians of North America—Great Lakes region.

398.2
Peyton, John L. *The Stone Canoe and Other Stories*. Illus. by author. McDonald & Woodward (0-939923-07-6), 1989. 151p. B/W illus. (Interest level: 3-8).

The author has carefully retold a dozen legends he learned from an Ojibway grandmother. Appealing to all ages, these well-crafted stories focus on the relationship between humans and nature (e.g., the hardships of harsh winters, the whims of nature in a northern climate, and humans' interdependence with nature).
♦ The author has preserved the integrity and the humor of these nature stories, allowing them to be used for enactment or storytelling. Young people may select one legend and draw a simple storyboard to display as they tell it. Or, they may act out one of the longer stories, such as "The Stone Canoe."
1. Ojibway Indians—Legends 2. Indians of North America—Great Lakes region—Legends.

398.2
Snake, Sam. *The Adventures of Nanabush*. Compiled by Emerson Coatsworth and David Coatsworth. Illus. by Francis Kagige. Doubleday (0-385-14148-X; 0-385-14249-8 pbk), 1979. 85p. Color illus. (Interest level: 3-6).

This collection of 16 tales (retold by Sam Snake) introduces Nanabush (Nanaboozhoo), a hero, prankster, and magician of Ojibway legend. Nanabush's lively and engaging nature will appeal to young people, and his authentic portrayal can be a basis for a cross-cultural study of trickster heroes.
♦ Students may enjoy reading and retelling these tales. Or, they may compare and contrast the qualities of Nanabush with those of Anansi, Coyote, Merlin, or other traditional characters.
1. Ojibway Indians—Legends 2. Indians of North America—Legends.

398.2
Talespins. (Audiocassette). Produced by Pamela Vanden Ploeg, 1984. Available from Hillsdale. 1 cassette, (31 min.). $9.00. (Interest level: 3-8).

Many of these tales, spun from Michigan's history, were drawn from happenings that were part of settling the land. Other tales are based on legends that developed from later state history. The appealing and distinctive qualities of the storyteller's voice, the manner of presentation, and the variety of stories included enhance the value of this audiotape.
♦ After listening to some of the historical tales, young people may search old newspapers or check with

historical societies to find a local story they want to tell.
1. Michigan—History 2. Folklore—Michigan.

398.2
Weeks, George. *Sleeping Bear: Its Lore, Legends and First People*. The Historical Society of Michigan (0-9614-3446-5), 1989. 56p. B/W photos and illus. Available from the Cottage Book Shop of Glen Arbor. $7.95. (Interest level: 5-8).

"The Beautiful Maiden of Sleeping Bear" and "Leelinau, the Lost Daughter" are just two of the legends about this large sand dune on Michigan's western coast. Facts about the region from its prehistoric days to the present are included.
♦ After reading this book, young people can use a map to locate the Sleeping Bear Dunes in western Michigan. They may speculate how the legend developed, and they may research what might have been the actual cause of a phenomenon like the dunes.
1. Indians of North America—Legends 2. Folklore—Great Lakes region.

551
The Geology of Michigan. (18 min.).
How the Glaciers Changed Michigan. (22 min.).
The Rocks and Minerals of Michigan. (30 min.).
The Geology of Pictured Rocks National Lakeshore. (22 min.).
The Fossils of Michigan. (40 min.).

(Videocassette Series). Series produced by Laurence Jankowski (with the cooperation and assistance of the Michigan Geological Survey, Michigan Department of Natural Resources, the University of Michigan, Bowling Green State University, and the University of Toledo) for Instructional Video, 1992. Available from Instructional Video. $29.95 per videocassette. (Interest level: 7-8).

The Geology of Michigan presents an overview of millions of years of Michigan geologic history from the time when the state was covered by seas to the present day. *How the Glaciers Changed Michigan* explains where the ice was in the state and what effects it had. *The Rocks and Minerals of Michigan* is a study of the native bedrock and the minerals that have played important roles in Michigan history. *The Geology of Pictured Rocks National Lakeshore* explores the geologic history of this National Lakeshore Tourist attraction. *The Fossils of Michigan* shows the appearance of the state when ancient plants and animals lived in and among its shallow seas and marshes. These videos combine live action and still footage with voice-over narration to give the viewer accurate and detailed information about the natural phenomena of Michigan and the Great Lakes region. Although there is some repetition of information among the videos, they are excellent for earth science studies. Their format allows the narration to be interrupted for teacher and student discussion.
♦ Students may be guided to specific segments of the videos for a closer study of one topic. They may build a landform to illustrate the depths and heights created by the glaciers. Or, they may create a display of rocks and mineral samples from their own region.
1. Michigan 2. Rocks 3. Geology—Michigan 4. Mines and mineral resources—Michigan.

551.48
Great Lakes Water Level Facts. U.S. Army Corps of Engineers (No ISBN), 1987. 15p. B/W illus. (Interest level: 5-8).

Each page of this informative Great Lakes booklet includes a map or graph and a few paragraphs of clearly written text. The first section presents the physical features of the Great Lakes, and the second explains water levels of the lakes and the factors that affect their fluctuation.
♦ Students may create a relief map of the Great Lakes and the rivers or small lakes that connect them.
1. Great Lakes.

551.48
Henderson, Kathy. *The Great Lakes*. Childrens Press (0-516-01163-4), 1989. (New True Book). 45p. Color photos. (Interest level: 1-3).

This book provides an easy-to-read introduction to the Great Lakes. Large print and carefully selected illustrations aid in describing the history and significance of the lakes.
♦ Adults may guide young readers to understand the size of the Great Lakes in relation to places and things more familiar to them (e.g., the size of a smaller lake or the area of a state). Young people may research locks, discovering why they are needed and how they are used to move ships through the Great Lakes.
1. Great Lakes.

582.13
Lund, Harry C. *Michigan Wildflowers*. Altwerger and Mandel (0-96148-180-3), 1991. 121p. Color photos. (Interest level: 3-8).

Beautiful color photos and clear descriptive information help the reader to identify Michigan wildflowers from the common cornflower to the rare lady's slipper. Special attention is directed to rare or endangered species and the laws that protect them.
♦ Students may compare the species of wildflowers found in their own neighborhoods with those identified in the book. They may take individual or group nature walks to collect specimens.
1. Wildflowers—Michigan—Identification.

597
Creatures in the Great Lakes. (Videocassette). Produced by Richard Brauer, 1985. Available from

Hillsdale. VHS 1/2", Color, (20 min.). $140. (Interest level: 6-8).

This videocassette depicts the colorful creatures found in the waters of the Great Lakes. The film's technical quality and the natural beauty of the subject make this an aesthetically pleasing production.
♦ Using this tape and additional resources, young people may make a chart of the depths of the Great Lakes and the creatures that inhabit each depth. They could enlarge the chart to wall size to be displayed for others. They may wish to create a comparison chart of the creatures living in other large bodies of water, particularly oceans.

1. Freshwater animals 2. Great Lakes.

597.96

Holman, J. Alan. *Michigan Snakes: A Field Guide and Pocket Reference*. Michigan State University Cooperative Extension Service (No ISBN), 1989. 72p. B/W and Color photos and illus. (Interest level: 3-8).

This factual presentation describes the nature of each of the species of snakes found in Michigan. The color photos that provide identification of the various snakes enhance the book's appeal for those young readers fascinated by the subject matter.
♦ Young people may gain a better understanding of the significance of the species of snakes that live in the Great Lakes region by comparing them with the snake populations of other areas. Students may also explore differences between poisonous and nonpoisonous species and the relationship of snakes to their predators.

1. Snakes.

598

Gillette, John and **Mohrhardt, David**. *The Coat Pocket Bird Book*. Illus. by authors. Two Peninsula Press (0-9419-1205-1), 1984. 160p. Color illus. (Interest level: 3-8).

Eighty birds from the marshes, lakes, forests, fields, and residential areas of the Great Lakes region are described in pertinent detail. Colorful illustrations and a handy, reinforced paperback format enhance the work's usefulness.
♦ Students may research the reasons some birds thrive in particular environments. Young people in the Great Lakes region may take a bird watching walk to identify birds in their own neighborhoods; those in other areas may prepare a display comparing and contrasting local birds with those of the Great Lakes region.

1. Birds—Great Lakes region 2. Bird watching—Great Lakes region.

629.22

Simonds, Christopher. *The Model T Ford*. Silver Burdett (0-382-24122-3; 0-382-24117-7 pbk), 1991. (Turning Points in American History Series). 64p. B/W and Color illus. (Interest level: 5-8).

This introductory history of Henry Ford's Model T addresses the car as well as the related issues of mass production and the impact of the automobile on society. The author's style is straightforward, leading the reader toward an understanding of the Model T's effects on the history and economic development of Michigan and the United States.
♦ Students may compare and contrast the advantages of mass production versus handcrafting. If possible, they may visit local industries and craftspeople to observe various types of production. Or, they may invite speakers from local businesses to help them understand the economics of the issue.

1. Ford Model T automobile 2. Automobiles—History.

636

"The North American Beaver Trade." *Cobblestone* 3 (June 1982). B/W illus. (Interest level: 3-6).

The North American beaver is the focus of this issue of *Cobblestone*, a social studies magazine. Although published for children, it is also useful for teachers who are designing units of instruction. It includes varied activities and approaches to the topic—informational articles, letters, charts, legends, puzzles, and maps.
♦ Younger students may use the information and the drawing-a-beaver instructions to make visual displays depicting the beaver in American history. Older students may add research information describing the beaver and its positive and negative impacts on the environment.

1. Fur trade.

641.7

Eberly, Carole, ed. *Our Michigan Ethnic Tales and Recipes*. Illus. by Beverly Woodward. Eberly (0-9322-9603-3), 1979. 136p. B/W illus. (Interest level: 3-6).

This book provides a look at Michigan ethnic groups through legends, folklore, and foods. Subjects range from Sojourner Truth to Mother Waddles, a well-known Detroit friend of the hungry and homeless. Mother Waddles' soup kitchen recipes for fried green tomatoes and cornbread are included.
♦ Young readers may hold an ethnic fair organized around foods associated with their own cultural group or another cultural group that interests them. They can prepare or purchase the foods to sample on the day of the fair, share legends and folklore, and display representative books, realia, and clothing.

1. Ethnology—Michigan 2. Folklore—Michigan 3. Cookery—Michigan.

741.977

Weidenaar, Reynold. *A Sketchbook of Michigan*. Text by Anne Zeller. Baker Book House (0-8010-9620-0), 1980. 110p. B/W illus. (Interest level: 6-8).

These pen-and-ink drawings, some specific to Michigan, are a collection of landscapes, nature, historical events, buildings, recreational activities, and

people in the Great Lakes region. The text is written in a short, free verse style that creates a sense of personal memory.
- ◆ After quietly examining an insect or flower in its natural environment near their school, home, or favorite location, students may record their observations through poetry or art.
1. Michigan—Pictorial works.

784.4
Bunyan and Banjoes: Michigan Songs and Stories. (Audiocassette). Produced by Kitty Donohoe, 1987. Available from Hillsdale. 1 cassette, (35 min.). $7.95; $15 with accompanying booklet. (Interest level: 1-6).

This cassette brings to life the songs and the spirit of the loggers, the miners, the lakes, and the legends. The accompanying booklet, developed by Kitty Donohoe and Pasqua Cekola Warstler, contains stories, recipes, facts of Michigan history, and song lyrics, thus providing background activities for the tales.
- ◆ Young people may learn and sing for an audience some of the songs presented on this cassette tape. They may use the information in the booklet to prepare an introduction to their program and to link the songs.
1. Michigan—Songs and music 2. Songs, American.

789.2
Michigan in Song. (Audiocassette). Produced by the Michigan Traditional Arts Program and The Michigan State University Museum, 1990. Available from River Road Press. 1 cassette, (75 min.). $10 with booklet. (Interest level: 2+).

These entertaining and authentic compositions, performed by skilled folk artists, are those traditionally sung by the lumberjacks, the Great Lakes sailors, and the copper miners. A highlight is Woody Guthrie's "1913 Massacre," based on a tragic event in the history of Calumet, a copper mining town. The accompanying booklet, written by Eliot Singer and Yvonne R. Lockwood, includes the lyrics and the history of some of the songs.
- ◆ Because most of the melodies are easily remembered, young people may present a program of songs and legends as part of a study of the Great Lakes region. They may also use the melodies to write some verses about their own community's history.
1. Great Lakes—Songs 2. Songs, American.

811.3
Longfellow, Henry Wadsworth. *Hiawatha.* Illus. by Susan Jeffers. Dial (0-8037-0013-X), 1983. 24p. Color illus. (Interest level: 1-4).

Henry Schoolcraft, a Michiganian and folklorist, recorded the Native American legend upon which the poem is based. Large, distinctive illustrations of young Hiawatha and the forest scenes enhance this excerpt from Longfellow's poem.
- ◆ Young people may present portions of *Hiawatha* as a choral reading. When sharing the poem, they may include information about Henry Schoolcraft and the historical background Longfellow used for his poem.
1. Indians of North America—Poetry 2. Indians of North America—Legends.

912.774 (Reference)
Michigan Atlas and Gazetteer. DeLorme (0-8993-3221-8), 1987. 204p. Color maps. (Interest level: 5+).

This detailed resource provides comprehensive maps of every section of the state. Its usefulness for research is enhanced by an index and supplementary text that covers recreational, commercial, and historical sites.
- ◆ Young people may choose a community described in the book and write to its Chamber of Commerce or other community organizations to collect samples of newspapers, brochures, and photographs. The materials can be used for an oral report or a visual display.
1. Michigan—Maps 2. Michigan—Description 3. Outdoor recreation—Michigan.

912.774 (Reference)
Sommers, Lawrence. *Atlas of Michigan.* Michigan State University Press (0-8701-3205-9), 1977. 242p. B/W and Color illus. (Interest level: 7-8).

This atlas is a comprehensive study of many aspects of Michigan, addressing the state's history, culture, economy, and people. It includes a complete index and a thorough bibliography.
- ◆ Students may use this atlas in combination with a world atlas and a United States atlas to identify the kinds of information each provides. They can then prepare a mini-atlas for their own school, neighborhood, or community.
1. Michigan—Maps.

917.704
Dutton, Fred. *Life on the Great Lakes: A Wheelsman's Story.* Wayne State University and Great Lakes Historical Society (0-8143-2260-3), 1991. 173p. (Interest level: 6-8).

In a time when the great ships were steered by magnetic compass, wheelsmen had to use their own knowledge and experience in adjusting navigational information to suit the situation. Dutton's account ranges from routine procedures to extraordinary challenges.
- ◆ After reading parts of this work, students may research navigational tools currently in use. They may also research the process by which someone becomes a Great Lakes sea captain today.
1. Seafaring life—Great Lakes 2. Great Lakes.

917.74
Field, Ellyce. *Detroit Kids Catalog: Complete Guide to Michigan Sites*. Wayne State University Press (0-8143-2202-6), 1990. 448p. B/W illus. (Interest level: 3-8).

This unusual compilation of things to do and places to go throughout the state of Michigan includes traditional historic sites, cultural museums, and local events as well as unusual tours such as a tour of an old lumber camp. The book provides practical information for planning trips and a helpful map that highlights areas that can be visited in a brief period of time.

♦ Young people may play the role of travel agents, planning their own imaginary trip (group or individual) complete with itinerary, transportation, accommodations, reservations, food, clothing, and budget. They could also create advertisements promoting their trip to the public.

1. Michigan—Description—Guidebooks.

917.74
Great Lakes Education Booklet. Michigan Department of Natural Resources (No ISBN), 1990. 16p. B/W and Color illus. (Interest level: 4-8).

Produced in celebration of Earth Day, this excellent information booklet is intended to promote a sense of stewardship and responsibility for preserving the Great Lakes. Included are a well-designed verbal and visual presentation of basic facts about the lakes, flash cards that identify important fish of the Great Lakes, a resource map, a sand dune poster, and a resource guide with names, addresses, and phone numbers.

♦ Students may create wildlife flash cards to identify animal life in their own region. They may choose to write a biographic profile of a Great Lake, describing its size, age, "moods," history, etc.

1. Great Lakes region.

917.74
Michigan Student Desktop Map. Hillsdale Education, n.d. 18" x 23" with plastic lamination. Available from Hillsdale. $12.95. (Interest level: 4-8).

This versatile and colorful map provides an excellent visual orientation to the state of Michigan and the Great Lakes region. One side shows Michigan's topography, population centers, and boundaries with an inset map of Detroit, the state's largest city. The other side shows the Great Lakes region with an inset map of the world.

♦ Two accompanying sets of map lessons (appropriate for individualized progress) are available ($15.95 each): Linda Ecklund prepared a set for secondary students (7+), and David and Stella McConnell prepared a set for younger students (grades 4-7).

1. Michigan—Maps.

917.74
Warbach, Ozz. *Mother Nature's Michigan*. Michigan Department of Resources (No ISBN), 1990. 80p. Color illus. (Interest level: 4-5).

Cartoon illustrations depict Michigan's wildlife. Although the approach is entertaining, much information is presented on such topics as the beaver's life, home, habits, and its effect on the ecology of woods and water.

♦ Students may draw their own cartoons of regional wildlife. These can be designed to demonstrate how animals affect or are affected by the environment. The approach can be extended to other parts of the ecological cycle.

1. Wildlife—Michigan.

970
Clifton, James A., Cornell, George L., and McClurken, James M. *People of the Three Fires*. Michigan Indian Press and Grand Rapids Tribal Council (0-9617-7070-8), 1986. 118p. B/W photos. (Interest level: 6-8).

This authentic resource sensitively traces the ancient and new stories of the Ottawa, the Potawatomi, and the Ojibway American Indians, many of whom settled in the western and southwestern part of Michigan. A workbook and a guide to discussion questions and activities are also available.

♦ Young people may make a list of cultural elements (e.g., mythology, rituals, and lifestyle) and prepare a chart illustrating, comparing, and contrasting Native American tribes in different geographical regions of the country.

1. Ottawa Indians 2. Ojibway Indians 3. Potawatomi Indians.

970.1
Deur, Lynne. *Nishnawbe: A Story of Indians in Michigan*. River Road (0-938682-00-8), 1981. 51p. Illus. (Interest level: 3-6).

This highly readable and thoughtful history addresses all aspects of the culture of the three Woodland Indian tribes who made their homes in the territory now known as the state of Michigan. Varied illustrative materials (maps, photos, old prints, and drawings) increase this book's usefulness. A related teachers' guide, Deur's *Nishnawbe Teachers' Guide* (River Road, 1981) includes activities, vocabulary words, and critical thinking exercises.

♦ Young people may extend their understanding of Deur's work by reading aloud Barbara Esbensen's picture book *The Star Maiden: An Indian Tale* (*see* Minnesota—Nonfiction—398.2).

1. Ojibway—Indians 2. Ottawa—Indians 3. Potawatomi—Indians 4. Michigan—History.

971.3
Bonvillain, Nancy. *The Huron.* Chelsea (1-55546-708-3), 1989. (Indians of North America Series). 111p. B/W and Color illus. (Interest level: 5-8).

This well-crafted, attractive, and informative book identifies the distinct characteristics of the Huron culture. Maps and illustrations trace the history and settlements of the tribe from earliest times to the present.

Two other titles in this series are relevant to Michigan: *The Potawatomi* by James Clifton (1988) and *The Menominee* by Patricia Ourada (1990). Alice Osinski's *The Chippewa* (Childrens Press, 1992) is another excellent source for information on one of Michigan's major Native American tribes.
♦ If possible, a Native American storyteller may be invited to share a traditional tale with a group of students, or perhaps a librarian or teacher can retell a Native American legend. The storyteller can explain the story's relationship to a specific culture.
1. Huron Indians.

973.5
Berton, Pierre. *The Capture of Detroit.* McClelland and Stewart (0-7710-1425-2), 1991. (Adventures in Canadian History: The Battles of the War of 1812). 115p. B/W illus. (Interest level: 5-8).

In detailing an early battle in the War of 1812, this valuable resource focuses on the leaders in the Great Lakes region. It reveals the personal qualities of Tecumseh, General Hull, and others, assessing the effects of their strengths and weaknesses on the history of the region.
♦ After reading this account of the capture of Detroit, young people may research the factors and decisions that helped define the border between the United States and Canada.
1. Detroit (Mich.)—History 2. United States—History—War of 1812.

977
Anderson, Julie. *I Married a Logger: Life in Michigan's Tall Timber.* Avery Color Studios (0-9322-1254-9), 1951, 1989. 328p. B/W illus. (Interest level: 6-8).

This reminiscence of a woman who grew up in Chicago recounts her life as she sets up housekeeping in a logging camp in northern Michigan. She humorously relates the realities of frontier life, recording her experiences with heat, freezing cold, mosquitoes, flies, mud, manure, forest fires, death, and injury.
♦ The stories provide many possibilities for skits like those on "Saturday Night Live." Students may wish to prepare their own stories, perhaps based on Paul Bunyan-like adventures.
1. Michigan—History 2. Lumber and lumbering—Michigan.

977
Armour, David A., ed. *Attack at Michilimackinac 1763.* Illus. by Dirk Gringhuis. Mackinac State Historical Parks (No ISBN), 1991. 131p. (Interest level: 4-8).

Alexander Henry's story of adventures and dangerous travels in Canada and the Indian Territories between 1760 and 1764 includes a canoe voyage along the passages from the Great Lakes into the interior. The illustrations show tools and items the settlers traded with the Indians.
♦ The building and maneuvering of canoes is a compelling subject for some young people. Members of a group may research such aspects as materials, construction, effects of weather, navigation, and possible accidents. If possible, they may extend their research by interviewing a canoe maker or retail distributor.
1. Michigan—History 2. United States—History—French and Indian War, 1755-1763..

977
Barcus, Frank. *Freshwater Fury: Yarns and Reminiscences of the Greatest Storm in Inland Navigation.* Wayne State University Press (0-8143-1828-2), 1986. 182p. B/W illus. (Interest level: 6-8).

The great storm of 1913 is the subject of this collection of stories that range from tall tales to eyewitness accounts. In addition to tales of mystery ships, miracles, and courageous men are descriptions of the fury of the blizzard, its powerful winds, and its staggering effect on the seas.
♦ These stories can be used in creating an old-fashioned radio drama complete with special sound effects. Young people can research the actual methods used to create sound effects on old radio shows. Or, they may write a contemporary newscast script with on-the-scene reporters interviewing the eyewitnesses of the storm.
1. Storms—Great Lakes 2. Great Lakes region—History.

977
Halsey, John R. *Beneath the Inland Seas.* Michigan Department of State Bureau of History (No ISBN), 1990. 72p. B/W illus. (Interest level: 6-8).

Fascinating text and illustrations reveal Michigan's rich archaeological heritage of underwater shipwrecks, ancient forests, and ancient domestic sites. The author convincingly advances the argument that these submerged remains should not be pilfered and damaged but preserved as underwater museums.
♦ A science project may involve one group of readers in discovering how water, sand, and silt act to protect or destroy artifacts. Another group may debate the rights and responsibilities of sports divers who explore these sites. A third group may conduct a town meeting to decide whether the museum should re-

main underwater or be brought to the surface to be shared by more people.
1. Great Lakes—History 2. Archaeology—United States 3. Underwater exploration.

977
Marshall, James R., ed. *Shipwrecks of Lake Superior*. Lake Superior Port Cities (0-942235-00-2), 1987. 282p. B/W illus. (Interest level: 6-8).

This complete story of the *Edmund Fitzgerald* emphasizes the idea that the Lake Superior graveyard is itself a large historical collection, containing artifacts, skeletons, and other treasures. Although many ships are sunk too deep to see, many others are visited by divers.
♦ This book may spark student interest in diving as a sport. Young people can find out about required training, regulations, and restrictions that govern the sport. They can pinpoint Great Lakes and other inland diving sites on a map of the United States.
1. Great Lakes—History 2. Shipwrecks.

977
Michigan Wetlands. (Poster). Nongame Wildlife Fund, Natural Heritage Program, Wildlife Division, Michigan Department of Natural Resources, 1988. Color. Free upon request. (Interest level: 4-8).

This 22" x 32" poster depicts 50 species of plant and animal life in their wetlands habitats. The reverse side defines and describes wetlands, marshes, bogs, swamps, and the plants and animals that inhabit them as well as the regulations that protect them. The text and illustrations are clear, concise, and informative.
♦ Students may produce a similar poster of the animal and plant life of another selected area.
1. Wildlife—Michigan 2. Plants—Michigan.

977
Ratigan, William. *Great Lakes Shipwrecks and Survivals*. Rev. ed. Illus. by Reynold H. Weidenaar. Eerdmans (0-8028-7010-4), 1977. 333p. B/W illus. (Interest level: 5-8).

The stories in this collection, all structured around a ship's demise or survival on the Great Lakes, convey folklore, history, and information about navigation. Their elements of adventure and human interest will engage readers in this aspect of Great Lakes history.
♦ Students may research and describe the various navigational methods in use at the time of the shipwrecks and compare those to contemporary methods. They may also use maps to trace the course of the ships and to highlight the conditions that contributed to the wrecks.
1. Shipwrecks—Great Lakes 2. Great Lakes—History.

977 (Reference)
Tanner, Helen H. *Atlas of Great Lakes Indian History*. Cartography by Miklos Pinther. University of Oklahoma Press (0-8061-1515-7), 1987. (Civilization of the American Indian). 224p. B/W illus. (Interest level: 7-8).

This excellent reference source addresses the cultures and the conflicts of the Indian people in the Great Lakes region. The comprehensive index makes the work easily accessible, and the thorough bibliography is valuable for students doing research and for teachers preparing units of study.
♦ Young people may explore the history of the specific treaties and Native American land rights. After completing their research they may debate or discuss related issues such as fishing rights on the Great Lakes.
1. Indians of North America—Great Lakes region—History 2. Great Lakes region—Maps.

977.4
Barfknecht, Gary W. *Mich-Again's Day*. Friede (0-9608-5882-2), 1984. 264p. B/W photos. (Interest level: 6-8).

This collection of Michigan trivia acquaints the reader with odd, humorous, and informative facts about events, commemorations, celebrations, and accomplishments for every day of the year. Other titles in the author's entertaining series on Michigan trivia include: *Michillaneous I* (Friede, 1982) and *Michillaneous II* (Friede, 1985).
♦ Celebrations and local events offer many clues to the history, the economy, and the cultures represented in any community. Young people may create a promotional plan for attracting visitors to one of the events identified in the work.
1. Michigan—Social life and customs.

977.4
Clements, John. *Michigan Facts*. Clements Research (ISSN: 1051-7146), 1992. 437p. (Flying the Colors Series). 1 color photo. (Interest level: 7+).

This comprehensive study of the state of Michigan today offers a complete picture of life in Michigan. The most current statistics have been used to compile this information.
♦ Young people may translate descriptive data into a visual format to share with the class as a transparency.
1. Michigan.

977.4
Deur, Lynne. *Settling in Michigan and Other True Pioneer Stories*. Illus. by Don Blens. River Road (0-938682-22-9), 1992. 80p. (Interest level: 3-8).

Using Michigan pioneer and historical collections, Lynne Deur has adapted stories of early Michigan days told by the people who lived them. With minimal changes she has succeeded in making these stories more easily read and understood by young people.
♦ These stories can be part of a student reenactment of early days in Michigan. Students may organize a

chronological presentation including these and other personal accounts they find in their research.
1. Michigan—History.

977.4
Deur, Lynne and **Michel, Sara**. *The Making of Michigan*. River Road (0-9386-8217-2), 1987. 300p. B/W illus. (Interest level: 4-8).

This excellent resource leads the reader through Michigan's history from prehistoric times to the present. One of its most significant features is the time line at the end of each chapter. The three columns compare events in Michigan history with world events during the same time period.
♦ Young people may add a fourth column to the time line, highlighting events happening in their own regions during the identified period. They may enlarge the time line to poster or wall size for public display.
1. Michigan—History.

977.4
Graveyards of the Great Lakes. (Videocassette). Michigan Council for the Arts and Michigan Council for the Humanities, 1988. Available from Hillsdale. VHS 1/2", Color, (30 min.). $29.95. (Interest level: 5-8).

This well-executed presentation chronicles disastrous shipwrecks like that of the *Edmund Fitzgerald*. Voice-over explanations of the circumstances leading up to each crisis increase the production's effectiveness, and eyewitness accounts add to the dramatic tension. Underwater photography reveals the burial places of these broken ships and underscores the fear and tragedy of each event.
♦ Using evening television news as a model, young people may write individual scripts that report one of the shipwrecks. They may wish to research and include other events happening around the world near the time of the shipwreck.
1. Great Lakes—History 2. Shipwrecks.

977.4
Kozlak, Chet. *Great Lakes Fur Trade*. Trans. by Jean Pierre Belanger. Illus. by author. Minnesota Historical Society Press (0-87351-154-9), 1991. 32p. B/W illus. (Interest level: 3-4).

Illustrated with line drawings that depict the animals that were part of the fur trading cycle in the early days of the Great Lakes settlements, this work emphasizes the French role in the history of the area and explains how the animals were hunted, trapped, and used for their furs and for other commodities the people needed. A major strength of this work is its bilingual text (English and French).
♦ Young people may participate in an imaginary frontier trading day. They could barter models or illustrations of necessary food or clothing items. They may choose to play the roles of certain tradespeople—cobbler, innkeeper, logger, weaver—and decide what each would need and what each would have to offer for trade. Students might explore the meaning of economic terms such as *bargain, inflation,* and *fair trade*.
1. Fur trade—Great Lakes region.

977.4
McCollom, Anita. *Come Explore Michigan the Beautiful*. Avery Color Studios (0-9322-1248-4 pbk), 1986. 80p. B/W and Color illus. (Interest level: 3-6).

Through an impressive collection of historic and contemporary photographs, this book documents the story of Michigan's history. It is an excellent example of a history told chronologically in a visual format.
♦ Young people may use this book as a model to produce an album of captioned photographs that present their own local history. They may collect copies of photographs and information from local libraries, historical societies, and historians.
1. Michigan—Description and travel—Views.

977.4
McConnell, David B. *Forging the Peninsulas: Michigan Is Made*. Hillsdale (0-910726-75-2), 1989. 410p. B/W and Color illus. (Interest level: 4-8).

This comprehensive and well-written history of Michigan contains historical and contemporary accounts of Michiganians. Its impressive format includes a thorough index and bibliography and features a wide variety of illustrative material, including cartoons, graphics, and highlighted inserts.
♦ Students may host a mock White House "Born-in-Michigan" (or any state or region) party. They may begin with the celebrity invitation list that could include, for example, Lily Tomlin, Madonna, Ty Cobb, Henry Ford, and Aretha Franklin. Students may also prepare a biographical sketch to be read as each guest arrives and is "presented." The activity may also include costumes, menu, decorations, and performances (recorded or role-played).
1. Michigan—History

977.4
Massie, Larry B. *Copper Trails and Iron Rails: More Voyages into Michigan's Past*. Avery Color Studios (0-932212-60-3), 1989. 290p. Color photos; B/W drawings. (Interest level: 6-8).

Massie, a Michigan newspaper columnist, historian, and storyteller, has collected accounts of events and people in the state's history. The stories of copper and iron mining in the northern peninsula blend with the story of the first Oldsmobile and a biographical sketch of prizefighter Joe Louis. Like feature stories, these tales are written in a journalistic style.
♦ These accounts are ideal for storytelling. Young people may tell one these stories or a similar one that they collect from adult family or community members. They may contribute their own stories to a

school newsletter or the school column in a local paper.
1. Michigan—History.

977.4
Mitchell, John and **Woodruff, Tom**. *Great Lakes and Great Ships: An Illustrated History for Children.* Illus. by authors. Suttons Bay (0-9621446-1-7), 1991. 48p. Color illus. (Interest level: 3+).

This well-written and illustrated history presents in detail basic facts, dates, legends, and statistics, and, in the process, meets the needs, interests, and abilities of young readers. Charts, insets, and action-packed scenes are used to tell the story of the lakes and the ships that sailed them.

♦ Young people may draw a map (or use a prepared map) to trace the movement of ships through the canals, locks, and lakes. They may also design and solve math problems that enhance their understanding of the variations of depth, volume, and flow of the lakes.

1. Great Lakes—History 2. Ships.

977.4
The Schoolship. (A schooner on Lake Michigan). (Interest level: 5-8).

During the spring and fall seasons two Lake Michigan schooners become schoolships, floating classrooms for young science students. A new ship, the *Inland Seas*, is being designed and built specifically for shipboard education. Students of all ages enjoy and profit as the instructors/crew bring maritime science and history to life. School trips can be arranged by contacting the Inland Seas Education Association, and a videotape presenting a sixth-grade science class's experiences aboard the schoolship is available from the Instructional Media and Technology Center, Ann Arbor Public Schools.

1. Great Lakes region.

977.4
Stein, R. Conrad. *Michigan.* Childrens Press (0-5160-0468-9), 1987. (America the Beautiful Series). 144p. B/W and Color illus. (Interest level: 4-8).

This introductory work addresses Michigan's geography, history, government, economy, industry, culture, and historic sites. Maps and an index enhance its reference usefulness.

♦ Students may be encouraged to write a song or poem highlighting Michigan's state flower, bird, flag, or motto. They may also plan the itinerary for a trip through the state.

1. Michigan.

977.4
Thompson, Kathleen. *Michigan.* Raintree (0-86514-465-6 lib bind; 0-86514-540-7 pbk), 1988. 48p. B/W and Color illus. (Interest level: 4-8).

Based on the "Portrait of America" television series, this is a unique source of information about Michigan's history, economy, culture, and future. The format of the book reflects its television origins and may thus be familiar to students. The book includes maps and a chronology of the state's history.

♦ Young people may use the book's format to write their own script for a video featuring Michigan or another state. They may prefer to plan one complete program or a series of short reports for an evening news broadcast.

1. Michigan—History.

977.4
Wiles, Richard. *Fayette.* (Videocassette). Michigan Magic, 1992. (Michigan Magic Series). VHS 1/2", Color, (26 min.). $19.95. (Interest level: 6-8).

This travelogue (with an introductory sequence common to all of the films in this Michigan tourist series) is an excellent documentary. Fayette was a "company town" in the Upper Peninsula of Michigan in the 1860s. Photographs and live action provide an insightful depiction of life in this community structure that came into existence during the settlement period.

♦ Young people may use the film's model to create a similar mock-up of a company town with its company store, housing, and its restrictions that often led the residents into indebtedness.

1. Michigan—History 2. Frontier and pioneer life—Michigan 3. Fayette (Mich.)—History.

977.4
Wiles, Richard. *Magical Straits of Mackinac.* (Videocassette). Michigan Magic, 1991. (Michigan Magic Series). VHS 1/2", Color, (25 min.). $19.95. (Interest level: 6-8).

This video provides an excellent overview of the history and the culture of the area where two Great Lakes, Huron and Michigan, meet. Old footage, still photos, and current film document the story that includes the building of the Mackinac Bridge.

♦ This production is an exceptional model for a video project in which young people may feature their own locale. Their preparations could include collecting historical photographs, filming current scenes, and interviewing local historians and public figures.

1. Michigan—History 2. Great Lakes region—History.

977.4
Wiles, Richard. *Michigan Magic.* (Videocassette). Michigan Magic, 1990. VHS 1/2", Color, (30 min.). $19.95. (Interest level: 6-8).

This history of the Upper Peninsula of Michigan is part of a travel series that focuses on tourist attractions, especially the sites that are also historic landmarks of the area. Live action footage and older still photos combine to relate the history of Michigan and the Great Lakes.

♦ Students may produce two time lines of historic events, one for the Upper Peninsula and another for the Lower Peninsula. After comparing the two, young people may decide whether they feel the Upper Peninsula should be part of the state of Michigan, a designation still being challenged by some residents of that part of the state.
1. Michigan—Upper Peninsula—History.

Biography

920
Sikkenga, Raymond. *Doers and Dreamers: The Governors of Michigan*. River Road (093-868-215-6), 1987. 164p. B/W illus. (Interest level: 4-8).

Accurate, well-arranged one- to two-page accounts of 45 Michigan governors highlight their contributions to the state and the Great Lakes region. Small portraits of the governors accompany their biographical sketches.
♦ Young people may create visual representations of the career paths of the governors, some of whom began their careers as politicians and some of whom followed other professions and avocations before entering politics.
1. Governors—Michigan—Biography 2. Michigan—Biography.

920
Troester, Rosalie Riegle. *Historic Women in Michigan*. Michigan Women's Studies Association (0-961-9390-0-1), 1987. 257p. B/W illus. Available from Hillsdale. $14.95. (Interest level: 6-8).

Nineteen women who were forces in Michigan history are the subject of this collection. The book is a valuable research and reference tool because it features a wide range of backgrounds and achievements among its subjects.
♦ Young people may take on the roles of writers, hosts, audience members, and guests in a contemporary talk show format to explore the personalities of these historic women. Questions may focus on social structures, women's roles, and women's responses in particular periods of time.
1. Women—Michigan—Biography.

92 Beaumont, William
Burns, Virginia. *William Beaumont—Frontier Doctor*. Rev. ed. Enterprise Press (0-9604726-4-9), 1990. 159p. B/W illus. (Interest level: 6-8).

Michigan's Mackinac Island is the setting for the famous story of Dr. Beaumont's surgical procedure—creating a "window" in his patient's stomach so he could observe the digestive process. This fictionalized account involves the reader in the experiment of a young surgeon.

♦ Young people may research other physicians who have pioneered a new procedure that has advanced the care of patients.
1. Beaumont, William, 1785-1853 2. Physicians 3. Digestion 4. Mackinac Island (Mich.)—History.

92 Blackstone, Harry
Blackstone, Harry. *My Life as a Magician*. Pocket Books (0-6716-4436-X), 1992. 112p. (Interest level: 3-5).

Michigan-born magician Harry Blackstone writes the story of his life, explaining the influence of his father, also a magician. More notable for high-interest content than for style, this small book will delight aspiring young magicians.
♦ Students may plan and produce a stage show, using Blackstone's tricks. They can carry out all of the required roles: producer, director, advertising manager, and performer.
1. Blackstone, Harry 2. Magicians.

92 Cass, Lewis
Burns, Virginia. *Lewis Cass, Frontier Soldier*. Illus. by Carolyn V. Hall. Hillsdale Educational Publishers (0-9604726-1-4), 1980. 175p. B/W and Color illus. (Interest level: 6-8).

This excellent biography introduces an important Michigan historical figure, one whose leadership was key to the development of the territory. Cass was also nominated for the presidency of the United States in 1848. Photographs, an index, and a bibliography increase the work's value for research activities.
♦ After reading this biography, young people may write their own plan for the progress of a new settlement from a territory to statehood. Or, they may create a radio series featuring interviews with early leaders and settlers of the Great Lakes area.
1.Cass, Lewis, 1782-1866 2. Soldiers—United States.

92 Edison, Thomas Alva
Adler, David A. *Thomas Alva Edison: Great Inventor*. Illus. by Lyle Miller. Holiday (0-8234-8020-5), 1990. (First Biography Series). 48p. B/W illus. (Interest level: 2-5).

Edison's ingenuity and determination are brought to life through interesting details of his youth in Michigan, his struggles as an inventor, and the successes that brought him fame. This introductory work will meet the needs of the science as well as the social studies curriculum. Other biographies of Edison include Carol Greene's *Thomas Alva Edison: Bringer of Light* (Childrens Press, 1985) and Margaret Davidson's *Story of Thomas Alva Edison: The Wizard of Menlo Park* (Scholastic, 1990).
♦ Young people may experience some of Edison's excitement through hands-on experiments of their own. They may visit a local hands-on museum or create their own laboratory with teacher/library media specialist guidance. They may also trace the

development of one of Edison's inventions (e.g., the motion picture camera) to the present time.
1. Edison, Thomas Alva, 1847-1931 2. Inventors.

92 Ford, Gerald R.
Sipiera, Paul P. *Gerald Ford.* Childrens Press (0-516-01371-8), 1989. (Encyclopedia of the Presidents Series). 100p. B/W photos. (Interest level: 3-6).

This biography provides a well-written profile of Gerald R. Ford of Michigan, the thirty-eighth president of the United States. It assesses honestly Ford's life and the unique circumstances that brought him to the presidency. Many photographs depict the major events of his presidency.

♦ Readers may use a map of the United States to highlight the hometowns of the presidents. They may research details of the presidents' education, profession, political party, policy priorities, and major accomplishments. Older students may focus on issues faced by Ford (e.g., pardoning Richard Nixon and providing amnesty for those who avoided the draft).
1. Ford, Gerald R. 1913- 2. Presidents—United States.

92 Ford, Henry
Kent, Zachary. *The Story of Henry Ford and the Automobile.* Childrens Press (0-516-04751-3; 0-516-04751-5 pbk), 1990. (Cornerstones of Freedom). 32p. B/W and Color illus. (Interest level: 1-4).

This biography introduces the determined young man who, born on a farm, moved to Detroit with the ambition of producing a reliable and affordable automobile. The illustrated depiction of historic automobile models and the portrayal of "Crazy Henry" will attract and hold the interest of almost all readers.

♦ After reading about the first 50 years of automobile history, young people may create a bulletin board with photographs of their own family's cars or illustrations of models owned during the last 50 years (or more). Pictures can be mounted and displayed in chronological order. Students may use the family stories about the cars for an accompanying creative writing or storytelling project.
1. Ford, Henry, 1863-1947 2. Inventors 3. Automobile industry.

92 Johnson, Earvin (Magic)
Haskins, James. *Sports Great Magic Johnson.* Enslow (0-89490-348-9), 1992. 64p. B/W illus. (Interest level: 5-8).

This straightforward and realistic biography recounts the past sports successes of the Los Angeles Lakers basketball star from Lansing, Michigan. The work's unbiased approach deals honestly with Johnson's problems with the HIV virus. A biography accessible to younger students (fourth-grade level) is Robert Italia's *Magic Johnson* (Abdo and Daughters, 1992; available from Rockbottom).

♦ After reading Magic's story, young people may look for other examples of people who are trying to be positive in dealing with adversity in their lives. The stories may include those of friends and family members or headliners and history-makers. If appropriate, qualified speakers may be invited to answer young people's questions about AIDS and the HIV virus.
1. Johnson, Earvin (Magic), 1959- 2. Los Angeles Lakers (Basketball team) 3. Basketball—Biography 4. African-American athletes.

92 Parks, Rosa
Celsi, Teresa Noel. *Rosa Parks and the Montgomery Bus Boycott.* Millbrook (1-87884-114-9), 1991. (Gateway Civil Rights Series). 28p. B/W and Color illus. (Interest level: 4-6).

Rosa Parks has been living in Michigan for a number of years although she grew up in Alabama, where she experienced segregation as an African-American woman. Her story is told in clear, easily readable text, with special attention given to her role as an early civil rights leader when she refused to give up her seat on a bus. Another worthy work for grades three to six is Beatrice Siegel's *The Year They Walked: Rosa Parks and the Montgomery Bus Boycott* (Four Winds, 1992).

♦ Using dates and names found in these books and others, young people may make a time line illustrating the story of the Civil Rights Movement and of the courageous people who participated in it. Brief biographical sketches and pictures of activists like Rosa Parks could be inserted. The time line can be displayed as part of a Martin Luther King Day observance.
1. Parks, Rosa, 1913- 2. African Americans—Biography.

92 Pontiac, Ottawa Chief
Fleischer, Jane. *Pontiac: Chief of the Ottawa.* Illus. by Robert Baxter. Troll (0-89375-146-4), 1979. 48p. B/W illus. (Interest level: 3-6).

This factual biography introduces the Ottawa chief who united bands of Ottawa, Potawatomi, and Chippewa Indians near Detroit to support the French during the French and Indian War. This readable biography weaves the histories of Michigan, Detroit, and Native Americans around an effective organizer of American Indian tribes.

♦ Young people may research other Native American leaders of the past and the present. After collecting stories and quotes, they may create a visual presentation emphasizing the leaders' sense of responsibility for their own people and the personal sacrifices they were willing to make.
1. Pontiac, Ottawa Chief, ca. 1720–1769 2. Ottawa Indians 3. Michigan—History.

92 Tecumseh, Shawnee Chief
Kent, Zachary. *Tecumseh*. Childrens Press (0-516-06655-2), 1992. (Cornerstones of Freedom). 32p. (Interest level: 3-6).

In an attempt to protect his people from failed treaties, Tecumseh organized groups of Indians to fight against the invasion of settlers. Tecumseh and his followers helped to win Detroit for the British, only to lose it again in the battle that cost Tecumseh his life. This biography presents a passionate and forceful leader who commanded the respect of the British ,who made him a general, and of the Americans, who honored him after his death.
♦ From this biography and others, e.g., Jane Fleischer's *Tecumseh, Shawnee War Chief* (Troll, 1979) and Russell Shorto's *Tecumseh and the Dream of an American Indian Nation* (see Ohio—Biography), young people may identify the characteristics that made Tecumseh a hero to his people, comparing his heroic attributes with those of contemporary heroes.
1. Tecumseh, Shawnee Chief, 1768-1813 2. Shawnee Indians.

92 Truth, Sojourner
Claflin, Edward. *Sojourner Truth and the Struggle for Freedom*. Illus. by Jada Rowlan. Barron's (0-8120-3919-X), 1987. (Henry Steele Commager's Americans Series). 153p. (Interest level: 5-6).

This dramatic account vividly presents the message about slavery that Sojourner Truth conveyed to Northern audiences before the Civil War. Her life is presented not only as the history of a people, but also as the history of a courageous, determined reformer who made Michigan her home in her later years.
♦ Young people may make Sojourner Truth's life the subject of a documentary, tracing her life, the meaning of her name, the choices she made, and the people she met.
1. Truth, Sojourner, d. 1883 2. African-American women 3. Abolitionists 4. Feminism.

92 Truth, Sojourner
Krass, Peter. *Sojourner Truth*. Chelsea (0-1910-0215-2 pbk), 1988. (Black Americans of Achievement). 110p. (Videocassette).VHS 1/2", Color, (30 min.). $39.95. (Interest level: 5-8).

This book and its companion video chronicle the life of the famous former slave, women's rights activist, and abolitionist who made Michigan her home in the later years of her life. The use of varied media—narration, music, interviews, and live footage—make the video attractive to young people.
♦ After experiencing both the book and the video, students may make a list of facts unique to each resource.
1. Truth, Sojourner, d. 1883 2. African-American women 3. Abolitionists 4. Feminism.

92 X, Malcolm
X, Malcolm. *The Autobiography of Malcolm X*. Ballantine (0-345-35068-5), 1965, 1991. 460p. (Interest level: 6+).

Malcolm X tells his own personal story—the story of a Michigan youth who overcame the setbacks of crime and imprisonment, educated himself, and eventually became a leader of his people. This account was written with the assistance of award-winning African-American writer and historian Alex Haley.
♦ Students may read biographies of other leaders (from any period in time) who share Malcolm X's concern about racism (e.g., Martin Luther King, Toussaint L'Ouverture, Lewis Farrakhan). They may then stage a panel discussion in which student researchers role-play each biographical subject's answers to questions about his or her efforts to combat racism. The questions can be written in advance so each student can prepare to play his or her role.
1. X, Malcolm, 1925-1965 2. African Americans.

Fiction

Blos, Joan W. *Brothers of the Heart: A Story of the Old Northwest, 1837-1838*. Aladdin (0-689-71166-2), 1985, 1987. 162p. B/W illus. (Interest level: 5-8).

A dying Native American woman teaches a 14-year-old boy how to survive in the Michigan wilderness. Physically disabled, he also learns to survive in a frontier village. The award-winning author realistically portrays the hardships of Michigan pioneer life in the nineteenth-century.
♦ Young people may read other survival stories in order to prepare an annotated bibliography of their favorites.
1. Frontier and pioneer life—Michigan—Fiction 2. Michigan—Fiction 3. Indians of North America—Fiction 4. Physically handicapped—Fiction.

Brill, Ethel C. *Copper Country Adventure*. Illus. by Bruce Adams. Iron Mountain (0-9332-4905-5), 1987. 213p. B/W illus. (Interest level: 6-8).

The 16-year-old who inherits his uncle's copper mining interest on the Keweenaw Peninsula copes with his lack of know-how and the deceit of those who would take advantage of him. This fictional account offers many facts about Michigan copper mining in the mid-1800s.
♦ Students may adapt one or more chapters to share as a play or a reader's theater presentation.
1. Adventure and adventurers—Fiction 2. Keweenaw Peninsula (Mich.)—Fiction 3. Copper mines and mining—Fiction.

Chappel, Bernice M. *Reap the Whirlwind: A Documentary of Early Michigan*. Wilderness Adventure Books (0-9611-5968-5), 1987. 413p. (Interest level: 6-8).

This historical novel is set in the territory and state of Michigan from 1795 to 1866. The novel's central characters are members of the Parker family, who travel through the Erie Canal on a lake steamer to the frontier town of Detroit. This carefully researched account offers background information on Indian life, Underground Railroad activities, and Civil War battles.
♦ Young people may brainstorm the nineteenth-century conditions encountered when traveling by boat and steamer, comparing them with those of today's ships.
1. Michigan—Fiction 2. Erie Canal—Fiction.

De Angeli, Marguerite. *Copper-toed Boots.* Doubleday (0-385-07264-3), 1938, 1992. 96p. Color illus. (Interest level: 3-6).

Shad's pranks, his friends, his family relationships, his effort to get a dog, and his longing for copper-toed boots are all a part of country living in nineteenth-century Michigan. De Angeli's dedication suggests that this story was prompted by childhood tales told by her father.
♦ Each student may wish to interview a family member or adult to discover a childhood prank that could be recorded in a class collection.
1. Boots—Fiction 2. Dogs—Fiction 3. Country life—Michigan—Fiction 4. Michigan—Fiction.

Fuller, Iola. *The Loon Feather.* Harcourt Brace Jovanovich (0-15-653200-X pbk), 1984. 456p. (Interest level: 7-8).

The subject of this very well-written, appealing novel is the historical figure Oneta, the daughter of the Shawnee Indian chief Tecumseh. Strong characterizations reveal Oneta's unique position as one who bridged the gap between the French and the Indian cultures.
♦ Young readers may dramatize some of the vivid scenes that portray the differences between the customs of Indians and those of white people. The lively dialogue and descriptive narrative lend themselves to a dramatic presentation.
1. Chippewa Indians—Fiction 2. Michigan—History—Fiction.

Holling, Holling Clancy. *Paddle-to-the-Sea.* Illus. by author. Houghton Mifflin (0-395-15082-5), 1941, 1969. B/W and Color illus. (Interest level: 3-6).

After an Indian boy carves a toy canoe containing a small passenger, he launches it in Lake Nipigon where it begins its four-year journey through the Great Lakes and down the St. Lawrence River to the Atlantic Ocean. Full-page color illustrations and pencil drawings frame the text and extend the details of the geography, nature, and people of the region.
♦ Young people may choose to trace Paddle-to-the-Sea's path on a map of the Great Lakes and then update this story to describe a similar journey today, looking for things that remain the same and things that might have changed.
1. Great Lakes region—Fiction.

Love, Edmund. *A Small Bequest.* Wayne State University Press (0-8143-1925-4), 1973, 1987. (Interest level: 7-8).

Edmund Love's own state of Michigan is the setting for several of his books, including this episodic novel about two young adults who travel to northern Michigan in 1934 to check on a small piece of land that one of them has inherited. What ensues is a series of comic incidents that cause havoc in the lives of the two young men. One strength of this work is the successful portrayal of minor characters through humorous, gentle sketches.
♦ Using Love's character descriptions as models, young people may write character sketches based on real or imaginary people.
1. Michigan—Fiction.

Paddle-to-the-Sea. (Videocassette). National Film Board of Canada, 1967. Available from Janus Films. VHS 1/2", Color, (28 min.). $88, with shipping. (Interest level: 3-6).

Based on H.C. Holling's *Paddle-to-the-Sea* (*see* Michigan—Fiction), this animation brings to life the adventures of the carved canoe and its passenger as it plunges over Niagara Falls, encounters large ships, and sails with river logs on its four-year journey from Lake Nipigon to the sea. The narrator's explanations of the history, culture, and industry of the Great Lakes make this video version effective in establishing the setting and encouraging viewer empathy with the Indian boy who carved Paddle-to-the-Sea.
♦ Small groups could create a storyboard in preparation for a new film that will add more adventures to Paddle-to-the-Sea's journey. Others may wish to set Paddle-to-the-Sea in different waterways and plan an entirely new film.
1. Great Lakes region—Fiction.

Whelan, Gloria. *Next Spring an Oriole.* Illus. by Pamela Johnson. Random (0-394-99125-7), 1987. 160p. B/W illus. (Interest level: 3-6).

When her parents decide to move to frontier Michigan in 1837, 10-year-old Libby must leave behind a familiar and comfortable life. In the months that follow, she experiences the physical hardships, fears, and special joys of pioneer life. This account presents a solid depiction of cooperation between the Indians and the pioneers.
♦ Young people may prepare a map to trace Libby's journey and locate her family's land. Those familiar with the area may write a description of traveling along that same route more than 150 years later,

highlighting the changes in scenery, travel modes, and occupations of people encountered.
1. Michigan—Fiction 2. Frontier and pioneer life—Michigan—Fiction 3. Indians of North America—Fiction.

Whelan, Gloria. *The Pathless Woods*. Illus. by Walter Kessell. Lippincott (0-3973-1930-4), 1981 (out of print). 181p. B/W illus. (Interest level: 6-8).

This fictionalized account reflects Ernest Hemingway's summers at his family's vacation home on a lake in the northern lower peninsula of Michigan. His adventures convey the universal processes of growing up, becoming independent, and recognizing responsibilities.
♦ Students may be encouraged to embellish a summer experience and share the written account with the class.
1. Hemingway, Ernest, 1899-1961—Fiction 2. Michigan—Fiction.

Periodicals

977.4

Michigan History Magazine. Michigan Department of State, Bimonthly. $9.95 per year; $3 per back issue. (Interest level: 6-8).

This sketchbook of Michigan history has been in publication for more than 75 years, offering a lively view of Michigan. Each issue includes illustrated stories of Michigan's past and information about current events and historical observances.
♦ Librarians may request samples of state magazines from different regions of the United States. Young people may compare the contents and focus of the magazines, share stories from each issue, or use the information for state reports.
1. Michigan—History.

Professional Materials

912.13

The Great Lakes: An Environmental Atlas and Resource Book. Environment Canada, United States Environmental Protection Agency, Brock University, Northwestern University (0-662-15189-5), 1987. 44p. Color illus. Available from Great Lakes National Program Office, Environmental Protection Agency. (Interest level: Professional).

This excellent resource details many aspects of the Great Lakes, including people, settlements, natural processes, concerns, and management. Drawings, graphs, photographs, and charts (including a wall chart) enhance the text.
♦ Students may make a chart for a body of water and surrounding landmass that is familiar to them. Or, they might choose to discuss how to solve one of the Great Lakes' problems identified in this resource.
1. Great Lakes region 2. Water resources development 3. Natural resources—Great Lakes region.

917.74

Great Minds? Great Lakes! United States Environmental Protection Agency (No ISBN), n.d. B/W and Color illus. 23p. (Interest level: Professional).

This excellent introduction to the Great Lakes ecosystem is an abbreviated form of a longer curriculum plan called *Great Lakes in My World*. The information, discussion, and activity suggestions are integrated with social studies, history, and environmental education.
♦ An activity in the booklet asks students to draw a picture describing "industry emissions entering the sky and coming back down as rain." Another activity involves students in calculating family water usage and comparing the familiar with the unfamiliar in order to understand the amount of water in the Great Lakes.
1. Great Lakes 2. Ecology.

Minnesota

by Mary Alice Anderson and Elsie Husom

Nonfiction

001.9
Quast, Michael. *The Sasquatch in Minnesota.* Quast (No ISBN), 1989. 82p. B/W illus. (Interest level: 5+).

This account of one man's quest to prove the existence of Big Foot in Minnesota presents intriguing details on reported sightings of large, hair-covered, humanlike or apelike creatures in the Minnesota Northwoods. Although lacking in print quality, this resource will be valuable for those interested in exploring "strange creatures." It can be used in conjunction with Michael Quast's *Creatures of the North: The New Minnesota Sasquatch Encounters* (Quast, 1992).
♦ After doing research, students may debate the existence of Sasquatch in Minnesota, assessing the credibility of reported sightings and the views of skeptics.
1. Sasquatch—Minnesota.

004.6
DataNet. (Online database). Minnesota State Planning Agency. (Interest level: 5+).

Facts, statistics, and other information about Minnesota's natural resources, business, demographics, justice system, and health make up this database of databases. Although originally developed for Minnesota businesses, this easy-to-use database has much valuable current information for Minnesota science and social studies classes.
♦ By comparing data in a number of fields, students may select what they feel is the best Minnesota city or town in which to live, giving reasons based on the statistics on employment, school district rankings, crime, household earnings, etc. Or, they may select the lake near which they would prefer to build a cabin or home.
1. Minnesota—Information networks 2. Minnesota—Statistics.

133.0977
Scott, Beth and **Norman, Michael.** *Haunted Heartland.* Warner (0-446-35725-1 pbk), 1985. 485p. (Interest level: 5-8).

One chapter in this collection is devoted to ghost stories set in various Minnesota cities, including stories about ghosts at St. Mary's College in Winona, a house in St. Paul, and a Goodhue churchyard. The stories have been told by people who believe they are true and who purport to have seen ghosts. The book makes a very appealing topic readable, entertaining, and enjoyable for older students.
♦ Young people may write their own ghost stories and generate ideas about the origins of these stories.
1. Supernatural—Minnesota 2. Ghosts.

301.41
Stuhler, Barbara, ed. *Women of Minnesota: Selected Biographical Essays.* Minnesota Historical Society (0-87351-112-3), 1987. 402p. B/W photos. (Interest level: 6-8).

Sixteen full-length essays and more than 100 short sketches provide information on Minnesotans generally not included in standard history books or biographies. Women included in this book are those who contributed to Minnesota's political and cultural climate in the nineteenth and early twentieth centuries. This adult book is most suitable for students doing research and helps fill the need for gender-fair materials.
♦ Students using the book for research can practice correct note-taking and research skills. They may also try to locate information in other sources.
1. Women—Minnesota—Biography.

301.453
Hillbrand, Percie V. *The Swedes in America.* Lerner (No ISBN), 1991. (In America Series). 84p. B/W photos. (Interest level: 5-8).

———. *The Norwegians in America.* Lerner (No ISBN), 1991. (In America Series). 71p. B/W photos. (Interest level: 5-8).

These two titles provide background information about European ethnic groups, their stages of immigration to the United States, and their contributions to American life in areas such as education, agriculture, business, entertainment, and government. A significant portion of each title pertains to Minnesota and well-known Minnesotans. These readable books present information that is often difficult to locate and will be helpful to students seeking to understand Minnesota's heritages.
♦ An individual assignment for students might be to create their own family tree. A class or cooperative group assignment could be to survey classmates about their ethnic backgrounds and produce a graph or map to explain the ethnic makeup of the class.
1. Swedish Americans—History 2. Norwegian Americans—History 3. Immigrants—Minnesota—History.

306.08
Goldfarb, Mace. *Fighters, Refugees, Immigrants: A Story of the Hmong.* Carolrhoda (0-87614-197-1), 1982. Unpaginated. Color photos. (Interest level: 3-6).

Written by a doctor who worked in a refugee camp, this book provides background information on one of Minnesota's fastest growing minority groups—the Hmong people of Southeast Asia. Goldfarb describes life in the camp, the schools, and the hospitals. He also describes the beliefs of the refugees. Although little information is provided about Hmong life in the United States, the book has value because there is little available information about the Hmong.
♦ Young people may discuss how Hmong life is different from their own and also how the book's information helps them understand their Hmong classmates or neighbors.
1. Refugees—Thailand—Case studies 2. Hmong (Asian people)—Thailand—Case studies.

307.76
Fixico, Donald Lee. *Urban Indians.* Chelsea (1-55546-732-6), 1991. 103p. B/W and Color photos. (Interest level: 5-8).

This book describes the life of urban Indians from the ancient cities of Mesoamerica to the present. Attention is paid to the relocation of Native Americans by the Bureau of Indian Affairs in the mid-twentieth century. Little specific information is provided about the relatively large Native American population in metropolitan Minnesota, but the book will be useful in helping upper elementary students gain a general insight into the life of Native Americans not living on reservations. Information on the American Indian Movement (AIM), founded by Minnesotan Clyde Bellacourt, will also be useful.
♦ Students may evaluate whether the book helps dispel stereotypes perpetuated in literature and movies.

Students may compare the relocation of Native Americans during the mid-twentieth century to the destruction of Indian land by early white settlers.
1. Indians of North America—Urban residence
2. Indians of North America—Social conditions.

317.376
Donnelly's Demographics. (Online database). Donnelly Marketing Information Services/DIALOG Information Services. Subscription. (Interest level: 6+).

Containing census data from the United States Census of Population and Housing for 1980 and 1990, current year estimates, and five-year projections, this database covers demographics of industries, occupations, employment, methods of transportation, travel time to work, and other common census data. The database can be searched by geographic areas and by demographic characteristics such as mobility, housing, education, occupation, income, race, age, population, and household. This tool provides excellent opportunities for analysis of Minnesota's population.
♦ Students may compare data from selected Minnesota cities and towns and consider possible relationships between categories (e.g., number of people in the household with household income or the amount of education with the standard of living). Young people should be challenged to hypothesize explanations for possible relationships.
1. United States—Statistics 2. Census.

330.97
Gelbach, Deborah L. *From This Land: A History of Minnesota Empires, Enterprises and Entrepreneurs.* Windsor (0-89781-231-X), 1988. 382p. B/W and Color photos. (Interest level: 5-9).

From 1634 to the present and looking toward the future, the accounts in this source focus on Minnesota people, ideas, actions, and values. Beautifully illustrated, the thoughtful writing portrays a Minnesota of sharp contrasts, dynamic changes, ingenious industrialization, and dramatic valor.
♦ Students may create a huge wall collage showing significant dates, events, people, industries, institutions, and celebrations of the state.
1. Minnesota—Economic conditions—Pictorial works.

333.1
White Earth Reservation Curriculum Committee. *White Earth: A History.* Minnesota Chippewa Tribe (No ISBN), 1989. (Minnesota Chippewa Tribe Reservation History Series). 52p. B/W photos and illus. (Interest level: 5-9).

Beginning with Chippewa legends about how the land came to be and about the early days in the area now known as Minnesota, this book recounts the history of the Chippewa to the present time. This easily accessible account provides valuable information that

has been passed by word of mouth from one generation to another.
♦ Young people may produce a wall map showing locations of the Chippewa people in Minnesota at specified times. Following further investigation, students may record on the map the estimated population of each group at given times in the tribe's history.
1. Ojibway Indians—Reservation 2. Indians of North America—Minnesota 3. White Earth Indian Reservation (Minn.)—History.

333.78
Nielsen, Nancy. *Boundary Waters Canoe Area, Minnesota.* Crestwood (0-89689-465-0), 1989. 48p. Color photos. (Interest level: 2-6).

The striking illustrations in this book enhance geographical and historical information about a popular place to visit in northern Minnesota. Chapters such as "What to Bring Along," "Setting Up Camp," and "Portaging" help make it a suitable travel guide.
♦ Some students may have canoed or skied in the boundary waters and could share their pictures or remembrances. Other students may design a travel brochure using desktop publishing software.
1. Boundary Waters Canoe Area (Minn.)—Description 2. Minnesota—Description.

338.9
Larson, Don W. *Land of the Giants: A History of Minnesota Business.* Peat, Marwick, Mitchell/Dorn Books (0-934070-03-2), 1979. 176p. B/W photos. (Interest level: 6+).

This rich panorama presents Minnesota business from the early days of lumber, iron ore, and milling industries to modern enterprises of electronics and medical devices. Although the book's appearance may detract from its appeal, this account of the hard work, luck, financial panics and depressions, determination, and daring that made up Minnesota business serves as an excellent reference on a little-published topic.
♦ Small groups of students may select a specific industry of their state and research its history and predict its future. Students may use letters of inquiry and on-site visits as sources of information.
1. Business—Minnesota—History 2. Minnesota—Business—History.

364.1
Trenerry, Walter N. *Murder in Minnesota: A Collection of True Cases.* Minnesota Historical Society (0-87351-180-8), 1985. 252p. B/W photos and illus. (Interest level: 7-8).

Fifteen murders that occurred between 1858 and 1917 are presented in this collection that makes history come alive. Most murders were in St. Paul or Minneapolis, although some were in other Minnesota locations such as Brainerd and Winona. Historical information makes this intriguing look at social history most suited for better readers who have some knowledge of life in the nineteenth century and are patient enough to read through detail.
♦ Using desktop publishing software, students may create a newspaper story about one crime, write a biography of the murderer, or plot the 15 murder locations on a map of Minnesota.
1. Homicide—Minnesota—Case studies 2. Criminals—Minnesota—Biography.

364.15
Hunting, George. *Robber and Hero.* Minnesota Historical Society (0-87351-194-8), 1986. 125p. B/W photos. (Interest level: 6+).

From memories of those who witnessed the Northfield raid comes this account of the attempted bank robbery and the ensuing manhunt through Minnesota. This story recounts one of the most attention-getting robbery attempts in the American West, realistically portraying both heroes (bank worker and townspeople) and outlaws (the James and Younger brothers).
♦ Some students may research other bank robberies in the early years of Minnesota, while others may relate the exciting/horrible experience in an imaginary letter from one of Northfield's townspeople to friends and relatives. Still others may explore what makes a hero and compare today's heroes to those of the past.
1. Bank robberies—Northfield (Minn.) 2. Robbers and outlaws—Minnesota.

380
Peterson, Eric. *Minnie the Streetcar Boat.* Minnesota Transportation Museum (No ISBN), 1991. 24p. B/W illus. (Interest level: K-2).

This easy reading and coloring book details travel by streetcar boats in Minneapolis and Minnetonka in the early 1900s. The simple approach to a unique travel mode will be useful when studying the history of transportation as well as the history of Minnesota.
♦ Students can discuss different forms of transportation and reasons why streetcars or streetcar boats are no longer used. They could also draw pictures of other forms of transportation no longer used. Some Minnesota students may be able to visit the renovated streetcar boat *Minnehaha* or the Minnesota Transportation Museum in St. Paul.
1. Minneapolis (Minn.)—History 2. Transportation—History.

380.145
Gilman, Carolyn. *Where Two Worlds Meet: The Great Lakes Fur Trade.* Minnesota Historical Society (0-87351-156-5), 1982. 136p. B/W and Color photos and illus. (Interest level: 6+).

Based on an exhibition of the Minnesota Historical Society, this resource shows how the fur trade helped bring two radically different cultures closer together. Although some of the text may be too advanced, the

illustrations and captions alone make this a valuable resource.
♦ Students may enjoy researching and discussing the theory that trading possessions is actually trading cultures. Where do "two worlds meet" today? Does international trade bring cultures closer? Students could select products and show the interdependence of the world by mapping the origin of the resources that make up the products.
1. Fur trade—Great Lakes region—History.

387
Split Rock Light: Tribute to the Age of Steel. (Videocassette). Produced by Steve Hall, Fresh Pictures. Minnesota Historical Society, 1986. VHS 1/2", Stereo/color, (24 min.). $36.95. (Interest level: 5+).

The Split Rock Lighthouse played an important role in Minnesota's steel industry by alerting ships in the most dangerous area of Lake Superior. Firsthand accounts of the life of the lighthouse keeper's family as well as the history of the lighthouse make this work valuable.
♦ Groups of students may write an imaginary diary kept by a member of the lighthouse keeper's family. Students may consider such challenges as the arrival of inspectors, ways to keep from getting bored, and activities during storms.
1. Lighthouses—Minnesota—History 2. Split Rock Lighthouse—Minnesota—History.

394.2
Marsh, Carole. *Minnesota Festival Fun for Kids!* Gallopade (0-7933-3995-2), 1991. 36p. B/W illus. (Interest level: 1+).

This introduction to Minnesota addresses historic, educational, famous, and humorous events. The interdisciplinary approach includes many activities for language arts, math, and geography. Users are granted permission to photocopy the pages for each student.
♦ Young people may write to the chamber of commerce in a selected city to request more information on specific festivals or events mentioned. They may also construct a wall display of brochures and other information on festivals of Minnesota.
1. Festivals—Minnesota 2. Minnesota—Festivals.

394.26
Johnston, Patricia Condon. *The Minnesota Christmas Book.* Photos by Charles James Johnston. Johnston (0-942934-08-3), 1985. B/W photos. (Interest level: 5+).

Ethnic and cultural history and traditions, recipes from restaurants and family meals, and a look at some select businesses make up this unique resource that discusses home, church, politics, and business during the Christmas season. The impressive photographs and captivating text draw readers into this exploration of what effect Christmas has on life in Minnesota.

♦ Senior citizens from the community may talk to the class about their favorite holiday and how they celebrated it in the past. Students may share their own family traditions.
1. Christmas—Minnesota 2. Minnesota—Christmas.

398.2
Childs, Lucille. *Tibdo, A Dakota Legend.* Illus. by Patrick des Jarlait. Indian Elementary Curriculum Project, Minneapolis Public Schools (No ISBN), 1977. 15p. B/W illus. (Interest level: 1-5).

This Dakota Indian legend gives an explanation of how the wren came to make its specific sound. Pronunciations and definitions help in the oral reading and in understanding the story as well as the culture of the Dakota. Passed by word of mouth from generation to generation, this legend is best used as a read-aloud or in storytelling.
♦ Students may find other legends to explain natural events or phenomena and tell them to the class. They could also write their own mythical explanation of a natural occurrence. After brief research in the media center, the students may compare their "legends" with scientific fact.
1. Indians of North America—Legends 2. Dakota Indians—Legends.

398.2
Esbensen, Barbara. *The Star Maiden: An Indian Tale.* Little, Brown (0-316-24951-3), 1988. 32p. Color illus. (Interest level: 2-5).

This story about the origin of the water lily depicts the peaceful, "once upon a time" lifestyle of the Ojibway. The impressive pastel illustrations enhance the book's suitability for reading aloud.
♦ Students may write their own stories about the origin of other flowers. They may wish to research other Ojibway Indian legends and share them with the class.
1. Ojibway Indians—Legends 2. Indians of North America—Legends.

398.2
Osofsky, Audrey. *Dreamcatcher.* Illus. by Ed Young. Orchard (0-531-08588-0), 1992. Unpaginated. Color illus. (Interest level: 1-4).

An Ojibway family's daily life is depicted in this picture book about an Ojibway child who was protected from bad dreams by the "dreamcatcher," a spider-web-like net traditionally hung around cradles. Pastel drawings by Ed Young accentuate the dreamlike and mystical quality of this story.
♦ Teachers may read the book to children before showing them the pictures, asking them to interpret orally or visually what they imagine. Or, students may read on their own and discuss what they learned about the Ojibway culture.
1. Ojibway Indians 2. Indians of North America—Legends.

398.2
Schommer, Carrie. *Unktomi and the Ducks.* Illus. by Steve Premo. Indian Elementary Curriculum Project, Minneapolis Public Schools (No ISBN), 1978. 33p. B/W illus. (Interest level: 2-7).

Based on a Dakota Indian legend, this story explains how the wood duck got its red eye. This simply written, imaginative story should capture students' interest in legends and in discussions of how other natural phenomena came to be.
♦ After the teacher or media specialist clarifies that legends are often explanations of the origin of natural wonders, the students may write their own tales dealing specifically with Minnesota: Why does the gopher have big front teeth? How did the loon get to have white speckles? How did the chickadee get its name? How did the showy lady's slipper become pink as well as white? Students may tell their legends to another class.

1. Dakota Indians—Legends 2. Indians of North America—Legends.

427
Mohr, Howard. *How to Talk Minnesotan: A Visitor's Guide.* Viking Penguin (0-14-000284-6 pbk), 1987. 222p. B/W illus. (Interest level: 6-8).

With tongue in cheek, Mohr humorously presents words, phrases, proverbs, and customs common to Minnesota. He includes explanations of "Hotdish," "Discussing the Weather," "Travel," "Romance," and "Going to the Laundromat" in diverse, short chapters. The book is suitable for reading aloud and stimulating students to discuss the meaning of commonly used and heard phrases and words. It may have special appeal to better and more insightful readers.
♦ Students could have fun discussing "Minnesotaisms" and then producing a video for Minnesota newcomers. They may use *VCR Companion* (Broderbund Software) to produce captions and silly props that would help explain Minnesota.

1. English language—Provincialisms—Minnesota
2. Minnesota—Social life and customs—Anecdotes.

574.5
Bowen, Betsy. *Antler, Bear, Canoe: A Northwoods Alphabet Year.* Little, Brown (0-316-10376-4), 1991. 32p. Color illus. (Interest level: K-2).

Twenty-six words, such as *rendezvous, kayak,* and *dogsled,* that help describe the Northwoods are briefly explained. The book is ideal for reading aloud and for introducing more advanced vocabulary and spelling words to young students.
♦ Young people may practice spelling and cooperatively create their own alphabet list to describe their own geographical area. They may also create their own illustrations and make posters for each of their words.

1. Alphabet 2. Forests and forestry—Pictorial works 3. Seasons—Pictorial works.

574.97
Wilderness World of Sigurd F. Olson. (16mm film). Produced by Ray Christensen and Steve A. Kahlenbeck. Filmedia, 1980. Color, (29 min.). Available from Minnesota Historical Society. $39.95. (Interest level: 6+).

Based on books by Sigurd F. Olson, one of Minnesota's foremost interpretive naturalists, this film presents an insight into one man's life throughout the seasons in the Northwoods. The striking photography of northern Minnesota canoe country evokes a feeling of serenity and emphasizes the beauty of humans living in harmony with nature.
♦ Students may write a paragraph either comparing and contrasting two seasons in Minnesota or describing what one season means to them. They may plan a film about a season in their own community, including what music they would use and notes on necessary narration.

1. Olson, Sigurd F. 2. Naturalists—Minnesota 3. Wilderness areas—Minnesota.

598.4
Blacklock, Craig. *The Geese of Silver Lake.* Voyageur (0-89658-114-4), 1989. 64p. Color photos. (Interest level: 4-8).

Nature photographer Craig Blacklock explains a popular Rochester, Minnesota, attraction through photography and text, providing the "history" of the geese's journey and settlement in Rochester. Biological and environmental information are also provided. The book is ideally suited for integrating mandated environmental learner outcomes into the curriculum.
♦ Many students throughout the United States will be able to describe their experiences with seeing geese or flocks of birds. If possible, an ornithologist could speak to the class about environmental issues.

1. Silver Lake (Olmstead County, Minn.)—History 2. Rochester (Minn.)—Pictorial works 3. Canada goose 4. Geese—Minnesota—Rochester.

598.4
Esbensen, Barbara. *Great Northern Diver: The Loon.* Little, Brown (0-316-24954-8), 1990. Unpaginated. Color illus. (Interest level: K-3).

Loon habits, their unique calls, and other biological information about Minnesota's state bird are described in this carefully illustrated book. The book is suitable for reports or browsing.
♦ Students may listen to recordings of bird calls (e.g., *Voices of the Loon,* NorthWord, 1980) and prepare a call to share with the class.

1. Loons.

598.4
Klein, Tom. *Loon Magic for Kids.* NorthWord (1-55971-047-0), 1989. 48p. Color photos. (Interest level: 3-8).

Outstanding, concise text makes this work about Minnesota's state bird interesting for younger readers. Various loon species, loon habits, and habitats are explained. The book is well suited for integrating environmental education into the language arts curriculum.
♦ Young people may describe loons they have seen or discuss bird sounds they know. They may also describe their feelings when they listen to the sound of a loon or see pictures of a loon.
1. Loons.

599
Hoover, Helen. *The Gift of the Deer*. Illus. by Adrian Hoover. Knopf (0-394-41803-4), 1989. 210p. Pen-and-ink drawings. (Interest level: 6-8).

After living for four years in northern Minnesota, the author describes her observations of Peter (an orphaned deer), his extended family, and other animals. Readers familiar with Hoover's children's books and those who like animals will enjoy this reflective account.
♦ By discussing the patterns of forest life and the balance of nature described, young people may determine: "What is the gift of the deer?" The author quotes a friend who said, "You seem to feel that nature is always smiling. Surely it has some sinister aspects." Students may explore some of the sinister aspects of nature depicted in the book.
1. Deer—Minnesota.

610.92
Crofford, Emily. *Frontier Surgeons: A Story about the Mayo Brothers*. Illus. by Karen Ritz. Carolrhoda (0-87614-318-8), 1989. 56p. B/W illus. (Interest level: 3-6).

This is a readable account of medicine in the late 1800s and the contributions of Charles and Will Mayo. The book fills a gap by providing elementary reading material about medical history, the contributions of Minnesotans to medicine, and Rochester's role as a medical community.
♦ As students read, they can list early medical techniques that may seem strange by today's standards and also make a list of the techniques the Mayo Brothers developed. Students may also make a computer crossword puzzle from the many new vocabulary and spelling words the book provides.
1. Mayo, William James, 1861-1939 2. Mayo, Charles Horace, 1865-1939 3. Physicians—United States—Biography.

630.74
Marling, Karal Ann. *Blue Ribbon: A Social and Pictorial History of the Minnesota State Fair*. Minnesota Historical Society (0-87351-251-0; 0-87351-252-9 pbk), 1990. 328p. B/W photos and illus. (Interest level: 5+).

This well-researched, comprehensive history of the Minnesota State Fair is based on several thousand newspaper articles as well as the experiences and observations of those who attended it. Younger readers will enjoy the illustrations and captions, and more mature readers will find the text fascinating reading because of its anecdotal and statistical information, editorial opinion, and news reports.
♦ Students may recall their own experiences at local or state fairs. After interviewing adults, small groups may compare fairs of the past to those of the present. Other groups may predict how fairs will change in the future. A discussion topic for the class might be the ways fairs are representative of the times and the area in which they are held.
1. Fairs—History 2. Fairs—Minnesota—Pictorial works.

633.1
Regguinti, Gordon. *The Sacred Harvest: Ojibway Wild Rice Gathering*. Lerner (0-8225-2650-6), 1992. (We Are Still Here: Native Americans Today Series). 48p. Color photos. (Interest level: 4-8).

Through a story about Glen, an 11-year-old boy, the techniques of harvesting and processing wild rice on the Leech Lake Indian Reservation are explained. The work gives brief information about Ojibway history and spiritual beliefs about rice.
♦ Students may write a newspaper article about Glen, make a computer time line about the wild rice growth and harvest cycle, make a crossword puzzle of the new vocabulary words they learned from this book, or cook a wild rice dish.
1. Ojibway Indians—Minnesota 2. Wild rice.

634.9
Faces of the Forest. (Videocassette). Produced by Slavko Nowytski, Filmart. Minnesota Historical Society, 1978. VHS 1/2", Color, (17 min.). $36.95. (Interest level: 6+).

Using a "You Are There" approach, this video shows the northern Minnesota forests of the early 1900s through the words of settlers, fire fighters, and lumberjacks. Excellent photography and thought-provoking narration relate the activities of clearing the land, building log homes, carrying out the maple sugaring, fighting fires, and lumbering.
♦ Students may list useful items made from forest products. They may speculate about what life would be like without trees. If papermaking kits can be obtained, making paper from wood would be a good culminating activity.
1. Forests and forestry—Minnesota.

636
The Changing Farm in Early Minnesota. (Videocassette). Produced by Tom Woods and Kelley Huson. Minnesota Historical Society and Northwest Cable Company, 1987. VHS 1/2", B/W, (14 min.). Available

from the Minnesota Historical Society. $5, rental. Includes teacher's guide. (Interest level: 4-8).

Filmed on a living history farm near Minneapolis, the video explains subsistence farming, market farming, and new tools (e.g., the threshing, reaping, and washing machines) that affected farming between 1850 and 1880. Problems, changes, and daily living are set forth in an upbeat, lively narrative partially taken from family letters. A teacher's guide includes objectives, a glossary, and a written copy of the audio script.
- ♦ After viewing the video students can list the conveniences new to farmers in the mid-nineteenth century. They may also compare the problems farmers had then to those farmers have now.

1. Minnesota—Agriculture—History 2. Farms—History.

641.5
Kaplan, Anne R., et al. *The Minnesota Ethnic Food Book*. Minnesota Historical Society (0-87351-197-2), 1986. 449p. B/W photos. (Interest level: 5+).

The foods and traditions of various ethnic groups communicate their history and culture. This sampler of ethnic food preparations is an intriguing collection of information gathered from interviews and conversations, showing the direct correlation between the foods people eat and their identity.
- ♦ Students may prepare some of the recipes for a tasting party in which young people explain the significance of each dish and changes that have evolved from the original recipe. Students may also describe food traditions in their own homes.

1. Cookery—American 2. Minnesota—Ethnic groups—Cookery 3. Ethnology—Minnesota.

641.5943
Parnell, Helga. *Cooking the German Way*. Lerner (0-8225-0918-0), 1988. (Easy Menu Ethnic Cookbooks). 48p. Color photos. (Interest level: 5-8).

This recipe book features ethnic foods that can be easily made from commonly found ingredients. Background information, given with the recipes, introduces young people to German customs.
- ♦ As part of an ethnic unit, young people may prepare one of the recipes in class.

1. Cookery—German 2. Germany—Social life and customs.

641.59481
Munsen, Sylvia. *Cooking the Norwegian Way*. Lerner (0-8225-0901-0), 1988. (Easy Menu Ethnic Cookbooks). 48p. Color photos. (Interest level: 5-8).

Many of the recipes presented in this book will be familiar to children of Norwegian heritage. Color photos enhance the clearly presented directions.
- ♦ Young people may research the origins of the major ingredients of the various recipes. If members of the class have a Norwegian heritage, they may bring from home family recipes that are variations of those given in the book.

1. Cookery—Norwegian 2. Norway—Social life and customs 3. Cookery—Scandinavian.

664.132
Burns, Diane L. *Sugaring Season: Making Maple Syrup*. Illus. by Cheryl Walsh Bellville. Carolrhoda (0-87614-420-2), 1990. 48p. Color illus. (Interest level: 1-5).

Through a maple sugaring expedition, young readers learn how maple syrup is extracted. Detailed explanations and fine illustrations make the process easy to understand and enjoy. Although the setting is not defined, the process can be applied to Minnesota.
- ♦ Young people may brainstorm different uses of maple syrup. They may also use it for a taste treat, pancakes made in class, or maple sugar candy.

1. Maple syrup 2. Maple sugar.

708.977
The Timekeeper. (Videocassette). Produced by Kristie Duckwell. Minnesota Historical Society, 1980. VHS 1/2", Color, (20 min.). $36.95. (Interest level: 5+).

Vivid scenes of still photography made into video capture the efforts of the Minnesota Historical Society to preserve the history of Minnesota and make it live for those who visit the society's museum or use its holdings. Viewing the videocassette would make an excellent introduction for a field trip to any historical museum.
- ♦ Students may select/ and describe items that they think should be preserved for the future to give the real picture of what life is like today. Their choices should be justified. Students may make a scrapbook of sketches or a display of selected realia.

1. Museums—Minnesota 2. Minnesota—History.

741.64
Gág, Wanda. *Growing Pains*. Minnesota Historical Society (0-87351-173-5), 1984. 475p. B/W photos and illus. (Interest level: 7+).

As a young girl growing up in Minnesota, children's author Wanda Gág kept a diary of her intimate thoughts and feelings, her insights into herself and others around her, and her creative sketches. Although this somewhat ponderous collection by Gág will not be read in its entirety by many students, segments can be read aloud to show the energy and lively determination of an adolescent working through difficult times.
- ♦ In her diary Gág made a number of resolutions. Students may discuss how her resolutions reflected the times and compare them to resolutions made today. Students may also discuss how there can be a difference between "me" and "myself," as indicated by Gág.

1. Gág, Wanda, 1893-1946 2. Authors—United States—Biography 3. Illustrators—United States—Biography.

745
Moore, Willard B., et al. *Circles of Tradition: Folk Arts in Minnesota.* Minnesota Historical Society (0-87351-239-1), 1989. 162p. B/W and Color photos. (Interest level: 6-8).

Photographs and a detailed text present a variety of Minnesota art forms including Ojibway drums, Polish paper cuttings, Norwegian rosemaling, and Hmong tapestry. Although valuable as a source of hard-to-find information that vividly shows Minnesota's diverse cultural heritage, the reading level and subject matter of the text also make it suitable as a teacher resource.
♦ Students can use the pictures as an aid to help understand ethnic groups they learn about from other materials and as a source of ideas for developing their own folk art projects.
1. Folk art—Minnesota 2. Ethnic art—Minnesota.

745.0973
Marling, Karal Ann. *The Colossus of Roads: Myth and Symbol Along the American Highway.* Photos by Liz Harrison. University of Minnesota (0-8166-1302-8), 1984. 140p. B/W and Color photos. (Interest level: 5+).

Marling's travels through Minnesota were a search for and study of the giant roadside sculptures found in many Midwest towns and cities. The unusual topic and the bits of history revealed make this pleasurable and informative reading.
♦ Students may design a sculpture that would symbolize the spirit or history of their town or city, explaining why the specific item was selected. The design (on paper or in miniature) and the rationale could be presented to the city council for possible adoption.
1. Folk art, American—Psychological aspects
2. United States—Popular culture—Psychological aspects.

796.5
Paulsen, Gary. *Woodsong.* Illus. by Ruth Wright Paulsen. Macmillan (0-02-770221-9), 1990. 132p. B/W illus. (Interest level: 5-8).

This two-part account is a reflection of Paulsen's life in northern Minnesota and his narrative of participation in the Alaskan Iditarod sled dog race. Animal and adventure lovers will find the book fascinating and enjoy Paulsen's thoughtful descriptions of animal life and habits.
♦ Students could illustrate the book, create their own maps, or read similar adventure stories such as Scott Anderson's *Distant Fires* (see Minnesota—Nonfiction—917.7) or an animal story such as Jack London's *The Call of the Wild* (Macmillan, 1903, 1963). Readers familiar with Paulsen's books could compare and contrast this title to his other works such as *Hatchet* (Bradbury, 1987).
1. Outdoor life—Minnesota 2. Sled dogs 3. Sled dog racing.

796.5076
Sansome, Constance J. *Minnesota Underfoot: A Field Guide to the State's Outstanding Geologic Features.* Trailblazer (0-89658-036-9), 1992. 224p. B/W and Color illus. (Interest level: 7+).

This excellent resource for hiking, biking, auto, or "armchair" explorations of the state gives much geologic information that should spark a reader's interest in further exploration. It addresses many questions about how certain landforms developed and why the state is divided into certain specific land areas. The information is presented in a "keep reading" style.
♦ Young people may make a crossword puzzle using names, places, bits of information, and vocabulary from the text. If available, a computer software program may be used to facilitate the process. Each young person could contribute one or two terms and definitions to be compiled into one puzzle.
1. Hiking—Minnesota 2. Minnesota—Description—Guidebooks.

796.54
Boundary Waters Canoe Trip: An Adventure Travel Game. (Board game). Trailblazer, 1992. (Interest level: 5+).

This simulated canoe and portage trip is highly realistic. Young people can play it more than once, taking a different route and different lakes each time. Four hundred game cards give information about the history, natural history, and geography of the region. The game emphasizes wilderness safety, care of equipment, and exploration of the environment.
♦ Young people may play the game in small groups or as a whole class. If feasible, this activity could lead to a field trip to a wilderness preserve or park.
1. Camping—Minnesota 2. Canoes and canoeing—Minnesota 3. Wilderness areas—Minnesota.

799.1
Fellegy, Joe. *Classic Minnesota Fishing Stories.* Waldman (0-931674-04-2), 1982. 238p. B/W photos and illus. (Interest level: 5+).

This entertaining collection of tales and exaggerated episodes is for fishing enthusiasts of all ages. These "armchair" fishing trips are meant to be read independently, read aloud, or told to a group.
♦ If a storyteller lives nearby, he or she could be invited to tell stories to the class. The collection is a good resource for storytelling activities by students.
1. Fishing—Minnesota 2. Fishing stories, American—Minnesota.

808.8
Fosdick, C. J., et al. *Blossoms and Blizzards.* Pegasus Prose (0-9617240-3-X), 1986. 110p. B/W photos. (Interest level: 6+).

This collection of short stories captures the spirit of Minnesotans through the state's unpredictable seasons—from warm, humid summer to frigid winter. A

look into the past as well as glimpses of the future are shown with humor and optimism.
♦ Students may take or find a photo of some seasonal aspect of life in Minnesota, then write a poem about this aspect and create a "Poetree" wall in their classroom. (The wall could contain one large sketch of a tree for each of the four seasons.) Students could also create bumper stickers that would give the essence of Minnesota (e.g., "Survive a Minnesota winter—the rest is easy").
1. Literature—Collections—Minnesota 2. Minnesota—Literature—Collections.

808.83
Engels, Stephen E. *A Minnesota Christmas Anthology*. Partridge (0-9621085-0-2), 1988. 112p. B/W illus. (Interest level: 6+).

This collection of newspaper accounts, recollections of well-known as well as everyday people, recipes, poems, and stories of Minnesota Christmases capitalizes on the excitement of the season. Using these primary sources, this book gives an excellent insight into Minnesota history.
♦ After further research on holiday customs of different nationalities and ethnic groups in Minnesota, students may wish to share these customs with others on a special day.
1. Minnesota—Christmas 2. Literature—Collections—Minnesota.

808.84
Sandberg, Walt. *The Turn in the Trail: Northwoods Tales of the Upper Great Lakes*. Willow Creek (0-932558-14-3), 1980. 215p. (Interest level: 6+).

Fifty-seven humorous or mystifying stories about people and events that have reinforced the author's attachment to the "picturesque and productive woods and waters of the North" are colorfully related. Although the renditions are more appropriate for older students and adults, some would make excellent read-alouds for students in the younger grades.
♦ Students in small groups may make up a radio or television newscast with an interview and "on the scene" reports of the events and people highlighted in this collection.
1. Minnesota—Description 2. Essays—Minnesota.

810.8
Erwin, Jean. *The Minnesota Experience*. Adams Press (0-914828-04-5; 0-914828-05-3 pbk), 1979. 453p. (Interest level: 7-8).

The themes in this collection of essays and cuttings from longer fiction and nonfiction writings by old and new classic Minnesota authors (e.g., Borghild Dahl, F. Scott Fitzgerald, Carol Bly, and Garrison Keillor) reflect the state's land (both rural and urban) and people (both young and old). The collection provides an opportunity for middle and junior high school students to become familiar with respected adult authors and develop an awareness of Minnesota's ethnic and geographical mixture.
♦ Students may read one or more stories and then do further research on the setting or situation described by the author. Students may also wish to read a complete work by one of these authors.
1. Literature—Collections—Minnesota 2. Minnesota—Literature—Collections.

813.52
Anderson, William. *Laura Ingalls Wilder Country*. Illus. by Garth Williams. Harper/Perennial (0-06-055294-8), 1990. 119p. B/W and Color photos. (Interest level: 3-8).

The settings for the "Little House" books are vividly portrayed in brief text and photographs, including many from Wilder family photo albums. This well-designed book adds dimension to a popular author and series of books. Chapters on the plains area of Walnut Grove in western Minnesota, the Big Woods of Pepin, Wisconsin, and the Master Hotel in Burr Oak, Iowa, are included. (Pepin is across the Mississippi River from Minnesota; Burr Oak is just across the border.) These chapters are valuable as a pictorial account of the differences in southeastern and southwestern Minnesota landscape.
♦ Some students may have visited Wilder sites and museums and can share their own remembrances or photographs. Students may wish to photocopy pictures in the book and make a poster illustrating a "Little House" book.
1. Wilder, Laura Ingalls, 1867-1957 2. Authors, American—20th Century—Biography 3. Literary landmarks—United States.

813.54
Paulsen, Gary. *Clabbered Dirt, Sweet Grass*. Illus. by Ruth Wright Paulsen. Harcourt, Brace, Jovanovich (0-15-118101-2), 1992. 120p. Color illus. (Interest level: 6-8+).

This memoir of life on a northern Minnesota farm during the early 1940s is a poetic tribute to a disappearing way of life. The work contains a prologue and four long chapters, each of which depicts farm life and social culture during a different season. Some sections, such as that on butchering pigs, show the less pleasant aspects of farm life.
♦ Teachers may read aloud part or all of the book. Students may interview individuals who lived on farms in the 1940s, compare farm life then and now, or create additional illustrations. Other comparisons can be made to farm life by listening to Michael Cotter's *Dad's Stories and Farm Memories* (see Minnesota—Fiction, end of section). or reading Paulsen's description of northern Minnesota in *Woodsong* (see Minnesota—Nonfiction—796.5).
1. Minnesota—Farm life 2. Minnesota—Social life and customs.

818
Meier, Peg and Wood, Dave. *The Pie Lady of Winthrop and Other Minnesota Tales*. Minneapolis Star and Tribune (No ISBN), 1981. 244p. B/W illus. (Interest level: 5-8).

Two reporters for the *Minneapolis Star and Tribune* have collected articles that originally appeared in the "Neighbors" section of the newspaper. People from throughout Minnesota and with varying backgrounds—a priest, the daughter of a slave, a 10-year-old boy, a pianist, and an aspiring singer—are described in this collection. Communities such as Lanesboro and Sauk Center are included. This collection portrays the cultural diversity of Minnesota's people.
♦ After each student reads a different story, the class may list and discuss the variety of ethnic and social backgrounds revealed in this collection.
1. Minnesota—Biography 2. Minnesota—Social life and customs.

904.5
Marsh, Carole. *Minnesota's (Most Devastating) Disasters and (Most Calamitous) Catastrophes*. Gallopade (0-7933-0620-5), 1990. 35p. B/W illus. (Interest level: 3-8).

Much information and many little-known facts about Minnesota's weather, historic events, and disease epidemics are given in a lively question-and-answer format. The information given could pique a child's curiosity for further research.
♦ Students could interview senior citizens about the worst disaster they remember: Was it caused by humans, by nature, or by accident? What was it like? How did they feel about it? How did humans, as a whole, react to it? How did the natural world respond?
1. Natural disasters—Minnesota 2. Disasters—Minnesota.

910.9
Wenzel, Dorothy. *Ann Bancroft: On the Top of the World*. Dillon (0-87518-418-9), 1991. 61p. Color photos. (Interest level: 3-6).

This brief account of the adventurer, credited with being the first woman to reach the North Pole by dogsled, includes her early life in Minneapolis and her trips to Africa. One of the few juvenile biographies about a Minnesota woman, this book helps meet the need for gender-fair materials for young readers.
♦ Students may research periodical indexes to discover information about other polar expeditions or women explorers. They may discuss Bancroft's achievements and the special challenges she faced.
1. Bancroft, Ann 2. North Pole.

917.7
Anderson, Scott. *Distant Fires*. Illus. by Les Kouba. Pfeiffer Hamilton (0-938586-33-5), 1991. 156p. B/W illus. (Interest level: 6-8).

A Minnesotan describes the 1,700-mile canoe trip he and a friend took from Duluth, along the shores of Lake Superior, and through the Winnipeg River and eastern Manitoba to Hudson's Bay. The realistic descriptions of the adventure (complete with rapids, portages, mosquitoes, and inclement weather) will appeal to many young people. Anderson's reflective insights on the natural environment, historic Canadian trading posts, and the culture of the Cree Indians will entice more mature and thoughtful readers.
♦ Students may trace the canoe trip on maps of Minnesota, Ontario, and Manitoba; write a reflective descriptive journal of a similar challenge; or create their own illustrations. A Hypercard stack could be created to trace Anderson's route.
1. Canoes and canoeing—Canada 2. Canoes and canoeing—Minnesota 3. Canada—Description 4. Minnesota—Description.

917.7
Jefferson, Constance. *Minnesota in Maps: A Trailblazer Atlas*. Illus. by Constance J. Sansome and Lisa E. Jefferson. Trailblazer (0-9626025-0-7), 1991. 32p. Maps. (Interest level: 2-6).

This beginner-level atlas is divided into 12 chapters on such topics as lakes, rivers, streams, rocks, soils, animals, and people. Each section has one page of text and an easy-to-read map, making this a good introduction to locating places and legends in an atlas.
♦ Students may do further map research with print sources or *DataNet* (see Minnesota—Nonfiction—004.6), or they may create similar maps of their own county based on their research or recorded observations of life around them.
1. Minnesota—Maps.

917.7
Minnesota Map. (40" x 44" Map). High Touch Learning, 1991. $149.95, basic map set; $11.95, storage board package. Set includes teaching guide. (Interest level: K-8).

This Minnesota map provides students with a hands-on learning experience in which they use Velcro tabs to identify cities, bodies of water, mountains, hills, geographic regions, and regional names. The map is ideally suited for cooperative learning. For students of all abilities, the map provides means to integrate the study of Minnesota into virtually every subject.
♦ Students may create their own tabs to identify the Minnesota setting of fiction and nonfiction books, population, counties, historic and geologic sites, animal habitats, birthplaces of famous Minnesotans,

regional economies, or other aspects of Minnesota that pertain to the curriculum.
1. Minnesota—Study and teaching 2. Minnesota—Maps.

917.76
Lee, Carvel. *36 One-Day Discovery Tours: Fun Places to Drive within and from Minneapolis and St. Paul.* Nodin (0-931714-40-0), 1990. 80p. B/W illus. Available from Micawber's, Inc. (Interest level: 4-8).

Suburban, metropolitan, and rural sites from southeast to central Minnesota are described through an imaginary automobile tour. The guide gives locations of historical and recreational areas and includes listings of various museums and hotels.
♦ Young people may cooperatively select a trip, justify their choice, map their travel, and list sights to be seen. They may also wish to figure the cost of the journey.
1. Minnesota—Description and travel—Guidebooks 2. Minneapolis (Minn.)—Description—Guidebooks 3. Saint Paul (Minn.)—Description—Guidebooks 4. Wisconsin—Description—Guidebooks.

917.76
Lund, Duane R. *Our Historic Boundary Waters from Lake Superior to Lake of the Woods.* Nordell Graphic Communications (0-934860-13-0), 1980. 97p. B/W illus. (Interest level: 6+).

From the days of the earliest known inhabitants to the provisions of the congressional acts of the 1960s and 1970s, this history tells of the people, events, and culture of one of Minnesota's most colorful areas. The writing is matter-of-fact and filled with many little known but interesting details.
♦ To examine the events of this account in relation to United States history, students may use Tom Snyder's *TimeLiner* (Tom Snyder Productions, 1992) computer program to create a large wall display of a time line of the history of the Boundary Waters along with a time line of American historical events.
1. Minnesota—History 2. Boundary Waters Canoe Area (Minn.)—History.

917.76
Marsh, Carole. *Uncle Rebus: Minnesota Picture Stories for Computer Kids.* Gallopade (No ISBN), 1991. 35p. B/W illus. (Interest level: 1+).

Stories, poems, and riddles covering tourist attractions, people, history, transportation, sports, statistics, holidays, and foods of Minnesota are presented using a computer dingbat "rebus" font. *Uncle Rebus* can be purchased in either print or computer disk format. Users are given permission to print out copies of the activity pages for each student.
♦ Using their own computer graphics or dingbat font, students may create a state rebus, recording a story about some aspect of their state, an activity, or an event that is familiar to them.
1. Computer games—Minnesota 2. Minnesota—Teaching aids and devices.

917.76
Marshall, Alexander B. *Pathways through Minnesota.* Clark & Miles (0-9626647-0-7), 1992. 638p. B/W illus. (Interest level: 4+).

Much history can be gleaned from this insiders' guide to the best and most unusual travel selections in the "Land of 15,293 Lakes." Descriptions of places to visit throughout each region are valuable for anyone wishing to know the Minnesota of yesterday and today.
♦ Students may use the information to prepare a travel brochure for a visitor from another country. Perhaps the school could select a similar city or community from another country and exchange brochures, then correspond via electronic mail.
1. Minnesota—Description—Guidebooks.

917.76
McCarthy, Ann. *Minnesota: A Photographic Journey.* Crescent (0-517-00177-2), 1990. 128p. Color photos. (Interest level: 4+).

Minnesota's lakes (15,000+), its prairies, and the Twin Cities are highlighted in this overview of the state. The text is poetic, and the photographs are evocative. Whether used for browsing or research, the work communicates vividly the spirit and beauty of Minnesota.
♦ Young people may speculate how these photographs of forests, lakes, transportation systems, farms, and cities would be interpreted 100 years from now. They may also consider what differences could be predicted in photographs of the same sites if they were taken 100 years from now.
1. Minnesota—Description 2. Minnesota—Pictorial works.

917.76
Minnesota Overtures. (Videocassette). Produced by Russell Manning. Minnesota Office of Tourism, n.d. VHS 1/2", Color, (20 min.). Free. (Interest level: 3+).

The spectacular aerial and ground camera work of this videotape present an overview of Minnesota's unique natural beauty. The blend of pictorial splendor and expressive music portrays a Minnesota that can be enjoyed in such varied ways as attending some of the many festivals or events, participating in outdoor sports activities, visiting the Minnesota Zoo, or touring the state in any season of the year.
♦ Following the viewing of this videotape, students may script, shoot, and edit a videotape of their own town, or they may instead identify some of the many events and places that should be included in a videotape of their own area.
1. Minnesota—Travel 2. Minnesota—Tourist trade.

917.76
Olsenius, Richard. *Minnesota Travel Companion*. Bluestem (0-9609064-0-1), 1982. 252p. B/W photos. (Interest level: 6+).

This valuable resource follows the main travel routes and explains how the history of the state unfolded along these roads. This "snapshot" history of Minnesota's smallest towns and largest cities provides sufficient information without including so many details that the reading is laborious.
♦ Teams of students may each select one group (ethnic, religious, economic) and research its settlement in their community. Answers to questions of why, when, and how can be shared with the class.
1. Minnesota—Travel 2. Minnesota—History.

917.76
Stavig, Vicki. *Minnesota Guide*. 2nd ed. Dorn Communications (0-934070-23-7), 1983. 359p. B/W photos. (Interest level: 5+).

This typical guidebook gives information on travel, geography, culture, events, business, government, and tourist attractions of Minnesota. This resource contains much miscellaneous data in a very thorough coverage of Minnesota today.
♦ Students in small groups may plan walking, biking, or driving tours of Minnesota, considering such details as number of miles per day, sights to see, estimated expenses, and events to attend. Reports could be given to the class in a video or through a desktop or oral presentation with visual aids. Students may construct their own dictionary of Minnesota vocabulary in a takeoff on the brief list given in this book.
1. Minnesota—Description—Guidebooks 2. Minnesota—Tourist trade.

917.76
Umhoefer, Jim. *All Season Guide to Minnesota's Parks, Canoe Routes and Trails*. NorthWord (0-942802-06-3), 1984. 105p. B/W photos. (Interest level: 5+).

Maps, informative commentary, and mood-setting photographs present a vivid picture of Minnesota's natural vacation spots in any season. This guide provides a firsthand look at what there is to see and do at any of Minnesota's state parks.
♦ Working in small groups, students may select one park and design, write, and produce an advertising brochure to encourage people to visit the park. A simple desktop publishing program will facilitate the process.
1. Parks—Minnesota—Guidebooks 2. Minnesota—Description 3. Outdoor recreation—Minnesota.

917.76
Webb, Val. *Rochester Sketchbook*. Johnson (No ISBN), 1976. 182p. Brown/White illus. (Interest level: 5-8).

Ink drawings and an accompanying page of text depict familiar contemporary and historical sites in Rochester (e.g., various homes, St. Mary's Hospital, the Mayo Clinic, Mayowood, the Kahler Hotel, Silver Lake, and the Rochester Municipal Airport). The book explains Rochester's important role in the economy of southeast Minnesota.
♦ As a cooperative group project, students may brainstorm a list of places to illustrate in a book about their area and make a sketchbook.
1. Rochester (Minn.)—Description.

940.53
Smith, James P., et al. *Minnesota during World War II*. (*Roots*, Vol. 17, No. 2). Minnesota Historical Society (ISSN 0148-6659), 1989. 35p. B/W photos. (Interest level: 6+).

These diaries, essays, and publicity posters provide an account of how Minnesotans contributed to and were apprised of the war effort. The photographs draw the reader into the informative and accessible text. A memorable account that portrays the effect of war on individuals is the diary of Patricia Dooley.
♦ Students may make a two-column list that compares and contrasts the events and feelings of people during World War II with those of a more recent conflict such as "Desert Storm." Students may also interview senior adults who have memories of World War II and compare their experiences to those recorded by Smith.
1. World War II, 1939-1945—Minnesota 2. Minnesota—World War II, 1939-1945.

970.004
Clark, James E. *Ojibway Indians Coloring Book*. Illus. by Chet Kozlek. Minnesota Historical Society (0-87351-146-8), 1979. 31p. B/W illus. (Interest level: 1-5).

Through a series of sketches showing how the Ojibway Indians lived many years ago, this coloring book gives a look into the way of life, foods, artifacts, and tools of these early Minnesotans. The authentic, single-page illustrations can be used to complement the texts of other sources.
♦ Students may do research to find out more about what is pictured on a single page, make a transparency of the page, color the transparency, and use it in sharing what they have learned with other members of the class or with younger students.
1. Ojibway Indians—Social life and customs 2. Indians of North America—Minnesota.

970.004
Marsh, Carole. *Christopher Columbus Comes to Minnesota*. Gallopade (0-7933-3689-9), 1991. 36p. B/W illus. (Interest level: 4+).

In an attempt to explore the impact early white settlers had on Minnesota, the author gives an unusual perspective that is most effective when used with other

materials and discussed as a whole. The book contains a bibliography but no footnotes. There are creative activities and discussion items that a teacher could use to encourage students to think about how white settlements affected the Native Americans in Minnesota.
♦ The class could write a play or story addressing both Native American and white views on early settlements.
1. Indians of North America—Minnesota—History.

970.004
Stan, Susan. *The Ojibway*. Rourke (0-86625-381-5), 1989. 31p. Color photos and illus. (Interest level: 2-6).

Clear photos, graphs, and a concise text provide insight into the life of the Ojibway Indians from before the arrival of white people to the present.
♦ Students may look for newspaper or magazine articles about contemporary life of Ojibway and other northern Minnesota Indians. Discussion topics could include relationships between the tribal reservation government and the rest of the community and the possibilities for Indians' achieving economic success through industries such as tourism and gambling.
1. Ojibway Indians 2. Indians of North America.

973.0497
Brooks, Barbara. *The Sioux*. Rourke (0-86625-382-3), 1989. 31p. B/W and Color photos and illus. (Interest level: 2-6).

This brief text introduces different groups of Sioux Indians, the buffalo economy, and changes in the Indians' life with the arrival of white people. The author includes Minnesota history through the discussion of the 1862 Sioux uprising and a chapter on Chief Red Cloud. Colorful illustrations and photographs help make the book appealing for younger students.
♦ Students could draw maps that show the displacement and movement of the Sioux from early times through the Wounded Knee Massacre. Young people may also research current newspapers or magazines to learn how many Minnesota Sioux are achieving economic success.
1. Dakota Indians 2. Teton Indians 3. Indians of North America—Minnesota—History.

973.91
Hull, William H. *The Dirty Thirties*. Stanton (0-939330-03-2), 1989. 262p. B/W photos. (Interest level: 5+).

The brief remembrances of people who lived through the Depression of the 1930s (as told during their later years) give a picture of the spirit of the survivors. They describe black dust storms, heat that burst thermometers, blinding blizzards, drought, and the struggle to find food. These vignettes of life, many of which are from Minnesotans, are excellent for reading aloud and discussing.

♦ Students may pretend there was a time warp and that, as a result, a family who lived through the Depression reappears in the 1990s. Students may role-play or write scenes describing this family as they go to a supermarket or a shopping center.
1. United States—History—1919-1933 2. Depressions, Economic—1929—Personal narratives.

976.4
Wolf, Bernard. *In This Proud Land: The Story of a Mexican American Family*. Lippincott (0-397-31815-4), 1978. 96p. B/W photos. (Interest level: 4+).

This story of one extended migrant family depicts the way of life, needs, ambitions, joys, and problems of Mexican Americans who work in Texas in the winter and migrate to work in the sugar beet fields of Minnesota in the summer. The photos graphically reflect their struggles and their dignity.
♦ After researching migrant workers, students could role-play the Hernandez family deciding whether they should stay in Minnesota all year or migrate back and forth. In making their decision they could consider such factors as availability of jobs, potential salary, schooling for the children, housing, weather conditions, cost of travel, language differences, and prejudice encountered.
1. Mexican Americans—Social conditions 2. Migrant labor—Minnesota 3. Migrant labor—Texas.

977
Martin, Janet and Todnem, Allen. *Cream and Bread*. Redbird (0-9613437-0-2), 1984. 128p. B/W illus. (Interest level: 4+).

These reminiscences of bygone days in rural Scandinavian homes cover all of the Midwest. The traditions, anecdotes, slang, and recipes make this a fun journey back in time and provide insight into Minnesota's Scandinavian population.
♦ Students might research the traditions, slang words, and jokes, discerning which have been assimilated into other ethnic and cultural groups. Their findings could lead to a discussion of whether the United States is really a "melting pot" or a "salad bowl."
1. Norwegian Americans—Middle West 2. Scandinavian Americans—Social life and customs.

977.02
Merrick, George Byron. *Old Times on the Upper Mississippi: The Recollections of a Steamboat Pilot from 1854-1863*. Minnesota Historical Society (0-87351-204-9), 1987. 323p. B/W photos and illus. (Interest level: 6-8).

First published in 1909, the book includes chapters on topics such as engines, knowledge of the river, piloting, Indians, wolves, river towns, and gambling. Although it is an adult book, the short chapters make it appealing to capable students for leisure reading or research.

♦ This work offers young people the opportunity to practice note-taking skills with an original source.
1. Steamboats—Mississippi River 2. Mississippi River Valley—History 3. Pilots and pilotage—Mississippi River—Biography 4. Frontier and pioneer life—Mississippi River Valley.

977.6
Bray, Edmund C. *A Million Years in Minnesota*. 3rd ed. North Central Publishing (No ISBN), 1962. 49p. B/W and Color photos and illus. (Interest level: 4+).

Accepted interpretations and theories about the formation of Minnesota's physical features are included in this book. Many maps and photos help to relate the geology of today to that of prehistoric times.
♦ Students may write a futuristic story such as "When the Glacier Came Back" or "Return of the Ice Age." They may also map changes in their own area for any given period of time or draw a series of maps showing the changes through the years within a 50-mile radius of their home.
1. Minnesota—History 2. Geology—Minnesota.

977.6
Carley, Kenneth. *The Sioux Uprising of 1862*. Minnesota Historical Society (0-87351-103-4 pbk), 1976. 80p. B/W photos and illus. (Interest level: 4-8).

This brief but detailed and readable account chronicles an event that helped further the decline of the Sioux nation in Minnesota. Both Native American and white viewpoints are introduced; numerous photos and drawings extend the student's understanding of a complex situation. Information on prominent individuals, such as Chief Little Crow or Henry Sibley, is especially helpful.
♦ This book is most suitable for students doing research on Minnesota history in that it provides ample opportunity for students to apply correct research and note-taking skills.
1. Dakota Indians—Wars, 1862-1865.

977.6
Carpenter, Allan. *The New Enchantment of Minnesota*. Childrens Press (0-516-04123-1), 1978. 96p. Color photos and illus. (Interest level: 4-7).

This book is a wealth of information that covers Minnesota's history as well as present-day geology, politics, cultures, and education. Also presented are legends, quotes, and stories to add personal interest.
♦ By making posters, conducting debates before an imaginary legislature, or giving speeches to the masses, students may portray the Twin Cities' rivalry for the state capital. Another activity could be role-playing specific events (e.g., a cornhusking bee, preparation for going to fight in the Civil War, the celebration when Minnesota became a territory or state, or moving to the new land).
1. Minnesota.

977.6
The Dakota in Minnesota. (Videocassette). Minnesota Historical Society, 1973. VHS 1/2", Color, (12 min.). $5, rental. (Interest level: 5-8).

The displacement of the Dakota Indians is chronicled, beginning with changes made to their lifestyle during their seventeenth-century interactions with French traders in northern Minnesota and concluding with their eventual defeat at Wounded Knee in 1890. The video portrays the Dakota sympathetically in the brief explanations of the imposition of the white people's way of life on the Dakota, the 1862 Sioux uprising, and the role of Indian leaders such as Sitting Bull and Little Crow.
♦ After viewing the video students may mark the areas to which the Dakota were relocated as whites claimed their land in northern Minnesota, and they may discuss how settlers imposed their lifestyle on the Dakota. The *Minnesota Map* (see Minnesota—Nonfiction, 917.7) may be used for this activity. Students may want to discuss how displacement on reservations has led to problems for Native Americans today.
1. Dakota Indians 2. Indians of North America—Minnesota.

977.6
des Jarlait, Patrick. *Patrick des Jarlait: The Story of an American Indian Artist*. Lerner (0-8225-0642-4), 1975. 57p. Color illus. (Interest level: 5+).

Des Jarlait's autobiography shows how growing up on the Red Lake Indian Reservation in northern Minnesota greatly influenced his art. The dignity of Chippewa traditions, the natural beauty of the Red Lake area, and the artist's talents are all clearly portrayed in this account of a nationally known painter.
♦ To further their understanding of the Chippewa, some students may research the Chippewa traditions captured on canvas by the artist and share the stories behind the paintings with the class. Other students may draw or paint scenes depicting customs of their own families or heritage.
1. Indians of North America—Biography 2. Ojibway Indians—Biography.

977.6
Fairbanks, Evelyn. *Days of Rondo*. Minnesota Historical Society (0-87351-255-3), 1990. 182p. B/W photos. (Interest level: 5-8).

The author recalls growing up in St. Paul's black Rondo neighborhood during the 1930s and 1940s. Each of the 17 chapters depicts a different aspect of life (e.g., Daddy, Mama, visits to the South, friends, death, church, and camp), and each is suitable for reading aloud to students as well as for individual or cooperative group learning. The work offers readers and listeners the opportunity to become aware of the past treatment of African Americans and to compare and contrast it with the experiences of minorities today.

♦ The class may write a mini-neighborhood recollection with each student depicting one aspect of life or one person. Students could write impressions as Fairbanks did.

1. African Americans—Saint Paul (Minn.)—Biography 2. African Americans—Saint Paul (Minn.)—Social life and customs 3. Rondo—Saint Paul (Minn.)—Biography.

977.6
Finsand, Mary Jane. *The Town that Moved.* Illus. by Reg Sandland. Carolrhoda (0-8761-4200-5), 1983. 48p. Color illus. (Interest level: 2-5).

This story describes how the houses, office buildings, and stores of a small town in Minnesota were moved to another location when iron ore was discovered in the ground beneath the original town. This book is simply written, yet it contains a number of interesting facts. The unusual but true story will intrigue young people.

♦ After reading this book, students may discuss what would be involved in moving their town now. Would it be more difficult to move a town today than at the time of the book's setting? Young people should justify their responses.

1. Hibbing (Minn.)—History 2. Minnesota—History.

977.6
Gilman, Rhoda R. *Northern Lights: The Story of Minnesota's Past*. Minnesota Historical Society (0-87351-241-3), 1989. 231p. B/W and Color illus. (Interest level: 5-8)

———. *Northern Lights: Going to the Sources.* Minnesota Historical Society (0-87351-242-1), 1989. 215p. B/W and Color photos. (Interest level: 5-7).

These companion volumes with many primary sources may be used as part of a comprehensive curriculum for grades 5-7. With a teachers' guide, they make an excellent resource for students to use in studying the whys and hows of history rather than just the whats. In particular, *Going to the Sources* presents some excellent thinking activities for students.

♦ Each student may select a different ethnic group in Minnesota and write a diary entry of one of its members showing imaginary reachions to the various changes (modes of transportation, electronics, education, etc.) encountered over a 30-year time period.

1. Minnesota—History.

977.6
Holmquist, June D., ed. *They Chose Minnesota: A Survey of the State's Ethnic Groups.* Minnesota Historical Society (0-87351-231-6), 1981. 614p. B/W photos and illus. (Interest level: 6+).

Background information on 60 immigrant groups (why and how they came, where they settled, their problems and accomplishments) from the earliest known Indians to the Indochinese of the 1980s is found in this thoroughly researched account.

♦ Students may research their own ancestry in other library media resources or family records, through interviews with older members of their family, or by visits to the nearest historical society or county courthouse. They may role-play the adventures of an ethnic group coming to the United States during any time period (e.g., Vietnamese during the 1970s), including reasons for coming and reactions to what was already in place at the time of their arrival.

1. Minnesota—Ethnic groups 2. Minnesota—Social life and customs.

977.6
Johnson, Eldon. *Prehistoric Peoples of Minnesota.* 3rd ed. Minnesota Historical Society (0-87351-223-5), 1988. 35p. B/W photos. (Interest level: 5-8).

Charts, sketches, photographs, and text about archeological findings help piece together an understanding of very early cultures in what is now Minnesota. Although first published more than 30 years ago, this revised edition sheds new light on the subject. It is a fascinating and worthy reference for anyone from the mildly interested to the avid archeologist.

♦ Indian mounds are found throughout Minnesota. Students may research Minnesota Indian mounds: What was their purpose? What and who were buried there? What myths or tales are associated with mounds? How are mounds protected now?

1. Indians of North America—Minnesota—Antiquities 2. Minnesota—Antiquities.

977.6
Johnston, Patricia Condon. *Minnesota: Portrait of the Land and Its People.* American Geographic (0-938314-36-X pbk), 1987. 103p. Color photos. (Interest level: 5+).

This resource includes the geography and the history of the six major regions that make up the state. Effective photographs give the armchair traveler a realistic trip around Minnesota, providing a wealth of information for anyone studying the state.

♦ Students may stage a state fair with different groups representing each of the six regions. They could present travel brochures/videos to advertise a particular region, bring goods representative of a region for "trading," and role-play notable people of that region.

1. Minnesota—Description 2. Minnesota—Geography.

977.6
Johnston, Patricia Condon. *Minnesota's Irish.* Johnston (0-942934-07-5), 1984. 92p. B/W illus. (Interest level: 7+).

This informative source describes how the Irish contributed to the character and spirit of Minnesota

throughout its history. Rarely published topics covered in this book include writers, boxers, farm settlers, rogues, and religious leaders.
♦ Young people may make up a computer database of nationalities and ethnic groups represented in their community. They may consider: Where did they come from? How long have they been in the area? Are they maintaining traditional celebrations?
1. Irish Americans—Minnesota 2. Nationalism—Irish Americans—Minnesota 3. Minnesota—Nationalism.

977.6
Marsh, Carole. *Minnesota Dingbats: A Super Fun Book of Facts, Games, Stories, Poems, Riddles, Math Quizzes, Activities and More.* Gallopade (0-7933-3842-5), 1991. 36p. B/W illus. (Interest level: 3+).

Challenging brain puzzles offer an entertaining approach to information about Minnesota's history, motto, products, cities, people, places to visit, and statistics. The work is also available on a computer disk and includes permission to print out activity pages for each student.
♦ Students could make their own puzzles, brainteasers, or coded messages dealing with some aspect of Minnesota.
1. Word games—Minnesota 2. Minnesota—Teaching aids and devices.

977.6
Meier, Peg. *Coffee Made Her Insane and Other Nuggets from Old Minnesota Newspapers.* Neighbors (0-933387-01-6), 1988. 314p. B/W illus. (Interest level: 5+).

This collection of old newspaper clippings offers a unique way of exploring history by giving insight into the thoughts, actions, and feelings of both well-known and lesser-known Minnesotans. All readers should be able to find articles, ads, or bits of information to pique their interest.
♦ Each student could find a present-day newspaper item to compare and contrast with a similar one from Meier's collection, addressing such topics as ideas, culture, values, conveniences, language, education, newspaper writing style, or roles of women and children. The two newspaper accounts, along with a written comparison, could be posted on the bulletin board.
1. Minnesota—Social life and customs—History
2. Clippings (Books, newspapers, etc.)—Minnesota.

977.6
Minnesota State Capitol. (Videocassette). Script by Jeanne Emrich. Narrated by Leonard Bart. Minnesota Government Learning Center, Osseo TV Media Productions, 1988. VHS 1/2", Color, (12 min.). Available from Minnesota Historical Society. $26.95. (Interest level: 4-12).

This video blends history and current information on the workings of Minnesota government and the building in which government business is accomplished to aptly show the pride of Minnesotans in their government. This video tour through the current State Capitol Building acquaints the viewer with the many nuances of Minnesota's government, yesterday and today.
♦ Before a field trip to the State Capitol, Minnesota students could view this video, listing a number of items that catch their interest. Then, during the visit, they could look for these items in the paintings, carvings, and displays and, if possible, take slides or pictures of the item. When they return, they could research the story behind the item, then share it with the class. Students in other states may compare and contrast their own state capitol with Minnesota's and explore the reasons for differences and similarities.
1. Minnesota—State Capitol (St. Paul, Minn.) 2. Minnesota—Politics and government.

977.6
Moore, David L. *Dark Sky, Dark Land: Stories of the Hmong Boy Scouts of Troop 100.* Tessera (0-9623029-0-2), 1989. 191p. B/W illus. (Interest level: 5-8).

In this book scoutmaster Moore has collected the oral histories of Hmong boy scouts in his troop. The histories, illustrated with portrait drawings, primarily describe the boys' lives in Laos, their escape to Thailand, and their life in refugee camps. Each chapter also presents glimpses of the boys' life in Minneapolis and experiences at summer camp. These incredible, exciting tales of courage, survival, and adjustment to a new culture provide important information about one of Minnesota's growing minority groups.
♦ After having heard the stories read aloud, students may discuss the challenges these boys faced. In some schools, students may have the opportunity to interview Hmong classmates.
1. Hmong-American teenage boys—Minneapolis (Minn.)—Biography 2. Boy Scouts—Minneapolis (Minn.)—Biography 3. Minneapolis (Minn.)—Biography.

977.6
Morris, Lucy Leavenworth Wilder, ed. *Old Rail Fence Corners: Frontier Tales Told by Minnesota Pioneers.* Minnesota Historical Society (0-87351-108-5), 1976. 344p. B/W illus. (Interest level: 6+).

This excellent source for learning history from those who lived it recounts authentic incidents of life on the Minnesota frontier. Although the small print may discourage younger readers from a page-by-page perusal, the comprehensive index will lead readers to information on a variety of interests.
♦ To understand better the changes in Minnesota's life and culture, students could select one or two modern conveniences that are used for a specific common activity (e.g., dishwasher, shampoo, hair drier, vac-

uum cleaner, or microwave) and then research how the same activity was done in frontier days.
1. Frontier and pioneer life—Minnesota 2. Minnesota—History, Local.

977.6
Northwest Passage: The Story of Grand Portage. (Videocassette). Produced by Slavko Nowytski. Minnesota Historical Society, 1979. VHS 1/2", Color, (14 min.). $36.95. (Interest level: 6+).

This beautiful production of the history of an important fur trading area uses letters, journals, and papers of the Northwest Company employees and fur traders for the narration. It features artifacts and archival reproductions of clothing and homes of Minnesota's early residents. Renditions of authentic voyageur songs add spice to the account of problems, treaties, bargainings, and celebrations of Grand Portage, Minnesota.
♦ Small groups may speculate which invention that has come about since the fur trade era would have been the most useful to the fur traders. Each group may come to a consensus and report to the whole class.
1. Fur trade—Great Lakes region—History 2. Minnesota—History.

977.6
Porter, A. P. *Minnesota.* Lerner (0-8225-2718-9), 1992. 72p. Color photos. (Interest level: 3-6).

This look at Minnesota's geography, history, and daily life is brief but upbeat. The photography is vivid, and the book provides an excellent glimpse of contemporary Minnesota. Facts-at-a-glance, the glossary, and information about famous Minnesotans, such as Charles Lindbergh and Prince, help make the book appealing to those who may not be interested in research.
♦ Students may use the book for research or for browsing and exploring ideas for projects. Working in cooperative groups, students may create additional pages on other famous Minnesotans.
1. Minnesota—History 2. Minnesota—Description.

977.6
Reid, Robert L. *Picturing Minnesota 1936-1943: Photographs from the Farm Security Administration.* Minnesota Historical Society (0-87351-248-0), 1989. 200p. B/W photos. (Interest level: 3+).

This collection of photos documents the challenges of Minnesota conflict and change during the Great Depression and World War II. The photos cover life on farms and in small towns as well as large cities, contrasting poverty and prosperity, joy and sorrow, and optimism and pessimism. The photos tell a vivid story in themselves, with very little text needed.
♦ In an activity that combines creative writing and historical understanding, students may select any one photo and create a fictional story or poem about the people or scene shown, trying to capture the emotion and mood of the photo and times.
1. Minnesota—Description—1858-1950 2. Minnesota—Social life and customs—Pictorial works.

977.6
Stein, R. Conrad. *Minnesota.* Childrens Press (0-516-00469-7), 1991. (America the Beautiful Series). 144p. B/W and Color photos and illus. (Interest level: 3-8).

The easily accessible information in this work addresses Minnesota's geography, history, people, government, economy, and recreation. Folklore, anecdotes, first-person accounts, and literary excerpts enliven the factual presentation. A companion teachers' manual is filled with "suggested activities, teaching strategies, and skill-focused lessons to help students apply their new knowledge and insights."
♦ Young people may make up a geography wheel about a specific area showing the five themes of geography: (1) location, (2) place, (3) relationships, (4) movement, and (5) region.
1. Minnesota—History 2. Minnesota—Description.

977.6
Swenson, Grace Stagberg. *From the Ashes: The Story of the Hinckley Fire of 1894.* Rev. ed. North Star Press (0-8783-9047-2), 1988. (Interest level: 6-8).

Extensive photographs, drawings, and reproductions from newspapers vividly recount the 1894 fire that destroyed Hinckley, Minnesota, as well as the rescue attempts and the rebuilding process. The book is especially useful for research and may appeal to the same students who read William Hull's *All Hell Broke Loose* (*see* Minnesota—Nonfiction—977.7).
♦ Students may write a newspaper account of the story or produce a video news show about the fire, being sure to role-play interviews with survivors. If any students have visited the Hinckley Fire Museum, they may tell the others about it.
1. Hinckley (Minn.)—Fire, 1894.

977.6
Taylor, David V. *Black Minnesotans.* (*Roots*, Vol. 17, No. 1). Minnesota Historical Society (ISSN 0148-6659), 1989. 43p. B/W photos. (Interest level: 6+).

Although a minority in numbers, the African-American population has played an important role in the history of Minnesota as portrayed in this issue of a periodical of the Minnesota Historical Society. Personal memoirs, essays, and historical accounts are enhanced by the many photographs and illustrations that supplement the text.
♦ In groups or individually, students may write and illustrate a simple story based on the information about traditions, lifestyles, customs, and accomplishments of the people in this resource. An empha-

sis should be placed on capturing the feelings of the people and the times.

1. Minnesota—History—Blacks 2. African Americans—Minnesota.

997.6

Thompson, Kathleen. *Minnesota*. Raintree (0-86514-466-4), 1987. (Portrait of America Series). 48p. B/W and Color photos. (Interest level: 3-6).

The problems and benefits of living in Minnesota are apparent through discussions of the state's history, economy, culture, and future. The work includes a state chronology, pertinent statistics, and maps. The many quotations and easy reading style are appropriate for this age level.

♦ The class could listen to excerpts from live broadcasts of Garrison Keillor's "A Prairie Home Companion" on American Public Radio, for example, "News from Lake Woebegone: Spring, Summer, Fall, Winter," (Minnesota Public Radio, 1983).

1. Minnesota—History 2. Minnesota—Description.

977.6

Wheeler, Robert C., et al. *Voices from the Rapids: An Underwater Search for Fur Trade Artifacts 1960-73*. Minnesota Historical Society (0-87351-086-0), 1975. 115p. B/W photos and illus. (Interest level: 7+).

Based on the Quetico-Superior Underwater Research Project, this work relates the experiences, dangers, and discoveries of scuba divers as they pursue fur trade archaeology. The discovered artifacts reveal much historical information about the fur trade that was part of Minnesota's early history. Although somewhat laborious except for readers with an avid interest in archeology, this book is useful for research.

♦ The class may create a time capsule containing contemporary objects that students bring from home. They can include brief descriptions of each item and the significance it has today. If local ordinances permit, the time capsule could be buried and a map of its location left in the school media center for the future.

1. Minnesota—Antiquities 2. Fur trade—Minnesota 3. Ontario—Antiquities 4. Fur trade—Ontario.

977.604

Meier, Peg. *Bring Warm Clothes: Letters and Photos from Minnesota's Past*. Design by Michael Carroll. Minneapolis Tribune (0-932272-06-1), 1981. 332p. B/W photos and illus. (Interest level: 5+).

This collection of original writings by individuals from Minnesota's past provides a detailed and very readable account of ordinary people's lives. One can find stories, thoughts, dreams, and records of deeds and happenings, along with thoughtful insights that make history come alive.

♦ Students may choose any person mentioned in the book, research the time in which this person lived, and then create an imaginary story of this person's life. The class might have a Minnesota history day in which students come dressed as their "characters."

1. Minnesota—Social life and customs 2. Minnesota—Biography 3. Minnesota—Description.

977.66

Marsh, Carole. *Minnesota Bandits, Bushwackers, Outlaws, Crooks, Devils, Ghosts, Desperados, Heroes, Heroines, Rogues, and Other Assorted and Sundry Characters*. Gallopade (0-7933-0623-X), 1990. 35p. B/W illus. (Interest level: 5+).

The book's title is an apt description of its contents. Although the entire work does not specifically focus on Minnesota, the riddles, jokes, math problems, and suggested learning activities may inspire young people to do further research.

♦ Students may search for more information on specific characters or make up "wanted" posters that give some historical perspective on the individuals they have selected.

1. Eccentrics and eccentricities—Minnesota 2. Robbers and outlaws—Minnesota.

977.67

Smith, Robert Tighe. *Minneapolis-St. Paul: The Cities, Their People*. American Geographic (0-938314-47-5), 1988. 103p. Color photos. (Interest level: 4+).

Colorful writing, light reading, postcardlike photographs, and plentiful information make this book an excellent resource for classrooms and media centers. It covers the cities' history, economy, people, and politics, and the impact of Minnesota weather.

♦ Young people may discuss what makes a city or town a good place to live. They could compare demographic information on Minneapolis-St. Paul with other cities of comparable size. Then, they may write a description of their ideal city.

1. Minneapolis (Minn.)—Description 2. St. Paul (Minn.)—Description 3. Minneapolis (Minn.)—History 4. St. Paul (Minn.)—History.

977.7

Hull, William H. *All Hell Broke Loose*. Stanton Publications Services (0-939330-01-6), 1985. 236p. B/W photos. (Interest level: 5-8).

Through extensive interviews with the author, Minnesotans share their recollections and experiences as survivors of the 1940 Armistice Day blizzard. Intriguing titles ("Burning Anything to Keep the Baby Alive"), brief stories, and the sense of adventure and survival make this appealing reading even for reluctant readers.

♦ Students may interview someone who experienced the Armistice Day blizzard or another fierce storm. Using a desktop publishing program, students may

prepare a newspaper article based on their favorite account of a storm.
1. Minnesota—Blizzard, 1940 2. Blizzards—Minnesota.

977.76
Hall, Steve. *Fort Snelling: Colossus of the Wilderness.* Minnesota Historical Society (0-87351-208-1), 1987. (Minnesota Historical Sites Pamphlet Series). 44p. B/W and Color photos and illus. (Interest level: 5+).

This account of the first military post in the Northwest describes its construction, the life of the people within its walls, and its importance in the history of Minnesota and the United States. Illustrations deftly highlight significant people and events, and the style of writing makes this book very readable.
♦ Using computer desktop publishing software, groups of students may write and publish a newspaper that reflects the events during various time periods in the fort's history. Interviews, articles, jokes, ads, classified notices, and obituary items may be included.
1. Fort Snelling (Minn.)—History 2. Fortification—Minnesota—History.

977.76
Miller, Dana. *The Iron Range in Transition.* (*Roots*, Vol. 17, No. 3). Minnesota Historical Society (ISSN 0148-6659), 1989. 39p. B/W photos and illus. (Interest level: 6+).

From its flourishing economy of the past to its depressed status today, the Iron Range is realistically depicted in this issue of a Minnesota Historical Society periodical. The very readable text covers the region's history, its present, and a projection into its future.
♦ Young people may make a time line (including future projections) of the iron industry in Minnesota.
1. Iron Range region (Minn.) 2. Mines and mineral resources—Minnesota 3. Iron industry—Minnesota.

Biography

920
Diary: Asian Minnesotans. (Videocassette). KTCA, 1991. VHS 1/2", Color, (45 min.). Available from the Minnesota Department of Education, Learning Resources Unit. Free. (Interest level: 6+).

Asian Minnesotans portrayed in this film came from a number of different countries in different decades, but they faced similar challenges in living in the United States while still maintaining their own culture. This thought-provoking film clearly shows the feelings of young children, teenagers, and both young and older adults, all of whom struggled to deal with their multicultural identity in communities that were not always receptive to those who were different.
♦ A discussion on the similar emotions of all human beings when facing new and different experiences would be a good follow-up to this video. The discussion could lead into the causes and effects of prejudice, and students could examine some familiar stereotypes.
1. Minnesota—Biography 2. Asians—Minnesota—Biography.

920
Diary: Black Minnesotans. (Videocassette). KTCA, 1991. VHS 1/2", Color, (58 min.). Available from the Minnesota Department of Education, Learning Resources Unit. Free. (Interest level: 5-8).

African-American Minnesotans, including the sheriff of Cook County, a Minneapolis entrepreneur interested in education, and an African-American family in Faribault, share largely positive views of being African American in Minnesota. In their interviews they stress the values of hard work, education, respect, common sense, and family. The relatively slow pace of the video and lengthy discussions make this work most suitable for showing in small segments.
♦ After viewing the video, students may discuss the values and attitudes reflected.
1. Minnesota—Biography 2. African Americans—Minnesota—Biography.

920
Diary: Hispanic Minnesotans. (Videocassette). KTCA, 1991. VHS 1/2", Color, (58 min.). Available from Minnesota Department of Education, Learning Resources Unit. Free. (Interest level: 6-8).

Interviews with Hispanic individuals who live in urban and greater Minnesota reveal how they adapt to life in Minnesota and work to keep their culture alive. The video is best suited for mature students.
♦ Students may find this most meaningful if they view it in sections. For example, the segment on a businessman may be useful to help break down stereotypes.
1. Minnesota—Biography 2. Hispanic Americans—Minnesota—Biography.

920
Diary: Native American Minnesotans. (Videocassette). KTCA, 1991. VHS 1/2", Color, (36 min.). Available from Minnesota Department of Education, Learning Resources Unit. Free. (Interest level: 6-8).

Interviews with two male Native American Minnesotans in greater Minnesota reveal how they have struggled with their identity and chosen to return to their cultural roots in order to teach their children by example. Another interview focuses on a female Native American working to encourage economic development in urban Minneapolis. The video will be of greatest interest to mature students.
♦ Students may compare Native American ceremonies and discuss why rituals are important to some individuals as a way of maintaining culture while others

have chosen to preserve a way of life through focus on economic development.
1. Indians of North America—Minnesota—Biography.

92 Blacklock, Les
Minnesota Living History: Les Blacklock. (Videocassette). Osseo Public Schools, 1980. VHS 1/2", Color, (25 min.). (Interest level: 6-8).

Noted naturalist and photographer Les Blacklock is portrayed both at work in northern Minnesota and through interviews. Biographical background information, including how he trained himself, is combined with Blacklock's views of the natural world as a place that should be preserved and shared with others.
♦ Students may view this as a companion piece to Craig Blacklock's *The Geese of Silver Lake (see* Minnesota—Nonfiction—598.4). Young people may then discuss perseverance, nature, philosophy, and commitment to a goal.
1. Blacklock, Les—Biography 2. Photographers—Minnesota.

92 Dahl, Borghild
The Immigrant Experience: Borghild Dahl. (Videocassette). Produced by Lyn Lacy. Heritage Productions, n.d. VHS 1/2", Color and B/W, (30 min.). (Interest level: 4-8).

Borghild Dahl's life is chronicled from birth until her death at age 94. The video emphasizes how through self-reliance and determination she functioned as a student, teacher, author, and speaker even though she was almost blind since birth and eventually became totally blind. This video introduces both Dahl's writings and Minneapolis life in the early twentieth century. It is especially useful for noting the accomplishments of women and the visually impaired.
♦ Students may watch the video as a source of information about an author or as background for discussion about overcoming disabilities.
1. Dahl, Borghild 2. Blind 3. Minneapolis (Minn.)—History.

92 Eastman, Charles
Eastman, Charles. *Indian Boyhood.* Dover (0-486-22037-0), 1971. 247p. B/W photos and illus. (Interest level: 5-8).

A full-blooded Sioux Indian, who later became a doctor and writer, Charles Eastman describes his childhood in Minnesota and his experiences as a warrior in the 1870s and 1880s. He explains how he loved the Indian life but eventually adopted the white man's ways. Excerpts from this original source material are excellent for reading aloud to students.
♦ Students may draw pictures to illustrate Eastman's accounts of activities such as hunting, discuss what they learned about Indian life, or write about how they would cope with a choice between two cultures.
1. Eastman, Charles 2. Santee Indians.

92 Flat Mouth, Ojibway Chief
Lund, Duane R. *Minnesota's Chief Flat Mouth of Leech Lake.* Nordell Graphic Communications (No ISBN), 1983. 96p. B/W photos and illus. Available from Adventure Publications. (Interest level: 5-9).

This tribute to one of the most influential Indian leaders of the area now called Minnesota tells the story of Chief Flat Mouth's life, which spanned the transitions between the "old ways" of the Indians and the coming of the white people. The factual, nonemotional tone clearly relates his relationship with the white people and with other Indian tribes.
♦ Small groups of students may select a Minnesota Indian chief, such as Flat Mouth, Little Crow, Hole-in-the-Day, Great Marten, or Yellow Hair, and recount how each influenced the events of history. Posters, bulletin boards, or a variety of oral reports with visuals could be used to share the information gathered.
1. Flat Mouth, Chief 2. Indians of North America—Minnesota.

92 Hill, James J.
Empire Builder James J. Hill. (Videocassette). Minnesota Historical Society, 1982. VHS 1/2" and 3/4" U-Matic, Brown/White and color, (11 min.). $5, rental. (Interest level: 5-8).

Historical brown-and-white photographs recount the life and dreams of railroad builder James J. Hill. Historical information about St. Paul, the building of a railroad across the northern plains, and the era of unrestrained competition followed by problems with the U.S. Supreme Court are highlighted. Hill is romantically portrayed as an achiever of the American dream and a philanthropist.
♦ Students may engage in research, or the media specialist or teacher may provide background information on the American dream and governmental regulation of monopolies. Then the class may discuss the issues involved. Students may also research the impact of the railroad on the development of the West and Minnesota.
1. Hill, James J. 2. Railroads—History.

92 Humphrey, Hubert H.
Hubert H. Humphrey: Here's My Hand. (Videocassette). Produced by the Hubert H. Humphrey Institute of Public Affairs. Quest, 1989. VHS 1/2", B/W and Color, (14 min.). $29.95. (Interest level: 5-8).

Through Hubert Humphrey's speeches and the narrator's description, the video reveals this Minnesotan's belief that each of us can make a difference in the broadening of American opportunity through a commitment to civil rights. The video also briefly explains Humphrey's political role in education and nuclear disarmament. The brevity of the video makes it ideal for assisting young viewers in the development of listening, viewing, and note-taking skills.

♦ After sharing the video, young people may discuss Humphrey's role in national politics. The video can also be used to introduce a discussion about past and current civil rights issues.
1. Humphrey, Hubert H.

92 Kirtland, William
Kirtland, William. *Billy: A Story of a Minnesota Boy Growing Up*. Idaho Book & School Supply (No ISBN), 1985. 210p. B/W illus. (Interest level: 5-8).

Billy nostalgically remembers life in Bemidji and Littlefork, Minnesota, during the 1930s and 1940s, a time when young boys had a good day by making nine cents selling lemonade, going to the county fair, seeing a new calf, gathering scrap iron, or traveling by train. Although each chapter stands alone, recounting a specific incident, the entire work is suitable for reading aloud. Billy's mischievousness and humor add to the appeal.

♦ Students may compare Billy's childhood, adolescence, and family life to their own. Students may be encouraged to keep a journal so they can write their own autobiographical remembrances.
1. Kirtland, William 2. Bemidji (Minn.) 3. Littlefork (Minn.).

92 Lindbergh, Charles A.
Collins, David R. *Charles Lindbergh: Hero Pilot*. Illus. by Victor Mays. Chelsea (0-7910-1417-7), 1991. 80p. B/W illus. (Interest level: 2-4).

This brief biography emphasizes Lindbergh's youth in Little Falls, Minnesota, and his early interest in mechanics and airplanes. His later accomplishments as an aviator and his concern for the environment are briefly mentioned. This work fulfills the need for easy-to-read information about a famous Minnesotan and is especially suitable for young children. However, it is too brief to be of much value as a research tool.

♦ Readers could list new facts they learned about Lindbergh from this book and discuss how Lindbergh's childhood interests led to lifelong accomplishments.
1. Lindbergh, Charles A. 2. Air pilots.

92 Lindbergh, Charles A.
Lindbergh, Charles A. *A Boyhood on the Upper Mississippi: A Reminiscent Letter*. Minnesota Historical Society Press (0-8735-1069-0), 1972. 50p. B/W photos. (Interest level: 5-8).

In this book, written as a letter to the Minnesota Historical Society, Lindbergh describes growing up on the family farm at Little Falls. He also reflects on his father's position as a U.S. representative, his school days, his early flying, and his own limited farming experience. This book, written in 1969 and illustrated with many family photographs, fondly presents a nostalgic look at middle-class farm life in the early 1900s and is well suited for reading aloud to young students.

♦ Students may compare farm and school life of the early 1900s to that of the present. Young people who have visited the Lindbergh family home and state park could describe their experiences to the class. Others may wish to write to the Charles A. Lindbergh State Park for information about the Lindbergh family home and the park.
1. Lindbergh, Charles A. 2. Little Falls (Minn.) 3. Air pilots.

92 Lovelace, Maud Hart
Frisch, Carlienne. *"Betsy-Tacy" in Deep Valley: People and Places*. Friends of Minnesota Valley Regional Library (No ISBN), 1987. B/W photos. 58p. (Interest level: 3-6).

Inspired by her daughter, who said, "you must find out about the real characters," Carlienne Frisch provides in this booklet facts about "real-life" places mentioned in Lovelace's "Betsy-Tacy" books. Ms. Lovelace's recollections of life in early twentieth-century Mankato, Minnesota, are also included. Through this work, students can learn about the person in whose honor the annual Maud Hart Lovelace book award is given.

♦ Students could make posters of scenes from the Betsy-Tacy books, creating maps when appropriate.
1. Lovelace, Maud Hart, 1892-1980 2. Women authors—Minnesota.

92 Molter, Dorothy
Dorothy Molter: Living in the Boundary Waters. (Videocassette). Produced by J. Hadel and W. Black. Direct Cinema, 1987. VHS 1/2", Color, (42 min.). Available from the Minnesota Historical Society. $5, rental. (Interest level: 5-8).

This video, filmed from 1983 to 1986, chronicles the life of Dorothy Molter (otherwise known as the Root Beer Lady) through the seasons and provides insight into a contemporary legendary figure who was the Boundary Waters' last human resident. The Root Beer Lady reflects on learning to live in the woods, going to town to get supplies, planting flowers, enjoying the company of the 6,000 visitors who come each year, and living alone for 55 years. The video also includes interesting footage of northern Minnesota.

♦ Students can discuss what caused Dorothy Molter to be termed a living legend. They may write a paragraph that explains the differences between living alone and being lonely.
1. Molter, Dorothy 2. Boundary Waters Canoe Area (Minn.).

92 O'Meara, Walter
O'Meara, Walter. *We Made It through the Winter: A Memoir of a Northern Minnesota Boyhood*. Minnesota Historical Society (0-8735-1092-5), 1974. 128p. B/W photos. (Interest level: 6-8).

Journalist Walter O'Meara introduces life in Cloquet, Minnesota, during the early 1900s by describing

activities during each of the four seasons. His recollections of the logging industry in Cloquet and the family's methods of surviving winter are especially interesting. Descriptions of the ethnic groups that settled northern Minnesota add to an understanding of Minnesota's diverse cultures.
♦ Students may build a model of a house fortified for winter or make various layers of doll clothes as described by O'Meara.
1. Cloquet (Minn.)—History 2. Minnesota—Social life and customs 3. Journalists.

92 Paulsen, Gary
Interview with Gary Paulsen. (Videocassette). Hennepin County Library System, 1989. (The Northern Lights & Insights Minnesota Authors Series). VHS 1/2", Color, (28 min.). $14.95. (Interest level: 5-8).

This interview is part of The Northern Lights & Insights Minnesota Authors Series produced weekly on Twin Cities Regional Cable Channel 6. Paulsen discusses jobs he has had, their influence on his writing, dog racing, students' responses to him, the freedom that writers have in Minnesota, and survival techniques. Of particular significance is the importance he places on reading and the value of libraries, without which he would have become an "intellectual idiot."
♦ Librarians and teachers may use the video to reinforce the importance of reading and writing. After viewing the video students may relate aspects of Paulsen's interview to specific elements in one of his literary works such as *Popcorn Days and Buttermilk Nights* (see Minnesota—Fiction), *Tracker* (see Minnesota—Fiction), or *Woodsong* (see Minnesota—Nonfiction—796.5).
1. Paulsen, Gary 2. Authors—Minnesota.

92 Tapping, Minnie Ellingson
Tapping, Minnie Ellingson. *Eighty Years at the Gopher Hole: The Saga of a Minnesota Pioneer 1867-1947.* Exposition Press, 1958 (out of print). 228p. (Interest level: 7+).

These memoirs give a detailed picture of the daily life and thoughts of one pioneer woman during Minnesota's years of expansion. Although too detailed for total reading by elementary students, there are thoughtful chapters that would be interesting if shared aloud and discussed in class.
♦ Young people may make a pieced paper quilt, with each student responsible for showing one memorable event in the author's life. If available, a computer drawing program may be used to print out the pieces in color. Then students can piece them together for display.
1. Minnesota—History 2. Frontier and pioneer life—Minnesota.

Fiction

Bauer, Marion Dane. *Face to Face.* Clarion (0-395-55440-3), 1991. 176p. (Interest level: 5-8).

Hoping to escape bullies at school and his stepfather, Michael, a teenage boy living on a farm in southeastern Minnesota, goes to Colorado to visit his father. He faces the challenges of a father with whom he cannot communicate and a dangerous white-water rafting adventure. Although only one-third of this novel is set in Minnesota, it does depict a portion of greater Minnesota not generally portrayed in fiction and shows that urban and rural children face the same problems.
♦ Students can locate the Root River on a map and research more about this unglaciated part of the state. They may also discuss how Michael could have handled his problems differently.
1. Fear—Fiction 2. Fathers and sons—Fiction 3. Rafting (Sports)—Fiction 4. Farm life—Minnesota—Fiction.

Bellairs, John. *The Dark Secret of Weatherend.* Dial (0-8037-0074-1), 1984. 182p. (Interest level: 5-7).

Anthony of Hoosac (Winona), Minnesota, and his friend, the city librarian, explore an old mansion, travel throughout Winona County, and try to stop an evil wizard from destroying the world by changing the weather. This lighthearted yet suspenseful mystery and adventure will appeal to young mystery and supernatural fans. Hoosac is a fictional name for Winona; some readers will enjoy seeing Minnesota place names in print.
♦ Readers familiar with locations and buildings described in the novel can compare these descriptions to the real places. Other readers may write their own ending or adventure for the book.
1. Supernatural—Fiction 2. Librarians—Fiction 3. Minnesota—Fiction.

Calvert, Patricia. *When Morning Comes.* Scribner (0-684-19105-9), 1989. 153p. (Interest level: 7-10).

Feeling rejected by everyone who has ever meant anything to her, a teenage girl creates a new personality when she is sent to her fourth foster home. However, she longs for others to like her for what she really is. This book, intended for more mature readers, effectively shows what patience and acceptance can do for a troubled teen.
♦ Young people may wish to compare city life and country life for teenagers in order to discuss whether it is easier to get into trouble in cities, what creates the best living situation for teens, and what should happen to teens who get into trouble.
1. Foster home care—Fiction 2. Bee culture—Fiction 3. Self-acceptance—Fiction.

Chall, Marsha Wilson. *Up North at the Cabin.* Illus. by Steve Johnson. Lothrop, Lee & Shepard (0-688-

09732-4), 1992. Unpaginated. Color illus. (Interest level: 1-5).

In this delightful story of a young girl's vacation in the Northwoods, vivid imagery helps capture the summer magic. The vibrant illustrations enhance a work that captivates young and old alike.
♦ Members of the class may draw or paint (by computer or hand) a scene from their own favorite vacation or activity.
1. Forests and forestry—Fiction 2. Vacations—Fiction.

Christgau, Alice F. *The Laugh Peddler.* Illus. by Arvis L. Stewart. Young Scott (No ISBN), 1968 (out of print). 157p. (Interest level: 3-6).

Farm family life in the early 1900s is vividly portrayed in this story of an orphaned 12 year old trying to find a place for himself in his adoptive family. Richly drawn characters come alive for the reader and give an insight into the hopes and fears of Minnesotans at the turn of the century.
♦ Students may play the role of a "laugh peddler" and bring a filled sack of goodies to try to sell to the class. Library research is necessary to determine which items could not be made on the farm but were needed by farm families. Along with the pretended auctioning of the articles, the "laugh peddler" should relate stories of the time period.
1. Minnesota—Farm life—History 2. Adoption—Fiction.

Delton, Judy. *Mystery of the Haunted Cabin.* Illus. by Anne Sibley O'Brien. Houghton Mifflin (0-395-41917-4), 1986. 128p. (Interest level: 2-6).

A vacation near a northern Minnesota lake offers three children a summer of excitement and individual growth. This fast-paced story has believable children but a sometimes unconvincing mother.
♦ Students may map the route to the lake cabin and try to determine the town near which Horseshoe Lake is located. Their decision should be justified by matching clues in the story with a study of the geography of the region. They may also enjoy researching and sharing other stories of "haunted" homes.
1. Minnesota—Fiction 2. Mystery and detective stories 3. Vacations—Fiction.

Dorner, Marjorie. *Nightmare.* Warner (0-446-35016-8), 1989. 350p. (Interest level: 6-8).

A teacher in Holtan (Winona) stalks the abductor of her young daughter. This suspenseful, contemporary story will appeal to many readers who are familiar with the dangers of modern society that exist even in rural areas.
♦ Readers may list and discuss the techniques the author uses to build suspense, compare this work of fiction to real-life child abductions, or compare the book to "Don't Take My Daughter," the 1991 television movie version of this novel.
1. Kidnapping—Fiction.

Dygard, Thomas J. *Wilderness Peril.* Morrow (0-688-04146-9), 1985. 208p. (Interest level: 6-8).

A camping trip to the BWCA (Boundary Waters Canoe Area) brings unexpected adventure to two teenagers when they discover a stash of $750,000 and encounter the hijacker who hid it. This adolescent novel features fast action, realistic characters, and good camping lore.
♦ Using desktop publishing software, students may write and publish a newspaper on the events in the novel, including information about the BWCA, articles on camping, advertisements for camping gear, etc.
1. Camping—Fiction 2. Hijacking of airplanes—Fiction 3. Boundary Waters Canoe Area (Minn.)—Fiction.

Ericson, Stig. *Dan Henry in the Wild West.* Trans. from the Swedish by Thomas Teal. Delacorte (0-440-01659-2), 1976. 148p. (Interest level: 6+).

Written by the winner of Sweden's highest children's book award, this is a well-researched story of a teenage Swedish boy who comes to the United States in the 1870s to make his fortune. In his first three years in Minnesota, he learns how to farm, makes new friends, learns the language, and gets accidentally involved in the Northfield bank robbery.
♦ Students may determine how they would film this story as a movie, addressing such considerations as the selection of actors and actresses, the determination of setting, changes in the story line, adaptation of the title, and choice of music for the sound track.
1. Frontier and pioneer life—Fiction 2. Minnesota—History—Fiction 3. Swedish Americans—Fiction.

Hassler, Jon. *Four Miles to Pinecone.* Warne (0-7232-6143-1), 1977. 117p. (Interest level: 6-8).

An incident at his uncle's cabin in northern Minnesota causes a teenage boy to reexamine his decision to keep silent about a robbery he witnessed. This book, written by a popular author, appeals to reluctant readers for independent reading or as a read-aloud.
♦ Students may role-play the situation and brainstorm alternative ways of handling it.
1. Friendship—Fiction 2. Crime—Fiction.

Hassler, Jon. *Jemmy.* Atheneum (0-6895-0130-7), 1980. 175p. (Interest level: 5-8).

Jemmy is a half-white, half-Chippewa teenager who is forced to drop out of school to care for her alcoholic father and brother. She feels alienated and unsure of her identity until an artist and his wife help her find pride in her Chippewa heritage. For adolescents who do not demand fast-paced fiction, the thoughtful por-

trayal of Jemmy provides insight into problems of Native Americans in contemporary society.
♦ Students may locate Jemmy's reservation home on a map of Minnesota and discuss ways in which minority students are mistreated in their school or community.
1. Minnesota—Fiction 2. Ojibway Indians—Fiction 3. Poverty—Fiction 4. Identity—Fiction.

Koch, Ron. *Almost Summer.* Darron (No ISBN), 1986. 121p. (Interest level: 6-8).
This realistic book reveals how today's way of life on small Minnesota farms is being threatened. A farm family's losing battle to save the farm that has been in their family for generations is told from the perspective of a teenage son who conveys their emotional upheaval in the financial struggle.
♦ After exploring the "farm problem" by researching how many farmers in the United States have had to sell out in recent years, young people may construct a large "future's wheel" showing the effects the farm problem has on different aspects of business and personal life.
1. Minnesota—Fiction 2. Family farms—Minnesota—Fiction.

Latimer, Jim. *Going the Moose Way Home.* Scribner (0-684-18890-2), 1988. Unpaginated. Color illus. (Interest level: K-3).
While traveling near his home in Moosehead, Minnesota, Moose gets stuck in the snow, visits the store, sees a band, explores a blueberry bog, encounters a troll, and also meets several animals native to northern Minnesota. Moose shares in the celebration of Christmas, Easter, Hanukkah, and Valentine's Day. Minnesota's natural environment is humorously and lovingly portrayed in this attractive picture book that can be used to integrate environmental education into language arts programs.
♦ Students may list the animals Moose meets, draw their own illustrations, or create their own Moose adventures.
1. Moose—Fiction 2. Animals—Fiction 3. Minnesota—Fiction.

Lovelace, Maud Hart. *Betsy and Tacy Go Downtown.* Harper & Row (0-06-440098-0), 1971, 1943. 180p. (Interest level: 3-6).
In this book in the Betsy-Tacy series, Betsy and her friends explore the theater and public library, meet a new friend, and solve problems with their friend Winona. Readers will experience the quaint, pleasant mood of this Betsy story and learn about the horseless carriage, telephones, a Carnegie library, and a small southwestern Minnesota city at the turn of the century.
♦ Students may research the cost of articles in the early 1900s and compare with today's prices. Students may also explore the concept that young girls had to deal with the same problems with their friends as young girls do today. Additionally, they may identify current innovations and hypothesize which ones may be outmoded or commonplace by 2050.
1. Friendship—Fiction 2. Minnesota—Fiction.

Lund, Duane R. *White Indian Boy.* Nordell Graphic Communications (0-934860-17-3), 1981. 164p. B/W illus. (Interest level: 4-9).
This account of a 10-year-old boy's capture by Indians is based on the adventures of John Tanner, the Falcon of Boundary Waters. Vivid and realistic descriptions of Indian culture are revealed in a nonromanticized tone as the boy spends his teen years learning the ways of the tribe.
♦ After reading this book, students may want to plot a sequel to the story. Also, they may research the real life of John Tanner to discover how his teen years as an American Indian affected the rest of his life.
1. Indians of North America—Captivities—Fiction 2. Tanner, John—Fiction 3. Minnesota—History—Fiction.

Lund, Duane R. *The Youngest Voyageur.* Adventure Publications (0-934860-41-6), 1985. 93p. B/W illus. (Interest level: 5-10).
A 15-year-old boy, joining voyageurs for the first time on a two-year trapping expedition in the 1790s, grows into manhood through good and bad experiences. This easily read story blends fiction and reality as the main characters meet real-life people in exciting circumstances.
♦ Students may plan a voyageur's expedition including preparations, supplies, hand-drawn maps, trading goods, travel plans, etc. Activities could be combined with the MECC *Voyageurs* computer program (no longer published but found on the MECC Elementary Volume 6-Social Studies disk).
1. Fur trade—Great Lakes region—History 2. Minnesota—History—Fiction.

Martinson, Tom. *The Christmas Loon.* NorthWord (1-55971-092-6), 1990. 54p. B/W and Color photos. (Interest level: K-3).
Jenny discovers a pair of loons and later their chicks on a northern lake. She observes their growth and becomes concerned for the chick Oot's safety until she sees a loon flying over the beach in Virginia on Christmas Day. While not specifically set in Minnesota, this heartwarming story and beautiful photography will inform young children about nature and Minnesota's state bird.
♦ After reading the book, children may discuss what they have learned about the loon, animals to which they have become attached, or a special Christmas present.
1. Loons—Fiction.

Myran, Karen. *Around Hawley with Ingrid.* The Hawley Herald (No ISBN), 1981. 48p. B/W illus. (Interest level: 2-5).

The author personalizes the telling of the history of a small Minnesota town by taking a visitor from another country on a walking tour and explaining the historical sites. This unusual method of fictionalizing history is effective in relating not only the small town's history but also the impact of events in United States history.

♦ Young people may research their own town/city's history by interviewing senior citizens, visiting the local historical society, and reading past newspapers. As a summary experience, they may collaborate in the development of a map showing the historical sites of their city/town. This map could be loaned to the local historical society or the school library media center.

1. Minnesota—History—Fiction 2. Hawley (Minn.)—History—Fiction.

Okimoto, Jean Davies. *Blumpoe the Grumpoe Meets Arnold the Cat.* Illus. by Howie Schneider. Little, Brown (0-316-63811-0), 1990. 30p. Color illus. (Interest level: 1-3).

A shy pet's endearing ways charm the "grumpiness" out of a lonely man in this broadly appealing picture book story. The man's trip highlights many Minnesota cities and towns.

♦ Students may find on a Minnesota map the cities and towns named in the story. They may also tell about a Minnesota trip they could take, indicating the route on a map. The idea of grumpiness may also be discussed: When do they feel grumpy? What do they do to feel better?

1. Cats—Fiction 2. Minnesota—Fiction 3. Hotels, motels, etc.—Fiction.

Paulsen, Gary. *The Cookcamp.* Orchard (0-531-05927-8), 1991. 115p. (Interest level: 5-8).

A five-year-old boy from Chicago is sent to live with his grandmother, a cook for a group of men building a road in northern Minnesota during World War II. Paulsen clearly evokes images of the men living a mobile, hard-working life, of the boy's feelings of loneliness, and of his confusion about his soldier father, his mother, and the mother's boyfriend.

♦ Students may interview a senior citizen who worked in Civil Conservation Corps camps like those in northern Minnesota during the 1930s and 1940s or interview someone who has worked with a firefighting or logging crew, focusing on what camp life is like.

1. Grandmothers—Fiction 2. World War II, 1939-1945—United States—Fiction 3. Roads—Fiction 4. Minnesota—Fiction.

Paulsen, Gary. *Popcorn Days and Buttermilk Nights.* Lodestar (0-525-66770-9), 1983. 160p. (Interest level: 6-9).

Sent to his uncle's "jackpine savage" farm in the 1940s, a tough teen, through hard work and a supportive environment, begins to develop a feeling of self-worth and a sense of what is really important in life. Very human characters are portrayed, and imagery is abundant in this account of Minnesota farm life.

♦ An interesting study may be done on the differences between how "city folk" saw "country folk" (and vice versa) in the 1940s as well as the present day. Students may enjoy comparing Carley's "city part of brain" with his "country part of brain" and determining what made the difference.

1. Farm life—Minnesota—Fiction 2. Minnesota—Fiction.

Paulsen, Gary. *Tracker.* Bradbury, 1984. 90p. (Interest level: 5-8).

As 13-year-old John copes with his grandfather's impending death from cancer and tracks deer in the Minnesota woods for his family's winter meat, he becomes attached to a doe and begins to hate his role as a hunter. Little is specifically revealed about northern Minnesota, but the hunting theme by a popular Minnesota author makes this book appealing to many readers, including reluctant readers.

♦ Readers may collect quotes from the book that help explain the book's themes of death, life, and hunting.

1. Deer—Fiction 2. Hunting—Fiction.

Qualey, Marsha. *Everybody's Daughter.* Houghton (0-395-55870-0), 1991. 201p. (Interest level: 7-8).

Sixteen-year-old Beamer is struggling with her own identity, values, and friendships while living with her parents who are associated with the remnants of a 1960s commune in northern Minnesota. Saturday night visits from old commune friends are embarrassing to Beamer as she strives to become something other than everybody's daughter. Skiing, fishing, nuclear power-plant protests, and small town Minnesota life in the 1980s are depicted through an integral setting.

♦ Students may examine pictorial histories of the 1960s and discuss the values that led to the establishment of communes. They may also compare Beamer's problems to their own needs for establishing an identity.

1. Communal living—Fiction 2. Minnesota—Fiction 3. Identity—Fiction.

Schwandt, Stephen. *Guilt Trip.* Atheneum (0-689-31557-0), 1990. 184p. (Interest level: 6-8).

Edrich Limerick moves to his fifth new school in three years and soon becomes involved with a wealthy schoolmate and the mysterious murder of the director of a theatrical troupe. The racial, social, and economic diversity of Minneapolis is revealed through charac-

terizations and setting, although a change in geographical names could place this novel in any city.
♦ Readers may discuss how suspense is created and whether the author has perpetuated or diminished racial and economic stereotypes.
1. Mystery and detective stories 2. Minneapolis (Minn.)—Fiction.

Shaw, Janet. *Changes for Kirsten: A Winter Story.* (0-937295-44-2), 1988. 65p.
———. *Happy Birthday, Kirsten! A Springtime Story.* (0-937295-32-9), 1987. 59p.
———. *Kirsten Learns a Lesson: A School Story.* (0-937295-09-4), 1986. 69p. Also audiocassette tape (0-937295-11-6).
———. *Kirsten Saves the Day: A Summer Story.* (0-937295-38-8), 1988. 67p.
———. *Kirsten's Surprise: A Christmas Story.* (0-937295-18-3), 1986. 62p. Also audiocassette tape (0-937295-20-5).
———. *Meet Kirsten: An American Girl.* (0-937295-00-0), 1986. 59p. Also audiocassette tape (0-937295-02-7).
(The American Girls Collection). Color sketches by Renee Graef and vignettes by Paul Lackner. Pleasant. (Interest level: 2-5).

This series, particularly appealing to younger children, presents the story of one year in the life of a nine-year-old Swedish immigrant to Minnesota. It includes her travels and various experiences in a new land. Warm, true-to-life characters will keep readers following Kirsten's story through the series, which includes, in each volume, an appendix of factual information about the major event or place in the story.
♦ Students may want to write imaginary diary entries of Kirsten's experiences, such as traveling, meeting Native Americans, going to school when she could not speak English, and celebrating Christmas. They may write the diary from the viewpoint of Kirsten's cousin who must cope with this stranger who has come to "her" country.
1. Immigration and emigration—Minnesota—Fiction 2. Minnesota—History—Fiction.

Sneve, Virginia Driving Hawk. *Betrayed.* Holiday (0-8234-0243-6), 1975. 125p. Map. (Interest level: 6+).

This fictitious account of the events of the Santee Indian Raid on the Minnesota Lake Shetek settlement in 1862 provides insight into both the Indians' and white settlers' interpretations of the issues. Readers can easily relate to the emotions of the characters.
♦ Students may wish to research the events leading up to the raid and the subsequent fate of the Indian and white survivors. Reports to the class may be done via simulated interviews, character reminiscences, or newspaper accounts.
1. Santee Indians—Wars, 1862-1865—Fiction 2. Indians of North America—Captivities—Fiction 3. Indians of North America—Minnesota—Fiction.

Stevermer, Caroline. *River Rats.* HBJ/Jane Yolen (0-15-200895-0), 1992. 214p. (Interest level: 6-8).

Tomcat and other orphan survivors of a nuclear flash travel on a paddle wheeler up and down the portion of the Mississippi River that is in extreme southeastern Minnesota. Their travels are action-packed as they take on a survivor and face death from the Wild Boys. Southeastern Minnesota locations mentioned in this science fiction novel are actual and described realistically.
♦ Young people may research the real names of the locations the author uses. They may discuss survival techniques used by the orphans.
1. Science fiction 2. Mississippi River—Fiction.

Thomas, Jane Resh. *Courage at Indian Deep.* Clarion (0-89919-181-9), 1984. 128p. (Interest level: 3-9).

Uprooted from his city life and unable to make friends in his new school, a young teenager runs away and becomes involved in the rescue of a shipwrecked crew off the Minnesota shore of Lake Superior. This realistic portrayal of the problems of youth perhaps overdoes the element of heroism, but that treatment could lead to good class discussion.
♦ Students may research shipwrecks on Lake Superior or the history of shipping on Lake Superior. They may also listen to one of many recordings of "The Wreck of the Edmund FitzGerald" (e.g., Gordon Lightfoot's performance on the album *Summertime Dream* by Reprise Records, 1976).
1. Youth—Fiction 2. Minnesota—Fiction 3. Shipwrecks—Fiction.

Wilder, Laura Ingalls. *On the Banks of Plum Creek.* Illus. by Garth Williams. Harper & Row (0-06-026471-3), 1937, 1953. 338p. (Interest level: 2-6).

Laura and her family move to Minnesota, where they live in a dugout until a new house is built. This fourth title in the "Little House" series presents misfortunes caused by flood, blizzards, and grasshoppers.
♦ Students may build a replica of the Ingalls' family home or other three-dimensional displays of life on Plum Creek. Students familiar with the television series may compare the book to life as it was presented in the series.
1. Family life—Fiction 2. Frontier and pioneer life—Fiction 3. Minnesota—History—Fiction.

Wosmek, Frances. *A Brown Bird Singing.* B/W illus. by Ted Lewin. Lothrop, Lee and Shepard (0-688-06251-2), 1986. 98p. (Interest level: 3-6).

A nine-year-old Indian girl must decide whether she wants to stay with her adoptive white family or return to her father's tribe and live as an Indian. This heartwarming story realistically develops the conflicting emotions involved in making such a momentous decision. The text beautifully portrays the relationship between two diverse families in turn-of-the-century Minnesota.

♦ Students may be interested in comparing the schools of yesterday with those of today. The class could plan and carry out one day of school as it was in the early 1900s.

1. Adopted children—Fiction 2. Race relations—Fiction 3. Indians of North America—Fiction.

Yolen, Jane. *All in the Woodland Early.* Illus. by Jane Breskin Zalben. Caroline (1-878093-62-2), 1991. Unpaginated. Color illus. (Interest level: Preschool-3).

In this charming alphabet book a woodland hunt reveals animals and insects from A to Z. Music and lyrics enrich this lively and interesting portrayal of life in a North American woodland. Although this book does not specifically name Minnesota, the setting is similar and could be used in studying Minnesota Northwoods.

♦ Students may create their own ABC book by using the computer program *StoryBook Weaver* (MECC, 1990). Each child may create a page showing one letter of the alphabet.

1. Alphabet 2. Animals—Fiction.

(Story collections)
Dad's Stories and Farm Memories. (Audiocassette). Narrated and produced by Michael Cotter, n.d. (55 min.). (Interest level: 5-8).

Austin, Minnesota, storyteller Michael Cotter vividly recalls life during the 1930s and 1940s, describing his father's childhood school, his own parochial school, and the challenge of driving a team of horses to town. He humorously describes how time was measured by who taught at the one-room or by what dogs his family owned in a given year.

♦ The recollections are an excellent source for teaching listening skills and encouraging students to write or tell their own stories. Students may wish to interview parents for stories about their youth. The audiocassette can be used as a companion piece to William Kirtland's *Billy* (see Minnesota—Biography, Kirtland).

1. Agriculture—Social aspects—Minnesota 2. Short stories—Austin (Minn.) 3. Farm life—Austin (Minn.).

Periodicals

917.76
Minnesota Calls. Stolee Communications. Bimonthly. B/W and Color illus. $12 per year. (Interest level: 5+).

Each issue of this refreshing periodical carries articles about current Minnesota places, events, festivities, and people as well as the state's history. All advertisements are geared to Minnesota. Photographs and sketches enhance this journal, allowing it to be used as a class resource.

♦ Students may develop a proposal for a feature article on their own town/city. They could include their rationale for their selected topic and perhaps photographs.

1. Minnesota—Social life and customs.

Ohio

by Carolyn S. Brodie

Nonfiction

070.593
Woodyard, Chris. *Haunted Ohio: Ghostly Tales from the Buckeye State.* Kestrel Publications (0-96284-72-08), 1991. 212p. (Interest level: 4-8).

This well-documented collection includes interesting Ohio ghost stories and ghost lore, ranging from Native American tales to contemporary haunted houses. One particular story (pp. 73-74) shares the ghostly returns of Johnny Appleseed near the site of a monument dedicated to him on Route 21 close to the Noble-Washington county line.
♦ Students may plot the stories on an Ohio map as they read through the selections. Students may also want to investigate and research any of their own local area ghost stories or "camp fire stories" and record them for others.
1. Ghosts—Ohio—Fiction.

301.451
McCluskey, John E., ed. *Blacks in Ohio: 7 Portraits.* New Day/Karamu (0-913678-13-9), 1980. 81p. B/W illus. (Interest level: 3-8).

Pen-and-ink drawings enhance brief, documented biographical accounts of seven important Ohio African Americans. Profiled are Lucy Bagby Johnson, Charles Waddell Chesnutt, Jane Edna Hunter, Granville T. Woods, Lottie Pearl Mitchell, Garrett Morgan, and Zelma George.
♦ Students may further research the outstanding contributions of these individuals to Ohio and the rest of the country. Students may wish to compile their own biographies of African-American achievers, using as a model the *Book of Black Heroes* by Toyomi Igus and others (Just Us Books, 1991).
1. African Americans—Ohio—Biography.

317.71 (Reference)
Ohio Almanac. Orange Frazer (0-9619637-6-X), 1992. 668p. B/W illus. (Interest level: 3+).

This definitive source of factual information about the state of Ohio has been called "an encyclopedia of indispensable information about the Buckeye universe." Jim Borgman, *Cincinnati Enquirer*'s political cartoonist and winner of the 1991 Pulitzer Prize in his field, contributed 100 political cartoons, which add to the book's appeal.
♦ Using information from this extensive resource and other Ohio informational resources, an "Ohio Information Olympics" may be sponsored. Each event could involve answering questions in different categories, such as history, Ohio presidents, and inventions. Simulated gold, silver, and bronze medals could be awarded for the greatest number of correct answers in each category.
1. Almanacs, American—Ohio 2. Ohio—Yearbooks 3. Ohio—Statistics.

340.092
Driemen, John E. *Clarence Darrow.* Chelsea (0-7910-1624-2), 1992. (Chelsea House Library of Biography). 111p. Color illus. (Interest level: 5-8).

In 1925 Clarence Darrow, the famous American lawyer of the early 1900s, defended the right of John T. Scopes to teach the theory of evolution in public schools. This biography presents an insightful, candid look at Darrow, who began practicing law in Ohio in the early 1880s and was born in Kinsman, Ohio, near Youngstown.
♦ Older students may be interested in researching the careers of famous American lawyers.
1. Darrow, Clarence, 1857-1938 2. Lawyers.

386.22
Hartford, John. *Steamboat in a Cornfield.* Crown (0-517-56141-7), 1986. 40p. B/W illus. (Interest level: 3+).

A humorous, rhyming text describes a 1910 incident on the Ohio River when the steamboat *Virginia* went aground in a cornfield. Photographs made this event a popular news item of the day.

♦ Students may locate information about the different types of boats (e.g., steamboats, flatboats, keelboats, and pirogues) that were used on the Ohio River. Students may choose to research the history of the steamboat *Virginia*. As reporters, the students may also wish to write a newspaper article about the event Hartford describes, including a headline and illustration.

1. Steamboats 2. Shipping—Ohio River—History 3. Ohio River—Navigation—History.

386.48
Gieck, Jack. *A Photo Album of Ohio's Canal Era, 1825-1913.* Kent State University Press (0-87338-353-2), 1988. 310p. B/W photos and illus. (Interest level: 4+).

This attractive pictorial description of life on the Ohio Canal provides much detailed information about the important role the Ohio Canal played in the growth and settlement of nineteenth-century Ohio.

♦ Using the illustrations as a guide, students may create models of boats that were common on the Ohio Canal in different time periods. Students may trace the Ohio Canal on a modern day map.

1. Canals—Ohio—Pictorial works 2. Ohio—Transportation.

386.4809
Ohio's Canal Era. (Videocassette). Produced by Jack Gieck. Available as parts 1, 2, and 3. Cinemark, 1991. VHS 1/2", Color, (20 min. each). $24.95 each. (Interest level: 4+).

Filmed at more than 24 locations throughout Ohio, this video uses archival photographs, visits to restored sections of canals, and interviews with professional staffs of these historic areas to examine the building and operation of this 813-mile transportation system, its effect on Ohio's economic development, and its subsequent decline with the beginning of the railroad era. This extensive, well-researched documentary provides many historical and contemporary comparisons. It has three parts: Part 1 concentrates on the construction of the canal; Part 2 explores the route of the canal; and Part 3 describes the Milan Canal in central Ohio and the Miami and Erie Canal.

♦ Students may be interested in comparing Gieck's book *A Photo Album of Ohio's Canal Era, 1825-1913* (see preceding entry) with information provided in the videos. Students may also create a poem about the formation and history of the canal system.

1. Canals—Ohio—History 2. Railroads—Ohio—History 3. Ohio—Economic conditions.

392.36
Shemie, Bonnie. *Houses of Bark: Tipi, Wigwam and Longhouse: Native Dwellings of Woodland Indians.* Tundra (0-88776-246-8), 1990. 24p. Color illus. (Interest level: 2-6).

Colorful, detailed, full-page illustrations depict Woodland Native American dwellings that were prevalent in the Canadian wilderness and around the Great Lakes area. The comprehensive text makes this a good source of information for Native American study.

♦ Using the examples in the book, students may make sample dwellings from pieces of bark, twigs, and wood. Students may play some of the games that Native American Woodland children might have played as described in Allan McFarlan's *Handbook of American Indian Games* (Dover, 1958).

1. Woodland Indians—Housing 2. Indians of North America—Housing 3. Houses.

500.9771
Lafferty, Michael B. *Ohio's Natural Heritage.* Ohio Academy of Science (0-933128-01-0), 1979. 324p. Color photos. (Interest level: 5+).

Numerous naturalist photographs and extensive research support this presentation of Ohio nature. The 19 chapters are divided into three sections: the land, natural regions, and the impact of humans. This comprehensive overview includes chapters by Martha Potter Otto on Native Americans as the first Ohioans and Ralph W. Dexter's survey of the history of naturalists in Ohio.

♦ Students may be interested in obtaining free pamphlets from the Ohio Department of Natural Resources (Fountain Square, Columbus, OH 43224) that feature information on such nature subjects as honeybees and bluebirds. Students may also wish to set up a simple nature habitat for birds and other creatures outside their classroom window.

1. Ohio—Description 2. Natural history—Ohio.

582.16
Ohio's Reptiles. (Slides). Text by Guy L. Denny. Photos by Alvin E. Staffan. Ohio Department of Natural Resources, n.d. 42 slides and guide. $18.25, with handling. (Interest level: K+).

Ohio's 43 species and subspecies of reptiles, including turtles, lizards, and snakes, are featured in a selection of vivid slides. A colorful 25-page guide provides additional information on locations and habitats. Other sets available include: *Ohio's Trees* (see following entry), *Discover Ohio, Ohio's Amphibians, Ohio's Birds, Ohio's Spring Wild Flowers,* and *Ohio's Stream Life.*

♦ A visit by a naturalist featuring a talk on reptiles (and possibly some visiting reptiles) may be of interest to students.

1. Reptiles—Ohio—Identification.

582.16
Ohio's Trees. (Slides). Text by Guy L. Denny. Photos by Alvin E. Staffan. Ohio Department of Natural Resources, n.d. 113 slides and guide. $22, with $3 handling. (Interest level: K+).

Vivid slides introduce 56 individual trees that are most commonly encountered in Ohio, including several ornamental trees now grown in Ohio but not native to the state. This excellent resource for the study of Ohio trees is accompanied with a guide that provides scientific names and close-up pictures. Other slide sets available include: *Ohio's Reptiles* (*see* preceding entry), *Discover Ohio, Ohio's Amphibians, Ohio's Birds, Ohio's Spring Wild Flowers*, and *Ohio's Stream Life*.
♦ Students may create a leaf collection and use the slides and guide to help identify trees native to Ohio. Students in other areas may take a field trip and locate any trees that are native to Ohio.
1. Trees—Ohio—Identification.

591.9771
Wildlife Histories: Notes on Ohio's Wildlife and Species. Ohio Department of Natural Resources (No ISBN), 1985. 80p. Illus. (Interest level: 3+).

This notebook offers individual pages of life histories and notes on Ohio wildlife, including fish, birds, and mammals. It also addresses habitats, food, and mating, making it an excellent resource for student reports.
♦ Students may research and prepare an illustrated report of an Ohio fish, bird, or mammal. These illustrated reports may be compiled for a scrapbook on Ohio wildlife. Using an Ohio map for reference, the class may also discuss where particular wildlife is located in the state.
1. Fish—Ohio 2. Mammals—Ohio 3. Birds—Ohio.

598.29771 (Reference)
Peterjohn, Bruce G. *The Birds of Ohio*. Illus. by William Zimmerman. Indiana University Press (0-253-34183-3), 1989. 237p. Color illus. (Interest level: K+).

This comprehensive reference resource provides information on Ohio birds. William Zimmerman illustrates the birds described with numerous detailed paintings.
♦ Students may want to mix some bird foods specially designed for different kinds of birds or create birdhouses or feeders such as those suggested in *Birdwise* by Pamela Hickman (Addison-Wesley, 1988). Students may then be interested in creating a bird sanctuary area visible from a classroom or library window and, using Peterjohn's book, record the different birds sighted. Students may also enjoy a visit from a naturalist or bird lover.
1. Birds—Ohio.

627.13
Boyer, Edward. *River and Canal*. Holiday (0-8234-0598-2), 1986. 48p. B/W illus. (Interest level: 2-8).

The design, construction, and operation of an imaginary nineteenth-century canal is explained from the perspective of Ezra Horne and Joshua Warren, who raised money to build an inland canal that follows two rivers to the Ohio Valley. Based upon the similar histories of real canals, this valuable source enhances a study of the Ohio and Erie Canal. It includes a list of canal sites and a glossary.
♦ Students may construct a model of a lock and dam system. Or, students may consult Alan Bridgewater's *I Made It Myself* (Tab Books, 1990) for instructions on decorating tin cans in the canal boat tradition.
1. Canals.

629.13
Freedman, Russell. *The Wright Brothers: How They Invented the Airplane*. Holiday (0-8234-0875-2), 1991. 129p. B/W photos. (Interest level: 3+).

This photobiography follows the lives of the Wright brothers and describes how they developed the first airplane. It includes original photographs taken by Wilbur and Orville Wright.
♦ As a reading follow-up, young people may choose to research early airplanes and create or retell an aeronautic adventure story.
1. Wright, Orville, 1871-1948 2. Wright, Wilbur, 1867-1912 3. Aeronautics—History—Biography.

629.13
Schulz, Walter A. *Will and Orv*. Carolrhoda (0-87614-669-8), 1991. 48p. Color illus. (Interest level: 2-5).

On a windy December 17, 1903, in Kitty Hawk, North Carolina, the Wright Brothers (of Dayton, Ohio) made history as they prepared the "Flyer" for the world's first engine-powered flight. Young Johnny Moon, one of only five observers of this historic event, paints a dramatic picture of this momentous 12-second ride.
♦ Young people may share important events that they have witnessed, either in person or through the media. Students may explore the history of flight with such resources as Andrew Nahum's *Flying Machine* (Eyewitness Books, Knopf, 1990) or Walter J. Boyne's *The Smithsonian Book of Flight for Young People* (Atheneum, 1988). They may also want to build a model aircraft similar to the Wright brothers' "Flyer," which is depicted in *Model Airplanes and How to Build Them* by Harvey Weiss (Crowell, 1975).
1. Wright, Orville, 1871-1948 2. Wright, Wilbur, 1867-1912 3. Aeronautics—History.

629.1332
Sullivan, George. *Famous Blimps and Airships*. Dodd, Mead (0-396-09119-9), 1988. 64p. B/W illus. (Interest level: 2-7).

The history of dirigibles is told through the highlighted events of 20 of the most famous airships of all time. Historical photographs illustrate an easy-to-read text that includes information on the Goodyear blimps, often based around the Akron area.

♦ Students may want to describe what they might see if they flew over their town or city while riding in a blimp. Roxie Munroe's *Blimps* (Dutton, 1989) may be used as an additional source of information.

1. Airships.

634.11
Greene, Carol. *John Chapman: The Man Who Was Johnny Appleseed*. Childrens Press (0-516-04223-8), 1991. (A Rookie Biography). 47p. B/W and Color illus. (Interest level: K-3).

This easy-to-read biography relates the story of how John Chapman distributed apple seeds and trees, making him a legendary American hero. The book includes a chapter on Chapman's "Ohio Years."

♦ Students may contribute to an apple tree display by making a large brown construction paper trunk and adding printed apples made by using real apples cut in half and a red stamp pad. Paper leaves painted with green tempera paint and sponges cut in the shape of a leaf will complete the project. Or, students may be interested in other apple activities as described in Paulette Bourgeois's *The Amazing Apple Book* (Addison-Wesley, 1990).

1. Appleseed, Johnny, 1774-1845 2. Apple 3. Frontier and pioneer life.

664.132
Burns, Diane L. *Sugaring Season: Making Maple Syrup*. Photos by Cheryl Walsh Bellville. Carolrhoda (0-86714-422-9), 1990. 48p. Color photos. (Interest level: 2-7).

Through easy-to-understand text and bright, clear photographs, this book carefully describes the making of maple syrup, an annual springtime event in Ohio. Explained are detailed steps from tapping the tree and collecting the syrup to cooking and packaging.

♦ Students may make a chart of the steps involved in preparing maple syrup. They may taste test real maple syrup, sugar, or candy. They may wish to watch the video *Sugaring Time* (American School Publishers, $37), based on the book of the same name by Kathryn Lasky (Macmillan, 1983).

1. Maple sugar.

778.930
Sieve, Jerry. *Ohio: Images of Nature*. Westcliffe (0-929969-33-2), 1990. 112p. Color illus. (Interest level: K+).

This photographic essay depicts the natural beauty of the state of Ohio during each of the four seasons. Jerry Sieve's outstanding, vivid, color photographs were taken as he logged over 15,000 miles on Ohio's highways, back roads, and trails.

♦ Students may want to identify the geographic locations of the photographs on a map of Ohio.

1. Ohio—Description—Pictorial works 2. Nature photography.

796.09771 (Reference)
Ohio Sports Almanac. Illus. by Jim Borgman. Orange Frazer (0-9619637-8-6), 1992. 240p. B/W illus. (Interest level: 4+).

Filled with statistics, records, and history, this is a complete and comprehensive source of information about high school, university, and professional sports in Ohio. Drawings by the *Cincinnati Enquirer*'s Pulitzer Prize-winning cartoonist, Jim Borgman, complement this work.

♦ Students may enjoy choosing a person from Ohio's list of national sports champions for further research, or they may wish to select an event to illustrate for a display. Students could prepare an "Ohio Sports" exhibit displaying books on the professional teams, pennants, posters, and a selection of factual information gleaned from the *Ohio Sports Almanac*. They may wish to write summarized information on appropriate cutout shapes (e.g., Cleveland Browns information written on a construction paper football).

1. Sports—Ohio—Dictionaries.

796.323
Zadra, Dan. *Cleveland Cavaliers*. Photos by Ron Koch. Creative Education (0-88682-200-9), 1989. Unpaginated. Color photos. (Interest level: 3-6).

This brief history of the Cleveland Cavaliers basketball team spans its beginning on February 7, 1970, through the 1988 playoffs. The book highlights a number of key players, including Lenny Wilkens, who now serves as head coach of the team.

♦ Students may want to follow the progression of a favorite NBA professional basketball team through the season by collecting newspaper and sports magazine articles for a scrapbook. They may also follow the team's travels across the country on a map of the United States. Students may want to write for information about the National Basketball Association (Olympic Tower, 645 Fifth Avenue, New York, NY 10022).

1. Cleveland Cavaliers (Basketball team)—History 2. Basketball.

796.357
Golenbock, Peter. *Teammates*. Illus. by Paul Bacon. Harcourt Brace Jovanovich (0-15-200603-6), 1990. Unpaginated. Color illus. (Interest level: 3-6).

This picture book presents one of the most moving moments in sports history when Brooklyn Dodgers baseball player Pee Wee Reese publicly supported his teammate Jackie Robinson during a game against the Cincinnati Reds. The watercolor illustrations are augmented with photographs of players, newspaper headlines, and baseball cards.

♦ Students may write a poem or essay that describes the qualities of a good teammate. The poems or essays may be used for a display with photographs of sports teams on which students have been mem-

bers. (Photocopies of original pictures may be made for the display.)
1. Robinson, Jackie, 1919-1972 2. Reese, Pee Wee, 1919- 3. Baseball 4. Race relations.

796.357
Humphrey, Kathryn Long. *Satchel Paige.* Watts (0-531-10513-X), 1988. 110p. B/W photos. (Interest level: 6+).
  This survey addresses the life and career of Satchel Paige, the Negro League pitching phenomenon who later became the first African-American pitcher of the American League with the Cleveland Indians in 1948. In a well-documented account, Humphrey's story culminates in 1971 as Paige becomes the first baseball player from the Negro League to be inducted into the National Baseball Hall of Fame.
♦ Students may be interested in locating information about the Negro Baseball League or investigating the achievements of other African-American baseball players.
1. Paige, Leroy, 1906-1982 2. Baseball—Biography 3. African-American athletes.

811.54
Adoff, Arnold. *Tornado! Poems.* Illus. by Ronald Himler. Delacorte (0-440-08965-4), 1977. Unpaginated. B/W illus. (Interest level: 2-6).
  The advent and aftermath of a tornado's destruction is related through poetry, accompanied with dramatic black-and-white illustrations. Adoff, a resident of Yellow Springs, Ohio, based this writing on his personal experience in a storm that devastated nearby Xenia, Ohio, on April 3, 1974.
♦ Young people may research the factors that create hazardous weather and design posters that identify precautionary steps for dangerous weather. If possible, a local meteorologist may speak about severe weather conditions and appropriate preparations that should be made.
1. Tornadoes—Poetry 2. Children's poetry.

811.54
Rylant, Cynthia. *Soda Jerk.* Illus. by Peter Catalanotto. Orchard (0-531-05864-6), 1990. 48p. Color illus. (Interest level: 4+).
  Through a unique series of poems, a young soda jerk observes the people and places in his small town. Catalanotto's paintings are based on the atmosphere in Saywell's Drugstore in Hudson, Ohio. The right side of the cover illustration features a half-portrait of Cynthia Rylant.
♦ Students may create poetry that gives insights into jobs they do now or occupations they plan to have in the future. Or, they may choose to describe the people and places around them by listing descriptive phrases or adjectives. While sipping on an ice cream soda, students may listen to poetry readings from *Soda Jerk* and participate in a discussion of the book.
1. Community life—Poetry 2. Poetry, American.

813.092
Meet the Newbery Author: Cynthia Rylant. (Videocassette). American School Publishers (87-909684), 1990. (Meet the Newbery Author Series). VHS 1/2", Color, (30 min.). $83. (Interest level: 3-8).
  Rylant provides insight into her writing through a candid discussion of her life. She invites the viewers into her home in Kent, Ohio, where she shares how personal experiences are evident in her work. Her warmth, honesty, and wit will inspire beginning writers.
♦ Selections from Rylant's autobiography *But I'll Be Back Again* (*see* Ohio—Biography, Rylant) may be shared prior to viewing the video.
1. Rylant, Cynthia, 1954- 2. Authors, American.

813.092
Meet the Newbery Author: Virginia Hamilton. (Videocassette). American School Publishers (87-912644), 1991. (Meet the Newbery Author Series). VHS 1/2", Color, (16 min.). $52. (Interest level: 4-8).
  From her home, a two-acre farm in Yellow Springs, Ohio, Virginia Hamilton relates her love for the land that has influenced her writing. A candid portrait of this award-winning author is told through iconographic video.
♦ Beginning with Virginia Hamilton's first book, *Zeely* (Macmillan, 1967), students may prepare a time line of her publications, including notes on the subject matter of each book. Educators may want to explore information about the annual Virginia Hamilton Conference held each spring at Kent State University or read about the conference in *Many Faces, Many Voices: Multicultural Literary Experiences for Youth,* edited by Anthony L. Manna and Carolyn S. Brodie (Highsmith Press, 1992).
1. Hamilton, Virginia 2. Authors, American.

913.031
Le Sueur, Meridel. *The Mound Builders.* Watts (0-531-02717-1), 1974. 62p. B/W illus. (Interest level: 3-6).
  This historical account of the Mound Builders of the eastern woodlands region features the Adena culture's Great Serpent Mound in Adams County, Ohio, and the Hopewell culture's Mound City near Chillicothe, Ohio. Photographs and historical documentation enhance the work's credibility.
♦ Students may be interested in locating the two featured sites on a present-day Ohio map. They may also compare the life of the Mound Builders with that of other Native American groups.
1. Mounds and Mound Builders.

917.7
Aylesworth, Thomas G. and **Aylesworth, Virginia L.** *Eastern Great Lakes: Ohio, Indiana, Michigan.* Chelsea (0-7910-1045-7), 1991. 64p. Color illus. (Interest level: 2-5).

This book contains a chapter on each of three states that border the Great Lakes, one of which is Ohio. A brief overview is provided on each state, including information on major cities, places to visit, events, and famous people.
♦ Students may locate on a map of Ohio the sites mentioned in this work.
1. Great Lakes region 2. Ohio 3. Indiana 4. Michigan.

917.71
Guide to Ohio. (Videocassette). Rand McNally (#429), 1990. (Rand McNally Videotrip Series). VHS 1/2", (50 min.). Available from VCRI. $22.99, with shipping. (Interest level: 2+).

This overview of the state is divided into five distinct regions: northeast, southeast, southwest, northwest, and central. Providing information on travel, culture, history, nature, and amusements, it is an excellent resource to introduce the state's attractions (e.g., the shore, islands of Lake Erie, historic villages, and riverboating on the Ohio River).
♦ Students may be interested in videotaping a "Guide to . . . " that features their own hometown. Or, students may locate travel brochures and information in order to create a display titled "Traveling in Ohio."
1. Ohio—Description.

917.71
Hochstetter, Nancy. *Travel Historic Ohio: A Guide to Historic Sites and Markers.* Guide Press (0-961-56995-6), 1986. 168p. B/W illus. (Interest level: 4+).

The complete inscriptions of Ohio's 198 historic markers located around the state and information on more than 50 Ohio Historical Society sites provide a continuing lesson on Ohio's colorful past. Maps indicate the county location of each marker and each historic site. An index to the cities that are nearest to marker locations is included.
♦ Students may design a postcard featuring the historic place that interests them.
1. Historic sites—Ohio—Guidebooks 2. Ohio—History, Local 3. Ohio—Description.

917.71
Ohio. (Videocassette). Turner Broadcasting System, n.d. (Portrait of America Series). VHS 1/2", (49 min.). Available from Ambrose Video Publishing. $99.95. (Interest level: K+).

Narrated by native Ohioan and actor Hal Holbrook, this video features the following: (1) the Wright brothers; (2) Ohio sports; (3) Cleveland; (4) new industries in Ohio (Amish, Smucker's); and (5) Ohio legends. These segments may be shown separately and are ideal for introducing a wide number of topics to students.
♦ Students may be interested in creating a video that features information on individuals or events important to Ohio history.
1. Ohio—Description.

917.71 (Reference)
Ohio Gazetteer. American Historical Publications (0-937862-80-0), 1985. 262p. (Interest level: 5+).

This historical gazetteer gives detailed information on the state's events as well as the people who have participated in them. It provides frequently sought, basic reference data.
♦ Students may compile a gazetteer of important historical information for their own community or for their own school. Basic reference information should be included.
1. Ohio—Gazetteers.

917.71
Traylor, Jeff and **Traylor, Nadean Disabato.** *Life in the Slow Lane: Fifty Backroads Tours of Ohio.* Backroad Chronicles (0-941467-03-1), 1989. 217p. B/W photos and maps. (Interest level: 4+).

Some of Ohio's most interesting backroads are identified in this work, which describes 50 car/bicycle touring routes. A guide to state parks/camping and to covered bridges is included.
♦ Students may transfer the touring routes to a large state map of Ohio. They may also wish to research covered bridges and construct a model of one.
1. Ohio—Description—Guidebooks.

917.71
Zimmermann, George. *Ohio, Off the Beaten Path.* Globe-Pequot Press (0-87106-442-1), 1991. 192p. B/W illus. and maps. (Interest level: 5+).

This guide explores the rich diversity of Ohio, first by sections and then by counties. Highlighted are the homes of presidents and inventors, festivals and special events, gristmills, Amish villages, and a town that was a station on the Underground Railroad.
♦ Students may write for information about the historic sites and points of interest that are included in this travel guide. After receiving the information, students may create a postcard that depicts the site or event, and on the reverse side they may write to a friend describing an imaginary trip.
1. Ohio—Description—Guidebooks.

970.471
Wilcox, Frank. *Ohio Indian Trails: A Pictorial Survey of the Indian Trails of Ohio.* 2nd ed. Edited by William A. McGill. Kent State University Press (0-87338-109-2), 1970. 144p. B/W and Color illus. (Interest level: 5+).

This detailed overview of the Ohio Indian Trails is enhanced by well-chosen artwork that illustrates the

Native American heritage. The book includes thorough maps and explanations of Ohio prior to pioneer settlement.

♦ Young people may follow the Indian trails on a present-day Ohio map and speculate why particular trails were important to the survival of Native Americans in Ohio.

1. Indian Trails—Ohio.

973.52
Nardo, Don. *The War of 1812.* Lucent (1-56006-401-3), 1991. (America's Wars Series). 112p. B/W illus. (Interest level: 6-8).

This account, which begins with a chronology of events, highlights the individuals who had important roles in the War of 1812. For example, Captain Oliver Hazard Perry contributed to the successful defense of the Great Lakes in what was considered to be a turning point in the war. This excellent resource includes detailed information as well as a glossary, bibliography, and a list of references.

♦ Using a map of the Great Lakes, students may plot the important battles that took place on these waters during the War of 1812. They may write to the Put-in-Bay Chamber of Commerce, P.O. Box 250, Put-in-Bay, OH 43456, for information about Perry's Victory and International Peace Memorial near his battle headquarters. The monument is the third tallest in the United States.

1. United States—History—1812-1815.

973.711
Gaines, Edith M. *Freedom Light: Underground Railroad Stories from Ripley, OH.* Illus. by Cliff Clay. New Day Press (0-913678-20-1), 1991. 36p. B/W illus. (Interest level: 4-8).

Based on the accounts of John Parker and John Rankin, this work describes the role of the Ohio River town of Ripley, 50 miles east of Cincinnati. Prior to the Civil War, Ripley played an important role in the Underground Railroad and other antislavery activities. Accompanying the detailed notes are vivid illustrations, a chronology, a map, and a bibliography.

♦ Students may find Ripley on an Ohio map and discuss why this town played such a vital role in the success of the Underground Railroad. They may write to the Ohio Historical Society for information about Ripley's Rankin House, which was a way station on the Underground Railroad and is now a historic site.

1. Underground Railroad 2. Ripley (Ohio)—History 3. African Americans.

977
Pearce, John, ed. *The Ohio River.* Photos by Richard Nugent. University of Kentucky Press (0-8131-1693-7), 1989. 188p. Color photos. (Interest level: 6+).

The Ohio River, known as the "Oyo" by Native Americans, played a vital role as a great pathway to the West. Documented with personal accounts and numerous photographs, this work traces the 1,000-mile river from its beginning at Pittsburgh to the Mississippi River.

♦ Students may follow the flow of the Ohio River on a map and research the importance of rivers as a form of transportation in the settlement of the country. Or, students may imagine a riverboat trip on the Ohio and, through creative writing, compare what they could possibly have seen 200 years ago to what they might see today.

1. Ohio River 2. Ohio River Valley.

977.1
Baker, Jim. *How Our Counties Got Their Names.* Pioneer Press (No ISBN), 1973. Unpaginated. B/W illus. (Interest level: K+).

A brief anecdote identifies the basis of each county name and the date the county was formed. The information is accompanied by a humorous cartoon and an outline map of Ohio with the county darkened.

♦ Using the book as a model, students in Ohio may add to the information provided for their county. Students in other states may create a list of counties for their state, identifying a historical fact for each.

1. Geographic names—Ohio 2. Ohio—History, Local.

977.1
Burke, Thomas Aquinas. *Ohio Lands: A Short History.* (No ISBN), 1991. 54p. B/W illus. (Interest level: 4-8).

This source explains how Ohio counties got their names and presents the history of Ohio from prehistoric times. Detailed drawings extend the history of the organization and establishment of counties under the Land Ordinance of May 20, 1785.

♦ Students would profit from hearing a surveyor talk about the significance of his or her job in defining land boundaries. The surveyor might also explain how surveying techniques have changed over the years.

1. Land use—Ohio 2. Ohio—Public Lands 3. Ohio—History.

977.1
Clements, John. *Ohio Facts: A Comprehensive Look at Ohio Today County by County.* Clements Research II (ISSN 1040-4872), 1988. (Flying the Colors Series). 438p. Color illus. (Interest level: 4+).

The extensive information about the 88 counties in Ohio includes details about land, economy, transportation, community services, and recreation. Other features of this book are a chronological history of each county, information about the 16 major market areas in Ohio, and numerous charts, maps, and graphs.

♦ Using frequency graphs or textual descriptions, students may compare a single aspect (e.g., industry, agriculture, or tourism) from county to county.
1. Ohio.

977.1
Couch, Ernie and **Couch, Jill**. *Ohio Trivia*. Rutledge Hill (0-934395-71-3), 1988. 191p. B/W illus. (Interest level: 4+).

Interesting Ohio trivia questions and answers address the following areas: geography, entertainment, history, arts and literature, sports and leisure, and science and nature.
♦ After studying Ohio, students may easily adapt *Ohio Trivia* for use with a trivia format game.
1. Ohio 2. Questions and answers.

977.1
Fox, Mary Virginia. *Ohio*. Watts (0-531-10392-7), 1987. (A First Book). 72p. B/W photos. (Interest level: 3-7).

In nine chapters this book addresses the land, history, industry, and people of Ohio. The brief overviews are an excellent introduction for further research.
♦ Using information from the book, students may create and display bumper stickers that promote the state of Ohio.
1. Ohio.

977.1
Kent, Deborah. *Ohio*. Childrens Press (0-516-00481-6), 1989. (America the Beautiful Series). 144p. Color photos. (Interest level: 4+).

This introduction to the state of Ohio covers its geography, history, government, economy, industry, agriculture, culture, historic sites, and famous people. The "Facts at a Glance" section provides several maps as well as extensive general information about the state and its people.
♦ Students may develop map skills by locating the major cities of Ohio and researching the importance of each city's role in the Ohio economy.
1. Ohio.

977.1
Ohio. (Map). Ohio Department of Transportation, 1992. Color. (Interest level: K-2).

Upon request, the Ohio Department of Transportation provides without cost the official map of the state of Ohio. Much information is attractively provided with the map: state agency phone numbers and addresses, state symbols, Ohio state park information, a list of famous Ohioans, and other travel information.
♦ Using the map as a center of study, students may locate the hometowns of famous Ohioans. Students may be interested in figuring the mileage from their home to historic sites, museums, or cities in Ohio.
1. Ohio—Maps 2. Ohio—Description.

977.1
Ohio. (18" x 20" puzzle). Created by George Gorycki. Great American Puzzle Factory (#807), n.d. Contains over 550 pieces. (Interest level: 2+).

This full-color puzzle of the state includes major cities, highlights a number of famous historic sites, and illustrates several crops and industries of the state.
♦ Students may put the pieces of the puzzle together and then identify the location of historic sites on an outline map of Ohio. Students may wish to create their own puzzle for Ohio, depicting certain cities and historical events.
1. Ohio 2. Puzzles.

977.1
Thompson, Kathleen. *Ohio*. Raintree (0-86514-455-9), 1987. (Portrait of America Series). 48p. Color photos. (Interest level: 2-8).

Especially valuable for the younger readers, this book discusses the history, economy, culture, and future of Ohio. A special feature includes an interview with Ivonette Wright Miller, a resident of Dayton, now more than 90 years old. In 1911, at the age of 15, she made her first flight in an early aircraft her uncles had built.
♦ This book about Ohio features the contributions that individuals have made to the state. Young people may want to interview leaders in their own community and record the contributions they have made thus far to the success and progress of their town. They may set up a display with photographs and written accounts of the accomplishments of individuals from their area.
1. Ohio.

977.1
Traylor, Jeff. *Ohio Pride: A Guide to Ohio Roadside History*. Backroad Chronicles (0-941467-04-X), 1990. 267p. B/W illus. (Interest level: 3+).

In 1953, as a part of Ohio's statehood sesquicentennial celebration, the Ohio legislature passed a bill authorizing the placement of historical markers at the corporation limits of towns along state highways. Traylor's unusual resource provides the text inscribed on each of the more than 250 Ohio-shaped historical markers. A page of detailed information on the historical relevance of each marker is included.
♦ Ohio students may want to create an alternative text of not more than 16 words for historical markers about their cities or towns. Students in other states may design an original marker for their own area.
1. Ohio 2. Historic sites—Ohio.

977.1
Vonada, Damaine. *Amazing Ohio: Illuminating Moments*. Orange Frazer (0-9619637-3-5), 1989. 157p. (Interest level: 5+).

This collection of factual information, divided into 20 chapters, includes Ohio myths, disasters, inventors,

hucksters, and feuds. This source is especially useful for locating unusual and interesting facts about the state.
♦ Students may create a mobile illustrating the inventions of Ohioans. Some students may choose a subject not included in this book, such as sports or presidents, and compile a list of amazing facts for a 21st chapter.
1. Ohio—History.

977.1
Vonada, Damaine. *Ohio: Matters of Fact*. Orange Frazer (0-9619637-5-1), 1990. 157p. B/W illus. (Interest level: 3+).

Divided into 31 sections, this valuable resource of Ohio facts includes "useful, educational, whimsical, inspirational, and unexpected information" on topics such as presidents from Ohio, famous inventors, and Ohio foods.
♦ Students in Ohio may locate trivia information to add to the various sections. Students of other states may want to begin a "Matters of Fact" book about their own state, which could be a year-long class project kept in a three-ring binder.
1. Ohio.

977.100497
King, Gwen. *What Indians Lived in Ohio?* Lake Erie Printing (No ISBN), 1991. 52p. B/W illus. (Interest level: 2-8).

This overview of the way of life of the Native American groups historically associated with Ohio emphasizes those from the northern part of the state. The title comes from a question often asked of King (who works in the Indian Museum on the Lake Erie College campus). This booklet is a valuable resource for researchers.
♦ Students may locate additional information on the Native Americans of Ohio and compare their ways of life to Native Americans in surrounding states.
1. Indians of North America—Ohio.

977.101
Ross, Jane Bark. *The Magic Moccasins: Life among Ohio's Six Indian Tribes*. Vimach Associates (0-917949-02-1), 1985. B/W illus. (Interest level: 4+).

The Delaware, Shawnee, Miami, Wyandot, Ottawa, and Mingo Native Americans are compared and contrasted in this descriptive text. Although life among these groups was similar, there were differences in religion, social life, local customs, government, and dress that this book points out.
♦ Using Ross' book as a starting point, students, divided into six groups, may further research a specific Native American group and present their findings to the rest of the class.
1. Indians of North America—Ohio.

977.136
Bloetscher, Virginia Chase. *Indians of the Cuyahoga Valley and Vicinity*. North American Indian Cultural Center (No ISBN), 1980. 112p. B/W illus. (Interest level: 6-8).

This resource covers all readily available information pertaining to the Indians of the Cuyahoga Valley. This easy-to-understand account addresses the prehistoric period (prior to 1700) and the historic period.
♦ Students may construct a time line history of the Cuyahoga Valley area in northeast Ohio, which has been called the "cradle of greatness" because so many important historical events have taken place there.
1. Indians of North America—Cuyahoga River Valley (Ohio)—History 2. Cuyahoga River Valley (Ohio)—History.

977.71
Hawley, Marcy and Vonada, Damaine, eds. *Particular Places: A Traveler's Guide to Inner Ohio*. Orange Frazer (0-9619637-4-3), 1990. 263p. B/W illus. (Interest level: 4+).

This travel guide provides specific information about 17 important tourist areas in Ohio. It includes many historical details and tips on the best places to visit.
♦ Because it is possible to travel anywhere in Ohio during a maximum time of about four hours, students may want to plan a "one-tank Ohio trip."
1. Ohio—Description.

Biography

920
Haskins, Jim. *Outward Dreams: Black Inventors and Their Inventions*. Walker (0-8027-6994-2), 1991. 101p. B/W illus. (Interest level: 6+).

This work documents a number of the achievements of African-American inventors. It includes a 10-page list of inventions with their patent numbers. Chapter 9 presents the inspiring story of Garrett Morgan, a Cleveland resident, who was responsible for the invention of the gas mask and the stoplight.
♦ Students may further explore Morgan's achievements in the February 1992 *Cobblestone* article "Black American Inventors." Students may construct the model replica of Morgan's stoplight depicted in that article (pp. 32-33). Students may also locate information about the importance of the gas mask in World War I. On a broader scope, students may research other African-American inventors or the history of other inventions important to everyone's health and safety.
1. Inventors—Biography 2. African Americans—Biography.

920.0771 (Reference)
Ohio Biographical Dictionary: People of All Times and All Places Who Have Been Important to the History and Life of the State. American Historical Publications (0-937862-58-4), 1986. 352p. (Interest level: 5+).

This comprehensive overview introduces important people in Ohio's history. One strength of this resource is that it provides hard-to-find biographical information on numerous minor figures.
♦ Students may select an individual from the dictionary as a project for further research. Through personal or telephone interviews, students may compile a biographical dictionary of important people in their own town, both past and present.
1. Ohio—Biography—Dictionaries.

92 Armstrong, Neil
Westman, Paul. *Neil Armstrong: Space Pioneer.* Lerner (0-8225-0479-0), 1980. (The Achievers Series). 64p. B/W photos. (Interest level: 4+).

Significant photographs enhance this description of the life of Neil Armstrong, originally from Wapakoneta, Ohio (now home of the Armstrong Air and Space Museum). Armstrong, as a member of the three-man Apollo 11 crew, became the first man to walk on the moon on July 20, 1969. To update recent biographical information on Armstrong consult Ray Spangenburg's *Space People from A-Z* (Facts on File, 1990).
♦ After studying about the moon and Neil Armstrong's historic walk, students may make a list of everything they would need to take for a futuristic weekend trip. Young people may compose a list of artifacts that they believe should be in an air and space museum.
1. Armstrong, Neil, 1930- 2. Astronauts—United States.

92 Bench, Johnny
Shannon, Mike. *Johnny Bench.* Chelsea (0-7910-1168-2), 1990. 64p. B/W photos. (Interest level: 4-8).

This detailed account introduces the outstanding catcher who was part of Cincinnati's "Big Red Machine" during the 1970s when they won four National League pennants and two World Series championships. Bench played for the Cincinnati Reds for 17 seasons, hitting 387 home runs, a league record for a catcher.
♦ Students may want to investigate the history of baseball pennants. They may trace chronologically the important events of the Cincinnati Reds baseball team or another team of their choice.
1. Bench, Johnny, 1947- 2. Baseball—Biography.

92 Blackwell, Elizabeth
Greene, Carol. *Elizabeth Blackwell.* Childrens Press (0-516-04217-3), 1991. (A Rookie Biography). 47p. Color illus. (Interest level: 3-5).

Blackwell, who grew up in Cincinnati, Ohio, became the first woman doctor in the United States, devoting her life to opening the field of medicine to women in both the United States and England. This easily read biography traces the life of a pioneering American woman.
♦ Following research, students may discuss the roles of women throughout history and create a display of "Women's Famous Firsts." Students may plan to recognize National Women's History Month, held annually during March. They may also contact the National Women's History Project (7738 Bell Road, Windsor, CA 95492) for more information.
1. Blackwell, Elizabeth, 1821-1910 2. Women physicians.

92 Dunbar, Paul Laurence
Gentry, Tony. *Paul Laurence Dunbar.* Chelsea (1-55546-583-8), 1989. (Black Americans of Achievement Series). 110p. B/W photos. (Interest level: 5+).

The brilliance of the first African American to gain international recognition as a poet is conveyed in this vivid account of the life of Paul Laurence Dunbar, who died at the age of 33 in his hometown of Dayton, Ohio. Phrases from Dunbar's poetry appear as chapter titles.
♦ Many of Dunbar's poems sensitively portray family life. Students may select a favorite poem for choral reading from *The Complete Poems of Paul Laurence Dunbar* (Dodd, 1980).
1. Dunbar, Paul Laurence, 1872-1906 2. Poets, American 3. African-American authors.

92 Dunbar, Paul Laurence
McKissack, Patricia. *Paul Laurence Dunbar: A Poet to Remember.* Childrens Press (0-516-03209-7), 1984. 127p. Illus. (Interest level: 4+).

This insightful biography features the turn-of-the-century African-American poet and novelist whose works were among the first to give an honest representation of African-American life. Dunbar's poetry is well known for its humor and spirit, even when addressing difficult situations.
♦ Young people may write poetry about their own experiences. They may share a Dunbar poem from Arnold Adoff's collection *I Am a Darker Brother* (Macmillan, 1970) aloud using background music.
1. Dunbar, Paul Laurence, 1872-1906 2. Poets, American 3. African-American authors.

92 Edison, Thomas Alva
Adler, David A. *Thomas Alva Edison: Great Inventor.* Illus. by Lyle Miller. Holiday (0-8234-0820-5), 1990. 48p. B/W illus. (Interest level: 2-5).

Born in Milan, Ohio, February 11, 1847, this genius was responsible for hundreds of inventions during his lifetime, including the electric light bulb, the phonograph, and the motion picture. This easily read biography provides an insightful portrayal of Edison's life.
♦ Noting that Edison was issued 1,093 patents, students may be interested in researching the history of the United States Patent Office. They may wish to

view *Patent Pending* (American Documents Series), a 60-minute video on patents, narrated by William Shatner (produced by Post-Newsweek Stations, Inc. for Republic Pictures Home Video, 1975; $14.95).

1. Edison, Thomas Alva, 1847-1931 2. Inventors.

92 Edison, Thomas Alva
Egan, Louise. *Thomas Edison: The Great American Inventor.* Illus. by Frank Ricco. Barron's Educational Series (0-8120-3922-X), 1987. (Solutions: Profiles in Science for Young People Series). 165p. (Interest level: 5-9).

The text recounts the life and achievements of the famous inventor, from his boyhood experiments to his search for electricity. This is a comprehensive source for information on the one-time resident of Milan, Ohio, whose birthplace is now a museum.

♦ Students may each draw an invention that they would like to construct to solve some problem in their everyday life. Students may view the 52-minute video *Thomas A. Edison* from the Famous Americans of the Twentieth Century Series (Questar Home Video, $29.95).

1. Edison, Thomas Alva, 1847-1931 2. Inventors.

92 Edison, Thomas Alva
Mitchell, Barbara. *The Wizard of Sound: A Story about Thomas Edison.* Illus. by Hetty Mitchell. Carolrhoda (0-87614-445-8), 1991. 64p. B/W illus. (Interest level: 2-5).

This brief biography recounts the life of the celebrated inventor, who moved with his family from his birthplace in Milan, Ohio, to Port Huron, Michigan, at the age of seven. The phonograph, his favorite invention, receives special emphasis.

♦ Students may make a list of the many possibilities the invention of the phonograph created, such as talking books for the blind, talking dolls, and recorded music. Students may write a newspaper article or present a TV news brief that announces and details Edison's invention of the phonograph.

1. Edison, Thomas Alva, 1847-1931 2. Inventors—United States.

92 Feller, Robert W. A.
Eckhouse, Morris. *Bob Feller.* Chelsea (0-7910-1174-8), 1990. 64p. B/W photos. (Interest level: 4-8).

Photographs enhance this account of Robert William Andrew Feller, who pitched for the American League's Cleveland Indians from 1936 to 1941 and 1945 to 1956. On April 16, 1940, Bob Feller pitched the only opening day no-hitter in major league history.

♦ Noting that Bob Feller was elected to the National Baseball Hall of Fame in 1962, students may want to write for information about this museum (P.O. Box 590, Cooperstown, NY 13326). A collector of baseball cards or a local dealer may be contacted to speak to students about his or her rare and unusual cards.

1. Feller, Bob, 1918-   2. Baseball players—Biography.

92 Garfield, James A.
Lillegard, Dee. *James A. Garfield.* Childrens Press (0-5160-1394-7), 1987. 100p. B/W photos and illus. (Interest level: 3-7).

This Ohioan, the twentieth president of the United States, was the last president born in a log cabin. This biographical account provides detailed information, along with numerous illustrations and political cartoons.

♦ Political cartoons are as popular today as they were in Garfield's time. Young people may want to bring in examples of political cartoons from local newspapers and discuss their meaning. They may want to research the history of the political cartoon and its role in American politics.

1. Garfield, James A. (James Abram), 1831-1881
2. Presidents—United States.

92 Gish, Lillian
Lanes, Selma G. *An Actor's Life for Me! Lillian Gish.* Illus. by Patricia Henderson Lincoln. Viking Kestrel (0-670-80416-9), 1987. 74p. B/W photos; Color illus. (Interest level: 4-8).

Legendary leading lady Lillian Gish, born in Springfield, Ohio, appeared in more than 150 films and 50 plays. Family photographs enhance this account of Gish's beginnings as a child actor in a traveling theatrical company.

♦ Young people may draw pictures depicting careers they hope to have in the future.

1. Gish, Lillian, 1896-1993 2. Actors, American.

92 Glenn, John
Westman, Paul. *John Glenn: Around the World in 90 Minutes.* Dillon (0-87518-186-4), 1980. 48p. B/W photos and illus. (Interest level: 2-4).

Enhanced with photographs of the time, this brief biography features the first American to orbit the earth. More recently serving as a United States senator from his native Ohio, Glenn ran for election three times before he won in 1974. Young people may update information on Glenn by consulting Ray Spangenburg's *Space People from A-Z* (Facts on File, 1990).

♦ Students may make a chronological time line of important American space achievements during the 1960s, beginning with Glenn's orbit of the earth.

1. Glenn, John, 1921-   2. Astronauts—United States
3. Legislators.

92 Grant, Ulysses S.
Kent, Zachary. *Ulysses S. Grant.* Childrens Press (1-516-01364-5), 1989. (Encyclopedia of Presidents). 100p. B/W photos and illus. (Interest level: 3-7).

This biographical account describes the military and political life of the 18th president of the United States,

born in Point Pleasant, Ohio. Numerous illustrations, photographs, and a historical chronology support the detailed information.
♦ Students may research and assess Grant's role during the Civil War and as president. Older students may find segments from *The Civil War* (a series of nine videos produced by PBS Video [CIVW-000], 1990; $350) useful in their research.
1. Grant, Ulysses S., 1822-1885 2. Presidents—United States 3. Generals—United States.

92 Harding, Warren G.
Wade, Linda R. *Warren G. Harding*. Childrens Press (0-516-01368-8), 1989. 100p. B/W photos and illus. (Interest level: 3-7).
This account examines the life and career of the Marion, Ohio, newspaperman who became the 29th president of the United States. Illustrations, an index, and a historical chronology enhance the work's research value.
♦ Students may wish to study the careers of all U.S. presidents to date and graph the frequency of the careers identified. Using this graph, they may write their interpretation of an ideal job description for someone who wants to run for the presidency.
1. Harding, Warren G. (Warren Gamaliel), 1865-1923 2. Presidents—United States.

92 Harrison, Benjamin
Clinton, Susan. *Benjamin Harrison*. Childrens Press (0-516-01370-X), 1989. 100p. B/W photos and illus. (Interest level: 3-7).
Born in North Bend, Ohio, this 23rd president of the United States was the only grandson of a president to become a president himself. Photographs and a historical chronology add to the detailed information.
♦ Students may want to trace careers in their own families and see whether there are any occupations that have been passed on through the generations.
1. Harrison, Benjamin, 1833-1901 2. Presidents—United States.

92 Harrison, William Henry
Fitz-Gerald, Christine Maloney. *William Henry Harrison*. Childrens Press (0-516-01392-0), 1987. 100p. B/W photos and illus. (Interest level: 3-7).
William Henry Harrison left his North Bend, Ohio, home in January 1841 and was inaugurated in March as the nation's ninth president, the one who had the shortest term in office. A historical chronology extends this straightforward account.
♦ Students may write a paragraph justifying whether or not they would want their own child to assume the role of president of the United States.
1. Harrison, William Henry, 1773-1841 2. Presidents—United States.

92 Hayes, Rutherford B.
Kent, Zachary. *Rutherford B. Hayes*. Childrens Press (0-516-01365-3), 1989. 100p. B/W photos and illus. (Interest level: 3-7).
Rutherford B. Hayes, born in Delaware, Ohio, in 1822, became the 19th president of the United States only after a vote of Congress, which took place 56 hours before his inauguration. This readable biographical account provides detailed information accompanied by numerous illustrations, photographs, and historical chronology.
♦ Students may investigate the election of United States presidents and construct a wall chart that defines the process, including how the election of a president may be determined by a congressional vote.
1. Hayes, Rutherford Birchard, 1822-1893 2. Presidents—United States.

92 La Salle, René-Robert Cavelier, Sieur de
Hargrove, Jim. *René-Robert Cavelier Sieur de La Salle*. Childrens Press (0-516-03054-X), 1990. 128p. B/W and Color illus. (Interest level: 4-8).
A French explorer, La Salle may have been in 1670 the first European to visit what is now Ohio; he is often credited with the "discovery" of the Ohio River. Illustrations, an index, and a historical chronology extend the usefulness of a text detailing France's claim to all of the Northwest.
♦ Students may follow the time line of La Salle's life, identifying other historic events taking place in the world. Or, students may locate information on other explorers who followed La Salle into the Ohio River Valley area.
1. La Salle, René-Robert Cavelier, Sieur de, 1643-1687 2. Explorers 3. Mississippi River Valley—Exploration.

92 McKinley, William
Kent, Zachary. *William McKinley*. Childrens Press (0-516-01361-0), 1988, 100p. B/W photos and illus. (Interest level: 3-7).
This work presents the early life, military career, and political life of the president who campaigned for the presidency from his front porch in Canton, Ohio. He was assassinated in 1901 during his second term in office. The clearly presented, unique details of McKinley's life will engage students' interest.
♦ Because McKinley was known to wear a scarlet carnation in his buttonhole for good luck, the Ohio legislature passed a resolution that made the carnation the official state flower. Students may want to research the significance of other state flowers.
1. McKinley, William, 1843-1901 2. Presidents—United States.

92 Oakley, Annie
Levine, Ellen. *Ready, Aim, Fire! The Real Adventures of Annie Oakley.* Scholastic (0-590-41877-7), 1989. 132p. B/W photos. (Interest level: 3-7).

Born in a log cabin on the Ohio frontier, Oakley was the world's most famous female sharpshooter. This account is enhanced with photographs of Annie; her husband of more than 50 years, Frank Butler; and posters from the Wild West Show.
♦ Students may be interested in locating more information on Buffalo Bill and the Wild West Show. Or, students may be interested in participating in a mock "sharpshooting tournament" using a Velcro target game.
1. Oakley, Annie, 1860-1926 2. Entertainers—United States 3. Shooters of firearms.

92 Oakley, Annie
Quackenbush, Robert. *Who's That Girl with the Gun? A Story of Annie Oakley.* Simon & Schuster (0-13-957671-1), 1988. 36p. B/W illus. (Interest level: 2-5).

Born in Darke County in western Ohio, Phoebe Ann Moses, better known as Annie Oakley, grew up as the provider of meat for her family. Quackenbush provides an amusing account of the star of Buffalo Bill's Wild West show for 17 years.
♦ Students may design a poster advertising Buffalo Bill's Wild West show.
1. Oakley, Annie, 1860-1926 2. Entertainers—United States 3. Shooters of firearms.

92 Pontiac, Ottawa Chief
Rothaus, James. *Pontiac: Indian General and Statesman.* Illus. by Harold Henriksen. Creative Education (0-88682-160-6), 1987. (We the People Series). 28p. B/W and Color illus. (Interest level: 2-4).

This biography examines the life of the Ohio-born Ottawa warrior who became a great war chief and united his people against the encroachment of the British by leading them in an attack on Fort Detroit in the 1760s. This large-print book briefly presents the accomplishments of Pontiac and his people who lived near the Great Lakes.
♦ Students may create a three-dimensional wigwam by using illustrations in the book, an encyclopedia, or Nancy Simon's *American Indian Habitats: How to Make Dwellings and Shelters of Natural Materials* (McKay, 1978). Students may locate more information about the Native Americans who lived around the Great Lakes area.
1. Pontiac, Ottawa Chief, ca. 1720-1769 2. Ottawa Indians.

92 Resnick, Judith
Bernstein, Joanne E. and Blue, Rose, with Gerber, Alan Jay. *Judith Resnick: Challenger Astronaut.* Lodestar (0-525-67305-9), 1990. 144p. B/W photos. (Interest level: 5-9).

With a doctorate in electrical engineering, Judith Resnik made history as one of the first women accepted in 1978 as a NASA scientist. She was later killed in the explosion of the space shuttle *Challenger*. This well-researched biography introduces the first Jewish person in space.
♦ Young people may participate in a flying papercraft contest, using the space shuttle glider model kit provided by NASA (U.S. GPO #730-106) or sample patterns from other sources such as *Fantastic Flying Paper Toys* by Richard E. Churchill (Sterling, 1989).
1. Resnick, Judith, 1949-1986 2. Astronauts—United States 3. Challenger (Spacecraft)—Accidents 4. Jews.

92 Rylant, Cynthia
Rylant, Cynthia. *But I'll Be Back Again: An Album.* Orchard (0-531-05806-9), 1989. 80p. B/W photos. (Interest level: 4-7).

In an autobiography arranged like a photograph album, Rylant relates her true story of childhood and teenage experiences growing up in West Virginia. This nationally acclaimed author and resident of Kent, Ohio, describes what was important to a young girl of the 1960s.
♦ After sharing some of the incidents of Rylant's life, young people may want to look at photographs from their own childhood and describe what they were thinking when the photograph was taken, or they may wish to begin a photograph album or journal of their own.
1. Rylant, Cynthia, 1954- 2. Authors, American 3. West Virginia—Social life and customs.

92 Spielberg, Steven
Hargrove, Jim. *Steven Spielberg: Amazing Filmmaker.* Childrens Press (0-516-03263-1), 1988. 128p. B/W and Color illus. (Interest level: 4-8).

Spielberg, born in Cincinnati, Ohio, has directed multiple top money-making motion pictures. His life and career are depicted and enhanced with photographs.
♦ Using information from a favorite book, each student may pretend that the book is being made into a movie and design a "coming attraction" poster.
1. Spielberg, Steven, 1947- 2. Motion picture producers and directors—United States.

92 Stowe, Harriet Beecher
Jakoubek, Robert. *Harriet Beecher Stowe.* Chelsea (1-55546-680-X), 1989. (American Women of Achievement Series). 112p. B/W and Color illus. (Interest level: 6-8).

Stowe's years in Cincinnati from 1832 to 1850 furnished her with many of the characters and incidents she used in writing *Uncle Tom's Cabin*. Stowe's life and literary accomplishments are detailed through a well-written and well-researched textual account.

♦ Students may contact Stowe House State Memorial, 2950 Gilbert Avenue, Cincinnati, Ohio, for an informative leaflet.

1. Stowe, Harriet Beecher, 1811-1896 2. Authors, American 3. Abolitionists.

92 Taft, William Howard
Casey, Jane Clark. *William Howard Taft*. Childrens Press (0-516-01366-1), 1989. 100p. B/W photos and illus. (Interest level: 3-7).

This biographical account examines the life and career of the lawyer, born in Cincinnati, Ohio, whose relatively unsuccessful presidency was followed by a rewarding term as chief justice of the Supreme Court. Reproductions of political cartoons that plagued his presidency will interest young people.

♦ Taft began the custom of having a U.S. president open the baseball season by tossing the first ball. Students may compile a trivia game or book about the presidents, using factual information from Joseph Nathan Kane's *Facts about the Presidents* (Wilson, 1989) or Barbara Seuling's *The Last Cow on the White House Lawn and Other Little-Known Facts about the Presidency* (Doubleday, 1978).

1. Taft, William H. (William Howard), 1857-1930 2. Presidents—United States.

92 Tecumseh, Shawnee Chief
Shorto, Russell. *Tecumseh and the Dream of an American Indian Nation*. Illus. by Tim Sisco. Silver Burdett (0-382-09569-3), 1989. (Alvin Josephy's Biography Series of American Indians). 136p. B/W illus. (Interest level: 5-7).

This exciting account of Tecumseh relates his repeated wars against the American colonists and gallant efforts to establish a united Indian nation. This well-researched biography concludes with Tecumseh's death on October 13, 1813, in the Battle of the Thames, north of Lake Erie.

♦ Tecumseh's Shawnee clan lived in a large village of roomy wigwams. Students may create cooperatively a mural of a village of wigwams.

1. Tecumseh, Shawnee Chief, 1768-1813 2. Shawnee Indians.

Fiction

Ackerman, Karen. *The Tin Heart*. Illus. by Michael Hays. Atheneum (0-689-31461-2), 1990. 32p. Color illus. (Interest level: 1-3).

This heartfelt picture book, set on the Ohio River during the Civil War, tells of two young girls, Flora and Mahaley, whose friendship is tested by the opposing political views of their families. As a symbol of their efforts to sustain their friendship, each wears half a tin heart made by Flora's father. The realistic setting is strengthened by the occupation of Mahaley's father, who runs a ferry boat across the Ohio River.

♦ Young people may describe on half of a paper heart their feelings when separated from a friend. They may also explore through discussion the ways friendships are tested today.

1. Friendship—Fiction 2. United States—History—Civil War, 1861-1865.

Collins, Judy. *My Father*. Illus. by Jane Dyer. Little, Brown (0-316-15228-5), 1990. Unpaginated. Color illus. (Interest level: 1-3).

Judy Collins' lyrical song of the same title is depicted with Dyer's soft illustrations of a young girl's coal-mining family. Their dream of leaving Ohio for the finer life of Paris, France, is finally realized many years later when the young girl grows up and rears her own children along the banks of the Seine.

♦ Young people may talk with older family members to see whether, when they grew up, they became what their parents wanted them to be.

1. Family life—Songs and music.

DeFelice, Cynthia. *Weasel*. Macmillan (0-02-726457-2), 1990. 119p. (Interest level: 5-8).

This exciting adventure story, set in Ohio in 1839, begins with a sudden knock on the cabin door of Nathan and Molly Fowler. A frontiersman explains that their father has been wounded by a cruel man called Weasel. As Nathan faces Weasel and cares for the farm and his father, he develops courage and learns forgiveness.

♦ After the teacher or librarian reads the brief first chapter of *Weasel*, students may brainstorm what they feel are possible events to come.

1. Frontier and pioneer life—Fiction 2. Ohio—Fiction.

Fleischman, Paul. *The Borning Room*. HarperCollins (0-06-023762-7), 1991. 101p. (Interest level: 5-9).

This reflective, sensitively written saga reveals a frontier Ohio family's history as seen through the eyes of Georgina while she lies dying in the room where she was born in 1851. Georgina shares scenes from the "the borning room" which, though seldom used, has been the place in the house for births and deaths, each having different, lasting effects on the family.

♦ Pretending that their family has lived in the same house or apartment for the last 30 years, each student may list the exciting events that happened in either the kitchen or living room.

1. Frontier and pioneer life—Fiction 2. Ohio—Fiction.

Follow the Drinking Gourd. (Videocassette). American School Publishers (0-07-540376-5), 1990. (The Children's Literature Series). VHS 1/2", Color, (11 min.). $35. Includes teacher's guide. (Interest level: 2-8).

Some runaway slaves were able to find their way northward to freedom by following the lyrics of the

song "The Drinking Gourd," based on the constellation of the Big Dipper, which always points to the North Star. This video uses Jeanette Winter's original acrylic paintings from the book of the same title, and the score for this production is based on plantation hymns such as "Mighty Rocky Road."
♦ Young people may choose to research the Big Dipper or another constellation that has been important for travel and navigation, creating or retelling a story about it.
1. Slavery—Fiction 2. Underground Railroad—Fiction 3. African Americans—Fiction.

Hamilton, Virginia. *Bells of Christmas.* Illus. by Lambert Davis. Harcourt Brace Jovanovich (0-15-206450-8), 1989. 59p. Color illus. (Interest level: 4-8).

Twelve-year-old Jason Bell of Springfield, Ohio, describes the close family celebration of Christmas in 1890. While enjoying the wonderful surprises of Christmas, Jason thinks of the Christmas of 1790 when pioneers in Conestoga wagons traveled along the historic National Road near his home. He wonders about horseless carriages and the Christmas of 1990.
♦ After sharing the story, young people may wish to complete a creative writing assignment on the Christmas of 2090 or create holiday ornaments of Christmas 1890 with popcorn, cranberries, and colored paper.
1. Christmas—Fiction 2. Family life—Fiction 3. Ohio—Fiction 4. African Americans—Fiction.

Hamilton, Virginia. *The House of Dies Drear.* Illus. by Eros Keith. Macmillan (0-02-742500-2), 1968. 256p. B/W illus. (Interest level: 6-9).

The new residents of an enormous house once used as a station in the Underground Railroad are frightened by mysterious sounds, events, and the discovery of secret passageways. Virginia Hamilton's suspenseful approach creates a drama of grave danger.
♦ Students may watch the videorecording *The House of Dies Drear* (Children's Television Workshop, 1984) and compare the book to the movie. Students may also select a scene from the book or movie for role-playing.
1. African Americans—Fiction 2. Mystery and detective stories 3. Ohio—Fiction.

Hamilton, Virginia. *M.C. Higgins, the Great.* Macmillan (0-02-742480-4), 1974. 288p. (Interest level: 7-9).

As strip mining moves closer to Sarah's Mountain in Ohio, 15-year-old M.C. is torn between trying to move his family and fighting to save the home they love. This 1975 Newbery Medal Award winner realistically depicts M.C. as he comes to terms with family, heritage, and his own desires.

♦ A panel of students may want to research strip mining to discover its effects on the environment and its possible alternatives.
1. Family life—Fiction.

Hamilton, Virginia. *The Mystery of Drear House: The Conclusion of the Dies Drear Chronicle.* Greenwillow (0-688-04026-8), 1987. 224p. (Interest level: 5+).

In this conclusion of the Dies Drear chronicle, Virginia Hamilton continues the saga of a family confronted with living in the home of a long-dead abolitionist. The suspense mounts with a series of dramatic events culminating in the family's decision of what to do with the treasure hidden for 100 years in a cavern near their home.
♦ Students may choose to research the role of abolitionists during the time of the Underground Railroad. Students may want to portray a character from the book and tell the story orally from a different perspective. Or, as the story unfolds, students may wish to compile a list of possible solutions for what should be done with the vast, hidden treasure.
1. African Americans—Fiction 2. Mystery and detective stories 3. Buried treasure—Fiction.

Hendershot, Judith. *In Coal Country.* Illus. by Thomas B. Allen. Knopf (0-394-88190-7), 1987. Unpaginated. Color illus. (Interest level: 2-5).

Judith Hendershot vividly describes her own childhood in a 1930s coal camp called Willow Grove, located near Neffs, Ohio. Rich pastel and charcoal illustrations depict the seasons as the text describes the memories associated with each special time of the year.
♦ After sharing the story, young people may draw their favorite season with pastels and charcoal on colored paper, or through personal written accounts they may share their own family traditions that are a special part of a particular season.
1. Coal mines and mining—Fiction.

Hickman, Janet. *The Valley of the Shadow.* Macmillan (0-02-743750-7), 1974. 215p. (Interest level: 7+).

Tobias, a 13-year-old Delaware Indian, interprets the events that led to the massacre by American militiamen of 96 Moravian Indians at Gnadenhutten, Ohio, in 1781 during the Revolutionary War. Hickman's deeply moving fictionalized account conveys the anguish and horror of this event.
♦ Young people may want to locate more information about the peace-loving Moravian missionaries of the Ohio country.
1. Moravian Indians—Fiction 2. Indians of North America—Fiction 3. Gnadenhutten, Ohio—History—Fiction.

Hickman, Janet. *Zoar Blue.* Macmillan (0-02-743740-X), 1978. 140p. (Interest level: 5+).

The lives of a young man and young woman are changed forever as the turbulence of the Civil War

affects the German pacifist community of Zoar, Ohio. Janet Hickman's story, finely tuned to human emotions, is rich in historic detail.
♦ Because letter writing was an important form of communication during this time period, students may write imaginary letters from the young people in this story to each other. Students should locate Zoar, Ohio, on a map.
1. Society of Separatists of Zoar—Fiction 2. United States—History—1861-1865, Civil War—Fiction 3. Zoar (Ohio)—Fiction.

Hurwitz, Joanna. *The Rabbi's Girls.* B/W illus. by Pamela Johnson. Morrow (0-688-01089-X), 1982. 192p. (Interest level: 4-6).

The town of Lorain, Ohio, in 1923 is the setting for 11-year-old Carrie Levin's newest home. This insightful story shares Carrie's tumultuous year, highlighting the birth of a sister and her sorrow over the death of her rabbi father.
♦ After reading about Carrie's account of her year in Lorain, students may want to keep a journal or diary.
1. Family life—Fiction 2. Jews—United States—Fiction 3. Lorain (Ohio)—Fiction.

In Coal Country. (Videocassette). American School Publishers (0-07-020558-2), 1990. (The Children's Literature Series). VHS 1/2", Color, (11 min.). $35. Includes teacher's guide. (Interest level: 2-6).

Daily life in a 1930s Ohio coal camp is described through the eyes of a young girl. Seven new pastel illustrations on colored papers were created by Thomas B. Allen for this production of Judith Hendershot's story of the same title (*see* Ohio—Fiction).
♦ Though the family depicted in the video did not possess material wealth, their lives were rich in other ways. Young people may wish to make a list of ways, other than material wealth, through which their own lives are enriched.
1. Coal mines and mining—Fiction.

Kellogg, Steven. *Johnny Appleseed.* Morrow (0-688-06417-5), 1988. Unpaginated. Color illus. (Interest level: 2-4).

This version of the story of Ohio's legendary hero is based on incidents from the life of John Chapman. Steven Kellogg's colorful, detailed illustrations humorously extend the text.
♦ Students may prepare apple dishes, following recipes such as those provided in "Fast & Fun: Apple Recipe Favorites" (Ohio Apple Marketing Program, P.O. Box 479, Columbus, OH 43216). Students may also choose apple activities depicted in *The Amazing Apple Book* by Paulette Bourgeois (Addison-Wesley, 1990).
1. Appleseed, Johnny, 1774-1845 2. Apple 3. Frontier and pioneer life—Middle West.

Lindbergh, Reeve. *Johnny Appleseed.* Illus. by Kathy Jakobsen. Little, Brown (0-316-52618-5), 1990. Unpaginated. Color illus. (Interest level: K-4).

Vivid, detailed folk art paintings (featuring the "Ohio Star" quilt design) and the lyrical text present the life of the legendary Johnny Appleseed. The work is loosely based on the experiences of John Chapman, who scattered apple seeds and planted apple trees in Ohio, Pennsylvania, and northern Indiana.
♦ After sharing the poem, young people may participate in the creative writing of a poem or paragraph from an apple tree's perspective.
1. Appleseed, Johnny, 1774-1845 2. Apple 3. Frontier and pioneer life—Middle West.

Lydon, Kerry Raines. *A Birthday for Blue.* Illus. by Michael Hayes. Whitman (0-8075-0774-1), 1989. Unpaginated. Color illus. (Interest level: 1-4).

The significance of Blue's birthday is recognized when, in his honor, his father plants seven small trees somewhere along the Cumberland Road that spanned southern Ohio in the mid-nineteenth century. Soft, pastel illustrations depict the joys and hardships of traveling cross-country in a Conestoga wagon.
♦ As described in Jane Lane's *How to Make Play Places and Secret Hidy Holes* (Doubleday, 1979), students may construct a replica of a covered wagon from a large appliance box. A smaller version from paper is featured in Laurie Carlson's *Kids Create* (Williamson, 1990).
1. Frontier and pioneer life—Fiction 2. Birthdays—Fiction.

McCloskey, Robert. *Lentil.* Viking Penguin (0-670-42357-2), 1940. Unpaginated. B/W illus. (Interest level: K-3).

The one desire of a young boy named Lentil, who lives in the imaginary town of Alto, Ohio, is to make music, but he cannot sing or whistle. After Lentil solves his problem by learning to play the harmonica, he saves the day by substituting for the band during the town's welcome home celebration for a local dignitary.
♦ Lentil was able to overcome his problem by thinking of an alternative solution. Young people may describe a problem and devise two or more solutions. They may wish to play the harmonica or, if possible, invite an individual from the community to play the harmonica for the group.
1. Ohio—Fiction 2. Harmonica—Fiction.

Merrill, Jean. *The Toothpaste Millionaire.* Houghton Mifflin (0-395-11186-2), 1972. 90p. B/W illus. (Interest level: 3-6).

A young girl describes how a young African-American school friend made more than a million dollars by creating and marketing a cheaper and better toothpaste. This humorous story is set in Cleveland, Ohio.
♦ After brainstorming about an everyday product (such as soap), students may choose to redesign the

packaging, invent new advertisement slogans, tape record jingles, and design posters displaying their new product.
1. Business—Fiction.

Myers, Christopher A. and **Myers, Lynne Born**. *McCrephy's Field*. Illus. by Normand Chartier. Houghton Mifflin (0-395-53807-6), 1991. 32p. Color illus. (Interest level: K-4).

When Joe McCrephy returns to his farm in Ohio after living in the West for 50 years, he hardly recognizes it. Through detailed, vivid watercolors, the changes that occurred as the farm went "back to nature" are illustrated: the fields turned ragged, the barn became gray with age, birds made nests in the growing trees, and a red fox dug a den in the field.
♦ Young people may want to make a list of ways the environment can be protected through ecology projects such as planting trees or recycling. The group may wish to engage in one of the activities listed.
1. Nature—Fiction 2. Barns—Fiction.

Polacco, Patricia. *Just Plain Fancy*. Bantam (0-553-05884-3), 1990. Unpaginated. Color illus. (Interest level: 1-5).

Naomi Vlecke, a young Amish girl, is horrified when an egg she has found hatches into a peacock. In this touching story Naomi tries to adhere to the simple ways of her people while carefully managing to keep "Fancy" a secret until he introduces himself at a community working bee in all his colorful glory.
♦ After sharing the story, young people may want to discuss or write about a secret they have *almost* successfully kept.
1. Amish—Fiction 2. Peacocks—Fiction 3. Eggs—Fiction.

Precek, Katherine Wilson. *The Keepsake Chest*. Macmillan (0-02-775045-0), 1992. 160p. (Interest level: 4-8).

Thirteen-year-old Meg Hamilton has problems adjusting when she moves from her beloved Colorado to an Ohio farmhouse. In this well-told, suspenseful story, Meg begins to probe the history of an old chest that she has found in the attic.
♦ Students may make a list of favorite or important things that they would like to save in a keepsake chest.
1. Moving, Household—Fiction 2. Ohio—Fiction 3. Genealogy—Fiction.

Rosen, Michael J. *Elijah's Angel: A Story of Chanukah and Christmas*. Illus. by Aminah Brenda Lynn Robinson. Harcourt Brace Jovanovich (0-15-225394-7), 1992. Unpaginated. Color illus. (Interest level: 1-6).

At Christmas-Hanukkah time, Elijah Pierce, a Christian barber in Columbus, Ohio, gives a carved wooden angel to a young Jewish friend who struggles with accepting this Christmas gift. Vibrant illustrations enhance this heartwarming story of the young friend who realizes that friendship is the same in any religion.
♦ Students may enjoy a demonstration of soap or wood carving.
1. Pierce, Elijah—Fiction 2. Wood carving—Fiction 3. Christmas—Fiction 4. Hanukkah—Fiction.

Sanders, Scott Russell. *Aurora Means Dawn*. Illus. by Jill Kastner. Bradbury (0-02-778270-0), 1989. 32p. Color illus. (Interest level: 1-5).

Vivid watercolors and lyrical text depict the covered wagon journey (1800) of the Sheldon family from Connecticut to Aurora, Ohio, in 1800. After the unforeseen hardships of the journey, the family finally arrives at their destination. Because the family sees their arrival as the first glimmering of hope in the unsettled place, they come to realize that the word *aurora* means dawn.
♦ Young people may wish to discuss and investigate how pioneers might have selected names for the towns and cities in their own area. If facts are not readily known, young people may want to write an imagined account of how they think their town was named.
1. Frontier and pioneer life—Fiction 2. Ohio—Fiction.

Sanders, Scott Russell. *Warm As Wool*. Illus. by Helen Cogancherry. Bradbury (0-02-778139-9), 1992. Unpaginated. Color illus. (Interest level: K-4).

When Betsy Ward's family moves from Connecticut to Ohio in 1803, she brings along a sockful of coins to buy sheep so that she can gather wool, spin cloth, and make clothes to keep her children warm. Richly detailed color illustrations depict the importance of the woman's role on the American frontier.
♦ Students may research what kinds of fibers are used in today's clothing. A guest speaker may demonstrate weaving, or students may be interested in weaving projects such as those suggested in Jenean Romberg's *Let's Discover Weaving* (Center for Applied Research in Education, 1975) or Alice Gilbreath's *Fun with Weaving* (Morrow, 1975).
1. Frontier and pioneer life—Fiction 2. Ohio—Fiction 3. Sheep—Fiction.

Taylor, Mildred D. *The Gold Cadillac*. Illus. by Michael Hays. Dial (0-8037-0343-0), 1987. 32p. Brown/White illus. (Interest level: 3-6).

Two African-American girls living in Toledo, Ohio, are proud of their family's brand new 1950 Cadillac Coupe deVille until they take it on a trip to Mississippi and encounter racial prejudice for the first time. This powerful and poignant story portrays growing up black in the United States during the 1950s.

♦ Students may want to trace the family's journey from Toledo to Mississippi, or students may discuss the symbolism of the gold Cadillac.

1. African Americans—Fiction 2. Prejudices—Fiction 3. Race relations—Fiction.

Willis, Patricia. *A Place to Claim as Home.* Clarion (0-395-55395-4), 1991. 166p. (Interest level: 4-8).

While the men are at war in 1943, 13-year-old orphan Henry is hired for the summer by the somewhat unfriendly Miss Morrison. This touching story depicts how loneliness can bring together people who need each other.

♦ Students may write poetry or prose about what the word *home* means to them. For interesting ideas students may look at the selections included in Michael J. Rosen's *Home: A Collaboration of Thirty Distinguished Authors and Illustrators* (HarperCollins, 1992).

1. Farm life—Fiction 2. World War II, 1939-1945—United States.

Winter, Jeanette. *Follow the Drinking Gourd.* Knopf (0-394-99694-1), 1988. 48p. Color illus. (Interest level: 2-6).

An old sailor named "Peg Leg Joe" travels through the South and subtly teaches the African-American folk song "The Drinking Gourd," which gives the directions for runaway slaves to journey northward across the Ohio River and Lake Erie to Canada. Powerful primitive and folk art illustrations follow one fugitive slave family's harrowing journey to freedom in the 1840s.

♦ After sharing the book, young people may use the clues in the song to draw a map showing the trail. They may also listen to other African-American folk songs and describe or illustrate their message or story.

1. Slavery—Fiction 2. Underground Railroad—Fiction 3. African Americans—Fiction.

Periodicals

977.1
Ohio Cues. Maumee Valley Historical Society. Quarterly. 1951-. Illus. $15 per year. (Interest level: 3+).

Published since 1951, *Ohio Cues* provides several pages of information in each issue on a specific theme related to Ohio history, such as "The Old Fashioned Fourth of July" or "County Names Honor Revolutionary Patriots and Heroes." Because many of the back issues of the past 40 years are available, this periodical provides much hard-to-locate information.

♦ After sharing several issues of *Ohio Cues*, students may be interested in selecting a theme and compiling an issue of their own magazine about Ohio or another state of their choice.

1. Ohio.

977.1
Ohio Magazine. Ohio Magazine, Inc., 1977- . Bimonthly. Color illus. $18 per year. (Interest level: 7+).

This overview of Ohio features both historical and contemporary articles on people, places, and events. Its contents include a wide range of well-written articles, informative columns, and numerous advertisements.

♦ Teachers and librarians preparing lengthy units of study on the state of Ohio will find this a useful source of information.

1. Ohio.

977.1
Timeline. Ohio Historical Society, 1984- . Bimonthly. Color illus. $18 per year. (Interest level: 4+).

Each issue includes several articles on Ohio history and related subjects. The articles within this excellent, well-researched, lively source for historical information are each supported with a bibliography of additional readings.

♦ Young people may examine the tables of contents for the last six issues, record the subjects included, and suggest other Ohio topics not considered in those issues.

1. Ohio—History.

Professional Materials

375.09771
Ohio Studies. Ohio Department of Education (No ISBN), 1985. (Minimum Standards Leadership Series). 68p. (Interest level: Professional).

This K-12 curriculum on the study of Ohio suggests several teaching strategies and includes sections on textbooks, sources for media, and lists of films.

♦ Students who are seeking information from Ohio state agencies, historical societies, restorations, and museums will find the list of addresses to be very helpful.

1. Education—Ohio—Curricula 2. Ohio.

977.1
Britton, J.D. *Ohio History Resource Guide for Teachers.* Ohio Historical Society (No ISBN), 1991. 131p. B/W illus. (Interest level: Professional).

This comprehensive guide to materials intended to assist educators in teaching Ohio history includes background information and 18 project ideas with lesson plans for grades 3 through 11.

♦ Students may want to complete some of the activities or projects suggested in this resource (e.g.,

imaginary trip around Ohio, Ohio symbols, pioneer buck kit, or the oral history project).
1. Ohio—History—Study and teaching (Secondary)
2. Ohio History—Study and teaching (Elementary).

977.1
Knepper, George W. *Ohio and Its People.* Kent State University Press (0-87338-337-X), 1989. 508p. B/W illus. (Interest level: Professional).

This comprehensive historical work is often cited as the definitive source of information on Ohio. Because it is thoroughly documented, it is an excellent resource for a professional to use as background information when teaching Ohio history.
1. Ohio—History.

Wisconsin

by Jane Roeber

Nonfiction

328.77 (Reference)
Wisconsin Legislative Reference Bureau. *State of Wisconsin Blue Book.* Published biennially in odd-numbered years. Distributed by Wisconsin Document Sales, Department of Administration. (Interest level: 5-8).

Contents include biographical information about the state's constitutional officers; Supreme Court justices; and members of the United States Congress, State Assembly, and State Senate; as well as information on Wisconsin history, symbols, governmental departments, various statistics, and much more. In addition to updated information on persons and agencies, each volume contains a special feature article and an index to the feature articles in prior *Blue Books*.
♦ In order to become acquainted with the range of information included, students should be allowed to spend time browsing through the book. Then they may select a page or section and redesign it to be more visually interesting.
1. Wisconsin—Politics and government 2. Wisconsin—Statistics.

355
Stevens, Michael E., ed. *Letters from the Front, 1898-1945.* State Historical Society of Wisconsin (0-87020-268-5 pbk), 1992. (Voices of the Wisconsin Past Series). 175p. (Interest level: 7-8).

This documentary history is told through the letters of 62 Wisconsin men and women serving in the United States armed forces in the Spanish-American War, World War I, and World War II. The feelings and philosophies of ordinary people reveal the realities of war—its discipline, combat situations, and prison camps.
♦ After students research further and develop a more complete understanding of the era, they may select one of these letters and compose a reply.
1. Military history 2. Wisconsin—History.

378.775
Schultz, Gwen. *The Bucky Badger Story.* Illus. by Bertha Schumacher. Hammock & Inglenook (0-915988-51-8), 1981. 80p. B/W and Color photos and illus. (Interest level: 4-8).

Fiction and facts about the mascot of the University of Wisconsin—Madison are presented in this entertaining and readable history. Natural history about badgers in the wild is included along with information about other badger symbolism in the state.
♦ Students may learn and perform the song "If You Want to Be a Badger." The words and music are printed in the book.
1. University of Wisconsin—Madison—History
2. Badgers.

394
Lowery, Linda. *Earth Day.* Illus. by Mary Bergherr. Carolrhoda (0-87614-662-0), 1991. (On My Own Series). 48p. Color illus. (Interest level: K-4).

This book describes the efforts of Gaylord Nelson, former United States senator from Wisconsin, in creating the original Earth Day in 1970. It also presents subsequent environmental concerns leading to a worldwide Earth Day in 1990. Included are practical suggestions for making every day an Earth Day as well as contact information for several environmental activist groups.
♦ As a class project, students may select one or more of the "every day/Earth Day" suggestions to carry out.
1. Earth Day, 1970 2. Earth Day, 1990 3. Environmental protection.

394
Patent, Dorothy. *Christmas Trees.* Illus. by William Muñoz. Dodd, Mead (0-396-09056-7), 1987. 64p. Color photos. (Interest level: 3-7).

The author describes both the Christmas tree traditions and the Christmas tree industry (planting, shearing, harvesting, and shipping). Although Wisconsin is

not specifically addressed, the book has relevance to the state's Christmas tree industry.
♦ Students may discuss ecologically responsible ways to dispose of Christmas trees after the holiday.
1. Christmas trees.

398.2
Arnold, Caroline. *The Terrible Hodag.* Illus. by Lambert Davis. Harcourt, Brace, Jovanovich (0-15-284750-2), 1989. 30p. Color illus. (Interest level: K-2).

Lumberjack Ole Swenson befriends the Hodag (a mythic creature with the head of an ox, feet of a bear, back of a dinosaur, and tail of an alligator) to their mutual benefit. Hodag stories have long been associated with Wisconsin logging camps, and this version can introduce for discussion an element of ecological awareness.
♦ Students may draw their own conception of the Hodag's appearance.
1. Folklore—United States.

398.2
Benton-Banai, Edward. *The Earth's First People: A History-Coloring Book of the Ojibway Indians.* Illus. by Joe Liles. Indian Country Communications (No ISBN), 1975. (A Mishomis Book, book No. 4). 20p. B/W illus. (Interest level: 1-4).

This series, adapted from *The Mishomis Book* (*see* Wisconsin—Nonfiction 970, Benton-Banai), also includes *The Great Flood: A History-Coloring Book of the Ojibway Indians,* book No. 5 (1979); *The Ojibway Creation Story: A History-Coloring Book of the Ojibway Indians,* book No. 1 (1975); *Original Man and His Grandmother-No-No-Mis: A History-Coloring Book of the Ojibway Indians,* book No. 3 (1976); and *Original Man Walks the Earth: A History-Coloring Book of the Ojibway Indians,* book No. 2 (1976). Although described as coloring books, they are informative picture books with brief texts. Originally developed for classroom use, the series is equally suitable for public library collections and home libraries of both Native and non-Native Americans.
♦ Young readers may match the vocabulary words and pictures at the end of each volume. Older readers may write a brief story incorporating some of the vocabulary.
1. Ojibway Indians—Legends 2. Ojibway Indians—History.

398.2
Brooke, William J. *A Telling of the Tales: Five Stories.* Illus. by Richard Egielski. Harper & Row (0-06-020689-6 lib bind), 1990. 132p. B/W illus. (Interest level: 3-7).

"The Growin' of Paul Bunyan" is one of the classics retold here with a modern twist of introducing him to Johnny Appleseed. Their differing philosophies about trees are immediately apparent. The ecological angle seems somewhat forced, but preferences for trees horizontal or trees vertical provide a starting point for discussion.
♦ Students may create similar interviews between Paul and Gaylord Nelson (using Jeffrey Shulman and Teresa Rogers' *Gaylord Nelson, see* Wisconsin—Biography, Nelson) or John Muir (using Ginger Wadsworth's *John Muir, Wilderness Protector, see* Wisconsin—Biography, Muir).
1. Short stories 2. Tall tales 3. Fairy tales.

398.2
Gard, Robert E. and **Sorden, L. G.** *Wisconsin Lore.* NorthWord (0-942802-79-9 pbk), 1987. 348p. (Interest level: 5-8).

Eleven chapters of tales, proverbs, yarns, home remedies, superstitions, and other folklore reflect the area's unique folk history and the traditions of those who settled the state. Although written for the general adult reader, the book's anecdotal nature makes it accessible to young people. The appendix of place name origins is an added bonus.
♦ From either the chapter on superstitions or the chapter on proverbs students may choose one list and, for one week, keep track of whether they hear these expressions in daily conversations.
1. Folklore—Wisconsin 2. Legends—Wisconsin 3. Wisconsin—History.

398.2
Gleiter, Jan and **Thompson, Kathleen.** *Paul Bunyan and Babe the Blue Ox.* Illus. by Yoshi Miyake. Raintree (0-8172-2119-0 lib bind), 1985. 32p. Color illus. (Interest level: 2-4).

Tales about Paul Bunyan's infancy, tree-felling exploits, crew of helpers, and his trusty ox, Babe, are retold here in a straightforward manner. The understated language and depiction of Paul in a noncaricatured style make this a quieter tall tale.
♦ Paul's growing of a gigantic stalk of corn is one of the less familiar tales in this narration. Students may decorate a classroom, library, or hall with a Bunyanesque stalk (perhaps bearing "ears" of books).
1. Paul Bunyan (legendary character) 2. Folklore—United States 3. Tall tales.

398.2
Johnston, Basil H. *By Canoe and Moccasin: Some Native Place Names of the Great Lakes.* Illus. by David Beyer. Waapoone (0-9692185-1-6 pbk), 1986. 45p. B/W illus. (Interest level: 5-8).

In nine brief stories the author recounts how Nanabush, a legendary Ojibway hero of superhuman powers, traveled throughout the Great Lakes region defending his tribe. This work includes Ojibway place names; the English language equivalents, where relevant; and a pronunciation guide.
♦ Using the book's regional map, students may locate the eight sites that are now in the area known as Wisconsin, find the references to them in the stories,

and compare that information with entries in Robert Gard and L. G. Sorden's *Romance of Wisconsin Place Names* (*see* Wisconsin—Nonfiction—977.5).
1. Ojibway Indians—Legends.

398.2
Kellogg, Steven. *Paul Bunyan.* Morrow (0-688-03850-6 lib bind), 1984. 40p. Color illus. (Interest level: K-4).

Kellogg's brisk retelling (accompanied by his own distinctive humorous drawings) carries Paul from childhood in Maine; through the Appalachians with his loggers; across the Great Lakes, Great Plains, and Rockies; over Texas and Arizona; and into the Pacific. It suggests he now lives in Alaska. The multiple lighthearted images on every page give this version very pleasing visual appeal.
♦ Paul's lumbermen cool off with a blizzard of popcorn balls at one point. Young students may enjoy a batch of popcorn—served from the largest possible bowl—as a related treat.
1. Paul Bunyan (Legendary character) 2. Folklore—United States 3. Tall tales.

398.2
McCormick, Dell J. *Paul Bunyan Swings His Axe.* Caxton (0-87004-093-6), 1936, 1987. 111p. B/W illus. (Interest level: 3-7).

This classic Bunyan book, illustrated by the author, features 17 stories in easily read chapters. Endpaper maps make it easy to locate the site of each adventure. The Round River will be of special interest to Wisconsin readers.
♦ Students may come to school dressed as Paul Bunyan's lumber crew for a day devoted to tall tales.
1. Paul Bunyan (Legendary character) 2. Folklore—United States 3. Tall tales.

398.2
Osborne, Mary Pope. *American Tall Tales.* Illus. by Michael McCurdy. Knopf (0-679-90089-6 lib bind), 1991. 115p. Color illus. (Interest level: 3-7).

This collection contains nine entertaining chapters focusing on nine familiar and not-so-familiar folk heroes: Davy Crockett, Sally Ann Thunder, Ann Whirlwind, Johnny Appleseed, Stormalong, Mose, Febold Feboldson, Pecos Bill, John Henry, and Paul Bunyan. The author provides brief background notes for each character and a map showing the sites of various exploits.
♦ Students may try to emulate the woodblock printing technique of artist McCurdy or use a less demanding medium to create portraits of the folk heroes.
1. Folklore—United States 2. Tall tales.

398.2
Rounds, Glen. *Ol' Paul: The Mighty Logger.* Illus. by author. Holiday (0-8234-0269-X), 1936, 1976. 93p. B/W illus. (Interest level: 4-8).

Originally published in 1936 and illustrated by the author, this collection of 10 Bunyan escapades is written as a first-person narrative. The informal narration flows naturally and robustly as though aimed at adults as well as children.
♦ The author suggests that he himself was recommended by Ol' Paul as the biggest liar Bunyan ever had in his camp. Students may hold a liar's contest to come up with new Bunyan inventions and/or adventures.
1. Paul Bunyan (Legendary character) 2. Folklore—United States 3. Tall tales.

398.2
San Souci, Robert. *Larger Than Life: The Adventures of American Legendary Heroes.* Illus. by Andrew Glass. Doubleday (0-385-24907-1), 1991. 59p. Color illus. (Interest level: 3-6).

Paul Bunyan's story is told along with tales of John Henry, Stormalong, Slue-foot Sue and Pecos Bill, and Strap Buckner. San Souci's version has Paul become more ecologically aware at its close than most retellings, but the narration does not lose its zest or become didactic.
♦ Students may create a Wisconsin map showing where state and national forests exist today as reforested areas where Paul and his loggers clear-cut.
1. Folklore—United States 2. Tall tales.

398.2
Shephard, Esther. *Paul Bunyan.* Illus. by Rockwell Kent. Harcourt (0-15-259749-2), 1924, 1985. 284p. B/W illus. (Interest level: 4-8).

The 21 chapters in this classic compilation of Paul Bunyan's exploits are written in the first-person as though being narrated by a companion lumberjack. The informal style and dialect may not appeal to every reader. Contemporary children will probably skip over Kent's drawings; however, this is a rich collection of adventures.
♦ Each student may make use of the first-person literary device to retell one adventure, experiencing with the group the oral tradition from which the tales originally sprang.
1. Paul Bunyan (Legendary character) 2. Folklore—United States 3. Tall tales.

500.977
Wilkins, Marne. *The Long Ago Lake: A Child's Book of Nature Lore and Crafts.* Chronicle (0-87701-632-1 pbk), 1990. 160p. B/W illus. (Interest level: 5-8).

Drawing on experiences from her 1930s childhood near Elkhorn, Wisconsin, and in summer camp near Hayward, the author describes a range of craft projects and practical instructions for outdoor activities. Scattered throughout the text are informal comments and advice on being a responsible person while enjoying the outdoors. The book was originally published by the Sierra Club.

♦ Using the author's ideas about responsibility, students may design a poster that could be displayed at county and state parks.
1. Natural history—Wisconsin 2. Naturecraft 3. Handicraft.

572
Herda, D. J. *Ethnic America: The North Central States.* Millbrook (1-56294-016-3), 1991. (The American Scene Series). 64p. Color photos. (Interest level: 5-8).

In five chapters—on American Indians, Europeans, African Americans, Asians, and Hispanics—the author presents a generalized look at the history and contemporary status of ethnic groups in nine states: Ohio, Indiana, Michigan, Illinois, Wisconsin, Minnesota, Iowa, and North and South Dakota. The book's format allows only a superficial treatment of a complex subject. Although no mention is made of Hmong immigrants, and some photo captions are misleading, useful information about U.S. immigration policies is provided.
♦ Students may show on a world map the diverse ethnic backgrounds represented in their classroom.
1. Ethnology—Middle West 2. United States—Social life and customs.

610
Epstein, Samuel and **Epstein, Beryl.** *Dr. Beaumont and the Man with the Hole in His Stomach.* Illus. by Joseph Scrofani. Putnam (0-698-30680-5 lib bind.), 1978. (Science Discovery Series). 62p. B/W illus. (Interest level: 3-6).

Treatment of a gunshot wound to the stomach of Alexis St. Martin, a French-Canadian voyageur on Mackinac Island (1822), was the beginning of the scientific study of digestion carried out over the next three decades as United States Army doctor William Beaumont and his patient moved to army posts in Wisconsin, New York, and Washington, DC. A briskly paced, straightforward narrative style and realistic drawings bring frontier life and early medical research into sharp focus.
♦ Students may compare and contrast what happened to St. Martin with what would occur in a medical emergency today.
1. Beaumont, William, 1785-1853 2. St. Martin, Alexis, 179[7]-1880 3. Physicians 4. Digestion.

620
Murphy, Jim. *Tractors: From Yesterday's Steam Wagons to Today's Turbocharged Giants.* Lippincott (0-397-32051-1 lib bind), 1984. 60p. B/W photos. (Interest level: 4-8).

In a readable text the author traces two centuries of the development of machinery important to Wisconsin's farm and manufacturing sectors. Of special interest is the coverage of J. I. Case, the nineteenth-century inventor and founder of one of the largest manufacturers in Racine, Wisconsin.
♦ Students may search for information on how plowing and harvesting were done by manual labor and horsepower. Reading p. 341 of Cheryl Bellville's *Farming Today Yesterday's Way* (*see* Wisconsin—Nonfiction—636) could be an excellent starting point.
1. Tractors—History.

631.2
Apps, Jerry. *Barns of Wisconsin.* Illus. by Allen Strang. Wisconsin Trails (0-915024-14-4 pbk), 1977. 143p. B/W and Color illus. (Interest level: 5-8).

The purposes, construction, ethnic variations, and decorative features of barns are encompassed in this historically oriented volume intended for the general adult reader. Even a scanning of the book's contents will enable the reader to see familiar rural structures in a new light.
♦ Using the floor plans and excellent illustrations as a guide, students may construct a scale model of a barn.
1. Barns 2. Wisconsin—History.

633
Bial, Raymond. *Corn Belt Harvest.* Houghton Mifflin (0-395-56234-1), 1991. 48p. Color photos. (Interest level: 2-6).

The cultivation, harvesting, and processing of one of the world's most abundant grains are clearly described in brief text and photos. Located on the fringe of the Corn Belt, Wisconsin has a significant annual corn harvest, which urban students will understand more fully through this book.
♦ Over a period of a week students may read labels and keep a log of all the foods they eat containing corn products.
1. Corn.

634
Cranberries: Wisconsin's Native Fruit. (Videocassette). University of Wisconsin—Stevens Point, University Telecommunications, 1990. VHS 1/2", (26 min.). $23. (Interest level: 6-8).

Produced with the cooperation of individual cranberry growers and the Ocean Spray Company, this video provides clear information about the cultivation, harvesting, processing, and packaging of cranberries, which are a major state crop. Brief segments on Native Americans' use of the berries and on pre-mechanical harvesting techniques are of special interest.
♦ Students may gather and publish a collection of cranberry recipes, using family favorites and cookbooks from the library. Historic recipes may be sought and highlighted.
1. Cranberry.

634
Jaspersohn, William. *Cranberries.* Houghton Mifflin (0-395-52098-3), 1991. 32p. Color photos. (Interest level: 1-4).

The cultivation and harvesting of cranberries are clearly pictured in a series of photographs accompanied by a very brief text. Although the pictures are not from Wisconsin, the book is important because students should understand an industry in which Wisconsin ranks second in the nation.
♦ Students may plan a party to sample cranberry juice, cranberry sauce, cranberry bread, dried cranberries, and perhaps such exotic foods as cranberry mustard and cranberry chutney.
1. Cranberry.

634
Kurz, Ann. *Cranberries from A to Z: An Educational Picture Book.* Cranberry Originals Press (0-9622784-0-8), 1989. 32p. Color illus. (Interest level: K-6).

Much detailed information about cranberry cultivation and industry is included in this alphabet picture book's drawings and brief text, making it useful for older children as well as the young. An excellent glossary, botanic drawings of the cranberry plant, and a map of major cranberry growing areas in the United States and Canada are valuable features.
♦ Older students may develop their own informative alphabet about another Wisconsin product of their choosing. Product possibilities could range from corn to Cray computers, from tractors to Trek bicycles.
1. Cranberry.

634.9
The Fallin' of the Pine: Logging on the Chippewa River, 1850-1900. (Videocassette). University of Wisconsin—Eau Claire, Office of University Research, 1984. VHS 1/2", B/W and Color, (14 min.). To obtain a free copy send a new VHS tape, return address label, and return postage to: Dr. Daniel J. Perkins, Department of Communication & Theatre Arts, Fine Arts Building 176, University of Wisconsin—Eau Claire, Eau Claire, WI 54702-4004, (715) 836-3419. (Interest level: 7-8).

Black-and-white archival photographs are contrasted with color views of the river today in ways that convey the magnitude of nineteenth-century logging operations. Life in the lumber camps is also described with readings from ordinary workers. Although slow-moving initially, the film brings the era into perspective.
♦ Verses of the folk song "Fallin' of the Pine" are sung as transitional devices. Students may write additional verses.
1. Logging 2. Rivers—Wisconsin 3. Wisconsin—History.

636
Bellville, Cheryl Walsh. *Farming Today Underground Rail's Way.* Carolrhoda (0-87614-220-X lib bind), 1984. 40p. Color photos. (Interest level: K-5).

Simple text and clear photographs present a year's cycle of farm work by a contemporary Wisconsin dairying family who have chosen to farm with horses rather than mechanical power. A glossary gives excellent explanations of terms that will be unfamiliar to most urban children and many rural children as well.
♦ Students may write captions for the book's photographs as though the students are participating in the work being performed.
1. Dairying 2. Draft horses 3. Horses 4. Farm life—Wisconsin.

637
Giblin, James Cross. *Milk: The Fight for Purity.* Crowell (0-690-04574-3 lib bind), 1986. B/W photos. (Interest level: 3-8).

This study traces human uses of cow's milk from the Middle Ages to the present era, technologies for safer consumption, and modern crises such as radioactivity. Although not addressing Wisconsin's dairy industry in any specific way, the book enhances knowledge of ongoing processes ensuring consumer safety in an industry for which Wisconsin is noted.
♦ Students may use this volume and others to design an informative and attractive milk carton with nutritional data, dairy cow descriptions, processing facts, etc.
1. Milk 2. Dairying.

637
Ross, Catherine and **Wallace, Susan.** *The Amazing Milk Book.* Illus. by Linda Hendry. Addison-Wesley (0-201-57078-4), 1991. 80p. B/W illus. (Interest level: 3-6).

Originally published by Kids Can Press, Ltd. (Ontario), the book has a Canadian viewpoint at times, but the excellent collection of facts and activities will enrich any study of Wisconsin. This mixture of lore, legends, projects, and technologic explanations is an appropriate way to garner knowledge about a leading Wisconsin industry.
♦ Students may select an activity from the several described in the text. Although instructions for making butter, yogurt, cottage cheese, and ice cream are included, the invisible ink project is the simplest.
1. Milk 2. Dairying.

637
Turner, Dorothy. *Milk.* Illus. by John Yates. Carolrhoda (0-87614-361-3 lib bind), 1988. 32p. Color photos and illus. (Interest level: K-3).

This picture book addresses how cows produce milk, how milk is processed, and what various milk products are the result. Inclusion of other milk-givers

besides cows and a multicultural approach provide an additional dimension.
♦ Students may follow the directions included to make their own yogurt.
1. Milk 2. Dairy products.

637
Ziegler, Sandra. *A Visit to the Dairy Farm.* Childrens Press (0-516-01496-X), 1987. (Field Trip Books). 31p. Color photos. (Interest level: K-3).

A Milwaukee, Wisconsin, elementary school class visits a Wisconsin dairy farm to learn about raising cows and milking them. The simple narrative conveys informative basic concepts about the dairy industry.
♦ A field trip similar to the one recorded in this book would be the optimal follow-up. A visit to a processing/packaging plant would be an alternative.
1. Dairying 2. Farm life.

639
Herda, D. J. *Environmental America: The North Central States.* Millbrook (1-878841-08-4), 1991. (The American Scene Series). 64p. Color photos. (Interest level: 5-8).

The states of Ohio, Indiana, Michigan, Illinois, Wisconsin, Iowa, Minnesota, and North and South Dakota are addressed in this survey of current environmental problems and attempted solutions. In this introduction to a complex subject, specific Wisconsin references are made to Fox River pollution, Dane County groundwater contamination, a Portage County agricultural compost project, and the International Crane Foundation at Baraboo.
♦ Using the final chapter, "What We Can Do," students may select one or more activities to pursue as a class or as individuals.
1. Conservation of natural resources 2. Pollution 3. Environmental protection.

639.9
McNulty, Faith. *Peeping in the Shell: A Whooping Crane Is Hatched.* Illus. by Irene Brady. HarperCollins (0-06-024135-7 lib bind), 1986. 58p. B/W illus. (Interest level: 3-8).

The author recounts the unusual circumstances under which a whooping crane chick was hatched at the International Crane Foundation in Baraboo, Wisconsin. The clear, straightforward explanations of mating and of the hatching process are examples of scientific writing at its best.
♦ Having read this book, students who are interested in wildlife preservation may read a more detailed account in Dorothy Patent's *The Whooping Crane: A Comeback Story* (*see* following entry).
1. Whooping cranes 2. Birds—Protection 3. Eggs—Incubation 4. International Crane Foundation.

639.9
Patent, Dorothy. *The Whooping Crane: A Comeback Story.* Illus. by William Muñoz. Clarion (0-89919-455-9), 1988. 88p. B/W and Color photos. (Interest level: 4-8).

Detailed here are 50 years of ongoing research and rescue work on behalf of the whooping crane, which nearly became extinct in the 1940s. The efforts of the International Crane Foundation in Baraboo, Wisconsin, are briefly mentioned in the discussion of the complexities of hand-rearing birds.
♦ By consulting library indexes, students may obtain more recent reports of progress in raising whooping cranes and returning them to natural habitats.
1. Whooping cranes 2. Birds—Protection 3. Wildlife conservation.

641
Hachten, Harva. *The Flavor of Wisconsin: An Informal History of Food and Eating in the Badger State.* State Historical Society of Wisconsin (0-87020-204-9), 1981. 363p. B/W photos. (Interest level: 7-8).

The early chapters and the 400 recipes representing diverse ethnic backgrounds and periods of history provide lively browsing in this introduction to social history. Thirty-two pages of archival photos, dating from the 1870s to the 1950s, provide special insights into food purchasing, preparation, and eating.
♦ Students may plan a week of family menus using recipes from as many different heritages as possible.
1. Cookery—American—History.

641
Walker, Barbara. *The Little House Cookbook: Frontier Foods from Laura Ingalls Wilder's Classic Stories.* Illus. by Garth Williams. HarperCollins (0-01-446090-8), 1989. 240p. B/W illus. (Interest level: 2-8).

Quotations and illustrations from Wilder's books accompany the more than 100 authentic recipes in this collection. More than a cookbook, Walker's readable volume is a social history providing insights into domestic methods and traditions.
♦ Depending on available facilities and resources, students may prepare a recipe such as popcorn with milk.
1. Cookery—American 2. Wilder, Laura Ingalls, 1867-1957 3. Frontier and pioneer life.

641.3411
Nottridge, Rhoda. *Apples.* Illus. by John Yates. Carolrhoda (0-87614-655-8 lib bind), 1991. (Foods We Eat Series). 32p. Color photos. (Interest level: 2-4).

Although no specific mention is made of Wisconsin orchards, this work can serve as an introduction to a Wisconsin product. The history, cultivation, and nutritional value of apples are briefly described. A glossary and recipes—for baked apples, Waldorf salad, and apple muffins—are special features.

♦ Students may explore Johnny Appleseed legends and illustrate them.
1. Apple.

664
Apps, Jerry. *Mills of Wisconsin and the Midwest*. Illus. by Allen Strang. Wisconsin Trails (0-915024-22-5 pbk), 1990. 128p. B/W and Color illus. (Interest level: 5-8).

The function and operation of flour, feed, and lumber mills are described in relationship to Wisconsin's nineteenth- and twentieth-century industrial development. Although the adult-level text may be difficult for some students, excellent drawings help explain the mechanics of water- and steam-powered mills.
♦ Students may research the location of mills and former mills in their region and the contemporary uses of remaining buildings.
1. Mills and millwork 2. Wisconsin—History.

720.977
Visser, Kristin. *Frank Lloyd Wright and the Prairie School in Wisconsin: An Architectural Touring Guide*. Prairie Oak Press (1-879483-07-6), 1992. 252p. B/W photos. (Interest level: 6-8).

A summary biography and a brief introduction to the Prairie School movement precede a city-by-city description that includes photographs of more than 80 buildings designed by Wright or his contemporaries. The book's usefulness is enhanced by information about access for the public and a clearly written glossary of 19 architectural terms.
♦ Wright agreed with his mentor Louis Sullivan that "form follows function." Students may use that precept to plan graphically or verbally a school or library of the future.
1. Architecture, Modern 2. Wright, Frank Lloyd, 1867-1959.

750
Moon, Marjorie Nelson. *A Is for Art: An Alphabetical Tour of the Milwaukee Art Museum*. Milwaukee Art Museum/Burton and Mayer (0-317-91187-2), 1988. 26p. Color reproductions. (Interest level: K-8).

This presentation of full-color reproductions of 26 works in the Milwaukee Art Museum's collection can be viewed as an ABC concept book, an introduction to art appreciation, or an illustration of the results of philanthropy. The varied styles of painting and sculpture can be studied as examples of artistic movements and social history.
♦ Students may create their own visual alphabet by observing objects in their school building and neighborhood.
1. Art history 2. Milwaukee Art Museum.

759
Garthwaite, Chester. *Threshing Days: The Farm Paintings of Lavern Kammerude*. Wisconsin Folk Museum (0-9624369-1-7), 1990. 103p. Color illus. (Interest level: 5-8).

Twenty-one color reproductions of self-taught artist Lavern Kammerude's realistic paintings reveal details of Wisconsin country life in the 1920s and 1930s. Although written at an adult level, the readable text accompanying each picture will help younger viewers' understanding of now unfamiliar practices and customs.
♦ Students may make posters advertising the farm auction (p. 71) or the county fair (p. 55).
1. Kammerude, Lavern, 1915-1989 2. Artists 3. Country life—Wisconsin 4. Farming—Wisconsin.

784
Peters, Harry B. *Folk Songs Out of Wisconsin: An Illustrated Compendium of Words and Music*. State Historical Society of Wisconsin (0-87020-165-4 pbk), 1977. 321p. B/W photos. (Interest level: K-5).

This collection of approximately 200 songs reflects social history through the music of farm families, schoolchildren, sailors, and lumberjacks. Diverse ethnic groups are represented, thus reflecting another facet of state history.
♦ Students may choose songs that complement or supplement a topic they are studying, then perform them musically or as a choral speaking presentation.
1. Folk songs, American—Wisconsin.

789.2
A Kingdom of Fiddlers: Old-Time Music in the Rural Community. (Videocassette). Wisconsin Folk Museum, 1991. VHS 1/2", B/W and Color, (18 min.). $19.95. (Interest level: 6-8).

Black-and-white archival and contemporary color photographs accompany narration and musical samples that explain the role of music in rural Wisconsin neighborhood gatherings in the years before World War I. There is thought-provoking commentary on the factors—such as radio, movies, automobiles—that had an influence on the gradual decline of neighbor-centered activity.
♦ Students may consult pages 82-85 in Chester Garthwaite's *Threshing Days* (see Wisconsin—Nonfiction—759), which include the painting *House Party* that reinforces the content of *A Kingdom of Fiddlers*. They may want to discuss social customs that might change or disappear in the twenty-first century.
1. Farm life—Wisconsin 2. Music, American.

789.2
Wiscandia: Scandinavian Folk Music. (Sound recording). Bob and Becky Wernerehl/Wiscandia, 1990. (50 min.). Available from Wisconsin Folk Museum. $8. (Interest level: 5-8).

Fifteen pieces of traditional Norwegian and Swedish music (waltzes, polkas, marches, etc.) are played on authentic instruments by the four members of the musical group Wiscandia. The music has been accu-

789.2
Wisconsing/David HB Drake. (Sound recording). Makin' Jam, Etc., 1989. (50 min.). $9.95. (Interest level: 4-6).

Drake recorded 12 folk songs (combined with facts and gently humorous stories about Wisconsin's farms, forests, rivers, lakes, and people) before an audience of children in Shawano, Wisconsin, who joined in on some sing-along activities. Wisconsin life today and in earlier times is evoked with accuracy and appreciation.
♦ Young people may be encouraged to participate in the sing-along activities.
1. Folk music, Wisconsin.

791
Clement, Herbert and **Jando, Dominique**. *The Great Circus Parade*. Illus. by Tom Nebbia. Gareth Stevens (0-8368-0159-8), 1989. 110p. Color photos. (Interest level: 5-8).

More than 200 color pictures show the preparations for an annual Circus Parade in Milwaukee and a rich sample of the parade itself. A brief text gives historical information about circus parades in general and the Milwaukee tradition in particular. Also provided is information about the State Historical Society of Wisconsin's Circus World Museum at Baraboo.
♦ Students may research additional material about clowns and use face paints to create their own clown face and persona.
1. Circus 2. Milwaukee (Wis.) 3. Clowns.

813
Giff, Patricia Reilly. *Laura Ingalls Wilder: Growing Up in the Little House*. Illus. by Eileen McKeating. Viking Kestral (0-670-81072-X pbk), 1987. (Women of Our Time Series). 56p. B/W illus. (Interest level: 2-6).

This introduction to Laura Ingalls Wilder interweaves events in her life with explanations of how each book came to be written. Although an elementary-level book, this one is well balanced and includes information beyond the "Little House" aspects of Wilder's life.
♦ The book mentions Wilder's enjoyment of letters from young readers. Students may imagine themselves as Wilder and compose a response to someone who enjoyed Wilder's first book, *Little House in the Big Woods* (*see* Wisconsin—Fiction), which was set in Wisconsin.
1. Wilder, Laura Ingalls, 1867-1957 2. Authors, American 3. Frontier and pioneer life.

rately researched, and brief cover notes give background information.
♦ Students may use selected songs when learning traditional dances or to set a mood when presenting related oral reports.
1. Folk music, Scandinavian.

813
North, Sterling. *Rascal: A Memoir of a Better Era*. Illus. by John Schoenherr. Dutton (0-525-18839-8), 1963. 189p. B/W illus. (Interest level: 4-8).

In 1918 Sterling North, an 11-year-old boy, acquired a pet raccoon named Rascal who shared his boyhood adventures in rural southern Wisconsin. Written with nostalgia and humor and without cloying sentimentalism, the memoir depicts not only one family's experiences but also conveys a realistic sense of place and community during World War I.
♦ Students may compare and contrast young people's recreations in Brailsford Junction in 1918 to their own community today.
1. North, Sterling, 1906-1974 2. Raccoons—Legends and stories 3. Country life—Wisconsin.

912.775 (Reference)
Robinson, Arthur N. and **Culver, Jerry**. *The Atlas of Wisconsin: General Maps and Gazetteer*. University of Wisconsin Press (0-299-06530-0), 1974. 111p. (Interest level: 5-8).

This basic general atlas of the state provides 28 pages of maps devoted to topography, government, and natural and cultural resources. Nondetailed maps of 17 cities are included. The comprehensive gazetteer has over 14,000 entries for parks, lakes, streams, landforms, and rural localities as well as cities, villages, and towns.
♦ Students may be given a list of sites with unusual names to locate as they familiarize themselves with the volume. Among the many possibilities are such unusual names as Ubet, Graveyard Springs, and Swishtail Bluff.
1. Wisconsin—Atlases.

912.775 (Reference)
Wisconsin Atlas and Gazetteer. 3rd ed. DeLorme Mapping Company (0-89933-247-1), 1992. 104p. (Interest level: 6-8).

Aimed more at the traveler than Robinson and Culver's atlas (*see* preceding entry), this volume includes keys to such attractions as bicycle routes, lighthouses, trout streams, ski hills, and factory tours. Definitions of geologic terms, an explanation of the township grid, and the topographic details shown on each of the 81 regional (quadrangular) maps make this a reference tool of substance.
♦ Students may begin by using the map key to locate the quadrangle in which a specific community is situated. Then, by referring to that map and the legend of symbols used, they may list the "points of interest" identified by the mapmakers.
1. Wisconsin—Atlases.

917.75
Wisconsin Library Association. *Wisconsin Literary Travel Guide*. Wisconsin Library Association (No

ISBN), 1989. 64p. B/W archival photos. (Interest level: 7-8; Professional).

More than 100 past and contemporary Wisconsin authors are cited in this guide, which is coded, from Antigo to Whitewater, to match the grid of the state's official road map. Brief information is provided about the authors and their works. Classroom relevance might be limited because fewer than 20 children's book creators are mentioned.

♦ Students may choose an author from their community or state and use library resources to discover how many of that author's books are still in print and whether they are available in the school or public library.

1. Authors, American 2. Authors—Wisconsin.

917.7504

Visser, Kristin and **Minnich, Jerry**. *Wisconsin with Kids*. Prairie Oak Press (1-879483-01-7), 1991. 264p. (Interest level: 5-8).

This family guide, divided into 13 regional chapters, presents a wealth of information about things to see and do in all parts of the state. Some lodging, dining, and shopping suggestions are also included. Concise descriptions convey accurate data and directions, but additional maps would be useful.

♦ Having selected an area of the state unfamiliar to them, students may use the guidebook to plan an investigative visit to its historic sites, modern industrial plants, or natural attractions.

1. Wisconsin—Description—Guidebooks.

917.758

Cook, Diane. *Wisconsin Capitol: Fascinating Facts*. Prairie Oak Press (1-879483-02-5), 1991. 110p. B/W photos. (Interest level: 5-8).

This personal collection of facts about the Wisconsin capitol includes its construction, decorative features, grounds, and lore. A chronology and a compilation of "startling statistics" enhance the work's usefulness.

♦ Students may choose one or more facts to use as the basis for creating a picture postcard of the capitol.

1. State capitols (Madison, Wis.) 2. Wisconsin—Politics and government 3. Madison (Wisc.)—History.

917.758

Wisconsin Department of Administration. *Wisconsin State Capitol Guide and History*. 33rd ed. Wisconsin Department of Administration (No ISBN), 1990. 60p. Color photos. Available from Capitol Tours, Division of Building and Grounds. (Interest level: 4-8).

This official guidebook, based on the original 1917 edition, incorporates much new information. Building history, architectural and decorative features, and recent restoration projects are described. Floor plans, biographical notes about architects and artists, and high-quality photography make this an outstanding introduction to the capitol for all ages.

♦ Students may imagine that they have been commissioned to decorate a capitol hallway and create a mural representing ideas about historic and contemporary Wisconsin that they feel are important.

1. State capitols (Madison, Wis.) 2. Wisconsin—Politics and government.

970

Benton-Banai, Edward. *The Mishomis Book: The Voice of the Ojibway*. Illus. by Joe Liles. Indian Country Communications (No ISBN), 1988. 114p. B/W illus. (Interest level: 5-8).

Fifteen chapters written in the voice of Mishomis (Grandfather) tell the Ojibway creation story, relate other traditional teachings, and present tribal history and contemporary concerns. The author is a Wisconsin Ojibway whose culture-based educational philosophy is well known and who, in this unique and important book, enlightens both Native and non-Native Americans.

♦ A map showing Ojibway migration westward is included, and students may prepare similar maps for other Native American groups to show relocations caused by tribal conflicts and encroachment by non-Native Americans.

1. Ojibway Indians—History 2. Ojibway Indians—Legends.

970

Cohen, Fay G. and **Heuving, Jeanne**, eds. *Tribal Sovereignty: Indian Tribes in U.S. History*. Daybreak Star Press (No ISBN), 1981. 44p. B/W photos. (Interest level: 6-8).

This history addresses the nature of tribal sovereignty from before contact with white people to the recent past, presenting clear descriptions of Indian nations' relationships with the United States government. This book serves as an excellent overall introduction to a frequently misunderstood subject. The book is of special interest for its description of the attempt to terminate the Menominees' tribal status in Wisconsin.

♦ Students may use newspaper indexes to discover the process by which Menominee sovereignty was restored.

1. Indians of North America—History.

970

Thunder in the Dells. (Videocassette). Ooteck Productions, 1990. VHS 1/2", Color, (29 min.). $59.95. (Interest level: 6-8).

Lance Tallmadge, director of the Wisconsin Dells Stand Rock Ceremonial, narrates this production that features Winnebago dance, song, and basketry traditions together with a brief introduction to tribal history. The video's strength is its presentation of clearly contemporary Native Americans who demonstrate and reflect on the traditions that they maintain and share with family members and non-Native Americans.

♦ The narrator says racism often comes from ignorance or fear. Students may discuss one or more ideas from the video that they think can help dispel ignorance and fear.

1. Winnebago Indians 2. Wisconsin—History.

970

Winnebago Women: Songs and Stories. (Videocassette). Jocelyn Riley/Her Own Words, 1992. VHS 1/2", Color, (19 min.). $95 with an accompanying discussion leader's guide available at a cost of $20. (Interest level: 7-8).

Five contemporary Wisconsin Winnebago women describe their interests in the traditional crafts of beadwork, appliqué, and basketry. They also discuss their preservation of techniques learned from mothers and grandmothers, creation of new designs, and teaching of new generations. Still photographs are less dynamic than moving pictures; therefore, students may need some advance preparation about the production of this video.

♦ One woman describes her experience as a student at the Neillsville, Wisconsin, Indian School, where speaking her Winnebago language was prohibited. Students may imagine themselves in similar circumstances and discuss what they could do to change the regulation.

1. Winnebago Indians.

973.7

Zeitlin, Richard H. *Old Abe, the War Eagle: A True Story of the Civil War and Reconstruction.* State Historical Society of Wisconsin (0-87020-239-1), 1986. 113p. B/W photos and maps. (Interest level: 7-8).

Old Abe was a bald eagle that served as mascot of the Eighth Regiment, Wisconsin Volunteer Infantry. His presence in 30 battles and his postwar symbolic appearances are vividly described. This book provides a unique angle from which to view the events of the Civil War era.

♦ Students may investigate the use of the eagle as a national symbol and its meaning to Native Americans.

1. Wisconsin—History 2. United States—History—Civil War, 1861-1865.

973.91

Votes for Women?! 1913 U.S. Senate Testimony. (Videocassette). Jocelyn Riley/Her Own Words, 1990. VHS 1/2", B/W and Color, (17 min.). $95 with an accompanying discussion leader's guide available for $20. (Interest level: 7-8).

Verbatim testimony from the April 1913 hearings on the issue of women's suffrage (testifying against: Kate Wiggin of New York; testifying for: Belle Case LaFollette of Wisconsin) is read as examples are shown of pro and con political cartoons, posters, buttons, banners, etc. The passionate speeches and colorful artifacts remain timely because there continues today public debate about the civil rights of various groups in the United States

♦ The Nineteenth Amendment to the Constitution, allowing women to vote, was not passed until 1920, nor have all men and minorities always had voting rights. Students may imagine themselves belonging to one of the disenfranchised groups and prepare "testimony" on their behalf.

1. United States—History.

977

Bratvold, Gretchen. *Wisconsin.* Lerner (0-8225-2700-6), 1991. (Hello USA Series). 72p. B/W and Color photos. (Interest level: 2-5).

Although brief, this introduction to Wisconsin state history, geography, geology, peoples, industry, and culture provides a wealth of data. A time line, biographical notes on 20 famous persons, and a chapter on environmental concerns are valuable features.

♦ On a map of Wisconsin students may locate four of the "places to visit" suggested in the book, identify at least four more they would recommend as worth visiting, and give the reasons for their choices

1. Wisconsin.

977

Fradin, Dennis B. *Wisconsin in Words and Pictures.* Illus. by Robert Ulm. Childrens Press (0-516-03948-2), 1977. 48p. Color photos and illus. (Interest level: 2-5).

This accessible introduction to Wisconsin history addresses prehistoric and contemporary times. It provides pronunciation guides and Wisconsin "firsts" throughout the text. Although published in the late 1970s, the volume is not unduly dated.

♦ Students may choose one of the "firsts" mentioned—or another fact of particular interest from the text—and create an illustrated bookmark from it.

1. Wisconsin—History.

977

McCall, Edith. *Biography of a River: The Living Mississippi.* Walker (0-8027-6915-2 lib bind), 1990. 162p. B/W illus. (Interest level: 5-8).

The Mississippi's story unfolds from descriptions of the area's earliest inhabitants to today's river users. Integral to the story are the explorations, trading, and settlement that helped shape Wisconsin history. A readable text, glossary, and maps make this a usable book.

♦ Students may create a collage of pictures showing all of the types of watercraft that have traveled on the Mississippi.

1. Mississippi River—History 2. Mississippi River Valley—History.

977

Regguinti, Gordon. *The Sacred Harvest: Ojibway Wild Rice Gathering.* Illus. by Dale Kakkak. Lerner

(0-8225-2650-6), 1992. (We Are Still Here Series). 48p. Color photos. (Interest level: 3-8).

In photos taken on the Leech Lake Reservation in Minnesota, a contemporary Ojibway father and son are pictured harvesting and processing wild rice. The traditional customs and the contemporary lives described in this outstanding book parallel those of Wisconsin Ojibway communities.
♦ Ojibway reservations in Minnesota are shown on the map on page 19. Students may make a map locating the Ojibway communities in Wisconsin before reading Edward Benton-Banai's *The Mishomis Book* (*see* Wisconsin—Nonfiction—970) for more understanding of tribal history.
1. Ojibway Indians 2. Indians of North America—Social life and customs 3. Wild rice.

977
Tanner, Helen H., ed. *Atlas of Great Lakes Indian History*. University of Oklahoma Press (0-8061-1515-7), 1986. (Civilization of the American Indian Series). 224p. B/W illus. (Interest level: 7-8).

In this volume, 33 maps by Miklos Pinther are arranged in chronological order (1640-1871) to show changing Indian communities as they were affected by white settlement, tribal conflicts, and government treaties. The accompanying explanatory essay for each map contributes important perspectives.
♦ Students may use Map 29 ("Black Hawk War 1832") as they read the novel *Sparrow Hawk* by Meridel LeSeuer (*see* Wisconsin—Fiction).
1. Great Lakes Indians—History.

977
Thompson, Kathleen. *Wisconsin*. Turner/Raintree (0-86514-448-6 lib bind), 1986. (Portrait of America Series). 48p. Color photos. (Interest level: 3-6).

This book gives insights into Wisconsin's unique character, introducing such varied topics as seventeenth-century meetings between French explorers and Wisconsin Indians, Progressive party politics, modern agriculture and industry, and the American Birkebeiner ski race. A time line of historical events is a useful reference point.
♦ From the chapter "Sons and Daughters of the Middle Border" students may select one individual about whom they want to read more in encyclopedias or biographies.
1. Wisconsin.

977.015
Stein, R. Conrad. *The Story of Marquette and Jolliet*. Illus. by Richard Wahl. Childrens Press (0-516-04630-6), 1981. (Cornerstones of Freedom). 31p. B/W illus. (Interest level: 3-6).

Briefly recounted is the 1673 exploratory canoe voyage of Father Jacques Marquette and military leader Louis Jolliet from Quebec through the Great Lakes, to Green Bay, and along the Fox, Wisconsin, and part of the Mississippi rivers. The book does not question the assumption that claiming lands for a European crown was acceptable. It does identify differences between Indian tribes encountered along the way.
♦ Students may write a script from the point of view of a tribe that has not yet had contact with white explorers but that has received messages about them from other tribes to the east with whom they communicate.
1. Mississippi River—Discovery and exploration 2. Jolliet, Louis, 1645-1700 3. Marquette, Jacques, 1637-1675 4. Explorers.

977.5
Current, Richard N. *Wisconsin: A History*. Norton (0-393-05624-4), 1977. (The States and the Nation Series). 226p. B/W photos. (Interest level: 7-8).

This brief interpretive history concentrates on persons and happenings distinctive to the state. Although written for the general adult reader, the work is also accessible to upper-grade students.
♦ From the chapter "Circuses and Such" students may choose one of the Wisconsin celebrities and describe why they would like to know that person better.
1. Wisconsin—History.

977.5
Gard, Robert E. and Sorden, L. G. *Romance of Wisconsin Place Names*. NorthWord (0-942802-88-8 pbk), 1988. 308p. (Interest level: 5-8).

This comprehensive volume includes explanations of approximately 3,000 alphabetically arranged Wisconsin place names—ethnic, geologic, commemorative, and nostalgic. The accessible and informal writing is appropriate for young people as well as the intended adult reader.
♦ Working as a class, students may prepare a map of one Wisconsin county, appending explanations of place names they find interesting.
1. Wisconsin 2. Geographic names—Wisconsin.

977.5
The Great Peshtigo Fire. (Videocassette). Wisconsin Educational Communications Board, 1971. VHS 1/2", Color, (28 min.). Available from Wisconsin Educational Television, Tape Dubbing Service. $15. With a written request for a tape, purchasers should send a new videotape of sufficient length to record the program. An invoice will be sent with the product. (Interest level: 6-8).

Archival photographs, color paintings, and compelling narrative featuring actors speaking the words of fire survivors combine to convey powerfully the drama of the October 8, 1971, tragedy and its aftermath. The full scope of the fire is perhaps better understood through the visual presentation than through reading about its destructive power.
♦ Students may prepare statistical comparison charts (injuries, deaths, property damage, etc.) between the

Peshtigo fire and the Chicago fire, which happened on the same day.
1. Wisconsin—History 2. Peshtigo (Wis.)—Fire 3. Fires.

977.5
Her Own Words: Dane County, Wisconsin Pioneer Women's Diaries. (Videocassette). Jocelyn Riley/Her Own Words, 1986. VHS 1/2", Color, (15 min.). $95 with an accompanying discussion leader's guide available for $20. (Interest level: 6-8).

Still color photographs with voice-over narration taken from the diaries of five mid-nineteenth-century Wisconsin pioneer women forcefully re-create the times. Juxtaposed pictures of artifacts and landscapes enhance the women's observations of nature, daily life, and motherhood.
♦ Students may write a comparison of observations in the video with characters' feelings in Carol Brink's *Caddie Woodlawn* (*see* Wisconsin—Fiction) or Laura Ingalls Wilder's *Little House in the Big Woods* (*see* Wisconsin—Fiction).
1. Frontier and pioneer life—Wisconsin.

977.5
Milwaukee, wie geht's? A History of German Milwaukee, 1839-1989. (Videocassette). Transatlantic Media/Institute für Film und Bild/Milwaukee County Historical Society, 1990. VHS 1/2", Color, (30 min.). Available from the Milwaukee County Historical Society. $29.95. (Interest level: 7-8).

Milwaukee's strong German cultural traditions in food, music, publishing, and industry are surveyed through archival materials and modern videography. Coverage of anti-German sentiment during World War I is insightful. However, a segment filmed at a contemporary gift shop selling Native American "crafts" and "Wild West" souvenirs to German visitors shows that other stereotypes still persist.
♦ By using the most recent census records available, students may discover the ethnic diversity of their community (or state) and prepare a comparison with data from an earlier census.
1. Milwaukee (Wis.) 2. German Americans 3. Frontier and pioneer life—Wisconsin.

977.5
Minnich, Jerry, ed. *The Wisconsin Almanac (Being a Loosely Organized Compendium of Facts, History, Lore, Remembrances, Puzzles, Recipes, and Both Household and Gardening Advice with Which to Offer Elucidation, Assistance, and Occasional Amusement to the Conscientious Reader).* North Country (0-944133-06-1), 1989. 262p. B/W illus. (Interest level: 5-8).

The subtitle of this almanac conveys the range of information contained in this informal compilation. Browsing through the almanac month by month is an effortless way to learn bits of history and traditions. The absence of an index makes tracking specific subjects difficult.
♦ Students may use the almanac to create questions for a "Knowledge Bee."
1. Wisconsin—History 2. Folklore—Wisconsin.

977.5
Prairie Cabin: A Norwegian Pioneer Woman's Story. (Videocassette). Jocelyn Riley/Her Own Words, 1991. VHS 1/2", Color, (17 min.). $95 with an accompanying discussion leader's guide available for $20. (Interest level: 6-8).

Based on research done in Wisconsin and Minnesota, Jocelyn Riley has created an authentic narration that is a composite of several strong nineteenth-century women's recollections about their new life on the unfamiliar prairie. The colorful still photographs of household artifacts, foods, buildings, and landscape are coupled effectively with insightful narrative about differences in plants, birds, weather, trees, and topography.
♦ The narrator says she is glad she copied the words to so many songs before leaving Norway. Students may list songs from the United States they would take with them if they were to move permanently to a place with a different language and culture.
1. Frontier and pioneer life—Middle West.

977.5
Stein, R. Conrad. *Wisconsin*. Childrens Press (0-516-00495-6), 1987. 144p. (America the Beautiful Series). B/W and Color photos. (Interest level: 4-8).

This survey begins with a consideration of topography and incorporates historic details with information on politics, the economy, the arts, and leisure activities. The carefully selected and positioned photographs add to the text's impact. Useful maps, biographical notes, and a list of important dates are also provided.
♦ Using the information in this book and others, students may make topographic salt maps.
1. Wisconsin.

977.5
Travel Historic Wisconsin. Guide Press (No ISBN), 1989. 125p. (Interest level: 5-8).

Compiled with the assistance of the State Historical Society of Wisconsin, this book contains the text of each of the 276 historical markers placed by the Society around the state. A map is keyed to the descriptive entries, which are presented both by community (from Albion to Wittenberg) and by highway location.
♦ Young people may discuss the types of information recorded on the markers and speculate about current individuals and events in Wisconsin or other states that might inspire future markers.
1. Wisconsin—History 2. Wisconsin—Description and travel.

977.5
A Vision Shaped in Stone. (Videocassette). Wisconsin Public Television Network, 1987. VHS 1/2", Color, (30 min.). Available from Wisconsin Educational Television, Tape Dubbing Service. $15. With a written request for a tape, purchasers should send a new videotape of sufficient length to record the program. An invoice will be sent with the product. (Interest level: 6-8)c

This history of the three Capitol buildings in Madison, Wisconsin, emphasizes the symbolic nature of the present structure, created to reflect a belief in and respect for how government acts on behalf of the people. The design and decorative elements of the present Capitol are placed in the context of turn-of-the-century political and social history (e.g., the LaFollette Progressive movement and the influence of the 1893 Chicago Columbian Exposition).

♦ Students may compare this video to Diane Cook's *Wisconsin Capitol: Fascinating Facts* (*see* Wisconsin—Nonfiction—917.758) and the Wisconsin Department of Administration's *Wisconsin State Capitol Guide and History* (*see* Wisconsin—Nonfiction—917.758), developing a rationale for which item they would recommend to a new resident of the state.

1. State capitols 2. Wisconsin—Capitol.

Biography

92 Barnum, Phineas Taylor
Tompert, Ann. *The Greatest Showman on Earth: A Biography of P. T. Barnum.* Dillon/Macmillan (0-87518-370-0), 1987. (People in Focus Series). 120p. B/W photos. (Interest level: 6-8).

Barnum's energetic life as a showman and civic leader in nineteenth-century Bridgeport, Connecticut, is described. His entry into the circus world and impact on this entertainment form are emphasized. The Barnum and Bailey Circus was sold after Barnum's death to the Ringling Brothers Circus of Baraboo, Wisconsin. Although the Baraboo connection is not made in this biography, the book provides good historical background on circus development in the United States.

♦ Circus sideshows exploited people with physical differences (such as Siamese twins). Young people may write a reaction to that practice in the form of a hypothetical letter to the editor.

1. Barnum, P. T. (Phineas Taylor), 1810-1891 2. Circus 3. Entertainers.

92 Bennett, Henry Hamilton
Views of a Cameraman. (Videocassette). Wisconsin Educational Television Network, 1983. VHS 1/2", B/W and Color, (30 min.). Available from Wisconsin Educational Television, Tape Dubbing Service. $15. With a written request for a tape, purchasers should send a new videotape of sufficient length to record the program. An invoice will be sent with the product. (Interest level: 7-8).

H. H. Bennett's own pioneering landscape and portraiture photographs illuminate the narrative describing the career of this inventive, inspired early (1857) settler in Kilbourn (now Wisconsin Dells). Although its pace in parts may seem slow to students accustomed to watching MTV, those with any interest at all in filmmaking or the Dells as a recreation area will be intrigued with Bennett's techniques and results.

♦ A museum or a private collection may make available a stereoscope (a device for which Bennett took many photographs). Students may look through it and then compare what they see with a postcard and a hologram.

1. Bennett, Henry Hamilton, 1843-1908 2. Photographers 3. Wisconsin.

92 Kherdian, David
Kherdian, David. *Root River Run.* Illus. by Nonny Hogrogian. Carolrhoda (0-87614-274-9), 1984. 160p. B/W illus. (Interest level: 6-8).

Racine, Wisconsin, 1940-47, is the setting for these 25 autobiographical vignettes describing the family, friends, and activities of a first-generation Armenian American. A glossary of Armenian words included in the text is useful as one reads the unique portrayal of this closely knit Armenian-American community.

♦ Early twentieth-century massacres of Armenians in Turkey led to emigration to the United States. Students may study recent and current media to find instances of similar genocidal atrocities.

1. Kherdian, David, 1931- 2. Authors, American 3. Armenian Americans—Biography.

92 LaFollette, Belle Case
Belle: The Life and Writings of Belle Case LaFollette. (Videocassette). Jocelyn Riley/Her Own Words, 1987. VHS 1/2", Color, (15 min.). $95, with an accompanying discussion leader's guide available for $20. (Interest level: 6-8).

Belle Case LaFollette, the first woman to graduate from the University of Wisconsin Law School, was an activist for women's right to vote. She became an influential voice for education through her speeches and writings in *LaFollette's Magazine* (later *The Progressive*). Although less famous today than her husband Robert LaFollette, Sr. (congressman, governor, and United States senator), Belle's place in state and national history is assured.

♦ In the video, students will hear Belle's comments about typewriters and see photographs of her own typewriter. They may do time studies assessing the time it takes to write a paragraph by hand, on a manual typewriter, on an electric typewriter, and on a personal computer. The assessments should in-

clude the time it takes for making corrections and duplicate copies.
1. LaFollette, Belle Case, 1859-1931 2. Wisconsin—History 3. Journalists.

92 Marty, Anna Arnold
Jacobson, Gloria. *Two for America: The True Story of a Swiss Immigrant.* Illus. by Don Cliff. Ski Printers (0-9618399-7-0 pbk), 1989. 36p. B/W and Color illus. (Interest level: 2-6).

Anna Arnold Marty's girlhood in rural Canton Uri, Switzerland, her emigration to the United States in 1908 at age 17, and her subsequent life in New Glarus, Wisconsin, are vividly described by her daughter. The text, a model of how family stories should be preserved and shared, is enriched by the inclusion of German words used in the family (with translation and pronunciation provided).
♦ Holiday and food traditions are important in Anna's biography. Students may interview family members or other adults to discover what traditions from their childhoods they remember most clearly and fondly.
1. Wisconsin 2. Switzerland 3. Immigration and emigration.

92 Meir, Golda
Adler, David A. *Our Golda: The Story of Golda Meir.* Illus. by Donna Ruff. Viking (0-670-53107-3), 1984. 52p. B/W illus. (Interest level: 4-8).

Eight-year-old Golda and her family emigrated from Russia to Milwaukee in 1906. A description of her 15 years there is included in this chronicle of her achievements as a spokesperson for Jewish rights and a leader of the Israeli government. Anecdotes personalize this survey of a historic figure's life, but young readers may lack sufficient background about the Nazi movement and Arab-Jewish conflicts to understand some of the material.
♦ Golda's Russian-Jewish heritage was important to her. Students may make (or imagine) a culture box of things they would want to take along if they were to move to a new country.
1. Meir, Golda, 1898-1978 2. Women politicians 3. Israel—Politics and government.

92 Meir, Golda
Keller, Mollie. *Golda Meir.* Watts (0-531-04591-9), 1983. (Impact Biography Series). 119p. B/W photos. (Interest level: 6-8).

In addition to providing well-documented examples of Meir's contributions to the development of modern Israel, this book presents readable historic background about Zionism and international events affecting the 1948 creation of the Jewish state. Although this is a comprehensive Meir biography for young people, details about her Milwaukee years are addressed equally in the other works listed on this page.
♦ Students may conduct research about other women who have been leaders of their nations' governments.
1. Meir, Golda, 1898-1978 2. Women politicians 3. Israel—Politics and government 4. Zionism.

92 Meir, Golda
McAuley, Karen. *Golda Meir.* Chelsea House (0-87754-568-5), 1985. (World Leaders Past & Present Series). 112p. B/W photos. (Interest level: 4-8).

As part of a series based on the premise that individuals make a difference in history, this work emphasizes the years of Meir's political leadership in Israel. However, it also touches upon her childhood in Russia and youth in Milwaukee and Denver. The inclusion of many photographs enhances and augments the text, bringing this recent history to life.
♦ Students may choose one of the photographs and compose a newspaper-of-the-time caption for it or a sound bite upon which radio or television journalists could have focused.
1. Meir, Golda, 1898-1978 2. Women politicians 3. Israel—Politics and government.

92 Mountain Wolf Woman
Lurie, Nancy O., ed. *Mountain Wolf Woman: Sister of Crashing Thunder: The Autobiography of a Winnebago Indian.* University of Michigan (0-472-06109-7), 1961. 142p. B/W photos. (Interest level: 7-8).

In 1958, at age 75, Mountain Wolf Woman recorded her life story for cultural anthropologist Nancy Lurie, describing Wisconsin Winnebago family life and customs in decades of change. This authentic narrative offers advanced students an understanding of both tribal traditions and one individual's perspective.
♦ On a time line representing Mountain Wolf Woman's span of years, students may indicate major social events and technological discoveries.
1. Mountain Wolf Woman, 1884-1961 2. Winnebago Indians.

92 Muir, John
Force, Eden. *John Muir.* Silver Burdett (0-382-09965-6), 1990. (Pioneers in Change Series). 146p. B/W photos. (Interest level: 6-8).

This well-researched biography emphasizes Muir's broad interests and curiosity about the natural world and examines his influence as a speaker and writer. Two chapters address Muir's farm and college years in Wisconsin.
♦ The class may brainstorm present-day issues that would have concerned Muir and, in small groups, speculate how Muir would react today.
1. Muir, John, 1838-1914 2. Naturalists 3. Nature conservation.

92 Muir, John
Muir, John. *The Story of My Boyhood and Youth.* University of Wisconsin (0-299-03650-2), 1913, 1965. 228p. B/W illus. (Interest level: 7-8).

Eight candid, lively essays describe the author's first 11 years as a child in Scotland, the next 11 years on a Wisconsin farm, and his 4 years as a University of Wisconsin student. An adult-level book first published in 1913, this remains a truly readable autobiography, providing excellent insights into Muir's sense of wonder about the natural world.
♦ Muir followed no established course of study as a university student. Young readers may lay out the classes they would choose to take now, given the opportunity for similar flexibility.
1. Muir, John, 1838-1914 2. Naturalists 3. Nature conservation.

92 Muir, John
Naden, Corinne J. and Blue, Rose. *John Muir: Saving the Wilderness.* Millbrook (1-56294-110-0), 1992. (A Gateway Biography). 48p. B/W and Color photos. (Interest level: 2-4).

This narrative provides a basic survey of Muir's life with emphasis on his dedication to conservation. The photographs will help young readers visualize unfamiliar places, and the sketches of Muir's Wisconsin farm home and his self-timing desk will help bring him to life in their imagination.
♦ After studying the picture of the desk (on display in the Wisconsin State Historical Society Library in Madison), students may list their own choices of books to put in such a desk for assignments and recreation.
1. Muir, John, 1838-1914 2. Naturalists 3. Nature conservation.

92 Muir, John
Tolan, Sally. *John Muir: Naturalist, Writer, and Guardian of the North American Wilderness.* Gareth Stevens (0-8368-0099-0), 1990. (People Who Have Helped the World Series). 68p. B/W and Color photos. (Interest level: 5-8).

From Muir's early childhood in Scotland and youth in Wisconsin through his adult career as a naturalist and environmental activist, this book reveals his intellect and determination. It also serves as an introduction to conflicts between preservation and conservation. Sidebar quotations from Muir and others, a chronology and glossary, archival reproductions, and a list of contemporary environmental organizations enhance the appearance and practical value of the volume.
♦ Young people may use one or more of the inspiring quotations from or about Muir as the basis for a poster.
1. Muir, John, 1838-1914 2. Naturalists 3. Conservationists.

92 Muir, John
Wadsworth, Ginger. *John Muir, Wilderness Protector.* Lerner (0-8225-4912-3), 1992. 144p. B/W photos. (Interest level: 4-8).

Although two chapters are devoted to Muir's early years in Wisconsin, this book concentrates principally on his adult life and conveys the breadth and depth of his studies and travels. Archival photographs and reproductions of several of Muir's own sketches reinforce the reader's sense of acquaintance with the naturalist.
♦ In order to create a base map and an overlay, students may do research to discover what areas of the country were considered wilderness in Muir's lifetime and what areas today could be described as wilderness.
1. Muir, John, 1838-1914 2. Naturalists 3. Nature conservation.

92 Nelson, Gaylord
Shulman, Jeffrey and Rogers, Teresa. *Gaylord Nelson: A Day for Earth.* Illus. by Larry Raymond. Twenty-First Century Books/Henry Holt (0-941477-40-1), 1992. (Earth Keepers Series). 68p. B/W illus. (Interest level: 8-12).

The 32-year political career and environmental commitment of Nelson, the originator of Earth Day, is traced from his boyhood in Clear Lake, Wisconsin, through his service as state senator, governor, and U.S. senator. Insightful descriptions of political realities and grassroots impacts outweigh minor inaccuracies such as reference to a "spire" atop the Wisconsin Capitol and the "suburb" of Crestwood. ("Statue" and "neighborhood" are correct.)
♦ Students may write to a local, state, or federal official expressing their concern about a specific environmental problem.
1. Nelson, Gaylord, 1916- 2. Legislators 3. Conservationists.

92 O'Keeffe, Georgia
Berry, Michael. *Georgia O'Keeffe.* Chelsea (1-55546-673-7), 1988. (American Women of Achievement Series). 112p. B/W photos and Color reproductions. (Interest level: 5-8).

This basic introduction to Georgia O'Keeffe's life and artistry emphasizes her lifelong independent spirit, from her southern Wisconsin childhood through old age. A good selection of photographs complements the text. Those in color are of paintings not frequently reproduced; those in black and white reveal elements of O'Keeffe's distinctive style.
♦ Having looked at O'Keeffe's paintings in this and other books, students may examine an object through a magnifying glass and draw it as an abstraction.
1. O'Keeffe, Georgia, 1887-1986 2. Painters, American 3. Women artists.

92 O'Keeffe, Georgia
Gherman, Beverly. *Georgia O'Keeffe: The "Wideness and Wonder" of Her World*. Atheneum (0-689-31164-8), 1986. 131p. B/W photos. (Interest level: 6-8).

This comprehensive, readable biography reflects the author's depth of feeling for O'Keeffe's singular artistic style and her strong character. The photographs are well chosen and carefully positioned. Notes, a bibliography, and an index add substance.
♦ Students may research sculptor Louise Nevelson in order to compare the career of another woman artist who was a contemporary of O'Keeffe's.
1. O'Keeffe, Georgia, 1887-1986 2. Painters, American 3. Women artists.

92 O'Keeffe, Georgia
Turner, Robyn Montana. *Georgia O'Keeffe*. Little, Brown (0-316-85649-5), 1991. (Portraits of Women Artists for Children). 32p. B/W photos and Color reproductions. (Interest level: 3-7).

O'Keeffe's Wisconsin childhood, education in the East, and artistic development are encapsulated accurately. In addition to biographical details, well-reproduced examples of O'Keeffe's work and perceptive accompanying commentary make this a valuable introduction to art appreciation.
♦ Students may examine real flowers and compare sizes and details to the way O'Keeffe painted them.
1. O'Keeffe, Georgia, 1887-1986 2. Painters, American 3. Women artists.

92 Wilder, Laura Ingalls
Anderson, William. *Laura Ingalls Wilder: A Biography*. HarperCollins (0-06-020114-2 lib bind), 1992. 240p. B/W archival photos. (Interest level: 4-8).

William Anderson provides two chapters on Wilder's early childhood in Wisconsin in a biography that carefully and clearly records her 90 years as daughter, sister, teacher, wife, mother, and author. Background information on Wilder's parents' families (true Wisconsin pioneers) and on the Homestead Act (which influenced family moves) provides an extra dimension to this definitive biography for children.
♦ Wilder referred to her earliest memories of home as "the pictures that hang in my memory." Students may verbally or visually prepare a "gallery" of early childhood recollections that they would want to share with children of the next generation.
1. Wilder, Laura Ingalls, 1867-1957 2. Authors, American 3. Frontier and pioneer life.

92 Wilder, Laura Ingalls
Anderson, William. *Laura Ingalls Wilder Country: The People and Places in Laura Ingalls Wilder's Life and Books*. Illus. by Leslie A. Kelly. Harper Perennial/HarperCollins (0-06-055249-8 cloth; 0-06-097346-3 pbk), 1990. 119p. Color photos. (Interest level: 2-6).

Documentary and modern photographs present Laura Ingalls Wilder's family, landscapes familiar to her, and artifacts from Wisconsin, Minnesota, Iowa, Kansas, and South Dakota. The nine chapters paralleling her nine books add to appreciation of their respective times and places, and the chapters devoted to Wilder's adult life and home further acquaint the reader with her.
♦ In public library, historical society, or newspaper resources, young people may find nineteenth-century pictures of their community that reflect life circa 1870 (when the Ingalls lived in Pepin, Wisconsin). One picture may serve as the basis for young people to write a paragraph that tells about nineteenth-century life.
1. Wilder, Laura Ingalls, 1867-1957 2. Frontier and pioneer life.

92 Wilder, Laura Ingalls
Anderson, William. *Little House Country: A Photo Guide to the Home Sites of Laura Ingalls Wilder*. Illus. by Leslie A. Kelly. Terrell (0-96-10088-8-1), 1989. 49p. Color photos. (Interest level: 1-6).

This slim volume is devoted primarily to Laura Ingalls Wilder's homes and their surrounding landscapes. Anderson's *Laura Ingalls Wilder Country* (see preceding entry) is richer in both text and visual information, but *Little House Country* has good introductory information for children reaching beyond the stories for the first time.
♦ Using a contemporary road atlas, students may trace the routes along which the Ingalls family moved and may compute the mileage and time required to cover the distance by horse-drawn wagon versus today's automobiles.
1. Wilder, Laura Ingalls, 1867-1957 2. Authors, American 3. Frontier and pioneer life.

92 Wright, Frank Lloyd
Murphy, Wendy Buehr. *Genius! The Artist and the Process*. Silver Burdett (0-382-09905-2), 1990. 128p. B/W photos. (Interest level: 5-8).

This biography of Wisconsin's (and perhaps America's) most famous architect accurately describes the evolution of Wright's often controversial approaches to design construction and business, as well as his dramatic private life. Although generally enhancing the text, the placement and quality of the photographs are not entirely effective.
♦ Students may observe and list purely decorative, non-useful architectural features in their school or neighborhood buildings in contrast to Wright's functional approach.
1. Wright, Frank Lloyd, 1867-1959 2. Architects.

Fiction

Benton-Banai, Edward. *Generation to Generation.* Illus. by Joe Milner-Benjamin. Indian Country Communications (No ISBN), 1991. 21p. B/W illus. (Interest level: 7-8).

Aunah-Quad, the narrator's grandfather, is the central figure in this simply told, contemporary northern Wisconsin story about family relationships. Although this slim booklet is physically modest, its spiritual content is strong. Advanced non-Native American readers will find it gives them insight into an unfamiliar culture that they can respect.
♦ Although most of the family members of the book follow traditional Ojibway ways, some do not; the resulting tension is a point for readers to discuss.
1. Ojibway Indians—Fiction 2. Family life—Fiction.

Brink, Carol Ryrie. *Caddie Woodlawn.* Illus. by Trina Schart Hyman. Macmillan (0-02-713670-1), 1973. 274p. B/W illus. (Interest level: 4-6).

Based on stories the author heard from her grandmother, this lively novel of pioneer farm life in 1864 in west central Wisconsin centers on the adventures of 11-year-old Caddie. The glow of this book, awarded the Newbery Medal in 1936, is somewhat shadowed by its presentations of stereotypes and by its patronizing depiction of Native Americans.
♦ Through discussion, young people may compare nineteenth-century (and 1930s) stereotypes of Native Americans with contemporary attitudes.
1. Frontier and pioneer life—Wisconsin—Fiction 2. Wisconsin—Fiction.

Brink, Carol Ryrie. *Magical Melons.* Illus. by Marguerite Davis. Macmillan (0-689-71416-5), 1944, 1990. 208p. B/W illus. (Interest level: 3-7).

Fourteen stories about Caddie Woodlawn and her family depict work and play in a small Wisconsin farming community from 1863 through 1866. With the exception of "The Circuit Rider's Story," a chapter that perpetuates several Native American stereotypes, the collection can be broadly recommended as an entertaining source of information about life and customs.
♦ Young people may select one of the games, recreations, or celebrations described in the book and write a poem comparing it to a present-day activity.
1. Frontier and pioneer life—Wisconsin—Fiction 2. Wisconsin—Fiction.

Butler, Beverly. *My Sister's Keeper.* Putnam (0-396-07803-6), 1980. 220p. (Interest level: 7-8).

When 17-year-old Mary James comes to Peshtigo, Wisconsin, in the hot, dry autumn of 1871 to help in the household of her pregnant elder sister, she becomes caught in family tensions, as well as in one of history's most devastating forest fires. The social customs and daily life of the era are clearly shown and the forest fire and its aftermath are accurately and realistically presented.
♦ Students may research in contemporary periodicals the ways government and other organizations respond to massive fire disasters today and prepare a television feature story to share with the school.
1. Wisconsin—Fiction 2. Brothers and sisters—Fiction 3. Forest fires—Fiction.

Carter, Alden R. *Up Country.* Putnam (0-399-21583-2), 1989. 256p. (Interest level: 7-8).

Milwaukee high school student Carl Stagger's life is shaped and shadowed by his mother's alcoholism and his own involvement with thieves until circumstances force him to live temporarily with relatives in a small northern Wisconsin town. This book realistically presents the court system and welfare bureaucracies, showing their impact on individuals even though urban-rural contrasts may be exaggerated.
♦ In a classroom discussion students may explore ways they would help a friend with problems similar to Carl's.
1. Alcoholism—Fiction 2. Family problems—Fiction 3. Country life—Fiction 4. Wisconsin—Fiction.

Enright, Elizabeth. *Thimble Summer.* Holt (0-8050-0306-1), 1938. 124p. B/W and Color illus. (Interest level: 4-6).

Spirited nine-year-old Garnet Linden is the central figure in this chronicle of a 1930s summer on a southwestern Wisconsin farm. The joys of Garnet's family and friends and their economic concerns, the beauty and power of nature, the hard work of farming, and the pleasures of small town celebrations are illuminated by the clarity of the prose in this 1939 Newbery Medal-winning novel.
♦ Young people may write a letter to Garnet inviting her to join in a summertime activity they like and telling her why, based on the book, they think she would enjoy it, too.
1. Wisconsin—Fiction.

Eunson, Dale. *The Day They Gave Babies Away.* Illus. by Douglas Gorsline. New Chapter (0-942257-21-9), 1990. 64p. B/W illus. (Interest level: 4-8).

Robert and Mamie Eunson emigrated from Scotland to Eureka, Wisconsin, in 1855. When they both died in 1868, their 12-year-old son had to spend Christmas Day finding new homes for his five younger siblings and himself. First published in 1946 and based on the experience of the author's family, this unusual Christmas story is not maudlin but reveals courageous strength, humor, and love.
♦ Students may research diphtheria and typhoid to discover how these diseases were eventually eradicated in the United States.
1. Wisconsin—Fiction 2. Frontier and pioneer life—Fiction.

Le Sueur, Meridel. *Sparrow Hawk.* Illus. by Robert Desjarlait. Holy Cow! Press (0-930100-22-0), 1987. 177p. B/W illus. (Interest level: 6-8).

The Illinois-Iowa border in the 1830s is the setting for most of this novel about Sparrow Hawk, a Sauk youth, who displays his loyalty to Black Hawk and involves himself in a corn-growing enterprise with Huck, a white friend. The story's climax is the Battle of Bad Axe in Wisconsin, where Black Hawk's Sauk band is defeated. This novel will enhance young people's understanding of a historic period on the American frontier.

♦ On a contemporary map students may locate each of the rivers and forts mentioned in the narrative.

1. Black Hawk, Sauk chief, 1767-1838—Fiction
2. Sauk Indians—Fiction   3. Frontier and pioneer life—Fiction.

McCall, Edith. *Better Than a Brother.* Walker (0-8027-6783-4), 1988. 133p. (Interest level: 4-8).

The household responsibilities and the friendships of a turn-of-the-century tomboy are the motifs of this novel set on the Lake Monona shore near Madison. Blended into the narrative are descriptions of now unfamiliar pastimes such as iceboating and businesses such as ice cutting and storage.

♦ On New Year's Eve, December 31, 1899, friends play a party game of imagining things that might be invented in the twentieth century. Considering the potential of today's technology, young people may describe products that they imagine might be possible in the twenty-first century.

1. Family life—Fiction   2. Wisconsin—Fiction.

North, Sterling. *The Wolfling: A Documentary Novel of the 1870s.* Illus. by John Schoenherr. Scholastic (0-590-30254-X pbk), 1980. 256p. B/W illus. (Interest level: 4-8).

In 1873 12-year-old Robbie Trent, a character based on Sterling North's father, learns about natural history through observation of Wolf, his wolf-dog pet, and through his friendship with his neighbor Thure Kumlein, the self-taught naturalist who was later on the staff of the Milwaukee Public Museum. Clear descriptions of the Lake Koshkonong region and of farm life make this documentary novel a useful history lesson.

♦ Kumlein predicted the eventual extinction of the passenger pigeon. Students may research which birds of Wisconsin or other states are presently endangered and write a newspaper editorial about their status.

1. Wisconsin—Fiction   2. Farm life—Fiction.

Osofsky, Audrey. *Dreamcatcher.* Illus. by Ed Young. Orchard (0-531-05988-0 lib bind), 1992. 28p. Color illus. (Interest level: K-3).

In a time long ago an Ojibway baby watches family activities and then sleeps, protected from bad dreams by the web of the dream net hung on the cradleboard. Games and tasks of daily living are accurately portrayed in this picture book, which also describes the construction of a dreamcatcher and beliefs surrounding it.

♦ In the book grandmother asks the big sister, "What did you see today that was beautiful; what did you hear that was pleasing?" After quiet reflection, students may answer that question for themselves through prose, poetry, or a picture.

1. Ojibway Indians—Fiction   2. Family life—Fiction.

Pellowski, Anne. *Betsy's Up-and-Down Year.* Illus. by Wendy Watson. Philomel (0-399-20970-0), 1983. 160p. B/W illus. (Interest level: 2-5).

Betsy Kolb (of *Willow Wind Farm,* see Wisconsin—Fiction, Pellowski) is a contemporary Wisconsin third grader concerned with imperfect teeth and fashionable shoes, sibling rivalry and cooperation, and traditions of family and community. Unlike the other books in this series, no Polish words or expressions are used and translated. A genealogical chart of the five generations of Betsy's family is provided.

♦ Upper-grade students may research and draw their own family trees.

1. Wisconsin—Fiction   2. Farm life—Fiction
3. Brothers and sisters—Fiction.

Pellowski, Anne. *First Farm in the Valley: Anna's Story.* Illus. by Wendy Watson. Philomel (0-399-20887-9), 1982. 191p. B/W illus. (Interest level: 2-5).

Set in 1876 in Trempealeau County, Wisconsin, this is chronologically the first of five books based on five generations of the author's family. This story centers on six-year-old Anna, one of 10 children born in this country to parents who emigrated from Poland. Authentic details of nineteenth-century farm life and family traditions abound. A map of the valley and a genealogical chart will especially interest those who read the other books in this series.

♦ Students may dye hard-boiled eggs in natural dyes as the Pellowski family did.

1. Wisconsin—Fiction   2. Frontier and pioneer life—Fiction   3. Farm life—Fiction   4. Polish Americans—Fiction.

Pellowski, Anne. *Stairstep Farm: Anna Rose's Story.* Illus. by Wendy Watson. Philomel (0-399-20814-3), 1981. 175p. B/W illus. (Interest level: 2-5).

Chronologically the third novel based on the author's family, this 1930s story, set in rural Trempealeau County, Wisconsin, has inquisitive five-year-old Anna Rose as its central character. Cooperation among family members and farm life realities are strongly emphasized throughout the book.

♦ Younger children may arrange spice and herb jars alphabetically as Anna Rose did when she began to explore the alphabet and reading. Older readers may

describe their recollections of learning the alphabet and beginning to read.
1. Wisconsin—Fiction 2. Farm life—Fiction 3. Family life—Fiction.

Pellowski, Anne. *Willow Wind Farm: Betsy's Story.* Illus. by Wendy Watson. Philomel (0-399-20781-3), 1981. 176p. B/W illus. (Interest level: 2-5).

Seven-year-old Betsy Kolb, who lives with her nine siblings on a contemporary (1967) farm in the Latsch Valley (Wisconsin), is the great-great-grandchild of the Valley's original Polish settlers. Continuity of family and community traditions and responsibilities is shown in a nonpedantic way.
♦ The class may play the "Mama's Going to Buy You . . ." game described in the final chapter.
1. Wisconsin—Fiction 2. Farm life—Fiction 3. Family life—Fiction 4. Brothers and sisters—Fiction.

Pellowski, Anne. *Winding Valley Farm: Annie's Story.* Illus. by Wendy Watson. Philomel (0-399-20863-1), 1982. 192p. B/W illus. (Interest level: 2-5).

Set in 1908, this is chronologically the second novel about the farms and customs of the Pellowski and Dorawa families in Trempealeau County, Wisconsin. The juxtaposition of "new" things such as automobiles and ice cream cones with traditional ways reveals an evolving modern society.
♦ Students may imagine they are in a one-room, multiple-grade schoolhouse and speculate how their roles and activities would differ from those in a modern single-grade classroom.
1. Wisconsin—Fiction 2. Farm life—Fiction 3. Family life—Fiction.

Riley, Jocelyn. *Only My Mouth Is Smiling.* Morrow (0-688-01087-3), 1982. 222p. (Interest level: 6-8).

Merle, the 13-year-old narrator of this contemporary novel, and her two younger siblings cope with the tensions of living with an unstable mother who has taken them to northern Wisconsin in search of a simpler way of life. Unusual characters and a realistic portrayal of attitudes in a small lake-country community make this a provocative novel for discussion.
♦ Students may imagine themselves as Lake Lune acquaintances of Merle and write a series of journal entries containing observations of her situation.
1. Mentally ill—Fiction 2. Family life—Fiction 3. Wisconsin—Fiction.

Schwandt, Stephen. *Hold Steady.* Holt (0-8050-0575-7), 1988. 161p. (Interest level: 6-8).

Seventeen-year-old Brendon Turner, his younger brother, and his mother are central characters in this contemporary novel set on Washington Island, Door County, Wisconsin, where they are spending their first summer without their father and husband. Legends about the Porte des Mortes Strait and the geography of the island and peninsula play roles in the ways the family faces its grief. A map of the island is included.
♦ Students may select passages to present as dramatic readings (e.g., dialogues revealing character development or descriptions they consider symbolically important).
1. Death—Fiction 2. Fathers and sons—Fiction 3. Wisconsin—Fiction.

Speerstra, Karen. *The Earthshapers.* Illus. by George Armstrong. Naturegraph (0-87916-108-1), 1980. 80p. B/W illus. (Interest level: 5-8).

Set in 900 A.D. along the Mississippi River, this novel describes the world of the effigy Mound Builders through the story of 12-year-old Yellow Moon and her extended family. Apparently based on sound archaeological findings, the book includes a map reflecting the trading patterns of this culture.
♦ The author lists the moons (months) of the year with such names as Cold Moon (January) and Moon of the Berries (August). Students may create a calendar with descriptive names revealing important aspects of their culture today.
1. Indians of North America—Fiction.

Wilder, Laura Ingalls *Little House in the Big Woods.* Illus. by Garth Williams. HarperCollins (0-06-026439-6), 1954. 237p. B/W illus. (Interest level: 1-6).

Pioneer farm life circa 1870 near Pepin, Wisconsin, is described in this first book of the Little House series, based on Wilder's early childhood remembrances. Clear descriptions of games, tastes, and activities such as threshing and maple sugaring help today's readers visualize the era's daily life.
♦ The Ingalls family was part of a westward flood of settlers primarily engaged in agriculture. Contemporary children may interview a family member or other adult to discover what influenced a decision to settle in a particular location.
1. Frontier and pioneer life—Wisconsin—Fiction 2. Wisconsin—Fiction.

Zeier, Joan T. *The Elderberry Thicket.* Atheneum (0-689-31612-7), 1990. 154p. (Interest level: 4-8).

The summer of 1938 brings further challenges to the Parsons, a rural Wisconsin family already hard hit by the Depression, when Mr. Parsons must leave to look for a new job. Although plot events are not unique to the state, the book conveys an authentic sense of Wisconsin farming community structure and of a summer's natural cycles.
♦ Individuals such as the visiting nurse and the neighboring farm wife are important adult helpers to the Parsons family. Students may describe the people and organizations they know about in their communities who help families today.
1. Self-reliance—Fiction 2. Country life—Fiction 3. Wisconsin—Fiction.

Periodicals

917.75
Wisconsin Trails. Wisconsin Tales and Trails (ISSN 0095-4314), 1960-. Bimonthly. Color photos. (Interest level: 5-8).

Each issue offers a wide range of articles on such topics as historic sites, scenic attractions, celebrations, historic and contemporary individuals, and various traditions. This general-audience publication is noted for excellent illustrations and well-researched articles, indexed in *Access* since 1978.
♦ Students may use this magazine as a reference source in many Wisconsin-related projects.
1. Wisconsin—Description and travel.

Professional Materials

Catalog File
School Resources from the State Historical Society of Wisconsin. Publication Sales, State Historical Society of Wisconsin (SHSW). Annual. (Interest level: Professional).

This descriptive flyer contains information about, and an order form for, SHSW materials deemed useful for classrooms (grades 4-12) whether or not the materials were originally prepared for that specific purpose. Brief information about SHSW gift shop resources is also provided. Requesting the current copy of *School Resources from the State Historical Society of Wisconsin* ensures having up-to-date information. (It is worth noting that the SHSW Museum Shop, 30 N. Carroll on Capitol Square, Madison, WI 53703, has a fine collection of print and nonprint materials from many sources, but no catalog of its inventory exists.)

016.977
Kruse, Ginny Moore, with Grobe, Deana; Lincoln, Elizabeth; and Lundstrom, Marie. *On Wisconsin: Books for Young Readers about Wisconsin People, Places, and Topics.* Cooperative Children's Book Center (CCBC) (No ISBN), 1993. (Interest level: Professional).

More than 150 carefully selected books relating in various ways to Wisconsin are listed; the majority are in print. In addition to standard bibliographic data, a descriptive annotation for each is provided. Titles cover the age range of preschool through high school. A nonselective *CCBC Wisconsin Identification Record* is published annually to document new books with a Wisconsin connection for children and young adults. The CCBC is a noncirculating library for adults with an academic or professional interest in children's and young adult literature. CCBC information services are funded by the School of Education, University of Wisconsin—Madison and the Wisconsin Department of Public Instruction Division for Library Services. For information about available CCBC publications on Wisconsin themes, send a stamped, preaddressed envelope to Publications, Cooperative Children's Book Center, 4290 Helen C. White Hall, 600 N. Park Street, Madison, WI 53706-1385.
1. Wisconsin—Bibliography 2. Children's literature—Bibliography—Wisconsin.

016.977
Wisconsin Division for Library Services. *American Indian Resource Manual for Public Libraries.* Wisconsin Department of Public Instruction, Division for Library Services (No ISBN), 1992. 150p. Available from Publication Sales, Wisconsin Department of Public Instruction. (Interest level: Professional).

Aimed primarily at the specific needs of Wisconsin libraries and emphasizing Wisconsin Native American tribes, this manual also contains information of broader application. Selective bibliographies of in-print adult and juvenile materials, approaches to materials evaluation and collection development, and suggestions for adult and children's programs are featured. An author/title index, a publishers directory, and reproducible clip art add to the practical value of the publication.
1. Indians of North America—Bibliography 2. Public libraries—Materials.

920
Lindgren, Merri V. *CCBC Resource List for Appearances by Wisconsin Book Creators.* 3rd ed. Cooperative Children's Book Center (CCBC) (No ISBN), 1993. Available from Friends of the CCBC, Inc. (Interest level: Professional).

More than 50 Wisconsin authors and illustrators of books for young people are included in this directory. Information about their published works and about the types of appearances they are willing to make is provided. Practical suggestions about all phases of arranging book creator appearance programs in schools and libraries are useful.
1. Authors—Wisconsin.

Directory of Publishers and Vendors

Below are the names and addresses of publishers and companies from whom materials cited in this book can be ordered.

Abdo Daughters
P.O. Box 36036
Minneapolis, MN 55435

AIMS Media Inc.
9710 De Sota Ave.
Chatsworth, CA 91311

Adams Press
59 Seymour Ave., SE
Minneapolis, MN 55414

Addison-Wesley Publishing Co., Inc.
Rte. 128
Reading, MA 01867

Adventure Publications
P.O. Box 269
Cambridge, MN 55008

Agency for Instructional Technology (AIT)
Box A
1111 W. 17th St.
Bloomington, IN 47404-3098

Aladdin Publishing Co.
P.O. Box 364
Palmer, AK 99645

Altwerger and Mandel Publishing Co.
6346 Orchard Lake Rd.
West Bloomfield, MI 48322

Ambrose Video Publishing
1290 Ave. of the Americas
Suite 2245
New York, NY 10104

American Geographic Publishing
P.O. Box 5630
Helena, MT 59604

American Library Association (ALA)
Publishing Services
50 E. Huron St.
Chicago, IL 60611

American School Publishers
155 N. Wacker Dr.
Chicago, IL 60606

Ann Arbor Public Schools
2555 S. State St.
Ann Arbor, MI 48104

Atheneum Publishers
866 Third Ave.
New York, NY 10022

Atlas Video, Inc.
4915 St. Elmo Ave.
Suite 305
Bethesda, MD 20814

Avery Color Studios
Box 275, Star Rte.
Au Train, MI 49806

Baker Book House
P.O. Box 6827
Grand Rapids, MI 49516

Ballantine/Del Rey/Fawcett/Ivy Books
201 E. 50th St.
New York, NY 10022

Bantam Doubleday Dell Publishing Group, Inc.
Affil. of Bertelsmann
666 Fifth Ave.
New York, NY 10103

Barron's Educational Series
Box 8040
250 Wireless Blvd.
Hauppauge, NY 11788

Bluestem Productions
P.O. Box 334
Wayzata, MN 55391

Bobbs
Imprint of Macmillan
866 Third Ave.
New York, NY 10022

Boyds Mills Press
910 Church St.
Honesdale, PA 18431

Bradbury Press
Imprint of Macmillan
866 Third Ave.
New York, NY 10022

Britannica Educational Corp.
310 S. Michigan Ave.
Chicago, IL 60618

Broderbund Software
17 Paul Dr.
San Rafael, CA 94903

Capitol Tours, Division of Building and Grounds
4 E. State Capitol
Madison, WI 53702

Carolrhoda Books, Inc.
241 First Ave., North
Minneapolis, MN 55401

The Caxton Printers, Ltd.
312 Main St.
Caldwell, ID 83606

Charles A. Lindbergh State Park
Rural Rte.
Little Falls, MN 56345

Chelsea House Publishers
95 Madison Ave.
New York, NY 10016

Children's Press
5440 N. Cumberland Ave.
Chicago, IL 60656

Children's Television Workshop (CTW)
1 Lincoln Plaza
New York, NY 10023

Chronicle Books
275 Fifth St.
San Francisco, CA 94103

Cinemark, Inc.
1761 Karg Dr.
Akron, OH 44313

Clarion Books
215 Park Ave., South
New York, NY 10003

Clark & Miles Publishing
1670 S. Robert St.
Suite 315
St. Paul, MN 55118

Clements Research
16850 Dallas Pkwy.
Dallas, TX 75248

Cobblestone Publishing, Inc.
30 Grove St.
Peterborough, NH 03458

Congress of Illinois Historical Societies and Museums
Old State Capitol
Springfield, IL 62701

Conner Prairie Press
13400 Allisonville Rd.
Noblesville, IN 46060

Cooperative Children's Book Center
4290 Helen C. White Hall
600 N. Park St.
Madison, WI 53706-1385

Coronet/MTI Film & Video
108 Wilmot Rd.
Deerfield, IL 60015

Corps of Engineers, Detroit District
P.O. Box 1027
Detroit, MI 48231

The Cottage Book Shop
Glen Arbor, MI 49636

Michael Cotter
Rte. 3, Box 47
Austin, MN 55912

Cranberry Originals Press
P.O. Box 25
Port Edwards, WI 54469

CRM Films
2215 Faraday
Carlsbad, CA 92008

Creative Education, Inc.
Box 227
123 S. Broad St.
Mankato, MN 56001

Crowell Junior Books
Imprint of HarperCollins Childrens Books
10 E. 53rd St.
New York, NY 10022

Crown Publishing Group
Affil. of Random House, Inc.
201 E. 50th St.
New York, NY 10022

Darron Publishing
P.O. Box 1753
St. Cloud, MN 56302

Daybreak Star/United Indians of All Tribes
P.O. Box 99100
Seattle, WA 98199

Delacorte Press
666 Fifth Ave.
New York, NY 10103

Dell Publishing
666 Fifth Ave.
New York, NY 10103

DeLorme Mapping Company
P.O. Box 298
Freeport, ME 04032

Dial Books for Young Readers
375 Hudson St.
New York, NY 10014

Dillon Press
Imprint of Macmillan Children's Book Group
866 Third Ave.
24th Floor
New York, NY 10022

Doubleday
666 Third Ave.
New York, NY 10103

Dover Publications, Inc.
31 E. 2nd St.
Mineola, NY 11501

Dutton Children's Books
375 Hudson St.
New York, NY 10014

Eagle's View Publishing Company
706 W. Riverdale
Ogden, UT 84405

Eberly Press
1004 Michigan Ave.
East Lansing, MI 48823

Eliza Records
3304 Rittenhouse St., NW
Washington, DC 20015

Enslow Publishers, Inc.
Box 777
Bloy St. & Ramsey Ave.
Hillside, NJ 07205

Enterprise Press
8600 S. Fenner Rd.
Laingsburg, MI 48848

Experience America, Inc.
P.O. Box 250
Cedar City, UT 84721

Eye Gate Media
3333 Elston Ave.
Chicago, IL 60618

Facts on File, Inc.
460 Park Ave., South
New York, NY 10016

Four Winds Press
Imprint of Macmillan Children's Book Group
866 Third Ave.
New York, NY 10022

Friede Publications
2339 Venezia Dr.
Davison, MI 48423

Friends of Minnesota Valley Regional Library
Box 3446
100 E. Main St.
Mankato, MN 56001

Friends of the CCBC, Inc.
P.O. Box 5288
Madison, WI 53705

Gallopade Publishing Group
235 E. Ponce de Leon Ave.
Suite 100
Decatur, GA 30030

Gareth Stevens, Inc.
River Center Bldg.
Suite 201
1555 N. River Center Dr.
Milwaukee, WI 53212

Globe Pequot
P.O. Box Q
Chester, CT 06421

Great American Puzzle, Inc.
16 S. Main St.
South Norwalk, CT 06854

Great Lakes National Program Office
United States Environmental Protection Agency
230 Dearborn Ave.
Chicago, IL 60604

Great Lakes Shipwreck Historical Society
111 Ashman St.
Sault Ste. Marie, MI 49783

Greenwillow Books
1350 Ave. of the Americas
New York, NY 10019

Grey Castle Press
Pocket Knife Square
Lakeville, CT 06039

Guild Press of Indiana
6000 Sunset Ln.
Indianapolis, IN 46208

Hammock & Inglenook
P.O. Box 1246
Madison, WI 53701-1246

Harcourt Brace Jovanovich, Inc.
6277 Sea Harbor Dr.
Orlando, FL 32887

HarperCollins Publishers, Inc.
10 E. 53rd St.
New York, NY 10022

The Hawley Herald
Hawley, MN 56549

Hawthorne Education Services
800 Gray Oak Dr.
Columbia, MO 65201

Heartland Press
520 Second Ave.
Spencer, IA 51301

Hennepin County Library
A.S.D. Secretary
12601 Ridgedale Dr.
Minnetonka, MN 55343

Heritage Productions
10255 Scarborough Rd.
Bloomington, MN 55437

High Touch Learning, Inc.
Box 754
Houston, MN 55943

Hinckley Fire Museum
Hinckley MN 55037

Historic Landmarks Foundation of Indiana
3402 Boulevard Pl.
Indianapolis, IN 46208

Holiday House, Inc.
425 Madison Ave.
New York, NY 10017

Holy Cow! Press
P.O. Box 3170
Mount Royal Station
Duluth, MN 55803

Henry Holt & Co., Inc.
115 W. 18th St.
New York, NY 10011

Hillsdale Educational Publishers
P.O. Box 245
39 North St.
Hillsdale, MI 49242

Holt, Rinehart & Winston, Inc.
6277 Sea Harbor Dr.
Orlando, FL 32887

Houghton Mifflin Co./Houghton Mifflin Software
One Beacon St.
Boston, MA 02108

William H. Hull
6833 Creston Rd.
Edina, MN 55435

Idaho Book and School Supply
5286 Chinden Blvd.
Boise, ID 83714

Illinois Department of Conservation
524 S. Second St.
Springfield, IL 62701-1787

Illinois Historical Society
Union Station
Springfield, IL 62701

Illinois State Historical Society
Old State Capitol
Springfield, IL 62701

Illinois Writers' Guild
5016 34th Ave.
Moline, IL 61265

Indian Country Communications
Rte. 2, Box 2900-A
Hayward, WI 54843

Indian Elementary Curriculum Project
Hans Christian Andersen Complex
1098 Andersen Lane
Room C207
Minneapolis, MN 55407

Indian Museum
c/o Lake Erie College
391 W. Washington
Painesville, OH 44077

Indiana Department of Commerce
Agriculture Division
1 North Capitol
Suite 700
Indianapolis, IN 46204-2288

Indiana Department of Natural Resources
Map Sales Section
402 W. Washington St., W160
Indianapolis, IN 46204

Indiana Historical Bureau
State Library and Historical Building
Room 408
140 North Senate Ave.
Indianapolis, IN 46204

Indiana University
Media and Teaching Resources
Bloomington, IN 47405

Indiana University Press
10th & Morton Sts.
Bloomington, IN 47405

Inland Seas Education Association
P.O. Box 4223
Traverse City, MI 49685-4223

Instructional Video
P.O. Box 21
Maumee, OH 43537

Janus Films
888 7th Ave.
Fourth Floor
New York, NY 10106

Jocelyn Riley/Her Own Words
P.O. Box 5264
Madison, WI 53705

Johns Hopkins University Press
Johns Hopkins University
Baltimore, MD 21211-2190

Johnson Publishing Co., Inc.
820 S. Michigan Ave.
Chicago, IL 60605

Just Us Books
301 Main St.
Suite 22-24
Orange, NJ 07050

Karamu House
2355 E. 89th St.
Cleveland, OH 44106

Kent State University Press
Kent State University
Kent, OH 44242

Kestrel Publications
1811 Stonewood Dr.
Beavercreek, OH 45434

Alfred A. Knopf, Inc.
201 E. 50th St.
New York, NY 10022

Lake Superior Port Cities
P.O. Box 16417
Duluth, MN 55816

Lerner Publications Company
241 First Ave., North
Minneapolis, MN 55401

JB Lippincott Co.
227 E. Washington Sq.
Philadelphia, PA 19106

Little, Brown & Company, Inc.
34 Beacon St.
Boston, MA 02106

Lodestar Books
375 Hudson St.
New York, NY 10014

Lothrop, Lee & Shepard Books
1350 Ave. of the Americas
New York, NY 10019

Lucent Books
P.O. Box 289011
San Diego, CA 92198-0011

Mackinac State Historical Parks
P.O. Box 873
Mackinaw City, MI 49701

Mackinac Island State Park Commission
P.O. Box 30028
Lansing, MI 48909

Macmillan Educational Distribution Center
Front and Brown Sts.
Riverside, NJ 08370

Makin' Jam, Etc.
Rte. 1, Box 246 A
Bowler, WI 54416

Maumee Valley Historical Society
1031 River Rd.
Maumee, OH 43537

McClelland & Stewart Ltd.
481 University Ave.
Suite 900
Toronto, ON M5G 2E9
Canada

McDonald & Woodward Publishing Company
P.O. Box 10308
Blacksburg, VA 24062

McGraw Hill Book Co.
School Division
1221 Ave. of the Americas
New York, NY 10020

David McKay Company, Inc.
Subs. of Random House, Inc.
201 E. 50th St.
Brooklyn, NY 11229

MECC (Minnesota Educational Computing Consortium)
3490 Lexington Ave., North
St. Paul, MN 55126

Micawber's, Inc.
525 N. Third St.
Minneapolis, MN 55401

Michigan Department of Natural Resources
P.O. Box 30028
Lansing, MI 48909

Michigan Department of State
Lansing, MI 48918-1805

The Michigan Indian Press
Grand Rapids Inter-Tribal Council
45 Lexington, NW
Grand Rapids, MI 49504

Michigan Magic
P.O. Box 794
Escanaba, MI 49829

Michigan State University
Cooperative Extension Service
Agriculture Hall, Room 10
East Lansing, MI 48824-1039

The Millbrook Press, Inc.
2 Old New Milford Rd.
Brookfield, CT 06804

Milwaukee County Historical Society
910 N. Old World Third St.
Milwaukee, WI 53203

Minnesota Chippewa Tribe
P.O. Box 217
Cass Lake, MN 56633

Minnesota Department of Education
Learning Resources Unit
605 Capitol Sq.
St. Paul, MN 55101

Minnesota History Center
345 Kellogg Blvd., West
St. Paul, MN 55102

Minnesota Office of Tourism
240 Bremer Building
419 N. Robert St.
St. Paul, MN 55101

Minnesota Public Radio
45 E. Eighth St.
St. Paul, MN 55101

Minnesota Transportation Museum, Inc.
26120 Bird Bluff Rd.
Shorewood, MN 55331

William Morrow & Company, Inc.
1350 Ave. of the Americas
New York, NY 10019

Morrow Junior Books
105 Madison Ave.
New York, NY 10016

National Geographic Educational Service
P.O. Box 98019
Washington, DC 20090

National Geographic Society
1145 17th St., NW
Washington, DC 20036

Naturegraph
Box 1975
Happy Camp, CA 96309

Neighbors Publishing
P.O. Box 15071
Minneapolis, MN 55415

Neil Armstrong Air and Space Museum
I-75 and Bellefontaine St., Box 1978
Wapakoneta, OH 45895

New Chapter Press
Old Pound Rd.
Old Pound, NY 10576

New Day Press/Karamu House
2355 E. 89th St.
Cleveland, OH 44106

Nongame Wildlife Fund
P.O. Box 30028, Dept. P.
Lansing, MI 48909

Nordell Graphic Communications
102 N.E. Sixth St.
Staples, MN 56479

North American Indian Cultural Center
1062 Triplett Blvd.
Akron, OH 44306

North Central Book Distribution
N57 W13636
Carmen Ave.
Menomonee Falls, WI 53051

North Country Press
P.O. Box 440
Belfast, ME 04915

North Star Press
P.O. Box 451
St. Cloud, MN 56302

NorthWord Press, Inc.
P.O. Box 1360
Minocqua, WI 54548

Jeffrey Norton Publishers, Inc.
On-the-Green
Guilford, CT 06437

Ohio Department of Education
65 S. Front St.
Columbus, OH 43215

Ohio Department of Natural Resources
ODNR Publications
4383 Fountain Square Dr.
Columbus, OH 43224

Ohio Department of Transportation
25 S. Front St.
Columbus, OH 43215

Ohio Historical Society
1982 Velma Ave.
Columbus, OH 43211-2497

Ohio Magazine, Inc.
62 E. Broad St.
Columbus, OH 43215

Ootek Productions
S. 12229 Round River Trail
Spring Green, WI 53588

Orange Frazer Press
P.O. Box 214
37-1/2 W. Main St.
Wilmington, OH 45177

Orchard Books
387 Park Ave., South
New York, NY 10016

Oryx Press
4041 North Central Ave. at Indian School Rd.
Phoenix, AZ 85012-3397

Osseo Public Schools
Educational Service Center
P.O. Box 327
11200 93rd Ave., North
Maple Grove, MN 55369

PBS Video
1320 Braddock Pl.
Alexandria, VA 22314-1698

Pfeifer Hamilton Publishers
1702 E. Jefferson St.
Duluth, MN 55812-2029

Philomel Books
Imprint of Putnam Publishing Group
200 Madison Ave.
New York, NY 10016

Pioneer Press
P.O. Box 28
102 Fourth St.
Terra Alta, WV 26764

Pleasant Company
P.O. Box 998
Middleton, WI 53562-0998

Prairie Oak Press
2577 University Ave.
Madison, WI 53705

Putnam, Inc.
200 Madison Ave.
New York, NY 10016

Quast, Inc.
379 7th Ave., South
Fargo, ND 58103

Quest Productions
2600 10th St.
Berkeley, CA 94710

Quest Publishing
2018 29th St.
Rock Island, IL 61201

Quinlan Press
131 Beverly St.
Boston, MA 02114

Raintree/Steck-Vaughn Publishers
310 W. Wisconsin Ave.
Milwaukee, WI 53203

Rand McNally Children's Books
Macmillan Publishing Company
3131 Mt. Pleasant St.
Racine, WI 53404

Random House, Inc.
201 E. 50th St.
New York, NY 10022

Reflections Press
A Division of T.I.S. Enterprises
P.O. Box 1998
Bloomington, IN 47402

River Road Publications
830 E. Savidge
Spring Lake, MI 49456

Rosen Publishing Group
29 E. 21st St.
New York, NY 10010

Rumpelstiltskin Productions
1326 E. Broadway
Mt. Pleasant, MI 48858

Rutledge Hill Press
513 Third Ave., South
Nashville, TN 37210

Scholastic, Inc.
730 Broadway
New York, NY 10003

The School Ship
Inland Seas Education Association
P.O. Box 4223
Traverse City, MI 49685

Scribner Book Companies/Macmillan
866 Third Ave.
New York, NY 10022

Silver Burdett & Ginn
250 James St.
Morristown, NJ 07960

Simon & Schuster
The Simon & Schuster Bldg.
1230 Ave. of the Americas
New York, NY 10020

Ski Printers
Blanchardville, WI 53516

Sterling Publishing Company, Inc.
387 Park Ave., South
5th Floor
New York, NY 10016-8810

Stolee Communications
P.O. Box 16344
Minneapolis, MN 55416

Stowe House State Memorial
2950 Gilbert Ave.
Cincinnati, OH 45206

Suttons Bay Publications
P.O. Box 361
Suttons Bay, MI 49682

Swiss Village Book Store
707 N. First St.
St. Louis, MO 63102

TAB Books, Inc.
Div. of McGraw Hill, Inc.
Box 40
Blue Ridge Summit, PA 17294-0850

Terrell
International Black Writers
P.O. Box 1030
Chicago, IL 60690

Tessera Publishing, Inc.
9561 Woodridge Circle
Eden Prairie, MN 55347

Ticknor & Fields
215 Park Ave., South
New York, NY 10003

Tom Snyder Productions
90 Sherman St.
Cambridge, MA 02140

Trailblazer Books
13030 Cannon City Blvd.
Northfield, MN 55057

Troll Associates
100 Corporate Dr.
Mahwah, NJ 07430

Tundra Books of Northern New York
Affil. of Tundra Books (Canada)
Box 1030
Plattsburgh, NY 12901

Two Peninsula Press
Michigan Book Central
P.O. Box 30034
Lansing, MI 48909

United States Environmental Protection Agency
Great Lakes National Program Office
230 Dearborn Ave.
Chicago, IL 60604

United States Government Printing Office
Superintendent of Documents
P.O. Box 371954
Pittsburgh, PA 15250-7954

University of Michigan Press
P.O. Box 1104
839 Green St.
Ann Arbor, MI 48106

University of Oklahoma Press
1005 Asp Ave.
Norman, OK 73019

University of Wisconsin—Stevens Point
University Telecommunications
Communication Arts Center
Stevens Point, WI 54481

University Press of Kentucky
663 S. Limestone St.
Lexington, KY 40508-4008

VCRI
P.O. Box 1179
Gillette, WY 82717

Viking Penguin, Inc.
375 Hudson St.
New York, NY 10014

Vimach Associates
3039 Indianola Ave.
Columbus, OH 43202

Vintage Books
201 E. 50th St.
New York, NY 10022

Waapoone Publishing
Lakefield, Ontario KOL 2HO
Canada

Phillip H. Wagner, Publisher
Wagner Office Systems
2800-2 S. Sixth St.
Springfield, IL 62703

Waldman House Press
525 N. Third St.
Minneapolis, MN 55401

Walker & Company
720 Fifth Ave., South
New York, NY 10019

Warne
Div. of Penguin USA
375 Hudson St.
New York, NY 10014-3657

Warner Books, Inc.
1271 Ave. of the Americas
New York, NY 10020

Franklin Watts, Inc.
387 Park Ave., South
New York, NY 10016

Wayne State University Press
Simons Building
5959 Woodward
Detroit, MI 48202

West Michigan Printing, Inc.
840 Ottawa Ave., NW
Grand Rapids, MI 49503

Albert Whitman
6340 Oakton St.
Morton Grove, IL 60053-2723

Wilderness Adventure Books
Box 968
320 Garden Lane
Fowlerville, MI 48836

Williams Publishing Co.
P.O. Box 185
Charlotte, VT 05445

Wisconsin Department of Public Instruction
P.O. Box 7841
Madison, WI 53707-7841

Wisconsin Document Sales, Department of Administration
202 S. Thornton Ave.
Madison, WI 53707

Wisconsin Education Television, Tape Dubbing Service
3319 W. Beltline Hwy.
Madison, WI 53713

Wisconsin Folk Museum
Mount Horeb, WI 53572

Wisconsin Historical Society
816 State St.
Madison, WI 53706

Wisconsin Library Association
4785 Hayes Rd.
Madison, WI 53704

Author Index

Aaseng, Nathan, 8, 9
Ackerman, Karen, 88
Adler, David A., 12, 43, 84, 107
Adoff, Arnold, 79, 84
Anderson, Joan, 15, 18
Anderson, Julie, 39
Anderson, Scott, 55, 57
Anderson, William, 56, 109
Andrews, Jan, 15
Apps, Jerry, 97, 100
Armour, David A., 39
Arnold, Caroline, 95
Arnosky, Jim, 2
Aylesworth, Thomas G., 5, 6, 23, 24, 80
Aylesworth, Virginia L., 5, 6, 23, 24, 80

Baker, David, 20
Baker, Jim, 81
Baker, Ronald L., 27
Barcus, Frank, 39
Barfknecht, Gary W., 40
Balterman, Lee, 3
Batson, Larry, 20
Bauer, Marion Dane, 15, 69
Baxter, Nancy Niblack, 24
Bellairs, John, 69
Bellville, Cheryl Walsh, 97, 98
Benton-Banai, Edward, 95, 102, 104, 110
Bernstein, Joanne E., 87
Berry, Michael, 108
Berry, S. L., 23
Berton, Pierre, 39
Bial, Raymond, 2, 3, 97
Blacklock, Craig, 52, 67
Blackstone, Harry, 43
Bloetscher, Virginia Chase, 83
Blos, Joan W., 45
Blue, Rose, 87, 108
Bonvillain, Nancy, 39

Bourgeois, Paulette, 78, 90
Bowen, Betsy, 52
Boyer, Edward, 77
Boyne, Walter J., 77
Brandenberg, Aliki, 29
Bratvold, Gretchen, 103
Bray, Edmund C., 61
Bridgewater, Alan, 77
Brill, Ethel C., 45
Brink, Carol Ryrie, 105, 110
Britton, J.D., 92
Brock, Kenneth J., 19
Brodie, Carolyn S., 79
Brooke, William J., 95
Brooks, Barbara, 60
Brooks, Gwendolyn, 4
Bunting, Eve, 8
Burke, Carol, 27
Burke, Thomas Aquinas, 81
Burns, Diane L., 54, 78
Burns, Virginia, 43
Bushey, Jerry, 2
Butler, Beverly, 110

Calvert, Patricia, 69
Carley, Kenneth, 61
Carlson, Laurie, 90
Carmony, Marvin, 27
Carpenter, Allan, 6, 27, 61
Carter, Alden R., 110
Casey, Jane Clark, 88
Cavan, Seamus, 24
Cavinder, Fred D., 27
Celsi, Teresa Noel, 44
Chall, Marsha Wilson, 69
Chambers, Catherine E., 30
Chappel, Bernice M., 45
Chappell, Carl L., 29
Childs, Lucille, 51

Christgau, Alice F., 70
Churchill, Richard E., 87
Claflin, Edward, 45
Clark, James E., 59
Clement, Herbert, 101
Clements, John, 40, 81
Clifford, Eth, 30
Clifton, James A., 38, 39
Clinton, Susan, 30, 86
Cobb, Vicki, 3
Cohen, Fay G., 102
Collins, David R., 9, 11, 68
Collins, Judy, 88
Cook, Diane, 102, 106
Cornell, George L., 38
Cotter, Michael, 56, 74
Couch, Ernie, 82
Couch, Jill, 82
Crofford, Emily, 53
Culver, Jerry, 101
Current, Richard N., 104

Davidson, Margaret, 43
Davis, James E., 4
Davis, Lauren, 5
De Angeli, Marguerite, 46
DeFelice, Cynthia, 88
DeLeeuw, Adele, 11
Delton, Judy, 70
Demuth, Patricia, 2
des Jarlait, Patrick, 61
Deur, Lynne, 38, 40, 41
Devaney, John, 14
Diller, Harriett, 15
Dolan, Edward R., 21
Dorner, Marjorie, 70
Driemen, John E., 75
Dutton, Fred, 37
Dygard, Thomas J., 70

Eastman, Charles, 67
Eberly, Carole, 36
Eckhouse, Morris, 85
Egan, Louise, 85
Engels, Stephen E., 56
Enright, Elizabeth, 110
Epstein, Beryl, 97
Epstein, Samuel, 97
Ericson, Stig, 70
Erwin, Jean, 56
Esbensen, Barbara, 38, 51, 52
Eunson, Dale, 110

Faber, Doris, 18
Fairbanks, Evelyn, 61
Fellegy, Joe, 55

Fertig, Dennis, 4
Fiday, Beverly, 15
Fiday, David, 15
Field, Ellyce, 38
Finsand, Mary Jane, 62
Fitz-Gerald, Christine Maloney, 30, 86
Fixico, Donald Lee, 49
Flatley, Dennis R., 1
Fleischer, Jane, 44, 45
Fleischman, Paul, 88
Force, Eden, 107
Fosdick, C. J., 55
Fox, Mary Virginia, 82
Fradin, Dennis B., 7, 27, 103
Freedman, Russell, 12, 77
Friermood, Elisabeth Hamilton, 30
Frisch, Carlienne, 68
Fuller, Iola, 46

Gág, Wanda, 54
Gage, Cully, 33
Gaines, Edith M., 81
Gard, Robert E., 95, 96, 104
Garthwaite, Chester, 100
Gelbach, Deborah L., 49
Gentry, Tony, 84
Gerber, Alan Jay, 87
Gherman, Beverly, 109
Giblin, James Cross, 98
Gieck, Jack, 76
Giff, Patricia Reilly, 101
Gilbert, Ruth, 18
Gilbreath, Alice, 91
Gillette, John, 36
Gilman, Carolyn, 50
Gilman, Rhoda R., 62
Gleiter, Jan, 95
Goldfarb, Mace, 49
Golenbock, Peter, 78
Goodman, Ailene S., 3
Greene, Carol, 12, 43, 78, 84
Gringhuis, Dirk, 33
Grobe, Deana, 113
Gross, Ruth Belov, 12

Haber, Louis, 9
Hachten, Harva, 99
Hale, Janet, 31
Hall, Steve, 66
Halsey, John R., 39
Hamilton, Virginia, 31, 79, 89
Hanfield, F. Gerald, 27
Hargrove, Jim, 5, 13, 86, 87
Hartford, John, 75
Hartman, Sheryl, 33
Haskins, James, 11, 44

Haskins, Jim, 4, 83
Hassler, Jon, 70
Hawke, Sharryl Davis, 4
Hawley, Marcy, 83
Hendershot, Judith, 89, 90
Henderson, Kathy, 35
Henry, Joanne Landers, 28, 31
Herda, D. J., 97, 99
Herman, Charlotte, 15, 16
Heuving, Jeanne, 102
Hickman, Janet, 89
Hickman, Pamela, 77
Hillbrand, Percie V., 48-49
Hochstetter, Nancy, 80
Holling, Holling Clancy, 46
Holman, J. Alan, 36
Holmquist, June D., 62
Hoose, Phillip M., 21
Hoover, Helen, 53
Howard, Ellen, 16
Hubbard, Kin, 20
Hull, William H., 60, 64, 65
Humphrey, Kathryn Long, 79
Hunt, Irene, 16
Hunting, George, 50
Hurwitz, Joanna, 90
Hyde, Charles K., 33

Igus, Toyomi, 75
Italia, Robert, 44

Jacobs, William Jay, 9, 13
Jacobson, Daniel, 23
Jacobson, Gloria, 107
Jagendorf, M. A., 18
Jakoubek, Robert, 87
Jando, Dominique, 101
Jaspersohn, William, 98
Jefferson, Constance, 57
Johnson, Eldon, 62
Johnston, Basil H., 95
Johnston, Patricia Condon, 51, 62

Kane, Joseph Nathan, 88
Kaplan, Anne R., 54
Katz, William Loren, 9
Keller, Mollie, 107
Kellogg, Steven, 1, 90, 96
Kelly, Joanne, 15, 16
Kent, Deborah, 10, 82
Kent, Zachary, 11, 14, 44, 45, 85, 86
Kherdian, David, 106
King, Gwen, 83
Kirtland, William, 68, 74
Klein, Tom, 52
Knepper, George W., 93

Koch, Ron, 71
Kozlak, Chet, 41
Krass, Peter, 45
Kriplen, Nancy, 18
Kruse, Ginny Moore, 113
Kurz, Ann, 98

Lafferty, Michael B., 76
Lamb, E. Wendell, 24
Lane, Jane, 90
Lanes, Selma G., 85
Larson, Don W., 50
Lasky, Kathryn, 78
Latimer, Jim, 71
Le Sueur, Meridel, 79, 104, 111
Lee, Carvel, 58
Lerner, Carol, 2
Levine, Ellen, 87
Light, Martin, 27
Lillegard, Dee, 85
Lincoln, Elizabeth, 113
Lindbergh, Charles A., 68
Lindbergh, Reeve, 1, 22, 90
Lindgren, Merri V., 113
Locker, Thomas, 16
Lomask, Milton, 10
London, Jack, 55
Long, Eleanor Rice, 31
Longfellow, Henry Wadsworth, 37
Love, Edmund, 46
Lovelace, Maud Hart, 71
Lowery, Linda, 94
Lund, Duane R., 58, 67, 71
Lund, Harry C., 35
Lundstrom, Marie, 113
Lurie, Nancy O., 107
Lydon, Kerry Raines, 90
Lyttle, Richard B., 21

Madison, James H., 32
Major, Charles, 31
Manna, Anthony L., 79
Marling, Karal Ann, 53, 55
Marsh, Carole, 51, 57, 58, 59, 63, 65
Marshall, Alexander B., 58
Marshall, James R., 40
Marston, Elsa, 23
Martin, Janet, 60
Martinson, Tom, 71
Massie, Larry B., 41
May, Julian, 19
McAuley, Karen, 107
McCall, Edith, 6, 103, 111
McCarthy, Ann, 58
McCloskey, Robert, 90
McClurken, James M., 38

McCluskey, John E., 75
McCollom, Anita, 41
McConnell, David B., 41
McCormick, Dell J., 96
McFarlan, Allan, 76
McFarland, Cynthia, 3
McGovern, Ann, 5
McKee, Carl R., 21
McKissack, Frederic, 1
McKissack, Patricia, 1, 84
McNulty, Faith, 99
Meier, Peg, 57, 63, 65
Merrick, George Byron, 60
Merrill, Jean, 90
Michel, Sara, 41
Micucci, Charles, 1
Miller, Dana, 66
Minnich, Jerry, 102, 105
Misselhorn, Roscoe, 7
Mitchard, Jacquelyn, 10
Mitchell, Barbara, 14, 85
Mitchell, John, 42
Mohr, Howard, 52
Mohrhardt, David, 36
Moon, Marjorie Nelson, 100
Moore, David L., 63
Moore, Willard B., 55
Morris, Lucy Leavenworth Wilder, 63
Morse, David, 19
Muir, John, 108
Munroe, Roxie, 78
Munsen, Sylvia, 54
Murphy, Jim, 22, 97
Murphy, Wendy Buehr, 109
Myers, Christopher A., 91
Myers, Lynne Born, 91
Myran, Karen, 72

Naden, Corinne J., 108
Nahum, Andrew, 77
Nardo, Don, 81
Naylor, Phyllis, 16
Newton, Stanley D., 34
Nicholson, Meredith, 31
Nielsen, Nancy, 50
Nolan, Jeannette Covert, 12
Norman, Michael, 48
North, Sterling, 101, 111
Nottridge, Rhoda, 99

O'Meara, Walter, 68
Ogden, R. Dale, 28
Okimoto, Jean Davies, 72
Olney, Ross R., 22
Olsenius, Richard, 59
Oppenheim, Joanne, 11

Osborne, Mary Pope, 96
Osinski, Alice, 39
Osofsky, Audrey, 51, 111
Ostendorf, Lloyd, 13
Otto, Simon, 34
Ourada, Patricia, 39

Parnell, Helga, 54
Patent, Dorothy, 94, 99
Paulsen, Gary, 55, 56, 72
Pearce, John, 81
Peat, Wilbur D., 29
Peavy, Linda, 10
Pellowski, Anne, 111, 112
Peterjohn, Bruce G., 77
Peters, Harry B., 100
Peterson, Eric, 50
Pevsner, Stella, 16
Peyton, John L., 34
Pfeiffer, Christine, 7
Polacco, Patricia, 91
Porter, A. P., 64
Precek, Katherine Wilson, 91

Quackenbush, Robert, 3, 87
Qualey, Marsha, 72
Quast, Michael, 48

Rahn, Joan Elma, 4
Ratigan, William, 40
Regguinti, Gordon, 53, 103
Reid, Robert L., 64
Riley, James Whitcomb, 22
Riley, Jocelyn, 112
Roberts, Naurice, 14
Roberts, Rich, 21
Robinson, Arthur N., 101
Rogers, Teresa, 95, 108
Romberg, Jenean, 91
Rosen, Michael J., 91, 92
Rosenthal, Bert, 21
Ross, Catherine, 98
Ross, Jane Bark, 83
Rothaus, James R., 21, 87
Rounds, Glen, 96
Rylant, Cynthia, 79, 87

San Souci, Robert, 96
Sandberg, Walt, 56
Sandburg, Carl, 14
Sanders, Scott Russell, 91
Sandin, Joan, 17
Sansome, Constance J., 55
Sayers, Evelyn M., 32
Schommer, Carrie, 52
Schultz, Gwen, 94

Schultz, Lawrence W., 24
Schulz, Walter A., 77
Schwandt, Stephen, 72, 112
Schwomeyer, Herb, 21
Scott, Beth, 48
Selden, Bernice, 11
Seuling, Barbara, 88
Shannon, Mike, 84
Shaw, Janet, 73
Shemie, Bonnie, 76
Shiels, Barbara, 10
Shephard, Esther, 96
Shorto, Russell, 45, 88
Shulman, Jeffrey, 95, 108
Siebert, Diane, 4
Siegel, Beatrice, 44
Sieve, Jerry, 78
Sikkenga, Raymond, 43
Simon, Charnan, 7
Simon, Nancy, 87
Simonds, Christopher, 36
Simons, Richard, 19
Sipiera, Paul P., 44
Smith, James P., 59
Smith, Robert Tighe, 65
Smith, Ursula, 10
Snake, Sam, 34
Sneve, Virginia Driving Hawk, 73
Snyder, Tom, 58
Sommers, Lawrence, 37
Sorden, L.G., 95, 96, 104
Spangenburg, Ray, 84, 85
Speerstra, Karen, 112
Stan, Susan, 60
Stanek, Muriel, 8
Stanley, Diane, 22
Stavig, Vicki, 59
Stein, R. Conrad, 6, 8, 42, 64, 104, 105
Stevens, Michael E., 94
Stevermer, Caroline, 73
Stewart, Gail, 5
Stone, Lynn M., 1
Stonehouse, Frederick, 33
Stuhler, Barbara, 48
Sullivan, George, 14, 77
Swain, Gwenyth, 28
Swenson, Grace Stagberg, 64

Tanner, Helen H., 40, 104
Tapping, Minnie Ellingson, 69
Tarkington, Booth, 31
Taylor, David V., 64
Taylor, Mildred D., 91
Teale, Edwin Way, 30
Terkel, Studs, 3
Thompson, Charles N., 29

Thompson, Kathleen, 8, 23, 42, 65, 82, 95, 104
Thomas, Jane Resh, 73
Todnem, Allen, 60
Tolan, Sally, 108
Tompert, Ann, 106
Traylor, Jeff, 80, 82
Traylor, Nadean Disabato, 80
Trenerry, Walter N., 50
Troester, Rosalie Riegle, 43
Turner, Dorothy, 98
Turner, Robyn Montana, 109
Umhoefer, Jim, 59

Van Steenwyk, Elizabeth, 15
Visser, Kristin, 100, 102
Vonada, Damaine, 82, 83

Wade, Linda R., 86
Wadsworth, Ginger, 95, 108
Walker, Barbara, 99
Wallace, Susan, 98
Warbach, Ozz, 38
Warburton, Lois, 8
Webb, Val, 59
Weeks, George, 35
Weidenaar, Reynold, 36
Weinberg, Larry, 13
Weiss, Harvey, 77
Wenzel, Dorothy, 57
Westman, Paul, 84, 85
Wheeler, Robert C., 65
Whelan, Gloria, 46, 47
White Earth Reservation Curriculum Committee, 49
Wilcox, Frank, 80
Wilder, Laura Ingalls, 73, 101, 112
Wiles, Richard, 42
Wilkins, Marne, 96
Willis, Patricia, 92
Wilson, George R., 29
Wilson, William E., 29
Winter, Jeanette, 92
Wisconsin Department of Administration, 102, 106
Wisconsin Division for Library Services, 113
Wisconsin Legislative Reference Bureau, 94
Wisconsin Library Association, 101
Witter, Evelyn, 9
Wolf, Bernard, 60
Wood, Dave, 57
Woodruff, Tom, 42
Woodyard, Chris, 75
Wormser, Richard, 13
Wosmek, Frances, 73

X, Malcolm, 45

Yolen, Jane, 74

Zadra, Dan, 78
Zeier, Joan T., 112

Zeitlin, Richard H., 103
Ziegler, Sandra, 99
Zimmermann, George, 80

Title Index

A Is for Art: An Alphabetical Tour of the Milwaukee Art Museum, 100
Abe Lincoln in Song and Story, 3
Abraham Lincoln (sound filmstrip), 12
Abraham Lincoln (videocassette), 12
Abraham Lincoln, President of a Divided Country, 12
Abraham Lincoln, Sixteenth President of the United States, 13
Abraham Lincoln: The Boy, The Man, 13
Across Five Aprils, 16
An Actor's Life for Me! Lillian Gish, 85
The Adventures of Nanabush, 34
Against All Opposition: Black Explorers in America, 4
All Hell Broke Loose, 64, 65
All in the Woodland Early, 74
All Season Guide to Minnesota's Parks, Canoe Routes and Trails, 59
Almost Summer, 71
Always the Young Strangers, 14
The Amazing Apple Book, 78, 90
The Amazing Milk Book, 98
Amazing Ohio: Illuminating Moments, 82
American Indian Habitats: How to Make Dwellings and Shelters of Natural Materials, 87
American Indian Resource Manual for Public Libraries, 113
American Tall Tales, 96
The Amish, 18
Animals That Changed History, 4
Ann Bancroft: On the Top of the World, 57
Antler, Bear, Canoe: A Northwoods Alphabet Year, 52
Apples, 99
Around Hawley with Ingrid, 72
Atlas of Great Lakes Indian History, 40, 104
Atlas of Michigan, 37

The Atlas of Wisconsin: General Maps and Gazetteer, 101
Attack at Michilimackinac 1763, 39
The Auction, 15
Aurora Means Dawn, 91
The Autobiography of Malcolm X, 45

Back in Those Days: Reminiscences and Stories of Indiana, 27
Barns of Wisconsin, 97
Be a Building Watcher on the Street Where You Live, 20
The Bears of Blue River, 31
Belle: The Life and Writings of Belle Case LaFollette, 106
Bells of Christmas, 89
Beneath the Inland Seas, 39
Benjamin Harrison, 30, 86
The Best of Kin Hubbard: Abe Martin's Sayings and Wisecracks, 20
Betrayed, 73
Betsy and Tacy Go Downtown, 71
"Betsy-Tacy" in Deep Valley: People and Places, 68
Betsy's Up-and-Down Year, 111
Better Than a Brother, 111
Billy: A Story of a Minnesota Boy Growing Up, 68, 74
Biography of a River: The Living Mississippi, 6, 103
The Birds of Ohio, 77
Birds of the Indiana Dunes, 19
Birdwise, 77
A Birthday for Blue, 90
"Black American Inventors," 83
Black Dance in America: A History through Its People, 11
Black Hawk, Frontier Warrior, 11
Black Minnesotans, 64

Black People Who Made the Old West, 9
Black Pioneers of Science and Inventions, 9
Blacks in Ohio: 7 Portraits, 75
Blimps, 78
Blossoms and Blizzards, 55
Blue Ribbon: A Social and Pictorial History of the Minnesota State Fair, 53
Blumpoe the Grumpoe Meets Arnold the Cat, 72
Bob Feller, 85
Book of Black Heroes, 75
The Borning Room, 88
Boundary Waters Canoe Area, Minnesota, 50
Boundary Waters Canoe Trip: An Adventure Travel Game, 55
Boyhood of Abraham Lincoln, 30
A Boyhood on the Upper Mississippi: A Reminiscent Letter, 68
Bring Warm Clothes: Letters and Photos from Minnesota's Past, 65
Bronzeville Boys and Girls, 4
Brothers of the Heart: A Story of the Old Northwest, 1837-1838, 45
A Brown Bird Singing, 73
The Bucky Badger Story, 94
Bunyan and Banjoes: Michigan Songs and Stories, 37
But I'll Be Back Again: An Album, 79, 87
By Canoe and Moccasin: Some Native Place Names of the Great Lakes, 95

Caddie Woodlawn, 105, 110
The Call of the Wild, 55
The Capture of Detroit, 39
CCBC Resource List for Appearances by Wisconsin Book Creators, 113
CCBC Wisconsin Identification Record, 113
The Cellar, 16
Changes for Kirsten: A Winter Story, 73
The Changing Farm in Early Minnesota, 53
Charles Lindbergh: Hero Pilot, 68
Chasing the Tornado, 19
Chicago (Aylesworth and Aylesworth), 6
Chicago, (Davis and Hawke), 4
Chicago (Pfeiffer), 7
Chicago (Stewart), 5
The Chicago Fire, 8
The Chickenhouse House, 16
Children of the Wagon Train, 24
The Chippewa, 39
The Christmas Loon, 71
Christmas on the Prairie, 18
Christmas Trees, 94
Christopher Columbus Comes to Minnesota, 59
Circles of Tradition: Folk Arts in Minnesota, 55
The Civil War, 86
Clabbered Dirt, Sweet Grass, 56

Clarence Darrow, 75
Classic Minnesota Fishing Stories, 55
A Clearing in the Forest: A Story about a Real Settler Boy, 31
Cleveland Cavaliers, 78
The Coat Pocket Bird Book, 36
Coffee Made Her Insane and Other Nuggets from Old Minnesota Newspapers, 63
The Colossus of Roads: Myth and Symbol Along the American Highway, 55
Come Explore Michigan the Beautiful, 41
Come Out Muskrats, 2
The Complete Poems of Paul Laurence Dunbar, 84
The Conners of Conner Prairie, 31
The Cookcamp, 72
Cooking the German Way, 54
Cooking the Norwegian Way, 54
Copper Country Adventure, 45
Copper Trails and Iron Rails: More Voyages into Michigan's Past, 41
Copper-toed Boots, 46
Corn Belt Harvest, 3, 97
County Fair, 2
Courage at Indian Deep, 73
Cows in the Parlor: A Visit to a Dairy Farm, 3
Cranberries, 98
Cranberries from A to Z: An Educational Picture Book, 98
Cranberries: Wisconsin's Native Fruit, 97
Cream and Bread, 60
Creatures in the Great Lakes, 35
Creatures of the North: The New Minnesota Sasquatch Encounters, 48

Dad's Stories and Farm Memories, 56, 74
The Dakota in Minnesota, 61
Dan Henry in the Wild West, 70
Daniel Boone and the Opening of the Ohio Country, 24
The Dark Secret of Weatherend, 69
Dark Sky, Dark Land: Stories of the Hmong Boy Scouts of Troop 100, 63
DataNet, 48, 57
The Day They Gave Babies Away, 110
Days of Rondo, 61
Deer at the Brook, 2
Detroit Kids Catalog: Complete Guide to Michigan Sites, 38
Diary: Asian Minnesotans, 66
Diary: Black Minnesotans, 66
Diary: Hispanic Minnesotans, 66
Diary: Native American Minnesotans, 66
The Dirty Thirties, 60
Discover Ohio, 76, 77
Distant Fires, 55, 57

Doers and Dreamers: The Governors of Michigan, 43
Donnelly's Demographics, 49
Dorothy Molter: Living in the Boundary Waters, 68
Dr. Beaumont and the Man with the Hole in His Stomach, 97
Dreamcatcher, 51, 111
Dreams into Deeds: Nine Women Who Dared, 10
Dune Boy: The Early Years of a Naturalist, 30

Early Indiana Trails and Surveys, 29
Earth Day, 94
The Earth's First People: A History-Coloring Book of the Ojibway Indians, 95
The Earthshapers, 112
Eastern Great Lakes: Ohio, Indiana, Michigan, 24, 80
Edith Herself, 16
Eighty Years at the Gopher Hole: The Saga of a Minnesota Pioneer 1867-1947, 69
The Elderberry Thicket, 112
Elijah's Angel: A Story of Chanukah and Christmas, 91
Elizabeth Blackwell, 84
Empire Builder James J. Hill, 67
Environmental America: The North Central States, 99
Ethnic America: The North Central States, 97
Everybody's Daughter, 72
Experiencing Indiana, 24
Explorers' Routes Map, 23

Face to Face, 69
Faces of the Forest, 53
Facts about the Presidents, 88
The Fallin' of the Pine: Logging on the Chippewa River, 1850-1900, 98
Family Farm, 16
Famous Blimps and Airships, 77
Fantastic Flying Paper Toys, 87
Farming the Land: Modern Farmers and Their Machines, 2
Farming Today Yesterday's Way, 97, 98
Fayette, 42
Fighters, Refugees, Immigrants: A Story of the Hmong, 49
First Farm in the Valley: Anna's Story, 111
The Flavor of Wisconsin: An Informal History of Food and Eating in the Badger State, 99
Flying Machine, 77
Folk Songs Out of Wisconsin: An Illustrated Compendium of Words and Music, 100
Follow the Drinking Gourd (videocassette), 88
Follow the Drinking Gourd (Winter), 92
Forging the Peninsulas: Michigan Is Made, 41
Fort Snelling: Colossus of the Wilderness, 66

The Fossils of Michigan, 35
Four Miles to Pinecone, 70
Frank Lloyd Wright and the Prairie School in Wisconsin: An Architectural Touring Guide, 100
Freedom Light: Underground Railroad Stories from Ripley, OH, 81
Freshwater Fury: Yarns and Reminiscences of the Greatest Storm in Inland Navigation, 39
From the Ashes: The Story of the Hinckley Fire of 1894, 64
From This Land: A History of Minnesota Empires, Enterprises and Entrepreneurs, 49
Frontier Surgeons: A Story about the Mayo Brothers, 53
Fun with Weaving, 91

Gaylord Nelson: A Day for Earth, 95, 108
The Geese of Silverlake, 52, 67
Generation to Generation, 110
Genius! The Artist and the Process, 109
The Geology of Michigan, 35
The Geology of Pictured Rocks National Lakeshore, 35
George Rogers Clark, Frontier Fighter, 11
Georgia O'Keeffe (Berry), 108
Georgia O'Keeffe (Turner), 109
Georgia O'Keeffe: The "Wideness and Wonder" of Her World, 109
Gerald Ford, 44
Giants of Jazz, 3
The Gift of the Deer, 53
Girders and Cranes: A Skyscraper Is Built, 3
The Glorious Fourth at Prairietown, 18
The Gobble-Uns'll Git You Ef You Don't Watch Out!, 22
Going the Moose Way Home, 71
The Gold Cadillac, 91
Golda Meir (Keller), 107
Golda Meir (McAuley), 107
"Good Morning, Mr. President," A Story about Carl Sandburg, 14
Grandaddy's Highway, 15
Graveyards of the Great Lakes, 41
The Great Circus Parade, 101
The Great Flood: A History-Coloring Book of the Ojibway Indians, 95
The Great Lakes, 35
The Great Lakes: An Environmental Atlas and Resource Book, 47
Great Lakes and Great Ships: An Illustrated History for Children, 42
Great Lakes Education Booklet, 38
Great Lakes Fur Trade, 41
Great Lakes in My World, 47
Great Lakes Region, 5, 25
The Great Lakes Region: The Heartland, 25

Great Lakes Shipwrecks and Survivals, 40
Great Lakes Water Level Facts, 35
Great Lives: Exploration, 10
Great Lives: Human Rights, 9
Great Lives: Invention and Technology, 10
Great Minds? Great Lakes!, 47
Great Northern Diver: The Loon, 52
The Great Peshtigo Fire, 104
The Greatest Showman on Earth: A Biography of P.T. Barnum, 106
Growing Pains, 54
A Guide to Free and Inexpensive Materials on Illinois History, 7
Guide to Ohio, 80
Guilt Trip, 72

Handbook of American Indian Games, 76
Handbook on Indiana History, 32
Happy Birthday, Kirsten! A Springtime Story, 73
Harold Washington, Mayor with a Vision, 14
Harriet Beecher Stowe, 87
Hatchet, 55
Haunted Heartland, 48
Haunted Ohio: Ghostly Tales from the Buckeye State, 75
Heartland, 4
Help! I'm a Prisoner in the Library, 30
Her Own Words: Dane County, Wisconsin Pioneer Women's Diaries, 105
Hiawatha, 37
Historic Women in Michigan, 43
Historical and Cultural Agencies and Museums in Illinois, 7
History of the Great Lakes States, 6
History on Tape: A Guide for Oral History in Indiana, 27
Hold Steady, 112
Home: A Collaboration of Thirty Distinguished Authors and Illustrators, 92
Hoosier Hersteria (A History of Indiana High School Girls Basketball), 21
Hoosier Historic Map, 23
Hoosier Landmarks: Indiana Properties Listed in the National Register of Historical Places, 28
Hoosier Hysteria, 21
Hoosiers: The Fabulous Basketball Life of Indiana, 21
The House of a Thousand Candles, 31
The House of Dies Drear (Hamilton), 31, 89
The House of Dies Drear (videocassette), 89
Houses of Bark: Tipi, Wigwam and Longhouse: Native Dwellings of Woodland Indians, 76
How Many Days to America?, 8
How Our Counties Got Their Names, 87 81ow the Glaciers Changed Michigan, 35

How to Make Play Places and Secret Hidy Holes, 90
How to Talk Minnesotan: A Visitor's Guide, 52
Hubert H. Humphrey: Here's My Hand, 67
The Huron, 39

I Am a Darker Brother, 84
I Made It Myself, 77
I Married a Logger: Life in Michigan's Tall Timber, 39
Ida B. Wells-Barnett, Woman of Courage, 15
If You Grew Up With Abraham Lincoln, 15
Illinois (Carpenter), 6
Illinois (Fradin), 7
Illinois (Stein), 8
Illinois (Thompson), 8
Illinois History, A Magazine for Young People, 17
Illinois Sketches, 7
The Immigrant Experience: Borghild Dahl, 67
In Coal Country (Hendershot), 89
In Coal County (videocassette), 90
In This Proud Land: The Story of a Mexican American Family, 60
Indian Boyhood, 67
Indian Clothing of the Great Lakes: 1740-1840, 33
Indian Lore, 24
Indiana (Aylesworth and Aylesworth), 23
Indiana (Carpenter), 27
Indiana (Ogden), 28
Indiana (Swain), 28
Indiana (Thompson), 23
Indiana: A History, 29
Indiana Days: Life in a Frontier Town, 30
Indiana Historic Indian Map, 23
Indiana: In Words and Pictures, 27
Indiana Map, 22
Indiana Place Names, 27
Indiana Puzzle, 22
Indiana University: Basketball Trivia, 21
The Indiana Way, 32
Indiana Writes, 27
The Indiana Book of Records, Firsts, and Fascinating Facts, 27
Indianapolis, 23
The Indianapolis Colts, 21
Indians of the Cuyahoga Valley and Vicinity, 83
The Indy 500, 22
An Interview with Bobby Knight, 20
Interview with Gary Paulsen, 69
The Iron Range in Transition, 66

James A. Garfield, 85
Jane Addams and Hull House, 10
Jane Addams: Pioneer in Social Reform and Activist for World Peace, 10
Janet Guthrie: First Woman at Indy, 22

Janet Guthrie: First Woman Driver at Indianapolis, 21
Jemmy, 70
Joel: Growing Up a Farm Man, 2
John Chapman: The Man Who Was Johnny Appleseed, 78
John Glenn: Around the World in 90 Minutes, 85
John Muir, 107
John Muir, Wilderness Protector, 95, 108
John Muir: Naturalist, Writer, and Guardian of the North American Wilderness, 108
John Muir: Saving the Wilderness, 108
Johnny Appleseed (Kellogg), 1, 90
Johnny Appleseed (Lindbergh), 1, 90
Johnny Bench, 84
Joshua's Westward Journal, 15
Judith Resnick: Challenger Astronaut, 87
Just Plain Fancy, 91

Katherine Dunham, 11
Keep an Eye on That Mummy, 18
Keep Stompin' Till the Music Stops, 16
The Keepsake Chest, 91
Kidding Around Chicago: A Young Person's Guide to the City, 5
Kids Create, 90
A Kingdom of Fiddlers: Old-Time Music in the Rural Community, 100
Kirsten Learns a Lesson: A School Story, 73
Kirsten Saves the Day: A Summer Story, 73
Kirsten's Surprise: A Christmas Story, 73

La Salle and the Grand Enterprise, 12
LaFollette's Magazine, 106
Land of the Giants: A History of Minnesota Business, 50
Land of the Sky Blue Waters, 34
Larger Than Life: The Adventures of American Legendary Heroes, 96
The Last Cow on the White House Lawn and Other Little-Known Facts about the Presidency, 88
The Laugh Peddler, 70
Laura Ingalls Wilder Country: The People and Places in Laura Ingalls Wilder's Life and Books, 56, 109
Laura Ingalls Wilder: A Biography, 109
Laura Ingalls Wilder: Growing Up in the Little House, 101
The Legend of Johnny Appleseed, 22
Lentil, 90
Let's Discover Weaving, 91
Letters from the Front, 1898-1945, 94
Lewis Cass, Frontier Soldier, 43
The Life and Times of the Apple, 1
Life in a Midwestern Small Town in the 1910s, 25

Life in the Slow Lane: Fifty Backroads Tours of Ohio, 80
Life on the Great Lakes: A Wheelsman's Story, 37
Limestone, 20
Lincoln, 13
Lincoln: A Photobiography, 12
The Little House Cookbook: Frontier Foods from Laura Ingalls Wilder's Classic Stories, 99
Little House Country: A Photo Guide to the Home Sites of Laura Ingalls Wilder, 109
Little House in the Big Woods, 101, 105, 112
Little Orphant Annie, 22
Log Cabin in the Woods: A True Story about a Pioneer Boy, 28
The Long Ago Lake: A Child's Book of Nature Lore and Crafts, 96
A Long Hard Journey: The Story of the Pullman Porter, 1
The Long Way to a New Land, 17
The Long Way Westward, 17
The Loon Feather, 46
Loon Magic for Kids, 52
Lore of the Great Turtle: Indian Legends of Mackinac Retold, 33

M.C. Higgins, the Great, 89
Magic Johnson, 44
The Magic Moccasins: Life among Ohio's Six Indian Tribes, 83
Magical Melons, 110
Magical Straits of Mackinac, 42
The Making of Michigan, 41
Many Faces, Many Voices: Multicultural Literary Experiences for Youth, 79
McCrephy's Field, 91
Meet Kirsten: An American Girl, 73
Meet the Newbery Author: Virginia Hamilton, 79
Meet the Newbery Author: Cynthia Rylant, 79
The Menominee, 39
The Miamis!, 24
Mich-Again's Day, 40
Michigan (Stein), 42
Michigan (Thompson), 42
Michigan Atlas and Gazetteer, 37
Michigan Facts, 40
Michigan History Magazine, 47
Michigan in Song, 37
Michigan Magic, 42
Michigan Snakes: A Field Guide and Pocket Reference, 36
Michigan Student Desktop Map, 38
Michigan Wetlands, 40
Michigan Wildflowers, 35
Michillaneous I, 40
Michillaneous II, 40
Milk, 98

Milk: The Fight for Purity, 98
Millie Cooper, 3B, 15
A Million Years in Minnesota, 61
Mills of Wisconsin and the Midwest, 100
Milwaukee, wie geht's? A History of German Milwaukee, 1839-1989, 105
Minneapolis-St. Paul: The Cities, Their People, 65
Minnesota (Porter), 64
Minnesota (Stein), 64
Minnesota (Thompson), 65
Minnesota: A Photographic Journey, 58
Minnesota Bandits, Bushwackers, Outlaws, Crooks, Devils, Ghosts, Desperados, Heroes, Heroines, Rogues, and Other Assorted and Sundry Characters, 65
Minnesota Calls, 74
A Minnesota Christmas Anthology, 56
The Minnesota Christmas Book, 51
Minnesota Dingbats: A Super Fun Book of Facts, Games, Stories, Poems, Riddles, Math Quizzes, Activities and More, 63
Minnesota During World War II, 59
The Minnesota Ethnic Food Book, 54
The Minnesota Experience, 56
Minnesota Festival Fun for Kids!, 51
Minnesota Guide, 59
Minnesota in Maps: A Trailblazer Atlas, 57
Minnesota Living History: Les Blacklock, 67
Minnesota Map, 57, 61
Minnesota Overtures, 58
Minnesota: Portrait of the Land and Its People, 62
Minnesota State Capitol, 63
Minnesota Travel Companion, 59
Minnesota Underfoot: A Field Guide to the State's Outstanding Geologic Features, 55
Minnesota's Chief Flat Mouth of Leech Lake, 67
Minnesota's Irish, 62
Minnesota's (Most Devastating) Disasters and (Most Calamitous) Catastrophes, 57
Minnie the Streetcar Boat, 50
The Mishomis Book: The Voice of the Ojibway, 95, 102, 104
The Mississippi, 6
Model Airplanes and How to Build Them, 77
The Model T Ford, 36
Mother Nature's Michigan, 38
The Mound Builders, 79
Mountain Wolf Woman: Sister of Crashing Thunder: The Autobiography of a Winnebago Indian, 107
Moving Hills of Sand, 19
Murder in Minnesota: A Collection of True Cases, 50
My Father, 88
My Life as a Magician, 43
My Sister's Keeper, 110

Mysteries in American Archeology, 23
The Mystery of Drear House: The Conclusion of the Dies Drear Chronicle, 31, 89
Mystery of the Haunted Cabin, 70
Myths and Moundbuilders, 23

Neil Armstrong: Space Pioneer, 84
The New Enchantment of Minnesota, 61
New Harmony: An Example and a Beacon, 28
Next Spring an Oriole, 46
Nightmare, 70
Nishnawbe Teachers' Guide, 38
Nishnawbe: A Story of Indians in Michigan, 38
"The North American Beaver Trade," 36
The North Central States, 23
Northern Lights: Going to the Sources, 62
The Northern Lights: Lighthouses of the Upper Great Lakes, 33
Northern Lights: The Story of Minnesota's Past, 62
Northwest Passage: The Story of Grand Portage, 64
The Northwoods Reader, 33
The Norwegians in America, 49
Notable Illinois Women, 9

Ohio (Fox), 82
Ohio (Kent), 82
Ohio (map), 82
Ohio (puzzle), 82
Ohio (videocassette), 80
Ohio (Thompson), 82
Ohio Almanac, 75
Ohio and Its People, 93
Ohio Biographical Dictionary: People of All Times and All Places Who Have Been Important to the History and Life of the State, 84
Ohio Cues, 92
Ohio Facts: A Comprehensive Look at Ohio Today County by County, 81
Ohio Gazetteer, 80
Ohio History Resource Guide for Teachers, 92
Ohio: Images of Nature, 78
Ohio Indian Trails: A Pictorial Survey of the Indian Trails of Ohio, 80
Ohio Lands: A Short History, 81
Ohio Magazine, 92
Ohio: Matters of Fact, 83
Ohio, Off the Beaten Path, 80
Ohio Pride: A Guide to Ohio Roadside History, 82
The Ohio River, 81
Ohio Sports Almanac, 78
Ohio Studies, 92
Ohio Trivia, 82
Ohio's Amphibians, 76, 77
Ohio's Birds, 76, 77
Ohio's Canal Era, 76

Ohio's Natural Heritage, 76
Ohio's Reptiles, 76, 77
Ohio's Spring Wild Flowers, 76, 77
Ohio's Stream Life, 76, 77
Ohio's Trees, 76
The Ojibway, 60
The Ojibway Creation Story: A History-Coloring Book of the Ojibway Indians, 95
Ojibway Indians Coloring Book, 59
Ol' Paul: The Mighty Logger, 96
Old Abe, the War Eagle: A True Story of the Civil War and Reconstruction, 103
Old Rail Fence Corners: Frontier Tales Told by Minnesota Pioneers, 63
Old Times on the Upper Mississippi: The Recollections of a Steamboat Pilot from 1854-1863, 60
On Location: Settings from Famous Children's Books—#1, 15, 16
On My Honor, 15
On the Banks of Plum Creek, 73
On the Downbeat—A Jazz Heritage, 20
On Wisconsin: Books for Young Readers about Wisconsin People, Places, and Topics, 113
One of the Third-Grade Thonkers, 16
Only My Mouth is Smiling, 112
"Oregon Trail," 24
Original Man and His Grandmother-No-No-Mis: A History-Coloring Book of the Ojibway Indians, 95
Original Man Walks the Earth: A History-Coloring Book of the Ojibway Indians, 95
The Ornery Morning, 2
Our Golda: The Story of Golda Meir, 107
Our Historic Boundary Waters from Lake Superior to Lake of the Woods, 58
Our Michigan Ethnic Tales and Recipes, 36
Outward Dreams: Black Inventors and Their Inventions, 83

Paddle-to-the Sea (Holling), 46
Paddle-to-the-Sea (videocassette), 46
Particular Places: A Traveler's Guide to Inner Ohio, 83
Patent Pending, 85
The Pathless Woods, 47
Pathways through Minnesota, 58
Patrick des Jarlait: The Story of an American Indian Artist, 61
Paul Bunyan (Kellogg), 96
Paul Bunyon (Shephard), 96
Paul Bunyan and Babe the Blue Ox, 95
Paul Bunyan of the Great Lakes, 34
Paul Bunyan Swings His Axe, 96
Paul Laurence Dunbar, 84
Paul Laurence Dunbar: A Poet to Remember, 84

Peeping in the Shell: A Whooping Crane Is Hatched, 99
Penrod, 31
People of the Three Fires, 38
A Photo Album of Ohio's Canal Era, 1855-1913, 76
Picturing Minnesota 1936-1943: Photographs from the Farm Security Administration, 64
A Picture Book of Abraham Lincoln, 12
The Pie Lady of Winthrop and Other Minnesota Tales, 57
Pinkerton: America's First Private Eye, 13
Pioneer Living: Education and Recreation, 25
Pioneer Living: Home Crafts, 25
Pioneer Living: Preparing Foods, 25
Pioneer Living: The Farm, 26
Pioneer Living: The Home, 26
Pioneer Living: The Village, 26
Pioneer Mill, 26
Pioneer Painters of Indiana, 29
Pioneer Plowmaker: A Story About John Deere, 11
A Place to Claim as Home, 92
Pontiac: Chief of the Ottawa, 44
Pontiac: Indian General and Statesman, 87
Popcorn Days and Buttermilk Nights, 69, 72
The Potawatomi, 39
Prairie Cabin: A Norwegian Pioneer Woman's Story, 105
Prairie-Town Boy, 14
Prairies, 1
Prehistoric Peoples of Minnesota, 62
The Problem Solvers: People Who Turned Problems into Products, 8
The Progressive, 106

The Rabbi's Girls, 90
Raccoons and Ripe Corn, 2
The Railroads: Opening the West, 1
Rascal: A Memoir of a Better Era, 101
Ready, Aim, Fire! The Real Adventures of Annie Oakley, 87
Reap the Whirlwind: A Documentary of Early Michigan, 45
René-Robert Cavelier Sieur de La Salle, 86
Rhymes of Childhood, 22
River and Canal, 77
River Rats, 73
The Rivers of Indiana, 19
Robber and Hero, 50
Rochester Sketchbook, 59
The Rocks and Minerals of Michigan, 35
The Role of Coal, 20
Romance of Wisconsin Place Names, 96, 104
Ronald Reagan, 14
Ronald Reagan, Fortieth President of the United States, 14

Ronald Reagan, President, 14
Root River Run, 106
Rosa Parks and the Montgomery Bus Boycott, 44
Rutherford B. Hayes, 86

The Sacred Harvest: Ojibway Wild Rice Gathering, 53, 103
Sand in the Bag and Other Folk Stories of Ohio, Indiana, and Illinois, 18
The Sasquatch in Minnesota, 48
Satchel Paige, 79
School Resources from the State Historical Society of Wisconsin, 113
The Schoolship, 42
Seasons of the Tallgrass Prairie, 2
Secrets of Limestone Groundwater, 19
Settling in Michigan and Other True Pioneer Stories, 40
Settling the Old Northwest, 26
Shipwrecks of Lake Superior, 40
The Sioux, 60
The Sioux Uprising of 1862, 61
Sister, 16
A Sketchbook of Michigan, 36
Skyscraper Going Up!, 3
Sleeping Bear: Its Lore, Legends and First People, 35
A Small Bequest, 46
The Smithsonian Book of Flight for Young People, 77
Soda Jerk, 79
Sojourner Truth, 45
Sojourner Truth and the Struggle for Freedom, 45
Sons of the Wilderness: John and William Conner, 29
Space People from A-Z, 84, 85
Sparrow Hawk, 104, 111
Split Rock Light: Tribute to the Age of Steel, 51
Sports Great Magic Johnson, 44
Sports Stars: Eric Dickerson, Record-Breaking Rusher, 21
Sports Stars: Larry Bird, Cool Man on the Court, 21
Stairstep Farm: Anna Rose's Story, 111
The Star Maiden: An Indian Tale, 38, 51
The State House: 1888 to Present, 28
State of Wisconsin Blue Book, 94
Steamboat in a Cornfield, 75
Steven Spielberg: Amazing Filmmaker, 87
The Stone Canoe and Other Stories, 34
The Story of Abraham Lincoln, President for the People, 13
The Story of Henry Ford and the Automobile, 44
The Story of Johnny Appleseed, 29
The Story of Marquette and Jolliet, 6, 104
The Story of My Boyhood and Youth, 108

The Story of the Black Hawk War, 5
The Story of the Chicago Fire, 8
The Story of the Haymarket Riot, 7
Story of Thomas Alva Edison: The Wizard of Menlo Park, 43
The Story of Walt Disney, Maker of Magical Worlds, 11
StoryBook Weaver, 74
Sugaring Season: Making Maple Syrup, 54, 78
Sugaring Time, 78
A Summer on Thirteenth Street, 16
Summertime Dream, 73
The Swedes in America, 48

Take Me Out to the Ball Game, 4
Talespins, 3418-
"Teaching Children to be Storytellers," 18–19
Teammates, 78
Tecumseh, 45
Tecumseh and the Dream of an American Indian Nation, 45, 88
Tecumseh, Shawnee War Chief, 45
A Telling of Tales: Five Stories, 95
The Terrible Hodag, 95
There'll Be a Hot Time in the Old Town Tonight: The Great Chicago Fire of 1871, 3
They Chose Minnesota: A Survey of the State's Ethnic Groups, 62
Thimble Summer, 110
36 One-Day Discovery Tours: Fun Places to Drive within and from Minneapolis and St. Paul, 58
Thomas A. Edison, 85
Thomas Alva Edison: Bringer of Light, 43
Thomas Alva Edison: Great Inventor, 43, 84
Thomas Edison: The Great American Inventor, 85
Threshing Days: The Farm Paintings of Lavern Kammerude, 100
Thunder in the Dells, 102
Tibdo, A Dakota Legend, 51
Time to Go, 15
The Timekeeper, 54
Timeline, 92
TimeLiner, 58
The Tin Heart, 88
The Toothpaste Millionaire, 90
Tornado! Poems, 79
The Town that Moved, 62
Tracker, 69, 72
Tractors: From Yesterday's Steam Wagons to Today's Turbocharged Giants, 97
Travel Historic Ohio: A Guide to Historic Sites and Markers, 80
Travel Historic Wisconsin, 105
Tribal Sovereignty: Indian Tribes in U.S. History, 102
True Stories about Abraham Lincoln, 13

The Turn in the Trail: Northwoods Tales of the Upper Great Lakes, 56
Two for America: The True Story of a Swiss Immigrant, 107

Ulysses S. Grant, 85
Ulysses S. Grant, Eighteenth President of the United States, 11
Uncle Rebus: Minnesota Picture Stories for Computer Kids, 58
Uncle Tom's Cabin, 87
United States Regions: The Midwest, 26
Unktomi and the Ducks, 52
The Unsung Heroes: Unheralded People Who Invented Famous Products, 9
Up Country, 110
Up North at the Cabin, 69
Urban Indians, 49

The Valley of the Shadow, 89
VCR Companion, 52
Views of a Cameraman, 106
Violent Storms, 19
Virgil I. Grissom: Boy Astronaut, 29
A Vision Shaped in Stone, 106
A Visit to the Dairy Farm, 99
A Visit with Russell Freedman, 12
Voices from the Rapids: An Underwater Search for Fur Trade Artifacts 1960-73, 65
Voices of the Loon, 52
Votes for Women?! 1913 U. S. Senate Testimony, 103
Voyageurs, 71

Walk in Peace: Legends and Stories of the Michigan Indians, 34
The War of 1812, 81
Warm As Wool, 91
Warren G. Harding, 86
We Came from Vietnam, 8
We Made It through the Winter: A Memoir of a Northern Minnesota Boyhood, 68
Weasel, 88
Western Great Lakes: Illinois, Iowa, Minnesota, Wisconsin, 5
What Indians Lived in Ohio?, 83
When Morning Comes, 69
Where Two Worlds Meet: The Great Lakes Fur Trade, 50
White Earth: A History, 49
White Indian Boy, 71
The Whooping Crane: A Comeback Story, 99
Who's that Girl with the Gun? A Story of Annie Oakley, 87
The Wild Donahues, 30
Wild Mammals of Illinois, 2

Wilderness Peril, 70
Wilderness to Washington: An 1811 Journey by Horseback, 31
Wilderness World of Sigurd F. Olson, 52
Wildlife Histories: Notes on Ohio's Wildlife and Species, 77
Will and Orv, 77
William Beaumont—Frontier Doctor, 43
William Henry Harrison, 30, 86
William Howard Taft, 88
William McKinley, 86
Willow Wind Farm: Betsy's Story, 112
Winding Valley Farm: Annie's Story, 112
Winnebago Women: Songs and Stories, 103
Winners: Women and the Nobel Prize, 10
Wiscandia: Scandinavian Folk Music, 100
Wisconsin (Bratvold), 103
Wisconsin (Stein), 105
Wisconsin (Thompson), 104
Wisconsin: A History, 104
The Wisconsin Almanac (Being a Loosely Organized Compendium of Facts, History, Lore, Rememberances, Puzzles, Recipes, and Both Household and Gardening Advice with Which to Offer Elucidation, Assistance, and Occasional Amusement to the Conscientious Reader), 105
Wisconsin Atlas and Gazetteer, 101
Wisconsin Capitol: Fascinating Facts, 102, 106
Wisconsin in Words and Pictures, 103
Wisconsin Literary Travel Guide, 101
Wisconsin Lore, 95
Wisconsin State Capitol Guide and History, 102, 106
Wisconsin Trails, 113
Wisconsin with Kids, 102
Wisconsing/David HB Drake, 101
The Wizard of Sound: A Story about Thomas Edison, 85
The Wolfling: A Documentary Novel of the 1870s, 111
Women of Minnesota: Selected Biographical Essays, 48
Woodsong, 55, 56, 69
The Wreck of the Edmund Fitzgerald, 33
The Wright Brothers: How They Invented the Airplane, 77

The Year They Walked: Rosa Parks and the Montgomery Bus Boycott, 44
The Youngest Voyageur, 71

Zeely, 79
Zoar Blue, 89

Subject Index

Abolitionists, 45, 88
Accidents—Fiction, 15
Actors, American, 85
Addams, Jane, 1860-1935, 10, 11
Adopted children—Fiction, 74
Adoption—Fiction, 70
Adventure and adventurers—Fiction, 45
Aeronautics—History, 77
Aeronautics—History—Biography, 77
African-American athletes, 21, 44, 79
African-American authors, 84
African-American women, 45
Africann Americans, 45, 81
African Americans—Biography, 4, 9, 11, 15, 44, 83
African Americans—Fiction, 89, 92
African Americans—Minnesota, 65
African Americans—Minnesota—Biography, 66
African Americans—Ohio—Biography, 75
African Americans—Poetry, 4
African Americans—Saint Paul (Minn.)—Biography, 62
African Americans—Saint Paul (Minn.)—Social life and customs, 62
Agricultural machinery, 2, 3, 11
Agriculture, 2, 3
Agriculture—Exhibitions, 2
Agriculture—Middle West, 2, 25, 27
Agriculture—Social aspects—Minnesota, 74
Air pilots, 68
Airships, 78
Alcoholism—Fiction, 110
Almanacs, American—Ohio, 75
Alphabet, 52, 74
America—Exploration, 4
American astronauts, 29
Amish, 18
Amish—Fiction, 91

Animals. *See* entries beginning with Mammals and names of individual animals, e.g., Racoon.
Animals and civilization, 4
Animals—Fiction, 71, 74
Animation (Cinematography), 11
Apple, 1, 29, 78, 90, 100
Appleseed, Johnny, 1774-1845, 1, 22, 29, 78, 90
Archeology—United States, 23, 24, 40
Architects, 109
Architecture—Indiana, 20
Architecture, Modern, 100
Armenian Americans—Biography, 106
Armstrong, Neil, 1930-, 84
Art. *See* entries beginning with Folk art.
Art history, 100
Artists, 100. *See* also entries beginning with Painters.
Asians—Minnesota—Biography, 66
Astronauts—United States, 84, 85, 87
Authors, American, 79, 87, 88, 101, 102, 106, 109
Authors, American—20th Century—Biography, 56
Authors—Minnesota, 69
Authors—United States—Biography, 14, 54
Authors—Wisconsin, 102, 113
Automobile industry, 44
Automobile racing, 22
Automobile racing drivers—United States, 22
Automobiles—History, 36
Autumn, 2

Badgers, 94
Bancroft, Ann, 57
Bank robberies—Northfield (Minn.), 50
Barns, 97
Barns—Fiction, 91
Barnum, P.T. (Phineas Taylor), 1810-1891, 106
Baseball, 79
Baseball—Biography, 79, 84
Baseball—Chicago (Ill.), 4

Baseball players—Biography, 85
Basketball, 21, 78
Basketball—Biography, 20, 44
Basketball—Biography—United States, 21
Basketball—Indiana—History, 21
Bears—Fiction, 31
Beaumont, William, 1785-1853, 43, 97
Beavers, 4
Bee culture—Fiction, 69
Bemidji (Minn.), 68
Bench, Johnny, 1947-, 84
Bennett, Henry Hamilton, 1843-1908, 106
Bird, Larry, 21
Bird watching—Great Lakes region, 36
Bird watching—Indiana Dunes State Park (Ind.), 20
Birds—Great Lakes region, 36
Birds—Indiana Dunes State Park (Ind.), 20
Birds—Ohio, 77
Birds—Protection, 99
Birthdays—Fiction, 90
Black Hawk, Sauk chief, 1767-1838, 5, 11
Black Hawk, Sauk chief, 1767-1838—Fiction, 111
Black Hawk War, 1832, 5
Blacklock, Les—Biography, 67
Blackstone, Harry, 43
Blackwell, Elizabeth, 1821-1910, 84
Blind, 67
Blizzards—Fiction, 30
Blizzards—Minnesota, 66
Boone, Daniel, 1734-1820, 24
Boots—Fiction, 46
Boundary Waters Canoe Area (Minn.), 68
Boundary Waters Canoe Area (Minn.)—Description, 50
Boundary Waters Canoe Area (Minn.)—Fiction, 70
Boundary Waters Canoe Area (Minn.)—History, 58
Boy Scouts—Minneapolis (Minn.)—Biography, 63
Brothers and sisters—Fiction, 110, 111, 112
Building, 3
Bunyan, Paul (Legendary character), 34
Buried treasure—Fiction, 89
Business—Fiction, 91
Business—Minnesota—History, 50
Business people—Biography, 9

Camping—Fiction, 70
Camping—Minnesota, 55
Canada goose, 52
Canada—Description, 57
Canals, 77
Canals—Ohio—History, 76
Canals—Ohio—Pictorial works, 76
Canoes and canoeing—Canada, 57
Canoes and canoeing—Minnesota, 55, 57
Cartoons and caricatures, 20

Cass, Lewis, 1782-1866, 43
Cats—Fiction, 72
Census, 49
Challenger (Spacecraft)—Accidents, 87
Chicago (Ill.), 5, 6, 7
Chicago (Ill.)—Description, 5
Chicago (Ill.)—Description—Guides, 5
Chicago (Ill.)—Fiction, 16
Chicago (Ill.)—Fire, 1871, 4, 8
Chicago Cubs (Baseball team), 4
Children—Museums, 18
Children's literature—Bibliography—Wisconsin, 113
Children's poetry, 79
Chippewa Indians—Fiction, 46
Choreographers, 11
Christmas—Indiana, 18
Christmas—Fiction, 89, 91
Christmas—Minnesota, 51
Christmas trees, 95
Circus, 101, 106
Civil rights, 15
Clark, George Rogers, 11
Cleveland Cavaliers (Basketball team)—History, 78
Clippings (Books, newspapers, etc.)—Minnesota, 63
Cloquet (Minn.)—History, 69
Clowns, 101
Clubs—Fiction, 16
Coal, 20
Coal mines and mining—Fiction, 89, 90
Collective settlements—Indiana, 28
Communal living—Fiction, 72
Community life—Poetry, 79
Computer games—Minnesota, 58
Conner, John, 29, 31
Conner, William, 29, 31
Conservation of natural resources, 99
Conservation of natural resources—Indiana, 29
Conservationists, 108
Cookery—American, 54, 99
Cookery—American—History, 99
Cookery—German, 54
Cookery—Michigan, 36
Cookery—Norwegian, 54
Cookery—Scandinavian, 54
Copper mines and mining—Fiction, 45
Corn, 2, 3, 97
Country life—Fiction, 110, 112
Country life—Michigan—Fiction, 46
Country life—Wisconsin, 100, 101
Courage—Fiction, 16
Cousins—Fiction, 16
Cranberry, 97
Crime—Fiction, 70

Criminals—Minnesota—Biography, 50
Cuyahoga River Valley (Ohio)—History, 83

Dahl, Borghild, 67
Dairy products, 99
Dairying, 3, 98, 99
Dakota Indians, 60, 61
Dakota Indians—Legends, 51, 52
Dakota Indians—Wars, 1862-1865, 61
Dancers, 11
Darrow, Clarence, 1857-1938, 75
Death—Fiction, 112
Deer—Fiction, 72
Deer—Minnesota, 53
Deere, John, 11
Depressions, Economic—1929—Personal narratives, 60
Detectives, 13
Detroit (Mich.)—History, 39
Dickerson, Eric, 21
Digestion, 43, 97
Disasters—Minnesota, 57
Disney, Walt, 1901-1966, 11
Dogs—Fiction, 46
Draft horses, 98
Dunbar, Paul Laurence, 1872-1906, 84
Dunham, Katherine, 11

Earth Day, 1970, 94
Earth Day, 1990, 94
Eastman, Charles, 67
Eccentrics and eccentricities—Minnesota, 65
Ecology, 2, 47
Edison, Thomas Alva, 1847-1931, 44, 85
Edmund Fitzgerald (Ship), 33
Education—Ohio—Curricula, 92
Eggs—Fiction, 91
Eggs—Incubation, 99
Energy resources, 20
English language—Provincialisms—Minnesota, 52
Entertainers, 106
Entertainers—United States, 87
Environmental protection, 94, 99
Erie Canal—Fiction, 46
Essays—Minnesota, 56
Ethnic art—Minnesota, 55
Ethnology—Michigan, 36
Ethnology—Middle West, 97
Ethnology—Minnesota, 54
Excavations (Archeology)—United States, 23
Explorers, 4, 6, 12, 86, 104
Explorers—Biography, 10

Fairs, 2
Fairs—History, 53
Fairs—Minnesota—Pictorial works, 53

Fairy tales, 95
Family farms—Minnesota—Fiction, 71
Family life—Fiction, 17, 73, 89, 110, 111, 112
Family life—Songs and music, 88
Family problems—Fiction, 110
Fantasy, 15
Farm life, 99
Farm life—Austin (Minn.), 74
Farm life—Fiction, 15, 16, 90, 92, 111, 112
Farm life—Illinois, 2
Farm life—Minnesota—Fiction, 69, 72
Farm life—Wisconsin, 98, 100
Farmers, 2
Farming—Wisconsin, 100
Farms—History, 26, 54
Fathers and sons—Fiction, 69, 112
Fayette (Mich.)—History, 42
Fear—Fiction, 69
Feller, Bob, 1918-, 85
Feminism, 45
Festivals—Minnesota, 51
Fire ecology, 2
Fires, 105
Fires—Chicago (Ill.), 4, 8
Fish—Ohio, 77
Fishing—Minnesota, 55
Fishing stories, American—Minnesota, 55
Flat Mouth, Chief, 67
Fletcher, Elijah, 31
Folk art, American—Psychological aspects, 55
Folk art—Minnesota, 55
Folk music, Scandinavian, 101
Folk music, Wisconsin, 101
Folk songs, 4
Folk songs, American—Wisconsin, 100
Folklore—Great Lakes region, 34, 35
Folklore—Michigan, 35, 36
Folklore—Old Northwest, 19
Folklore—United States, 95, 96
Folklore—Wisconsin, 95, 105
Food, 26
Football, 21
Football players—Biography, 21
Ford Model T automobile, 36
Ford, Gerald R. 1913-, 44
Ford, Henry, 1863-1947, 44
Forest fires—Fiction, 110
Forests and forestry—Fiction, 70
Forests and forestry—Minnesota, 53
Forests and forestry—Pictorial works, 52
Fort Snelling (Minn.)—History, 66
Fortification—Minnesota—History, 66
Foster home care—Fiction, 69
Fourth of July, 18
Freshwater animals, 36
Friendship—Fiction, 70, 71, 88

Frontier and pioneer life, 24, 25, 26, 78, 99, 101, 109
Frontier and pioneer life—Fiction, 16, 70, 73, 88, 90, 91, 110, 111
Frontier and pioneer life—Illinois—Fiction, 15
Frontier and pioneer life—Indiana, 28, 31
Frontier and pioneer life—Indiana—Fiction, 30, 31
Frontier and pioneer life—Michigan, 42
Frontier and pioneer life—Michigan—Fiction, 45, 47
Frontier and pioneer life—Middle West, 90, 105
Frontier and pioneer life—Minnesota, 64, 69
Frontier and pioneer life—Mississippi River Valley, 61
Frontier and pioneer life—Old Northwest, 24, 26
Frontier and pioneer life—West (U.S.), 9
Frontier and pioneer life—Wisconsin, 105
Frontier and pioneer life—Wisconsin—Fiction, 110, 112
Fur trade, 36
Fur trade—Great Lakes region, 41
Fur trade—Great Lakes region—History, 51, 64, 71
Fur trade—Minnesota, 65
Fur trade—Ontario, 65

Gág, Wanda, 1893-1946, 54
Garfield, James A. (James Abram), 1831-1881, 85
Geese—Minnesota—Rochester, 52
Genealogy—Fiction, 91
Generals—United States, 86
Geographic names—Indiana, 27
Geographic names—Ohio, 81
Geographic names—United States, 15
Geographic names—Wisconsin, 104
Geography, 25
Geography—Middle West, 25
Geology, 19
Geology—Michigan, 35
Geology—Minnesota, 61
German Americans, 105
Germany—Social life and customs, 54
Ghosts, 48
Ghosts—Fiction, 31
Ghosts—Ohio—Fiction, 75
Gish, Lillian, 1896-1993, 85
Glenn, John, 1921-, 85
Gnadenhutten, Ohio—History—Fiction, 89
Governors—Michigan—Biography, 43
Grandfathers—Fiction, 17
Grandmothers—Fiction, 72
Grant, Ulysses S., 1822-1885, 12, 86
Great Lakes, 35, 36, 37, 47
Great Lakes—History, 33, 40, 41, 42
Great Lakes—Songs, 37
Great Lakes Indians—History, 104

Great Lakes region, 5, 6, 24, 25, 33, 38, 42, 47, 80
Great Lakes region—Fiction, 46
Great Lakes region—History, 6, 39, 42
Great Lakes region—Legends, 34
Great Lakes region—Maps, 40
Grissom, Virgil I., 29
Guthrie, Janet, 22

Hamilton, Virginia, 79
Handicraft, 25, 97
Hanukkah—Fiction, 91
Harding, Warren G. (Warren Gamaliel), 1865-1923, 86
Harmonica—Fiction, 90
Harrison, Benjamin, 1833-1901, 30, 86
Harrison, William Henry, 1773-1841, 30, 86
Hawley (Minn.)—History—Fiction, 72
Hayes, Rutherford Birchard, 1822-1893, 86
Haymarket Square Riot, Chicago, (Ill.), 1886, 8
Hemingway, Ernest, 1899-1961—Fiction, 47
Hibbing (Minn.)—History, 62
High School Basketball (Girls)—Indiana, 21
Hijacking of airplanes—Fiction, 70
Hiking—Minnesota, 55
Hill, James J., 67
Hinckley (Minn.)—Fire, 1894, 64
Hispanic Americans—Minnesota—Biography, 66
Historic buildings, 20
Historic sites—Illinois, 7
Historic sites—Indiana, 28
Historic sites—Ohio, 82
Historic sites—Ohio—Guidebooks, 80
History. *See* names of states and regions, followed by History.
Hmong (Asian People)—Thailand—Case studies, 49
Hmong-American teenage boys—Minneapolis (Minn.)—Biography, 63
Homicide—Minnesota—Case studies, 50
Horses, 4, 98
Hotels, motels, etc.—Fiction, 72
Houses, 76
Houses—Fiction, 16
Hubbard, Kin, 20
Hull House (Chicago, Ill.)—History, 10, 11
Human rights, 9
Humphrey, Hubert H., 68
Hunting—Fiction, 72
Huron Indians, 39

Identity—Fiction, 71, 72
Illinois, 5, 7, 8
Illinois—Biography, 9
Illinois—Description, 2
Illinois—Description—Guidebooks, 7
Illinois—Fiction, 15, 16

Illinois—History, 5, 8, 11, 17
Illinois—History—Sources, 7
Illustrators—United States—Biography, 54
Immigrants—Minnesota—History, 49
Immigration and emigration, 107
Immigration and emigration—Fiction, 17
Immigration and emigration—Minnesota—Fiction, 73
Indian Trails—Ohio, 81
Indiana, 23, 24, 25, 27, 28, 29, 80
Indiana—Description, 19
Indiana—Fiction, 31, 32
Indiana—History, 19, 27, 28, 29, 31, 32
Indiana—History, Local, 27
Indiana—History—Fiction, 30, 31
Indiana—History—Resource guide, 32
Indiana—Maps, 23
Indiana—Pictorial works, 23
Indiana—Politics and government, 28
Indiana—Religion, 28
Indiana—Transportation—History, 29
Indiana Dunes State Park (Ind.), 19
Indiana State Capitol (Indianapolis, Ind.), 28
Indiana University, 21
Indianapolis (Ind.), 23
Indianapolis (Ind.)—History—Fiction, 31
Indianapolis Colts, 21
Indianapolis Speedway Race, 22
Indians of North America, 23, 24, 60
Indians of North America—Bibliography, 113
Indians of North America—Biography, 61
Indians of North America—Captivities—Fiction, 71, 73
Indians of North America—Cuyahoga River Valley (Ohio)—History, 83
Indians of North America—Fiction, 45, 47, 74, 89, 112
Indians of North America—Great Lakes region, 34
Indians of North America—Great Lakes region—Costume and adornment, 33
Indians of North America—Great Lakes region—History, 40
Indians of North America—Great Lakes region—Legends, 34
Indians of North America—History, 102
Indians of North America—Housing, 76
Indians of North America—Legends, 34, 35, 37, 51, 52
Indians of North America—Minnesota, 50, 59, 61, 67
Indians of North America—Minnesota—Antiquities, 62
Indians of North America—Minnesota—Biography, 67
Indians of North America—Minnesota—Fiction, 73
Indians of North America—Minnesota—History, 60
Indians of North America—Ohio, 83
Indians of North America—Poetry, 37
Indians of North America—Social conditions, 49
Indians of North America—Social life and customs, 104
Indians of North America—Urban residence, 49
Individuality—Fiction, 16
Industrialization, 27
International Crane Foundation, 99
Inventions, 10
Inventors, 11, 44, 85
Inventors—Biography, 9, 10, 83
Iowa, 5
Irish Americans—Minnesota, 63
Iron industry—Minnesota, 66
Iron Range region (Minn.), 66
Israel—Politics and government, 107

Jazz music, 3, 20
Jazz musicians—Biography, 3
Jennings, Ann, 31
Jennings, Jonathan, 31
Jews, 87
Jews—United States—Fiction, 90
Johnson, Earvin (Magic), 1959-, 44
Johnson, Oliver, 1821-1907, 28
Jolliet, Louis, 1645-1700, 6, 104
Journalists, 69, 107

Kammerude, Lavern, 1915-1989, 100
Keewenaw Peninsula (Mich.)—Fiction, 45
Kherdian, David, 1931-, 106
Kidnapping—Fiction, 70
Kirtland, William, 68
Knight, Bobby, 20

La Salle, René-Robert Cavelier, Sieur de, 1643-1687, 12, 86
Labor disputes, 8
Labor unions—History, 1
LaFollette, Belle Case, 1859-1931, 107
Land use—Ohio, 81
Large-print books, 12
Lawyers, 75
Learning disabilities—Fiction, 17
Legends—Mackinac Island (Mich.), 34
Legends—Wisconsin, 95
Legislators, 85, 108
Librarians—Fiction, 69
Libraries—Fiction, 30
Lighthouses, 33
Lighthouses—Minnesota—History, 51
Lime, 20
Lincoln, Abraham, 1809-1865, 3, 5, 12, 13, 30

Lindbergh, Charles A., 68
Literary landmarks—United States, 56
Literature—Collections—Minnesota, 56
Little Falls (Minn.), 68
Littlefork (Minn.), 68
Logging, 98
Loons, 52, 53
Loons—Fiction, 71
Lorain (Ohio)—Fiction, 90
Los Angeles Lakers (Basketball team), 44
Lovelace, Maud Hart, 1892-1980, 68
Lumber and lumbering—Michigan, 39

Mackinac Island (Mich.)—History, 43
Madison (Wisc.)—History, 102
Magicians, 43
Mammals—Illinois, 2
Mammals—Ohio, 77
Maple sugar, 54, 78
Maple syrup, 54
Maps, 23
Marquette, Jacques, 1637-1675, 6, 104
Mayo, Charles Horace, 1865-1939, 53
Mayo, William James, 1861-1939, 53
Mayors, 15
McKinley, William, 1843-1901, 86
Meir, Golda, 1898-1978, 107
Mentally ill—Fiction, 112
Mexican Americans—Social conditions, 60
Miami Indians, 24
Michigan, 24, 35, 40, 42, 80
Michigan—Biography, 43
Michigan—Description, 37
Michigan—Description—Guidebooks, 38
Michigan—Description and travel—Views, 41
Michigan—Fiction, 45, 46, 47
Michigan—History, 35, 38, 39, 41, 42, 44, 47
Michigan—History—Fiction, 46
Michigan—Maps, 37, 38
Michigan—Pictorial works, 37
Michigan—Social life and customs, 33, 40
Michigan—Songs and music, 37
Michigan—Upper Peninsula—History, 43
Middle West, 23
Middle West—Description, 5, 25
Middle West—Indiana, 27
Middle West—Poetry, 4
Middle West—Social life and customs, 25
Migrant labor—Minnesota, 60
Migrant labor—Texas, 60
Military history, 94
Milk, 98, 99
Mills and millwork, 26, 100
Milwaukee (Wis.), 101, 105
Milwaukee Art Museum, 100
Mines and mineral resources—Michigan, 35

Mines and mineral resources—Minnesota, 66
Minneapolis (Minn.)—Biography, 63
Minneapolis (Minn.)—Description, 65
Minneapolis (Minn.)—Description—Guidebooks, 58
Minneapolis (Minn.)—Fiction, 73
Minneapolis (Minn.)—History, 50, 65, 67
Minnesota, 5, 61
Minnesota—Agriculture—History, 54
Minnesota—Antiquities, 62, 65
Minnesota—Biography, 57, 65, 66
Minnesota—Blizzard, 1940, 66
Minnesota—Business—History, 50
Minnesota—Christmas, 51, 56
Minnesota—Description, 50, 56, 57, 58, 59, 62, 64, 65
Minnesota—Description—1858-1950, 64
Minnesota—Description—Guidebooks, 55, 58, 59
Minnesota—Description and travel—Guidebooks, 58
Minnesota—Economic conditions—Pictorial works, 49
Minnesota—Ethnic groups, 62
Minnesota—Ethnic groups—Cookery, 54
Minnesota—Farm life, 56
Minnesota—Farm life—History, 70
Minnesota—Festivals, 51
Minnesota—Fiction, 69, 70, 71, 72, 73
Minnesota—Geography, 62
Minnesota—History, 54, 58, 59, 61, 62, 64, 65, 69
Minnesota—History, Local, 64
Minnesota—History—Blacks, 65
Minnesota—History—Fiction, 70, 71, 72, 73
Minnesota—Information networks, 48
Minnesota—Literature—Collections, 56
Minnesota—Maps, 57, 58
Minnesota—Nationalism, 63
Minnesota—Pictorial works, 58
Minnesota—Politics and government, 63
Minnesota—Social life and customs, 56, 57, 62, 65, 69, 74
Minnesota—Social life and customs—Anecdotes, 52
Minnesota—Social Life and Customs—History, 63
Minnesota—Social life and customs—Pictorial works, 64
Minnesota—State Capitol (St. Paul, Minn.), 63
Minnesota—Statistics, 48
Minnesota—Study and teaching, 58
Minnesota—Teaching aids and devices, 58, 63
Minnesota—Tourist trade, 58, 59
Minnesota—Travel, 58, 59
Minnesota—World War II, 1939-1945, 59
Mississippi River, 6
Mississippi River—Discovery and exploration, 104
Mississippi River—Exploring expeditions, 6

Mississippi River—Fiction, 73
Mississippi River—History, 6, 103
Mississippi River Valley—Exploration, 86
Mississippi River Valley—History, 61, 103
Molter, Dorothy, 68
Moose—Fiction, 71
Moravian Indians—Fiction, 89
Motion picture producers and directors—United States, 87
Motion pictures—Biography, 11
Mounds and Mound Builders, 24, 79
Mountain Wolf Woman, 1884-1961, 107
Moving, Household—Fiction, 15, 91
Muir, John, 1838-1914, 107, 108
Museums—Illinois, 7
Museums—Indiana, 18
Museums—Minnesota, 54
Music, American, 100. *See also* entries beginning with Folk music, Folk songs, and Jazz.
Musicians, American, 20
Mystery and detective stories, 31, 70, 73, 89

Nationalism—Irish Americans—Minnesota, 63
Natural disasters—Minnesota, 57
Natural history—Ohio, 76
Natural history—Wisconsin, 97
Natural resources, 20
Natural resources—Great Lakes region, 47
Naturalists, 107, 108
Naturalists—Indiana, 30
Naturalists—Minnesota, 52
Nature—Fiction, 91
Nature conservation, 107, 108
Nature photography, 78
Naturecraft, 97
Nelson, Gaylord, 1916-, 108
New Harmony (Ind.), 28
Nobel prizes, 10
North Pole, 57
North, Sterling, 1906-1974, 101
Norway—Social life and customs, 54
Norwegian Americans—History, 49
Norwegian Americans—Middle West, 60

Oakley, Annie, 1860-1926, 87
Obedience—Fiction, 15
Ohio, 24, 80, 82, 83, 92
Ohio—Biography—Dictionaries, 84
Ohio—Description, 76, 80, 82, 83
Ohio—Description—Guidebooks, 80
Ohio—Description—Pictorial works, 78
Ohio—Economic conditions, 76
Ohio—Fiction, 88, 89, 90, 91
Ohio—Gazetteers, 80
Ohio—History, 81, 83, 92, 93
Ohio—History, Local, 80, 81
Ohio—History—Study and Teaching (Elementary), 93
Ohio—History—Study and Teaching (Secondary), 93
Ohio—Maps, 82
Ohio—Public Lands, 81
Ohio—Statistics, 75
Ohio—Transportation, 76
Ohio—Yearbooks, 75
Ohio River, 81
Ohio River—Navigation—History, 76
Ohio River Valley, 81
Ohio River Valley—History, 24
Ojibway Indians, 38, 51, 60, 104
Ojibway Indians—Biography, 61
Ojibway Indians—Fiction, 71, 110, 111
Ojibway Indians—History, 95, 102
Ojibway Indians—Legends, 34, 51, 95, 96, 102
Ojibway Indians—Minnesota, 53
Ojibway Indians—Reservation, 50
Ojibway Indians—Social life and customs, 59
O'Keeffe, Georgia, 1887-1986, 108, 109
Old Northwest—History, 24
Olson, Sigurd F., 52
Ontario—Antiquities, 65
Oral history—Handbooks, manuals, etc., 27
Oral history—Indiana, 27
Ottawa Indians, 38, 44, 87
Outdoor life—Minnesota, 55
Outdoor recreation—Michigan, 37
Outdoor recreation—Minnesota, 59
Outer Space—Exploration, 29

Paige, Leroy, 1906-1982, 79
Painters, American, 108, 109
Painters, American—1800-1899—Biography, 29
Painters—1800-1899—Indiana, 29
Parks, Rosa, 1913-, 44
Parks—Minnesota—Guidebooks, 59
Paul Bunyan (legendary character), 95, 96
Paulsen, Gary, 69
Peacocks—Fiction, 91
Peshtigo (Wis.)—Fire, 105
Photographers, 106
Photographers—Minnesota, 67
Physically handicapped—Fiction, 45
Physicians, 43, 97
Physicians—United States—Biography, 53
Pierce, Elijah—Fiction, 91
Pilots and pilotage—Mississippi River—Biography, 61
Pinkerton, Allan, 1819-1884, 13
Plants—Michigan, 40
Poetry, American, 4, 22, 23, 79
Poets, American, 14, 84
Polish Americans—Fiction, 111

Pollution, 99
Pontiac, Ottawa Chief, ca. 1720-1769, 44, 87
Porters—History, 1
Potawatomi Indians, 38
Poverty—Fiction, 71
Prairie ecology, 2
Prairie plants, 2
Prejudices—Fiction, 92
Presidents—United States, 5, 12, 13, 14, 30, 44, 85, 86, 88
Problem solving, 9
Promises—Fiction, 15
Public libraries—Materials, 113
Pullman Company—History, 1
Puzzles, 82

Questions and answers, 82

Raccoon, 2
Raccoons—Legends and stories, 101
Race relations, 79
Race relations—Fiction, 74, 92
Rafting (Sports)—Fiction, 69
Railroads—History, 1, 67
Railroads—Ohio—History, 76
Rats as carriers of disease, 4
Reagan, Ronald, 1911-, 14
Reese, Pee Wee, 1919-, 79
Reformers, 10, 11
Reformers—Biography, 9
Refugees—Thailand—Case studies, 49
Reptiles—Ohio—Identification, 76
Resnick, Judith, 1949-1986, 87
Riots—Chicago (Ill.), 8
Ripley (Ohio)—History, 81
Rivers—Indiana, 19
Rivers—Wisconsin, 98
Roads, 29
Roads—Fiction, 72
Robbers and outlaws—Minnesota, 50, 65
Robinson, Jackie, 1919-1972, 79
Rochester (Minn.)—Description, 59
Rochester (Minn.)—Pictorial works, 52
Rocks, 35
Rondo—Saint Paul (Minn.)—Biography, 62
Rylant, Cynthia, 1954-, 79, 87

Saint Paul (Minn.)—Description, 65
Saint Paul (Minn.)—Description—Guidebooks, 58
Saint Paul (Minn.)—History, 65
Sand dunes—Indiana, 19
Sandburg, Carl, 1878-1967, 14
Santee Indians, 67
Santee Indians—Wars, 1862-1865—Fiction, 73
Sasquatch—Minnesota, 48
Sauk Indians, 5, 11

Sauk Indians—Fiction, 111
Scandinavian Americans—Social life and customs, 60
School stories, 16
Science. *See* specific subjects within Science, e.g., Ecology.
Science fiction, 73
Scientists—Biography, 9
Seafaring life—Great Lakes, 37
Seasons—Pictorial works, 52
Self-acceptance—Fiction, 69
Self-reliance—Fiction, 112
Shawnee Indians, 45, 88
Sheep—Fiction, 91
Shipping—Ohio River—History, 76
Ships, 42
Shipwrecks, 40, 41
Shipwrecks—Fiction, 73
Shipwrecks—Great Lakes, 40
Shipwrecks—Superior, Lake, 33
Shooters of firearms, 87
Short stories, 33, 95
Short stories—Austin (Minn.), 74
Silver Lake (Olmstead County, Minn.)—History, 52
Skyscrapers—Design and construction, 3
Slavery—Fiction, 89, 92
Slavery—United States—Fiction, 31
Sled dog racing, 55
Sled dogs, 55
Snakes, 36
Social workers, 10, 11
Society of Separatists of Zoar—Fiction, 90
Soldiers—United States, 43
Songs, American, 3, 37
Spielberg, Steven, 1947-, 87
Split Rock Lighthouse—Minnesota—History, 51
Sports—Ohio—(Dictionaries), 78. *See also* names of individual sports, e.g., basketball.
St. Martin, Alexis, 179[7]-1880, 97
State capitols, 106
State capitols (Madison, Wis.), 102
Steamboats, 76
Steamboats—Mississippi River, 61
Storms, 19
Storms—Great Lakes, 39
Stowe, Harriet Beecher, 1811-1890, 88
Supernatural—Fiction, 69
Supernatural—Minnesota, 48
Swedish Americans—Fiction, 17, 70
Swedish Americans—History, 49
Switzerland, 107

Taft, William H. (William Howard), 1857-1930, 88
Tall tales, 95, 96
Tanner, John—Fiction, 71

Teale, Edwin Way, 30
Tecumseh, Shawnee Chief, 1768-1813, 45, 88
Teton Indians, 60
Tornadoes, 19
Tornadoes—Poetry, 79
Tractors—History, 97
Transportation—History, 50
Travelers, 29
Trees—Ohio—Identification, 77
Trucks—Fiction, 15
Truth, Sojourner, d. 1883, 45

Underground Railroad, 81
Underground Railroad—Fiction, 31, 89, 92
Underwater exploration, 40
United States—Antiquities, 23
United States—History, 103
United States—History—French and Indian War, 1755-1763, 39
United States—History—Revolution, 1775-1783, 11
United States—History—1783-1865, 26
United States—History—War of 1812, 39
United States—History—1812-1815, 81
United States—History—Civil War, 1861-1865, 88, 103
United States—History—Civil War, 1861-1865—Fiction, 16, 90
United States—History, 1865–1918, 25
United States—History—1919-1933, 60
United States—Immigration and emigration, 8
United States—Popular culture—Psychological aspects, 55
United States—Social life and customs, 97
United States—Statistics, 49
United States—Territorial expansion, 24
University of Wisconsin-Madison—History, 94

Vacations—Fiction, 70
Vietnamese Americans, 8
Voyages and travels, 31

Washington, Harold, 1922-1987, 15
Water pollution, 19
Water resources development, 47
Water supply, 19
Weather, 19
Wells-Barnett, Ida B., 1862-1931, 15
West (U.S.)—Biography, 9
West (U.S.)—History, 1
West Virginia—Social life and customs, 87
White Earth Indian Reservation (Minn.)—History, 50
Whooping cranes, 99
Wild rice, 53, 104

Wilder, Laura Ingalls, 1867-1957, 56, 99, 101, 109
Wilderness areas—Minnesota, 52, 55
Wildflowers—Michigan—Identification, 35
Wildlife—Michigan, 38, 40
Wildlife conservation, 99
Winnebago Indians, 103, 107
Wisconsin, 5, 103, 104, 105, 106, 107
Wisconsin—Atlases, 101
Wisconsin—Bibliography, 113
Wisconsin—Description—Guidebooks, 58, 102
Wisconsin—Description and travel, 105, 113
Wisconsin—Fiction, 110, 111, 112
Wisconsin—History, 94, 95, 97, 98, 100, 103, 104, 105, 107
Wisconsin—Politics and government, 94, 102
Wisconsin—Statistics, 94
Wisconsin Capitol, 106
Women—Biography, 9, 10, 11
Women—Michigan—Biography, 43
Women—Minnesota—Biography, 48
Women—United States—Biography, 10
Women artists, 108, 109
Women authors—Minnesota, 68
Women physicians, 84
Women politicians, 107
Wood carving—Fiction, 91
Woodland Indians—Housing, 76
Word games—Minnesota, 63
World War II, 1939-1945—Minnesota, 59
World War II, 1939-1945—United States, 92
World War II, 1939-1945—United States—Fiction, 16, 72
Wright, Frank Lloyd, 1867-1959, 100, 109
Wright, Orville, 1871-1948, 77
Wright, Wilbur, 1867-1912, 77

X, Malcolm, 1925-1965, 45

Youth—Fiction, 73

Zionism, 107
Zoar (Ohio)—Fiction, 90

www.ingramcontent.com/pod-product-compliance
Lightning Source LLC
Chambersburg PA
CBHW080540300426
44111CB00017B/2815